FOOTBALL FANATIC

FOOTBALL FANATIC

A Record-Breaking Journey through English Football

Ken Ferris

MAINSTREAM
PUBLISHING

EDINBURGH AND LONDON

For my father Ken and my son Lyle

First published in 1995 by Two Heads

This edition published in 2000 by
MAINSTREAM PUBLISHING COMPANY (EDINBURGH) LTD
7 Albany Street
Edinburgh EH1 3UG

ISBN 1 84018 200 8

A catalogue record for this book is available from the British Library

Typeset in 10 on 11.5 pt Times New Roman
Printed and bound in Great Britain by Creative Print Design Wales

CONTENTS

ACKNOWLEDGEMENTS

I thought it was all over – it is now. Until I had been on the pitch at more League grounds than most players, I never realised how much time and effort was involved in writing a travelogue. My love of football kept me going on those long journeys and sustained me through the 0–0 draws that inevitably cropped up from time to time among 93 League matches. But I could always fall back on the many people who gave me encouragement when I was flagging, some of whom accompanied me to a game here and there. I would like to take this opportunity to thank them all.

There are four very special people who backed me all the way on my mad journey across the country: my girlfriend Nicky, my son Lyle and my parents, Ken and Sadie. I am grateful to: Lyle and Nicky for keeping me company at the Rochdales and Grimsbys as well as the Liverpools and Evertons; my dad, who was always there to push me along when I was drowning in a sea of Premier and Endsleigh League fixtures and who worked out how many miles my journeys took, how many goals were scored and how many people watched all the games I saw; my mum, who also helped to keep me going and patiently transcribed hours of taped reports and interviews.

Another group of people who supported my efforts (their football teams are in brackets) were members of the JAG (James Alexander Gordon) Society at Reuters, who also helped to raise money for charity by sponsoring my record attempt. Their line-up includes: Iain Rodger (Chelsea), Graham Jones (Manchester City), Steve Meadows (Crystal Palace), Simon Wright (Arsenal), Rob Simpson and Dave Pape (Newcastle), Tony McCormack (Celtic) and his brother John (Arsenal), David Nowell (Notts County), and Dean Ratcliffe (Everton).

Others who supported my endeavour and also came to one or two fixtures were: my old pal at Reuters Simon Denyer, now sadly missed in London but taking the Big Apple by storm (Portsmouth); his girlfriend Sarah (Pompey too, I suppose); Dave Lewis (Barnet, sort of); Gareth Jones (Manchester City); Don Frier (Sunderland); and Richard Cheal (Norwich City). As you can see, I mostly travelled alone.

My thanks also go out to Douglas Cheal (Norwich), who thought my journey was fascinating, partly because he's as eccentric as I am; and to his wife, Pauline, who probably thought I was completely mad but never said so. Thank you for that, Pauline. Lou, Richie and Alfie also played their part, though I'm not exactly sure what it was!

Among those who provided information for the book I'd like to thank Alan Raybould and his mum Dorothy for their background on West Bromwich Albion and Neil Winton for information about Brighton's ground-sharing plans.

Mike Rich at Endsleigh supported my efforts all the way and probably opened more than a few doors with his backing for my record attempt. I hope it was worth it, Mike. A special mention should also go to Vic Curtis (Arsenal), who always asked me how my record attempt was shaping up and showed a keen interest in my travels. Thanks, Vic.

My colleagues on Reuters Financial Television were often bemused, and sometimes amazed, at the lengths to which I had to go to visit 93 League grounds whilst working full-time. They are: Jon Engel, Mark Jones, Mike Lawrence, Steve Clarke, Ed Brunetti, Clar Ni-Chonghaile, Sofy Fearnley-Whittingstall and Gwen Dunne.

I couldn't blow the final whistle without mentioning Dave Hefford, Barry Hughes and Paul Kemp – lifelong friends and still soccer mad, even though they support West Ham. Thanks also to: John Buckley, though he supports Manchester United and therefore knows what success is all about; the entire Ludlows football team from the Essex Independent Sunday League, who badly missed my silky skills on Sunday mornings for a whole season; and finally, Johnny Allen, their manager, who had a hand, or should I say foot, in breaking my toe, which meant that I missed a whole season and thus had enough time to reach all 93 grounds. Thanks, John.

All 93 League clubs welcomed me with open arms and gave me invaluable help throughout the season.

And there you have it: a group of individuals who in one way or another influenced my successful attempt to join the ranks of the immortal (or should that be insane) in *The Guinness Book of Records*. By the way, in case he thinks I've forgotten, I should also mention Brian Martin, the genial Irishman who is Jack Charlton's biggest fan!

PREFACE TO THE 2000 EDITION

Since the first edition of *Football Fanatic* appeared, several teams have moved to new grounds in the biggest shake-up of footballing venues since the turn of the last century. Bolton have left Burnden Park for the Reebok Stadium. Brighton's Goldstone Ground has closed. Derby have made the short journey from the Baseball Ground to Pride Park. Middlesbrough have forsaken Ayresome Park for the Cellnet Riverside Stadium. Northampton now play at the Sixfields Stadium instead of the County Ground. Stoke's Victoria Ground has given way to the Britannia Stadium at Trentham Fields. And Sunderland have moved to the Stadium of Light at the Wearmouth Colliery.

All these changes have resulted in improved facilities for the fans and are in tune with the face-lift being given to football in the 1990s. They're also safer venues at which to watch football. But despite all that, something has been lost. The old grounds had more character than the more sterile new stadiums with their executive suites, restaurants, bars and shops. Sentiment has given way to sponsors; memories to money; passion to profits. Something *has* been lost. Even the sort of people who go to football today have changed. They're more affluent – and have to be affluent to afford the prices being charged. They are more middle-class than working-class. Sitting in a plastic seat is more comfortable than standing on the terraces.

On the plus side there's far less trouble now than there was during the '70s and '80s. It also makes sense to put the new stadiums in out-of-town sites with good access and lots of parking. The smart, new facilities are also attracting supporters who visit their clubs to socialise hours before a game kicks off. That's attracting new business and more money into football; but most of it goes to line the pockets of the players, many of whom have no attachment to the team or the area beyond receiving a large chunk of the fans' hard-earned money. Progress comes at a price.

So I'm glad I wrote *Football Fanatic* when I did. I saw the last Tees–Wear derby between Middlesbrough and Sunderland at Ayresome Park and the last-ever game at Northampton's County Ground. I also captured the flavour of the Baseball Ground, Burnden Park, the Goldstone Ground, Roker Park and the Victoria Ground – places that were full of football folklore and can never be replaced. The Manor Ground at Oxford will also shortly pass into history as the club relocates to Minchery Farm.

Southampton, Reading, Blackpool, Luton and Everton are also planning to leave their ancestral homes before too long. Even the likes of Arsenal and Newcastle have toyed with the idea of moving. Is nothing sacred?

At the time of writing *Football Fanatic* there were already relatively new grounds at Chester, Walsall and Wycombe. But every other team was playing at its spiritual home. The book stands as a testimony to those grounds and to the people who made them great.

Ken Ferris

They said it was either a crazy idea or a brilliant idea. I guess most thought it was crazy, but there were a few football fanatics who had sympathy with my eccentricity.

It first struck me during a series of trips I made to Stafford in north-west England to visit a friend. As the train passed the Wolverhampton and Birmingham grounds (which are clearly visible from the British Rail line), the first inklings of the idea began to take hold.

I can't remember exactly when I made my mind up to do it, but once I had decided, there was no going back. I couldn't get it out of my head. I pondered the practicalities of doing it; I assessed the time and effort involved; I turned it over again and again in my mind, rocking to and fro between what a stupid idea it was and what a great idea.

My weekends in the North-West had also taken me past Stoke City's ground a number of times and within reach of Port Vale. I had already visited quite a few London grounds in my football supporting 'career', but my experience of away grounds was limited. (Away from White Hart Lane that is – so now you know I'm a Spurs fan.) Above all, though, I'm a football fan and this book is for all fans and covers most clubs no matter how small.

Then the idea grew. What would it be like to visit all the FA Premier and Football League grounds? What if I did that and wrote a book about my experiences, a sort of travelogue? But, wait a minute, hadn't I seen an entry in *The Guinness Book of Records* listing a supporter who'd visited all the League grounds in the fastest time? What if I tried to break that record?

I checked an old copy of the records book and found an entry for 'Most peripatetic football supporters'. Once I'd worked out how to say the word (not worth attempting if you're drunk!), I decided to look it up. The Collins dictionary defines it as 'itinerant, walking, travelling about'. The last definition was probably the most fitting for the Guinness entry, since even the most ardent supporter would struggle walking to 92 League grounds (plus the Berwick Rangers ground, of which more later).

The entry I found from the 1983 records book listed a Michael Jones and Bob Wilson of Shrewsbury as having visited all 92 League grounds (and Berwick Rangers' ground) in 264 days between 10 August 1968 and 30 April 1969. How come the record had stood for so long? Was nobody crazy enough to break it?

Next I looked up the most recent record. Sure enough, the latest edition showed a change. The new record-holder was a guy called Edward Wood of Quarndon, Derby, who had been everywhere from Arsenal to York in 243 days between 17 August 1991 and 15 April 1992. On four occasions he watched two matches in a day.

Could it be beaten? A quick back-of-the-envelope calculation told me that I would have to see three games a week for 25 weeks of the season and two games a week for the other nine weeks. A pretty tall order when you're working full-time.

Again I turned the idea over in my mind. Some days I was convinced it was madness. Other days I felt I could do it. But throughout my assessment of the wisdom of attempting such a daunting project I knew it would be fun (and it was, most of the time).

In May and June 1993 I had travelled to see England play away in Poland and Norway during the World Cup qualifying rounds. The qualifiers eventually led to the showdown with Holland in Amsterdam and a 2–0 defeat which saw England blow their chance of going to USA '94 for a tournament which Pete Davies called 'The Greatest Show on Earth' in his book *All Played Out* about Italia '90. It was the first time I'd seen England play away from Wembley and it whetted my appetite to become peripatetic.

I wanted to find out more about the previous record-holders. Were they mad? Had their wives and kids walked out, leaving them with a burning desire to fulfil a mad ambition by default? Maybe they were poor lonely souls with nothing else to do but wander around the country from ground to ground seeking a modicum of fame, no matter how small, in what was otherwise an empty existence.

The people I told about my plans reacted in one of three ways: either it was a fantastic challenge (a few); downright stupid (some); or very sad (most). I wasn't the only fanatic, though. Phil Ambler didn't attempt to break the record, but he did visit all 92 League grounds (he didn't go to Berwick-upon-Tweed, but he went to Darlington – by then the club were out of the League – and Macclesfield, then the temporary home of Chester City, to compensate).

Perhaps we needed therapy for the treatment of football fanatics. A specialised profession. 'Sit down on the couch. How long have you been obsessed with football? Why do you feel it necessary to fill your life playing, watching or thinking about football? What do you mean you considered suicide when your wife cancelled your subscription to Sky Sports?' The questions would be endless. The logic hard to justify.

I first came across Phil Ambler in a WH Smith sports books section. There on the shelf was a tome which immediately caught my eye: *Full Colour Views of the Football League Grounds*, photography by Phil Ambler. Inside the front cover it said, 'After a lifelong obsession to see all 92 clubs in the Football League a dream has come true. Taking just over a year and using my holidays I managed to visit all the clubs, actually taking 16 days to do so plus travelling 6,000 miles.'

That people like Phil existed intrigued me. Why would anyone travel 6,000 miles and spend all their annual holiday taking pictures of empty football stadiums? To pursue my interest I contacted the Ninety-Two Club.

The club is based in Whitchurch, Bristol, and its members are people who have visited all 92 League grounds during their lifetime. It even has honorary members. The most famous are Alan Durban, who played for Cardiff, Derby and Shrewsbury, and Derby manager Jim Smith, former boss at Colchester, Blackburn, Birmingham, Oxford and Queens Park Rangers. Another honorary member is the late Eric Northover, a Northampton director. Completing the list of personalities among the élite ranks of the Ninety-Two Club are Gilbert

Napthine (referee), Alan Smith (physiotherapist) and Hal Mason (match-programme editor).

By the end of my journey I hoped to have joined them and to have secured my place in history with an entry in *The Guinness Book of Records*. Along the way I discovered why former Soviet President Mikhail Gorbachev supports Wigan; how Huddersfield built the most futuristic stadium in Britain; whether Crewe's fans thought David Platt would become England captain; why Everton won the Championship playing at Anfield; what Ken Bates thinks wealthy young managers should do with their money; the names of the two most powerful women in British soccer; and how Paul Gascoigne perfected his famous free-kick technique in his early days at Newcastle.

I also crossed the paths of players, managers and chairmen, past and present, including Denis Law, Frank McLintock, Stan Bowles, Sammy Lee, John Beck, John Jackson, Matt Le Tissier, Alan Ball, Alan Shearer, Tim Flowers, Chris Sutton, Joey Jones, Bruce Grobbelaar, Jimmy Neighbour, Peter Taylor, Mick McCarthy, Terry McDermott, Pavel Srnicek, Barry Fry, Ray Clemence, Norman Hunter, Trevor Brooking, Graham Taylor, Alan Mullery, Paul Allen, Kerry Dixon, John Sillett, Alan Sugar, Mark Chamberlain, Frank Lampard, Harry Redknapp, Martin Allen, Don Hutchison, Joe Royle, Lou Macari, David Dein, Charlie George, Martin Peters, Les Sealey, Andy Townsend, Ronnie Whelan, Archie Gemmill, John McGovern, Jason McAteer, Alan Stubbs, Bernie Slaven, Gary Bennett, Phil Gray and Andy Sussex.

This book is certainly about football. But it's more than that. It's a personal account of what it's like to live and breathe football for a season.

Carlisle United v Exeter City – Brunton Park, 10 September 1994

Ken Bates sat back in the departure lounge at London's Heathrow Airport looking relaxed and self-assured. Chelsea's larger-than-life chairman, with his shock of white hair, had good reason to be pleased with life. His team were fifth in the Premiership after their best start for years – three wins in a row. Today they'd face their toughest test so far, away to Newcastle. With the inspirational Kevin Keegan at the helm, Newcastle were also unbeaten and heading for their best start since 1908.

As we waited to be called for our flight Bates's attention was drawn to an interview in the *Daily Mirror* with Chelsea manager Glenn Hoddle. The former Spurs and Monaco star claimed that a new breed of 'rich kid' managers was driving the fear factor out of English football. 'There is a new generation of financially independent young managers who don't have to live with the pressures of fear or failure and the negative football which that produces,' said Hoddle.

Bates smiled: 'If they're that financially independent, they should become chairmen and use their own money to buy players.'

As we boarded the bus which would take us the short distance across the tarmac to the early-morning British Airways flight to Newcastle I asked Bates to forecast the result of the match at St James's Park. 'It's going to be tough up there,' he said with a rueful expression. He had reason to be concerned.

The reason for his visit to Newcastle was clear. As for me, it was the first stop on a longer journey. I was headed for Brunton Park, home of Carlisle United and the remotest ground in the country. A local derby there was a visit from Newcastle, 58 miles to the east. I'd decided that the best time to visit this outpost of League football was in the late summer, before the winter set in. Besides, it was close enough for me to see the Middlesbrough v. Sunderland match at Ayresome Park the next day.

The train to Carlisle, the county town of Cumbria and its largest city, passed through breathtaking scenery. As I settled back to enjoy picture-postcard views of rolling hills, fields enclosed by stone walls and sparkling rivers I got my first glimpse of a real Carlisle supporter at a place called Haltwhistle, just over halfway from Newcastle. Surprisingly, he was the only fan on the train.

The journey to Carlisle took longer than I expected. Making connections between the plane and the trains delayed my arrival. Luckily, my B&B was *en route* to Brunton Park. I followed the Carlisle fans walking to the match, stopping briefly to drop off my heavy bag. Carlisle is so close to the Scottish border that there was once speculation United would join the Scottish League, like Berwick Rangers, who play in the Scottish Second Division even though their ground is in England.

Carlisle's links with Scotland crop up throughout its history. It's an ancient border fortress with a chequered past. The town was originally a Celtic settlement before becoming Roman during the building of Hadrian's Wall. The struggle with the Scots went on over centuries. In 1315 Robert the Bruce was repelled; and Bonnie Prince Charlie's troops held the town for a few months before surrendering to the Duke of Cumberland. Today it's the region's centre for trade and commerce and, despite the history, Carlisle are still in the English Football League. The other Cumbrian teams with a League history, Barrow and Workington, both failed to secure re-election in the 1970s, leaving Carlisle to fly the county flag alone.

I arrived at the main gates, which said 'Welcome to Carlisle United', and looked around the Main Stand. Simon Inglis in *The Football Grounds of Great Britain* was impressed when he visited the ground. 'At the back of the main stand is an excellent new entrance hall, tastefully designed in almost high-tech decor, with rubberized floors, tinted glass and potted plants; a welcome and encouraging relief from all those football ground entrances decked in formica, garish carpets and simulated wood.'

I approached the doorman, who looked like a redeployed bouncer, and asked if I could take a look at the club's new restaurant, Foxy's. The Cumberland fox, Carlisle's crest, had been discreetly used as a themed motif throughout the trendy eating-spot. It had to be an improvement on the 'Brunton pasty' I'd picked up outside the ground before the game. 'If you keep your match ticket you can come out for another one of those at half-time,' said the elderly gateman. 'Mind you, you'll have to make an appointment at the doctor's afterwards.'

The restaurant was one of Carlisle's latest innovations. All chrome and gold-plate on the outside, Edwardian splendour on the inside. *The Cumberland Sausage* fanzine described the place as 'airy, spacious, bright, smelling of pine and monogrammed deep-pile carpets and high-backed padded chairs around polished tables, looking through the plate glass at the back of balding farmers in the paddock.'

The greeter, dressed in pristine white suit with black bow-tie, told me business had been brisk since the place opened on the night of Mervyn Day's testimonial against Leeds before a crowd of about 8,000. The former West Ham, Orient and Leeds goalkeeper had been forced to retire with a knee injury and had become the assistant to Mick Wadsworth, Carlisle's director of coaching.

'Does the level of business in the restaurant reflect the team's performance?' I asked.

'Probably,' replied the well-dressed greeter.

Carlisle's chairman Michael Knighton would have been interested to hear of a possible connection. 'People don't stop eating good food because the team is losing,' according to Knighton. The theory had yet to be put to the test, since Carlisle were top of the Third Division after three wins and a draw.

Star of the show was striker David Reeves, the club's record buy and a snip at £121,000 from Notts County. 'Reevesy' scored 11 goals in 36 games during his first season and there was a sense of anticipation that he'd be even better this term. Reeves had already been picked for the PFA team of the season and couldn't stop scoring goals. 'I went to see him in a reserve match for County and after 15 minutes I said to our coach: "We must have him no matter what it costs,"' said Knighton. 'I did the deal that night and soon we will have big clubs trying to get him off us. But he is staying put. He is a First Division striker who has matured late.'

Not unlike his chairman. Remember him? The ball-juggler from Old Trafford with the dodgy moustache, whose 'modest' millions weren't enough to secure a future at Manchester United. Knighton promised to lead the Reds to a new era of prosperity on and off the field with talk of trophies in the boardroom and a £100 million company. 'The extraordinary thing was that I said at my first press conference there I am not a wealthy man, I'm a modest millionaire.'

Knighton's bid to buy Manchester United for £10 million ended with a High Court injunction after the close friends he'd invited to participate in his project failed to deliver. He says that he left United after achieving everything he set out to do and he helped transform a declining club into the force they are today.

It's hard to believe now that United were ever up for sale, never mind at a knockdown price. As Knighton acknowledges, Ryan Giggs must be worth more than that on his own. But when United's chief executive Martin Edwards put the club on the market in 1989, buyers weren't exactly queuing up outside Old Trafford. When Knighton showed up, United rushed into a contract, sparking off a period of uncertainty and, ultimately, embarrassment for all concerned.

'It's easy to forget that United had had a few bad years, that attendances were down to 23,000 and that Edwards was coming in for a lot of criticism,' said Knighton. 'I can't take credit for what has happened since, but there is no question I was a catalyst. I had a blueprint in 1989, and everything on it has come about.

'Prior to 1989 the club was losing money, but profits [in 1994–95] were £10.8 million and overall turnover £44 million. In all modesty, and I am a modest man, you did not have to be an economic genius to predict that. It was staring you in the face. It's much more of a financial risk coming here [to Carlisle], believe me. With United you couldn't fail.' When asked about the club now he replies, 'Manchester who? There is only one United – Carlisle United.'

Knighton's involvement with Carlisle began when he bought a majority share in the club, which was then rooted at the bottom of the Third Division. They'd already been languishing in the basement division for more seasons than they cared to remember. Then-manager Aidan Macaffery talked about his players becoming part-timers, as the club lost £6,000 a week.

Enter Knighton. He made it clear he didn't intend to spend anything on players. 'The club must grow within its means.' That meant any new signings were free transfers. Knighton was firm in his conviction that he'd not be waving a cheque book around like Blackburn's Jack Walker. Some of the supporters were upset by his tight hold on the purse strings, but Knighton knew he had to put the club on a sound financial footing. 'The fans want me to be a rich benefactor, but I haven't got the money.' He had learned his lesson.

Knighton's approach worked and within a couple of seasons he'd turned things around. The club was back in profit and the surplus was used to buy Reeves. 'I shall be eternally grateful the fans gave me the benefit of the doubt,' says Knighton.

Tony Smith of the Carlisle *Evening News & Star* summed up the town's feelings about the chairman. 'Everyone here thinks Michael Knighton walks on water. Eccentric or not, you can't knock his achievement.'

The girl behind the bar in the new sponsors' lounge testified to the change in atmosphere at Brunton Park since Knighton took over. 'The club was going nowhere a few years ago and support was dwindling, but since Mr Knighton came in everything has begun to improve.'

Foxy's restaurant was only one small part of Knighton's redevelopment plans. 'We've just finished the new restaurant and corporate facilities and my priority now is to create one of the greatest football clubs in the country.'

Knighton had recently been profiled in *The Times* for a series called 'The Power Players'. Journalist Simon Barnes had his own theory on Knighton's character. 'Knighton's life has been marked out by pain. Two events shaped his life in football: the first was a knee injury, which scuppered his aspirations towards a career as a professional footballer; the second was the [Manchester] United affair, a period of sustained public ridicule that ended, three years on, with his departure from Old Trafford.

'His life has been carved out of frustration, bitterness and disappointment, but Knighton lacks the taste for dwelling on these things. Instead, he is gifted, or cursed, with a kind of idiot optimism. You don't normally find this trait among men of finance, but it is something you see all the time among professional athletes. This is a belief, one held with marrow-deep sincerity, that ultimate victory will be theirs.'

Knighton had a ten-year plan for Carlisle but had also said that if the right offer came along he would sell tomorrow. He was full of contradictions. 'One day I will pay myself a gargantuan salary,' said the man whose efforts at Brunton Park had so far been modestly rewarded. So what exactly was his master plan for Carlisle, the team he expected to emulate the other United as future winners of the Premier League?

On the back of the programme was an artist's impression of the new all-seater East Stand, which the club planned to have finished by Christmas 1995. Knighton said it would house a museum of British football. 'We've got some marvellous stuff for a museum, lots of people will want to see it.'

Rob Pearson of *The Cumberland Sausage* takes up the story. 'So there we all were, making our merry way along Warwick Road, full of expectancy for the season ahead. A new season – a new start. Not only that, but the enticing prospect of seeing the fruits of a summer of hard work toward the construction of our glorious 6,000 all-seater stand.

'I had seen a vision of its towering splendour in my dreams two nights earlier. A monstrous, beautiful construction scraping the Cumbrian skyline, serving as a monument to the legend that is Carlisle United Football Club. Barely able to negotiate the Paddock turnstile in eager anticipation of the sight that lay before me, I took my first steps on Brunton Park terrace for the new season to find . . . the Scratchin' Shed (Popular Side) still there – with its bloody roof off. Congratulations all round to those involved with such a fantastic feat of engineering.'

The roof was removed from the Popular Side, also known as the Scratching Shed or Scratchers, 'before it fell down', according to Carlisle's commercial manager Martin Hudson. Basically, it was the cheapest way of making it safe. The plan, though, was to build a new East Stand to replace the Scratchers by the end of 1995.

It was expected to cost £1.5–2 million. So where would the money come from? The club would get about £1 million from the Football Trust – and the rest? Rising attendances had contributed more than £200,000 to revenue in 1993–94, and Knighton had high hopes for the future of Carlisle United Football Club. 'I predict that within ten years we will be among the ten wealthiest clubs in this country. We will be competing in Europe and will have one of the finest stadiums.'

Really? Or, as Simon Barnes put it in *The Times*, 'Earth to Knighton: Hello? Hello?'

Some of the supporters had sort of latched on to Knighton's dream. The fanzine *So, Jack Ashurst, Where's My Shirt?* (a reference to a shirt promised to one of the fanzine editors after a crucial match) was taking a light-hearted view of his dreams. 'Michael Knighton's ten-year plan hasn't allowed for more than three years in the Third Division, and coach Mick Wadsworth is well aware that the European Champions League won't wait.'

The comments were clearly tongue-in-cheek. Knighton's, on the other hand, had to be taken at face value. 'Two years ago only 1,500 people were coming here. Now our average is 6,000 and that figure is going to grow. We have plans for a new stadium and we have already started some work. And I believe we will fill it when we reach the First Division and then the Premiership.'

Carlisle have had one or two star players over the years, including Peter Beardsley. Cumbrians fan Roger Robson remembered Beardsley 'with the ball stuck to his foot, whether in a tackle or jinking into the box with panic all around'. But the club has never won a major trophy. Not that failure has stopped them packing the trophy cabinet with priceless items like the vase inscribed with Anglo-Italian Cup, recalling Carlisle's annihilation of Roma, or pennants from the club's Scottish cousins across the border like Alloa and St Mirren. The European Cup was strangely absent, as was the FA Cup, the League Championship and many other major trophies I could mention.

The only time Carlisle have graced the top division was in 1974, when they were in first place after three games but relegated at the end of the season. Former Carlisle manager Bill Shankly called their promotion to the First Division 'the greatest achievement in the history of the game'. When Shankly arrived at Brunton Park in 1949, he was less enthusiastic. He called the stadium 'a hencoop, a glorified hencoop. The stand and terraces and everything about the ground was in terrible condition, except for the pitch and that was always a good one.'

The club's present-day sports centre, a dark, windowless wooden building surrounded by barbed wire, was behind the Waterworks End. 'That's Colditz, our indoor sports centre. I know it looks terrible, but it pulls in 50K a year,' said Knighton. Carlisle's chairman hoped the brave new world he was planning for the club meant such eyesores would soon be a thing of the past. The aim was to raise the capacity to 28,000. 'I think we shall command 18,000 home supporters once we are up with the glamour people.'

The fans certainly deserve success. Carlisle has a population of only 78,000, yet the club regularly topped the Third Division's home attendance figure. There was always plenty of support at away games, which was remarkable when you consider a 'local' derby involves a trip of about 80 miles. Record season-ticket sales for the 1994–95 campaign showed the faith the supporters had in Knighton and his team.

The potential support was staggering and just needed a spark of success to be ignited. Apart from the odd cup run, the only real excitement in recent years had been local derby games with teams like Preston, variously described by *The Cumberland Sausage* as Carlisle's 'loveable rivals from the deep south' and 'the worst team in the world. Quite possibly.' Preston were voted as 'Most Disliked Opposing Team' in the fanzine's end-of-season poll, a quite staggering turnaround from almost every other year, when Burnley topped this category.

So why are Carlisle fans so loyal? The club has had some great players over the years, but never a great team, so their following can't be based on memories of a glorious past. They are, of course, the only team, in Cumbria and that must surely help to attract local support. But the club is in one of the most sparsely populated parts of the country and their catchment area is therefore tiny. *FourFourTwo* magazine believed the support was partly because the Cumbrians are 'a strange, hardy breed in themselves'. *The Cumberland Sausage* had a different theory: 'One can only suggest that some of us are simply born to be blue.'

Forty-seven-year-old Geoff Tomlinson, a United fan for nearly 40 years, was certainly 'born to be blue'. A week or so before my visit to Brunton Park he set out for the Bescot Stadium in the supporters' club coach to see United play Walsall. It would have been his 1,900th consecutive Carlisle match. Unfortunately the coach got stuck in a 27-mile traffic jam on the M6. After queuing for three and a half hours, the driver finally abandoned the journey, bringing to an end Tomlinson's extraordinary record.

I settled into my seat in the Main Stand next to a little blondie (the mascot) and her mum. The view across the countryside on what was a sunny Saturday afternoon was breathtaking. Most people have seen it on *Match of the Day,* since whenever Carlisle are featured (rarely) the coverage from Brunton Park invariably begins with the view over a pastoral scene once described by Brian James in his book *Journey to Wembley* as 'a frontier post of football indeed, guarded only by sheep'.

The teams ran onto the pitch to D-Ream's 'Things Can Only Get Better' – a fitting theme tune for the new era being championed by Knighton. Carlisle's 1–0 win over Exeter, thanks to a goal from livewire winger Rod Thomas, was one of many during the season that would see them streak away to a 20-point lead by the spring. Thomas was a former England teenage sensation, who burned out under the bright lights in London. He'd recaptured his form at Brunton Park.

I wandered into the sponsors' lounge for a beer after the game. Knighton's personal assistant was at the bar. A tall blonde with gorgeous blue eyes, she was originally from Essex but had moved to Carlisle with her parents. What was Knighton like to work for? 'He works hard,' she told me. I made tentative plans to meet her for a drink later that night.

After the match I went back to my B&B, Howard House. After a cup of tea and a short rest I walked into town to find a restaurant called Zapotec: the Kitchens of Mexico and Spain. The food was hot and spicy – unlike the waitresses. I sat back to read the fanzines I'd bought outside the ground that afternoon. As I looked at *The Cumberland Sausage* I suddenly wondered what the hell I was doing hundreds of miles from home, on my own, on a Saturday night. Was I a sad bastard? Or had I embarked on a wonderful journey that would be the envy of football fans everywhere? I'm not sure I knew then, but I do now. I was definitely a sad bastard.

After my meal I wandered the streets of Carlisle. Groups of youngsters dressed to kill were making their way to the pubs and clubs. I found the bar where Knighton's PA said she'd be going that night with a friend. She was supposed to be there at about 11 o'clock. It was 10.30, a little too early. I had a quick look around and then decided I couldn't stay awake much longer. I reluctantly gave up on the idea of a night on the town with a gorgeous blonde and wandered wearily back to my bed.

As I walked towards the market square a drunken Scotsman veered unsteadily along the street shouting abuse at the 'Fucking English'. I avoided him and weaved my way through the back streets to Howard House. So what's a guy to do on his own in a B&B after dark? Thank God for *Match of the Day*. More tea, a flick of the TV button and I was in my element. It didn't last long. I was knackered and even Blackburn Rovers couldn't keep me awake. Besides, a trip to Middlesbrough beckoned the next morning.

DIRTY NORTHERN BASTARDS

Middlesbrough v Sunderland – Ayresome Park, 11 September 1994

I woke up just in time for breakfast in the quaint dining-room of Howard House, just down the road from Brunton Park. At my table sat a young couple from Brighton who worked in a religious bookshop (business was booming apparently) and an elderly couple born in Salford who were searching for their roots.

After half an hour I'd heard enough about great-grandparents and long-lost cousins to last me a lifetime, although the bigamist with nine children, who lived for years at a time with each of his wives before returning to the other, raised an eyebrow or two, including mine. There were two Swedish couples at breakfast who were also tracing their family trees. All roads lead to Carlisle it seems!

I thanked my hosts and hit the road to Middlesbrough. I was looking forward to my first Tees–Wear derby – the last at Ayresome Park before Boro moved to their new £25 million, 32,000 all-seater Cellnet Riverside Stadium in the docks area on the banks of the River Tees.

The journey would take me first to Newcastle, where I had to change. The train from Toon Town left Central Station and crossed the River Tyne. There were so many different bridges over the river it looked as if someone had been let loose with a Meccano set. I gazed back on the city with an air of satisfaction. I'd been to the first League ground of my record attempt. Only 92 to go!

The train shuffled along the edge of the North Sea, where I was treated to glorious views of the coastline. The terrain was quite flat, but with the sun sparkling on the water the morning promised a great day ahead. It didn't quite turn out that way!

There were two Sunderland supporters from Carlisle on the train who often travelled to Roker Park. They'd been at the Carlisle–Exeter match the day before and had heard the half-time announcement over the Tannoy welcoming me to Brunton Park and wishing me luck with my record attempt.

But why didn't they support their home-town team, Carlisle? 'I don't know really,' said the ginger one with the friendly face. 'I just saw the name Sunderland in the paper one day when I was a kid and it stuck in my mind.' The other lad with the crew cut and big smile said he was hooked from the moment he saw his first game at Roker as a boy. They made the 150-mile round trip as often as they could, going to Carlisle games only if Sunderland were away or playing on a Sunday, like today.

The train sped across the Tyne and on towards Sunderland. It passed alongside the city towards Seaham, a coal port with a badly polluted coastline, before going through Hartlepool. 'The monkey-hangers,' said the lad with the crew cut. I gave him a blank look. 'Don't you know the story?' I again stared back blankly with a shake of the head. 'During the Napoleonic wars a French galleon is supposed to have drifted into the harbour at Hartlepool. Nobody was on board except a monkey in Napoleonic battle dress. The people of Hartlepool thought he was a spy so they hung him.'

The Sunderland fans were telling me that Newcastle supporters were the hardest when we were interrupted by half a dozen policemen boarding the train to keep an eye on the travelling away fans. The Sunderland lads were worried the police might check to make sure there were no troublemakers without tickets going to the match.

They decided it was time to get off and take a taxi. It was safer than being 'welcomed' at the main station by the Middlesbrough fans. I decided to join them. They'd arranged to pick up their tickets from a friend outside the ground – a Middlesbrough fan who had got them for the Holgate End amongst the home supporters.

I had a seat in the Main Stand as a guest of Boro's 100 club. The match was live on Tyne-Tees and the fans were watching the pre-match build-up in the bar, a sort of working man's club. Out on the pitch Middlesbrough were parading their new signing. The programme billed him as 'The Boy from Bolivia'. Name: Jaime Moreno, known to Bolivian fans as '*Il Pichon*', which roughly translated means 'Roadrunner'. Beep, beep. Club: FC Blooming, based thousands of feet above sea level at Santa Cruz de la Sierra, Bolivia's second city. What would he make of Middlesbrough?

The fanzine *Bread 'N' Boro* once listed the misconceptions outsiders have about Middlesbrough, which were picked up from a Boro exile. He'd had people tell him that it was near Newcastle and the locals are Geordies, or that it's near Birmingham; the blokes wear cloth caps and keep pigeons; they say 'Why aye, man'; everyone works for ICI; it stinks of pollution; and that it's spelt 'Middlesborough'.

Middlesbrough actually lies south of Hartlepool. It developed in the nineteenth century as a port and an iron and steel town. That explains why the industrial heart of the place is called the Ironmasters District, while the town was originally dubbed Ironopolis. ICI's Wilton petrochemical works are also nearby, though not everybody works there.

Boro were once sponsored by ICI, but their shirt advertising had gone. Some visitors to Ayresome Park were glad. The Tranmere fanzine *Give Us An R* noted that the ICI logo had put a lot of teams off tackling. 'It was a good idea really [that the ICI logo had gone] as everyone had been taking the piss out of this sponsorship deal for years due to all the chemical factories in the surrounding area. You always felt that when a Middlesbrough manager said he was experimenting with the defence it didn't just involve moving them about, but had more to do with a Mary Shelley novel.'

Towards the coast, some three miles from Boro's new ground, is the Redcar British Steel Corporation works. British Steel had also been one of the club's sponsors. However, relations between them and Middlesbrough were now strained to say the least. British Steel were not amused when they found out that Boro's new stadium was being constructed with German steel and they promptly withdrew their £10,000-a-year sponsorship. So much for community spirit!

Middlesbrough said the decision was made by Taylor Woodrow, the civil engineering firm in charge of building the stadium. And the Boro fans say they might have had more sympathy for British Steel if the company hadn't itself refurbished its Lackenby plate mill with – German steel! Nevertheless, the decision did upset families with a history of working in the Teeside steel industry and the ironstone mines.

Out on the Ayresome Park pitch Moreno was introduced to the crowd alongside the club mascot, Roary the Lion. Bryan Robson had fought off top sides from Spain and Colombia in the race for his signature (Moreno's not Roary's!). The 20-year-old forward cost £250,000 plus a further £125,000 based on appearances. That was probably a lot of pesos, but in the world of multi-million-pound British transfers it was peanuts.

Moreno was a product of the renowned Tahuici Football Academy (well, that's what it said in the programme). He'd won the latest of his 30 international caps during the 1994 World Cup Finals in the United States, when he came on as substitute against Germany and Spain. Apparently, his name is pronounced 'High-me'. In London it would sound Jewish. But with a North-East accent . . .

Captain Marvel was well pleased with his new arrival. Moreno got a noisy welcoming reception from the crowd whilst Roary jumped around him. I guessed Robson was hoping Moreno would soon be growling at opposing defences. He scored two goals on his debut in a 3–0 pre-season friendly win over Darlington, but was unable to take part in the serious business of League action until his work permit was approved.

Robson was angry at the delay. 'I'm sure no Boro fans need reminding about the wait we have had in gaining Jaime's work permit. I just find it strange that some players wait only a week for a permit, while for others, like Jaime, it's more like five or six weeks. Surely there should be a set pattern and clear rules to adhere to so that gaining a work permit or not is a straightforward process, no matter who you are.'

British clubs signing foreign players have to meet certain criteria. A permit is issued only to current internationals who've played for at least the previous two years in 75 per cent or more of their country's competitive games. British clubs also have to show they've conducted a genuine and thorough resident labour search in the EC countries. But that search is often neither genuine nor thorough. Middlesbrough's consisted of an attempt to sign Darren Anderton. No wonder Moreno's permit was delayed.

Robbo had signed him to give Boro an extra attacking option, particularly when regular strikers Paul Wilkinson or John Hendrie were injured. They certainly could have used their Bolivian import against Sunderland as their North-East rivals took a commanding two-goal lead.

I thought of the two Sunderland fans in the Holgate End celebrating among the home fans with a muted 'yep' followed by 'I could see that coming' or 'bit exposed at the back, weren't they'. I guessed that inside they were jumping up and down with the rest of the Sunderland fans, who were going barmy in the corner of the south stand at the opposite end of Ayresome Park.

Their joy was premature. Boro staged an amazing comeback with just 12 minutes to go. Alan Moore pulled one back for the home side before captain Nigel Pearson headed the equaliser. Hendrie should have hit the winner for Boro but missed a sitter, firing into the side netting, in an incredible finale to a fine match.

Earlier, Robson had suffered a kick in the balls from Shaun Cunnington, who was booked but could easily have been sent off. The crowd were incensed. 'You dirty northern bastards,' they shouted at Sunderland. I thought I was so far north already that shouting abuse at northerners wasn't kosher. But it seems anyone north of where you are is, er, north. In Aberdeen there's probably only one choice: 'You dirty southern bastards.'

After the match a taxi ride to the metro and a train from there got me back to the airport, but a mix-up over flight times meant I'd missed my plane to London. I then went on a wild-goose chase from the airport to the train station to the bus station, but all in vain. There was no transport back to London. I got another taxi to the airport hotel and rang someone to cover for me at work the next morning. That night I drifted off to sleep watching Woody Allen's *Play It Again Sam*. It had been a long weekend and I was shattered.

The next morning I bought a copy of *The Journal* to see how the local press viewed the match. The Robson incident had grabbed the headlines. 'When Robbo got up, and it took a while, he fixed [Craig] Hignett with the same sort of death mask grin Joe Frazier used to reserve for Mohammed Ali.'

I took the paper along to the dining-room. It was like a throwback to the '60s: garish diamond-shaped mirrors and plastic chandeliers with a patterned carpet like a TV whose horizontal hold needed adjusting. The breakfast buffet included three jugs containing pink, yellow and brown liquid

'What's in those?' I asked the waitress.

'Milk shake, sir,' she replied. Strange people these northerners.

THE ADAMS FAMILY

Wycombe Wanderers v Hull City – Adams Park, 13 September 1994

Wycombe Wanderers' Adams Park ground is the future of British football. I'm not kidding. It's the perfect purpose-built stadium. The right size, superb facilities, a friendly crowd and not a hint of trouble (except when Swansea come to town, I was told). And, of course, there were Cyrille Regis and Simon Garner to draw the fans.

Big Cyrille. Idol of the Hawthorns and Highfield Road. After brief spells at Villa and Wolves he was now spearheading the Wycombe attack. Super Si, former Blackburn favourite, had joined on a free from West Brom. The 30-something attack was still a force to be reckoned with in the Endsleigh Second Division.

Garner, known as the Godfather because he looks like Al Pacino, was a folk hero after treating the Wycombe fans to 'some of the most scintillating talent we have ever witnessed'. Well, we are talking about Wycombe fans here! Hard as it is to believe, Garner is a bigger God than Alan Shearer in the eyes of the true Blackburn fans, according to some of them. I'm not so sure they'd say that now Shearer & Co have delivered the Premier League title.

Big Cyrille was still a class above the rest even at his ripe old age. Always a powerful athlete, he looked in good shape as he pulled into the car park.

'Will you score against us tonight Cyrille?' asked one of the Hull fans who'd driven down for the match and were now hovering outside the players' entrance looking for free tickets.

'I might not be playing,' said Regis. 'Surely you are,' said the other Hull supporter.

'It's not good to be presumptuous,' smiled big Cyrille.

The Hull fans began talking about their team's rivalry with Grimsby. 'Codheads' they called them. (I didn't like to point out that Hull is also well known for its links with the fishing industry.) They travelled to most of City's away games, but they'd come to Adams Park especially to see the flower-beds which they'd heard were dotted around the ground. They were not disappointed.

Wycombe have created a lovely family atmosphere. Children mixed with grandparents and the disabled. Players stopped to sign autographs at the side of the pitch during their pre-match warm-up. Stewards welcomed fans with a smile. There were even tea trollies pushed around the stands in case you wanted a quick cuppa during the game.

The club is so down-home in its approach to professional football that the opening notes in the match programme don't mention the people's game until the 12th line. The introduction left me, well, lost for words. It was called 'Behind the Scenes' by John Goldsworthy. I'll let him take up the story:

'I have just arrived back from my daily morning walk, but as it was rather misty it was not a case of smelling the flowers on the way, but rather a case of studying the intricate spiders' webs, not usually visible, but because of the mist exposed as necklaces of pearls, very charming. If I keep this up I'll get a first class degree in Environmental Studies.' And very likely lose your job as a contributor to the match programme.

It got worse. After reading a quick reference to Hull and a debate over why they're known as the Tigers – the conclusion was that it derived from their shorts (it didn't explain why) and not from tigers, since Hull is a seaport, unless they imported tigers from India – I was left speechless once again.

'I have always associated Hull City with the name of Needler, because some years ago a gentleman of that name was an FA Councillor of some standing and also that gentleman's name was associated with chocolates. [Any idea what all this is about yet? Me neither.] I recollect the name on boxes and bars of chocolate, but not now, probably swallowed up by Cadbury's.'

The article then laments the fact that Wycombe missed a golden opportunity

25

to play a pre-season friendly with Skonto, the Latvian champions, because of fixture congestion. I was sure Adams Park would have been filled to the rafters for that one. The standing of the Latvian champions dawned on Wycombe when they heard Skonto had knocked Aberdeen out of the UEFA Cup.

Next came criticism of a *Daily Mail* special report which included uncomplimentary comments about Wycombe Hospital. This man knows no bounds. There was also a full account of his visit to see the British Grand Prix at Silverstone after an absence of 38 years. I'm sure he was missed.

He ended with an unforgettable list of places everyone should visit 'once in a lifetime'. They included: a big football match at Wembley; the Taj Mahal; Agra by moonlight (where?); Victoria Terminus (why?); Bombay; Florence; Italy (surely covered by the Florence trip?); the Icreflies in the jungle at Kogalia (of course!); Sri Lanka (get me Thomas Cook right away); and, wait for it, Adams Park (surely high on everyone's list of exotic destinations). Wouldn't you know that our man from Wycombe had done the lot. Been there, done that, got the T-shirt. But what had all this got to do with football and tonight's match in particular? I remain bewildered.

I had set off for Adams Park from London's Marylebone Station after work with an army of commuters. As I sat, crammed in with the dark-blue pin-stripe brigade and their smart briefcases, the surroundings gradually changed from the rows of houses and light industry around the City to the beautiful open countryside of Buckinghamshire.

Wycombe's nickname, the Chairboys, comes from the furniture industry which once dominated the area. The club was formed by a group of young furniture trade workers in 1884 under the name of North Town Wanderers – the area of the town where they lived. They were probably also named after the famous FA Cup winners, the Wanderers, who visited the town in 1877 for a tie with the original High Wycombe club. The name was changed to Wycombe Wanderers in 1887.

Despite the town's seeming prosperity, the taxi drivers who drove me to and from the ground talked about the number of factories that were closing. One sweet factory employing 300 people had shut down and moved to Banbury. G-Plan had also laid people off. Things weren't as good as they'd once been in High Wycombe (let alone Low Wycombe, which I never did find! Is there such a place?)

The exception was the football. Success on the pitch and a new stadium had brought the crowds in ever-increasing numbers to Adams Park. The ground is surrounded by high trees and must be one of the prettiest settings in the League, along with Shrewsbury and Rochdale. Surprisingly, the Wycombe pitch is the same size as Wembley, though that's where the comparison ends.

The club sold Loakes Park, their home for 100 years, to property developers for £3.5 million, and moved to their present ground at Hillbottom Road. The new stadium cost £3.75 million, with the difference coming from local business sponsorship. Adams Park was opened in 1990, three years before Wycombe were promoted to the Football League as Vauxhall Conference champions. They also won the FA Challenge Trophy that year, to complete a historic 'double'. Remarkably, they were then promoted to the Second Division via the play-offs in their first season in the League.

A tour of the ground before kick-off enabled me to take a look at the cantilevered stands on all four sides of the stadium: the Main Stand; the Bucks

Free Press Stand; the Hillbottom Terrace; and the Davenport Vernon Stand; which was once used to accommodate the visiting supporters who tonight, however, were standing on the terraces at the Hillbottom Road End. The ground holds just under 12,000, but was the perfect size for football at this level.

Next we wandered into the directors' lounge, where pride of place went to the 1994 *Evening Standard* Five-A-Side trophy. Framed newspaper cuttings of the club's 1931 Amateur Cup win lined the walls leading up to the executive lounge, whereas in the lounge itself was a portrait of Wycombe director and television commentator Alan Parry alongside the club's other directors.

It would be a busy few weeks for Alan. He'd had to miss the Wycombe–Hull match because he was commentating on Wolves versus Southend for Central. Then it was off to Heathrow for a flight to Barcelona and the opening Champions League tie with Galatasaray. On the Thursday morning Alan was flying from Spain to Italy, where he'd check into Aston Villa's team hotel to prepare for their big game against Inter Milan in the San Siro. A flight back to London on Friday and another Central extravaganza, Birmingham against Peterborough, on Sunday. In between, he hoped to slip up to Crewe to catch Wycombe's next match. 'Just think of it, Nou Camp to Gresty Road,' said Alan.

Refreshingly, Alan Parry really appreciates his jet-setting lifestyle. 'As I've said so often before, being paid to watch football is a dream come true for this little scruff from the back streets of Liverpool.'

Wycombe had started well following their play-off success the previous season. After six games they'd won four, drawn one and lost one. The fans next to me were sceptical about their chances of keeping this up. 'At Bradford it was like the Alamo. We were all waiting for Davy Crockett to come on as sub.' Wycombe had only lost 2–1 but it could have been six, I was reliably informed. Wycombe had lost the games they should have and won the games they shouldn't. It didn't sound as if they could keep it up.

Still, at least the fans could keep up with the latest news on their 'Blues Beeper' – if they wanted to. The *Adams Family* fanzine thought it was 'a mind-blowingly stupid idea. Do you really need some tacky blue box beeping its little heart out? It could be highly embarrassing. I can just picture the scenario. I've pulled Patsy Kensit, she takes me back to her flat and starts ripping her clothes off when suddenly, "Bleep, bleep, bleep" and I can't help myself. I shout, "Maybe some other time Patsy," and sprint to the nearest phone box to find out if it's true that we've signed some oafish centre-back on a free from Dulwich Hamlet.'

The fans weren't the only ones dreaming of gorgeous women. Wycombe's dressing-room was decorated with a picture of five stunners, backs to camera, shapely bottoms in full view. 'Chase the Blues Away' said the caption. Unfortunately, that's exactly what Hull did. They took the lead four minutes on and added a second after the break. Wycombe were so friendly even their announcer seemed excited. 'That's another goal for Hull,' he enthused.

'He doesn't have to sound so happy about it,' said the fan next to me on the Davenport Vernon Stand terraces. Even a late consolation from the Chairboys didn't cheer him up.

INTO THE LIONS' DEN

Millwall v Burnley – The New Den, 14 September 1994

Millwall's reputation leaves you wondering what the hell you'll be letting yourself in for when you visit their ground in south London. But my visit to the New Den, just off London's Old Kent Road, turned out to be a pleasant surprise. It's not just that I survived the experience without getting beaten up and dragged senseless into a back street. The new stadium is actually superb, the match was a five-goal thriller and, although Millwall lost, everyone seemed to get home in one piece.

I have to admit I'd never been to the old Den in the aptly named Cold Blow Lane but, by all accounts, the former home of the Lions was not the sort of place to be found on a cold, wet winter night. Eamon Dunphy, in his excellent book *Only a Game?*, described a visit to the Den as something most teams hated.

'I remember thinking, "Where is this?" Then you go and have a look at the pitch, which is bumpy, terrible. The away team dressing-room is a dungeon, no light, no window. The bathrooms are horrible. Then you get out there to face them – the Lions. And they come storming at you and most sides jack it in.'

In *The Football Grounds of Great Britain* Simon Inglis described Cold Blow Lane on a dark, wet night as 'the perfect setting for a Jack the Ripper horror film; dry ice wafting about the cobbled streets and under the low tunnels. There are mysterious yards full of scrap, malodorous goings-on behind high fences, tower blocks looming in the distance, even old tram lines embedded in the roads. They knew what they were dealing with when they called it Cold Blow Lane.'

The ground suffered bomb damage during the Second World War and was closed a record number of times because of crowd trouble in 1920, 1934, 1947, 1950 and 1978. The goal nets had a very close mesh to protect opposing goalkeepers from being hit by missiles thrown from the crowd. The last game there saw a pitch invasion, when balls and the goalposts were stolen. 'No one likes us, we don't care,' is the supporters' anthem.

So, would things be different at the new ground? This is variously called the New Den, the New London Stadium or Senegal Fields – the name of the site of the ground from the days when London's Docklands area actually employed tough local dockers to unload bulging ships from around the world. Maybe Derby's players could provide the answer after the pitch invasion during the 1994 play-offs, when their keeper was attacked. But if you ask most supporters, they'll tell you the incident was caused by a senseless minority bent on destroying the club's image. Most fans are well behaved.

On the night of my visit, the Burnley fans in the North Stand upper tier were so far away from the Millwall supporters in the rest of the ground that only Peter Pan could have got within fighting distance. The atmosphere inside the ground was great. Both sets of supporters were chanting for their teams, the compact new stadium (capacity just over 20,000) providing an excellent environment for modern football.

Later in the season Port Vale's marvellous fanzine *The Memoirs of Seth Bottomley* would prepare its readers for the trip to Millwall by organising an apocryphal Cockney Weekend:

> As soon as you reach London it's time for a 40-minute tube journey through some of London's most picturesque tunnels. You will spend the entire journey standing up in a crowded compartment with your face pressed against the armpit of someone who's just finished a ten hour shift at Smithfield Market, while in your left ear you'll have to endure the buzzing of a crap INXS album from a personal stereo belonging to a hairy Australian tourist who hasn't washed for a week.
>
> Next is a traditional taxi ride with a cheeky Cockney chappie cab driver. You will sit for about half an hour in a traffic jam while the driver keeps looking over his shoulder at you and rabbiting on about the government or Terry Venables, calling you 'guv' and charging you about twenty quid for the privilege, and then calling you all the names under the sun if you don't give him a tip. Alternatively, you can travel in a vomit-ridden mini-cab driven by an illegal immigrant from Morocco with no insurance and bald tyres.

I decided to avoid public transport and drive west from the London suburb of Redbridge past the gleaming Canary Wharf tower – the tallest building in Europe – in the heart of London's Docklands. The name apparently comes from the canaries imported from the West Indies in the nineteenth century and brought into the docks to be unloaded and shipped to high-class pet shops, where they were sold to wealthy ladies who needed the company.

The regeneration of London's Docklands is amazing. Glass and steel constructions have replaced many of the old tenements, with the docks now surrounded by new homes and refurbished warehouses. The high ceilings and raw brick have been preserved to provide a luxurious setting for wealthy City traders, accountants, property developers and others on above-average salaries.

The less well-off are in places like Millwall's home at New Cross – itself transformed by a rash of developments during the property boom of the 1980s. I drove to the New Den past some interesting pubs. There was the World Turned Upside Down, a suitable description for some of the turmoil caused by Millwall fans in the past, and the Thomas A Beckett on the Old Kent Road – famous because of the gym upstairs. Many a gritty London boxer, including Our 'Enry, cut his teeth (eyes, nose, etc.) training above the pub for a big fight. Opposite New Cross Gate station is the Rose, named after former *Double Your Money* star Monica.

Travelling fans are still wary of a trip to the Lions' Den. The Port Vale fanzine issued this warning on using the local hostelries:

> Remember where you are when using these pubs. Millwall supporters have a somewhat unsavoury reputation so it may be prudent not to steam into any of these houses shouting 'Johnny Rudge's Black & White Army' or

'Come and have a go if you think you're hard enough', as they're more than hard enough and would probably jump at the chance of having a go! A useful tip to blend into the surroundings, apart from shaving your head and tattooing KILL THE BILL on your forehead, is to remember the local pronunciation of Millwall. The l's are silent.

I parked in a back street near the ground, carefully hiding the radio and ensuring the alarm was set before walking to the stadium. I sat in the comfortable padded seats reserved for match sponsors in the executive area of the stand. The view from just above the halfway line was perfect. The same couldn't be said for the weather as the rain began to drizzle down on a warm autumn night.

The game itself was a slow starter, goalless at half-time. I headed for the press-room at the top of the main stand for some half-time refreshments. Tea and sandwiches were being served to reporters from the national papers, local radio and Clubcall line. Their main concern was to catch some of the Man United match against IFK Gothenburg in the Champions League. Millwall's first-half performance was hardly mentioned.

The reporter from the weekly *Burnley Express* had to write a match report plus a commentary and an interview with Burnley manager Jimmy Mullin. His deadline was three o'clock Friday afternoon, but he'd deliver his words of wisdom that night over the phone on his portable computer to avoid rushing back to Burnley in the morning. By the end of the second half he'd have much to write about.

I joined the Press for the second half. There wasn't a single woman amongst them. It seemed that the advent of female television sports presenters on Sky and the BBC hadn't transferred itself to the printed press corps, which was clearly still a bastion of male domination in a feminist world. Next to me in the press seats was a commentator from Radio Lancashire. Alongside him, providing the expert analysis, sat a Burnley player who'd been injured and was having trouble getting his place back after the record signing of Liam Robinson for £250,000 from Bristol City.

Former Spurs and Fulham star Alan Mullery was behind me, providing the colour commentary for London's Capital Gold. There was plenty of colour to add in the second half when former Derby winger Ted McMinn collided with Millwall full-back Tony Cunningham in a clumsy attempt to play the ball. Referee Mick Bailey pulled out the yellow card, then the red, implying that the unfortunate McMinn was being sent off for a second bookable offence. The problem was he hadn't committed the first one yet!

McMinn protested. He asked his manager what he should do. 'I told him to stay on the pitch,' Mullin explained after the match. The referee, realising his mistake, consulted his linesman. Not that either manager trusted his judgement.

'How can you have much faith in a linesman who earlier gave offside from a throw-in?' said Millwall manager Mick McCarthy.

There was only one possible outcome. The referee had to change his decision. At least he was brave enough to admit his mistake. And McCarthy, to his credit, said McMinn didn't deserve to get sent off. Millwall's manager was just upset at the standard of officiating. Not that he or his team could blame the ref for their first home defeat in 20-odd matches at the New Den. When asked to pinpoint the reason for losing, he just said: 'Bad defending.'

The winning goal in a 3–2 thriller had the Burnley fans on their feet. They'd already tried to build up the atmosphere with a Lancashire rendition of the Mexican wave in the first half. 'It's called the Mexican wave because the fans first began to do it in Mexico at the World Cup in 1986,' the man behind me explained to his female companion. She was obviously an expert on football!

After the match the journalists began to file their reports. One was shuffling pieces of yellow paper with scribbled notes all over them as if he couldn't make up his mind which bits to put where in his story. Another was giving his version of the McMinn mix-up. The *Burnley Express* reporter made his way downstairs to interview some of the players in their bar, while the rest of us waited for the managers to give us their words of wisdom at the post-match press conference.

Jimmy Mullin came into the press-room first. A former Huddersfield star, he'd guided Burnley out of the Third Division and into the Second Division play-offs. A remarkable victory in front of 44,000 fans at Wembley had launched them into the First Division.

Mullin asked for a beer and then sat poker-faced waiting for questions. Anyone would have thought that Burnley had just been slaughtered given his sombre appearance. If this is what he's like when they've won a five-goal thriller away from home, how does he react when they lose?

'Could you single out any of your players for praise tonight?' I asked.

'They were all brilliant, just brilliant. I couldn't have asked for any more from them. It was a great team performance. Sometimes, I put my arm around them in the dressing-room and they know they've played well.'

His demeanour was a topic of conversation among the hacks as they waited for McCarthy to emerge from the dressing-room. 'Why did you take Mark Kennedy off and bring Dave Mitchell on? Weren't you removing the player who would have provided the crosses for him?' McCarthy was asked.

'I don't know what game you were watching,' McCarthy snapped back. 'You tell me how many crosses he supplied while he was on the pitch.' A fair point, but Kennedy had played well.

McCarthy was a reporter's dream. Controversial. Always ready to tell it like he sees it. A journalist from *The Sun* told me McCarthy had once brought his son into the press-room and let him crawl around the floor with his toy car while he answered questions (McCarthy not the boy!). I was to meet the Millwall manager once again on my travels, at White Hart Lane, where he would be spying on FA Cup opponents Arsenal.

OLIVER HÄHNKE

Doncaster Rovers v Hereford United – Belle Vue, 16 September 1994

My visit to Doncaster in south Yorkshire was dominated by one man: Oliver Hähnke. If someone had told me I'd be sitting in the Main Stand at the club's Belle Vue stadium talking to a football-mad ice cream salesman from Berlin and his Brazilian girlfriend from Rio de Janeiro, I wouldn't have believed them. But that's exactly what happened.

I met Oliver at the refreshment bar before the match. I first noticed him because of the Brazilian baseball cap he was wearing.

'Have you come all the way to Doncaster from Brazil?' I asked, half-joking.

'No, I'm from Germany,' he replied in a soft accent.

'What are you doing here?' I asked, trying to work out why he had joined less than 2,000 die-hard Doncaster fans and 50-odd Hereford supporters on a cold Friday night.

The explanation was simple. Oliver was a football fanatic. Not just any football. He loved English football. He couldn't explain why, but he supported Everton, though he liked all English teams. Oliver's passion for the game was so strong that he spent a large part of his annual holidays travelling around England watching football. This year he'd hired a caravanette.

Oliver was one unique individual. If an English team was playing a German team, he wanted the English team to win. He rooted for Norwich when they beat Bayern Munich in the UEFA Cup in 1994. He planned to watch 15 games in three weeks on this trip, including Arsenal, Manchester United, Aston Villa, Ipswich, Everton, Wimbledon and any others he could fit into his schedule. He ended up driving 11,000 kilometres and seeing 25 matches, including England–Romania at Wembley. On the way home from England they stopped at the Kaiserslautern–Odense BK game. Why not?

At the end of the Doncaster–Hereford match he opened his wallet to show me all the tickets he'd already bought. He did have one slight problem. Arsenal's return Cup-Winners' Cup tie against Omonia Nicosia and Villa's UEFA Cup game against Inter Milan were on the same night. He had tickets for both matches, but not even football-mad Oliver Hähnke could get to two games at the same time.

Oliver watched and played football all over the world. He was a regular visitor to the national Maracana stadium in Brazil, and often played football on the beaches of Rio. He was a goalkeeper, though at present he couldn't play because of a foot infection picked up on those Rio beaches. He'd be out of action for months.

Oliver was lucky in that his girlfriend, Rosi, loved football too. Having said that, I'm not sure she enjoyed the Doncaster match. In her broken English she told me the weather was much warmer in Rio. I'm sure the football was better too, though, to their credit, Doncaster put on a show for her with some neat football and three goals.

Let's face it, how many men have a gorgeous Brazilian girlfriend who is happy to follow them all over England, come rain or shine, to watch Third Division Endsleigh League Football at places like Doncaster. Exactly. Oliver's last girlfriend, from Yugoslavia, wasn't quite so keen. 'She wasn't like Rosi,' he told me. Who is?

Rosi's favourite player was Romario, though she didn't like the way he sometimes dived to get penalties. He should stay on his feet more.

'Like Klinsmann,' I said cheekily.

'Even Germans hate the way Klinsmann dives all the time,' said Oliver. 'He's a good player, very quick, he should stay on his feet.'

I'd arrived at Doncaster, a town of just under 300,000, well before kick-off for a tour of the ground. It didn't take long. After Wycombe and Millwall, with their brand new purpose-built stadiums, a visit to Doncaster was like going back in time. They were lucky to have a sponsor for tonight's match, but it looked as if times were hard for the second-oldest League club in Yorkshire. The match sponsors received a football signed by the first team and a buffet was laid on for them in their own lounge, which looked like someone's front room.

Rovers moved to Belle Vue in 1922 after the supporters moved a pile of ash from the nearby coal tips to build up the banking and lay the foundation for the pitch. The fans also jacked up the Main Stand from the club's previous ground at Bennetthorpe, wheeled it along the road and put it on the northern terrace. It looked as if little had changed since the 1920s. There was talk about building a new stadium with the town's rugby club but, so far, that was all it amounted to, talk.

The ground is opposite the town's famous racecourse, which lies on the east side of Belle Vue on Town Moor. Parts of its magnificent grandstand date back to the late 1700s and its oldest classic race, the St Leger, was established in 1776. The St Leger is run during the second week of September, whereas the William Hill Lincoln Handicap in March begins the flat-racing season in Britain. On race days the horse-boxes are parked in the Belle Vue car park and traffic often comes to a standstill when horses are led across Bawtry Road.

The only other things Doncaster is famous for is railway engineering – the Great Northern Railway established its workshops there in the 1800s – and Europe's largest indoor leisure complex, the Dome. the Railway Plant Works no longer play much part in the town's industry. But the Dome sure does. Touted as the 'new heart of Doncaster', it completely overshadows the dilapidated Belle Vue stadium.

The football club had hoped the £22 million, council-built sports and leisure complex would be part of a refurbished football ground. It wasn't and the club can only cast envious glances at its next-door neighbour, which comes complete with leisure pools (the lagoons), ice rinks, squash courts, sports hall, saunas, steambaths, indoor bowling green, multi-screen cinema and social club. The Dome hosts the World Matchplay Snooker Championships, plus international boxing and basketball.

Inside Belle Vue the referee had arrived and was inspecting the pitch. The game had been switched from Saturday to avoid clashing with the RAF Finningley international airshow. It was difficult enough to attract supporters without competing with one of the biggest airshows of the year. The organisers expected a record attendance of more than 150,000 because the impending closure of Doncaster's RAF base in 1996, after 60 years service, meant this was the last show.

The referee was admiring the pitch, which was in perfect condition. Rovers can be proud of their playing surface. The owners of Wembley offered more than £10,000 for the Belle Vue turf in the 1970s but were turned down. Rovers knew the surface was only in such good condition because of the drainage beneath, where the ash lay. It used to be the largest in the League, until manager Billy Bremner, the former Leeds captain, decided his team wasn't fit enough to run around it for 90 minutes. To stop opponents taking advantage of their shortcomings, he had eight yards trimmed off the end!

I was taken beneath the Main Stand into the home dressing-room, where I met former Spurs and West Ham winger Jimmy Neighbour. He'd just been appointed assistant manager the previous Tuesday. 'We can't score enough goals, that's our problem; only five in eight matches so far this season. I want to change that,' he said. Neighbour's enthusiasm was infectious.

I told him I'd seen him play for Spurs. 'That was a long time ago,' he said. His job now was to motivate the Doncaster players. He was writing up the names of the Hereford team on a white blackboard with a marker pen when I interrupted him. The name Wilkins stood out (Graham not Ray).

'Have you any special plans for tonight?' I asked. 'You know, a man-to-man marker or anything like that.'

'Not really,' said Jimmy. 'I'd prefer to let the other team worry about us, especially when we're playing at home.'

I wished him luck on his home début and went in search of the trophy room. When I asked where the trophies were kept, Terry Burdass, the commercial manager, looked at me as if I was winding him up. But I wasn't. I knew from the programme that Doncaster were champions of the Third Division in the '30s and '40s and had won the Fourth Division title a couple of times.

There wasn't a trophy room as such, but the boardroom contained a wall cabinet with a few old trophies. Most of them were regional titles, but I was intrigued by a mini replica of the Jules Rimet Trophy, presented to the club by the Football Association to mark England's 1966 World Cup triumph. I hadn't seen one before but assumed every League club was given one after our victory over West Germany. They were.

The other interesting item in the panelled boardroom was a caricature of a group of policemen on each other's shoulders. They formed a pyramid like you sometimes see in an acrobats' circus act. The policeman on top was shining a torch across the pitch over the caption: 'I wish they'd fix those bloody floodlights.'

'Just goes to show what we have to put up with sometimes,' said the commercial manager.

We stopped by the office of the oldest manager in English professional football, 62-year-old Sammy Chung. His makeshift office was in a Portakabin in the Belle Vue car park. Hardly inspiring, but it didn't seem to bother the happy-go-lucky Mr Chung. He'd also only recently been appointed and was enjoying life.

Chung joined Reading in 1949 and became an accomplished inside-forward at Norwich and Watford. He then took a job as assistant to Bill McGarry at Watford before moving to Ipswich and Wolves. The partnership at Wolves took them to the UEFA Cup final in 1972, where they lost to Spurs, and victory in the 1974 League Cup final.

Chung took over from McGarry when Wolves were relegated in 1976. They were promoted at the first attempt, but Chung was sacked two years later. He had since coached abroad (in Sweden), at Stoke and at Colchester. In 1993 he set up a soccer academy in Wolves and settled back to a peaceful life outside football management.

'I thought someone was pulling my leg when the chairman Ken Richardson rang from Doncaster. I thought it had all gone past me actually. I'd been applying for jobs and was not even getting interviews,' said Chung, whose Chinese father came to Britain as an interpreter in 1914.

The Doncaster manager certainly has his own style. 'I used to have these big discussions with Brian Clough. He'd say, "It's all about management." I would argue, "No, it's about coaching, about technique, teaching guys the basics, how to head a ball." Clough said: "I don't teach them. I buy them because they can head the ball." This discussion went on until in the end we agreed, "I make 'em, you buy 'em.'"

I left Chung's office and walked across the car park towards the away supporters who'd just made the four-and-a-half-hour trip from Hereford. They were waiting for their team to arrive. Hereford's captain Dean Smith came across the car park towards the players' entrance and was immediately surrounded by fans. The previous day, manager Greg Downs, a member of Coventry's 1987 FA Cup winning side, had resigned and assistant manager John Layton was in charge for tonight's match.

The supporters wanted to know what was going on at the club. Smith chatted amiably to the fans. They were a dedicated bunch and they paid his wages, so it was in his interests to give them a few minutes of his time. But he seemed genuinely anxious to address their concerns. 'The players didn't want the boss to leave. But we're professionals and we just have to concentrate on our football,' he explained.

He left to prepare for the match and I asked a young fresh-faced fan what he thought of the latest developments. 'Well, the players may not have wanted Downs to leave, but I did. We were crap last season and we haven't started well this year either. We need some new faces to turn things around. We just can't score goals right now.'

I asked why he followed Hereford all over the country when they had such a crap team. 'I also like Arsenal and last season I started watching more of their games. The trouble is I live in Hereford. They're my local team, so I have to support them.'

And there you have it – fan loyalty. Football is unlike any other product. You can't just replace one team with another like you can when you don't like your wife, your job or your soap powder anymore. The clubs know this and for years they have subjected loyal fans to abject conditions inside Britain's football grounds. It took the law, in the form of Lord Justice Taylor's report, to wake them up to the decline in the facilities. Fans like Oliver Hähnke may never complain, but they shouldn't have to.

WHY ARE WE CHEERING?

Leicester City v Tottenham Hotspur – Filbert Street, 17 September 1994

At last, a Carling Premier League match to savour. Now, don't get me wrong; I enjoy football at all level – schoolboy internationals, GM Vauxhall Conference games, amateur football. But the Premier League is class. It was the main reason Oliver Hähnke had driven hundreds of miles from Berlin in a caravanette.

I was looking forward to today's match. For a start, I had the mouthwatering prospect of watching Germany's centre-forward Jürgen Klinsmann playing alongside England international Teddy Sheringham for Tottenham. Then there was the Romanian Ilie Dumitrescu, playing today without his compatriot Gica Popescu, who was still waiting for a work permit. And, finally, exciting England Under-21 star Julian Joachim was up front for Leicester, with Mark Draper behind him in midfield.

I hoped the football was going to be more attractive than the town. My *Blue Guide to England* gave a rather blunt description of the city. 'Leicester, the county town, is an unattractive place. The pervasive effects of its industry and manufacturing – in the outer sprawl of 20th century housing estates, inner ring of 19th century red-brick terraces and ghastly redevelopment of the centre – make it hard to appreciate the real points of interest, chiefly its Roman remains and several museums.' They might have added a visit to Filbert Street given the club's newly acquired Premier League status.

Leicester's prosperity since the seventeenth century has come from the hosiery trade, which explains the arrival of hundreds of Asian immigrants in the '50s and '60s. Today, about a third of the population of almost 300,000 is Asian and the city elected Britain's first Asian MP, Keith Vaz, in 1987. That was the reason for the popularity of the Indian restaurants on Belgrave Road – the site of Leicester City's first enclosed ground – which drew people from miles around. What I couldn't work out was why there was not a single Asian player in the Leicester team. There was a big enough pool of young talent to choose from; was it that they just weren't good enough?

The other interesting titbit I found out about Leicester was that Thomas Cook took his first step as a tour operator in the town with a railway excursion to Loughborough and back in 1841. So how come his company wasn't running the Leicester City travel club?

Having made my own way to the ground, I arrived just in time to meet Jack Curtis, a Leicester City official, who gave me a tour of Filbert Street, also known as the City Stadium. This really meant a look around the new Main Stand, sponsored by Carling, which had opened two years ago, and a walk up the tunnel and out onto the pitch. Jack just had time to show me around before getting back to reception and his main pre-match task of giving the mascots a tour. Their parents would accompany them and I sensed they were looking forward to it as much as their kids.

Jack Curtis had known great success in football. His Leicester district side had twice won the English Schools Trophy, the premier domestic schoolboy competition. One of those successes was at the expense of Manchester United just after the war. 'The first leg at Filbert Street was 0–0 and so was the second leg at Old Trafford. It went to extra-time and a lad I didn't rate very highly – a big lad he was – ended up scoring two goals. I'd originally asked why he was in the team at all! The lad in question never made it in the big time, though.'

Out on the pitch the stewards were receiving instructions as I took photos of the Spion Kop. 'We're the only club who still put that on the matchday tickets,' said Jack. 'Do you know how it got the name?' I did, but I wanted to hear Jack's version of the story. 'It comes from the Boer War,' he told me.

The Spion Kop was the name of a hill in South Africa fought for by British troops, drawn mainly from regiments in Lancashire, in January 1900. More than

300 soldiers died in the attack on the Boer Forces defending the hill, many of whom were from Liverpool. 'I suppose the slopes of the banking used for the terraces reminded them of the hill they defended in South Africa, so that's why they called it the Spion Kop,' said Jack.

I wondered how many of today's 22,000 crowd knew the origins of the Spion Kop (see also Liverpool v. Southampton). I had thought there was only one Kop – the famous terrace at Anfield, which I remembered as a sea of red and white flags and scarves before it became all-seater. But, as I was to discover on my travels, many other grounds around the country have stands called the Kop, including Bloomfield Road, the Racecourse Ground and Windsor Park. Arsenal claim to have had the first, but the club no longer uses the name at Highbury.

The Filbert Street pitch was in superb condition, surrounded by Leicester's redeveloping stadium. The Tottenham fanzine, the embarrassingly titled *Cock-a-Doodle Doo*, described the ground as 'an interesting mix. Two sides are small, low, cramped, old – seats tacked onto what were once terraces many years ago now. Visiting fans are allocated one or two East Stand blocks (along the side), probably around 2,000 seats.'

The City End (Spion Kop or South Stand) is also old (built in 1927), but a fairly large double-decker. The Main Stand, by total contrast, is a massive, spacious new stand, built two years ago at a cost of £5.35 million. After so long (the last time the two sides met was in 1986–87), it's almost like going to a new ground altogether.

Executive boxes lined the top of the North Stand in Filbert Street, home of the Captain's Club restaurant, while the Main, or Carling, Stand contained more luxurious executive facilities – including seats outside the boxes for those who wanted to soak up the atmosphere. The main entrance to the East Stand in Burnmoor Street is through houses, and the gateways pass underneath the bedrooms of the local residents!

The idea of watching a match behind glass didn't appeal to me. It's the crowd and the passion and the wind and the rain and all that goes with actually being out there in the elements that makes football such a great spectacle. Sitting in an executive box is like a halfway house between Sky Sports and actually going to the match.

After a walk around the edge of the pitch we popped our heads into the home dressing-room. It was already filling up with the Leicester players preparing for today's big match. Iwan Roberts, a bustling centre-forward signed from Huddersfield, passed me in the corridor to join his team-mates. The players' shirts were hanging on pegs around the dressing-room wall: DRAPER, AGNEW, BLAKE, JOACHIM. Their freshly washed bright blue-shirts were all ready for the day's action.

The Carling Stand was full of executive suites and sponsors' lounges, among them the Gordon Banks Suite and the Gary Lineker Suite – legends among the Leicester faithful. Curiously, there was no Peter Shilton Suite despite the fact that Shilts generated Leicester's then-record transfer fee of £340,000, when he followed in Banks's footsteps by signing for Stoke in November 1974.

I asked to see the trophy room. Leicester won the old Second Division Championship six times. They've never won the FA Cup, despite reaching the final four times, but they did win the Football League Cup for the first time in

1964, when sponsorship was unheard of and the Milk Marketing Board, Littlewoods and Coca-Cola had nothing much to do with football.

Unfortunately the trophies were still stored in boxes underneath the Carling Stand, or at least Jack thought that was where they were. 'They're planning a trophy room but they haven't got around to it yet,' he told me. After all, the Carling Stand had only been open for two years! Doncaster may not have won many trophies, and they may not have had a trophy room either, but at least I could see their trophies in the directors' boardroom. I was sure Leicester fans would eventually get the chance.

Outside the Gary Lineker Suite were framed pictures of the great man at the peak of his career playing for Leicester, Everton, Barcelona and Tottenham. But there were three pictures which caught my attention: the one, two, three goals he scored for England against Poland in the 1986 World Cup – the goals that turned Lineker into an international superstar. Inside, the sponsors were enjoying a three-course meal.

Jack Curtis knew Lineker quite well. 'A nice lad, Gary,' he said. Jack used to open the batting with a 16-year-old Lineker when he played for a local cricket team called Leicester Banks. 'I won't tell you how old I was,' said Jack. I couldn't tell exactly how old he was either, but he was a pensioner and a very proud man; proud of Leicester City and of the young players he'd helped over the years in his role as the head of schools football in the area.

Jack had worked with world-class players. Peter Shilton was one of his 'boys' as well as Lineker. Shilton got his break when England's first-choice Youth goalkeeper was ruled out of a match because of a verruca. 'Peter wasn't in the side. In fact, he wasn't even second choice. But when the team was announced, he was in goal. I was amazed. I asked him afterwards how he managed it. Apparently, the first-choice keeper was bandaging his foot before the match when the England manager saw him. "What's wrong with your foot, lad?" he asked him, "It's a verruca," he replied. And that was that. "Get changed, Shilton," he said to Peter.'

Jack was aware that football could be heartbreaking as well as exhilarating. Another of his protégés was playing for a young England team alongside Bobby Charlton at inside-forward with a promising career ahead of him. A serious injury ended his ambitions. 'So you see, it can fall both ways,' said Jack ruefully. 'I guess that's football.'

Jack Curtis was a man of principle. For him it was all about hard work and dedication. He was of the old school. I felt humbled in his company. Somehow I didn't feel I could have matched his standards. It's a different world today. Jack was the salt of the earth. The game was lucky to have people like him setting an example for young footballers.

By now the Leicester fans, and a few Spurs supporters, had started milling around outside Filbert Street's main entrance waiting for the rest of the players to arrive. The remaining Leicester players drove into the car park outside the Carling Stand before heading for the dressing-rooms, signing autographs along the way.

Joachim was the star attraction. He was surrounded by youngsters, some wearing shirts that bore his name. They thrust their programmes and autograph books in front of him, keeping him busy outside the main entrance for a good five minutes. He looked smart and sophisticated in his brown suit; a young man who knew he was going places. Already an England Under-21 international, many wise heads in the game believed it was only a matter of time before he stepped up a level to secure a full cap.

Mark Draper was the next Leicester star to turn up. The shaven-headed midfielder was a record signing from Notts County. He was to play a significant role in the afternoon's proceedings, pulling the midfield strings that would undo the Tottenham defence time and again in what was to be a very entertaining match.

I looked around the club car park to see what sort of wheels were privileged enough to be parked inside the ground. BMWs, Mercedes, a red Bentley, Jags, a red Ferrari. These people had money. And they seemed happy enough to spend some of it on football. The sponsors' lounges and pre-match meals were testimony to the luxury that could be bought at Filbert Street and many other grounds across the country. Football clubs were catering for the middle classes and it was changing the nature of the game.

The key to this new market was still success on the field and star attractions like Klinsmann, Dumitrescu and Popescu. As the Spurs team bus pulled into the car park the crowd reacted with a sense of anticipation and excitement. Soon they would get a glimpse of Klinsmann and co. He was first off the bus and raised a cheer from the home fans. They pointed and called out to each of the Spurs players in turn. 'Why are we cheering?' asked one Leicester fan. 'We're playing against them today!' Times have changed in football.

My dad had often told me how, as a boy, he went to watch football as much to see the star players coming to town as to see his own team, Leyton Orient, win. Lawton, Matthews, Finney, Shackleton. They were larger than life. Heroes. As big an attraction as the home team. Could it be that crowds are returning to those values? A nice thought, though maybe premature.

I took my seat in the stand to watch the pre-match build-up. After running through the team line-ups the announcer read out the odds on who would score first: Joachim 7–1, Klinsmann 7–2, Sheringham 5–1. 'Why not place your bets on the first goalscorer?' he said.

The match sponsors were Walkers Crisps. How did I know? Well, apart from the huge red and white crisp bag in the ad which covered most of the centre circle, there was a guy walking around the perimeter of the pitch wearing a Walkers crisp bag. He was throwing packets of crisps into the crowd, helped by two more tastefully dressed females. 'I'm getting hungry,' said the fan next to me. It was obviously working.

Shortly afterwards the club mascot, a large furry fox in a Leicester City kit, came out to shake hands with the fans. He was great. Baggy shorts with a big bushy tail sticking out the back. Leicester are known as the Foxes, because of the area's tradition for fox hunting, or the Filberts, after the name of the ground.

Leicester had the better of the first half and just before the interval Joachim made the breakthrough with a jinking run and curling shot past Spurs defender Stuart Nethercott and goalkeeper Ian Walker into the top corner. 'One, nil. And they don't come much better than that,' as David Coleman would have put it.

In the second half, Tottenham fought back. Mike Hazard, an old Spurs favourite who'd returned to White Hart Lane after spells at Chelsea and Swindon, came on for Colin Calderwood and started to make things happen. But despite Tottenham's attacking football, they couldn't score.

It was left to Leicester's new re-signing, David Lowe, to wrap up the game with a curling shot into the top corner. Two, nil. And that was that, or so I thought at the time. Then, with three minutes left, Tottenham scored. Sheringham looped over a cross to Klinsmann, who chested the ball down and volleyed into the back of the net.

The Leicester supporters around me became edgy. Spurs attacked again and hearts were in mouths. They needn't have worried. Leicester broke down the right again through Joachim, who rifled a low right-foot shot into the far corner. Three, one.

It must have been a good day for Leicester fans in more ways than one as I'm sure quite a few had a flutter on Joachim, scorer of Leicester's first and third goals. Not a bad day out: your team wins and you earn a few bob as well. Happy days at Filbert Street.

There was no way back for Spurs now. There was for me, though. I had to catch the train to London. I left the ground and followed the away fans being shepherded to the station by the police. They looked like a flock of sheep who'd lost their way as, huddled together, they gloomily contemplated the journey home.

It had been a great game full of exciting, attacking football; four great goals; end to end stuff. Klinsmann's goal alone was worth the entrance fee.

MONDAY NIGHT FOOTBALL

Ipswich Town v Norwich City – Portman Road, 19 September 1994

Portman Road on a wet Monday night. The Golden Lion down the High Street. Auntie Beryl. Catching the last bus home. If . . . you're drinking Bovril!

This was Monday Night Football in East Anglia, courtesy of Sky Sports. Plenty of passion, three goals (two penalties), six bookings, home débuts for Sedgeley of Ipswich and Sheron of Norwich and lots and lots of rain.

I came out of Ipswich station into a swirling drizzle which quickly covered my suit in a light film of raindrops. I could see the Portman Road floodlights towering above me as I crossed the River Orwell. They were originally paid for by supporters, who raised £15,000, and were used for the first time in a friendly against Arsenal in 1960. The water level in the river was very low, revealing an assortment of unwanted objects including an old chair. The river looked black and murky, like the night itself.

As I made my way to the ground I could feel the sense of anticipation building up among the fans around me. It may not be like a north London or Manchester derby, but Ipswich v. Norwich is the game of the season in East Anglia. There would be no love lost between the fans or the teams tonight.

'I haven't seen any Norwich fans yet,' said a small boy alongside me.

'Probably too scared to come tonight,' his pal replied.

But they had come. They made lots of noise in the corner of the East Stand and by the end of the night it would be hard to get them out of the stadium as they swayed and sang of victory at Portman Road for the first time in 12 years.

I passed by the stewards on the main gate and went to reception to pick up my ticket. As I waited Mick McGiven walked through the main reception. He had been manager in the 1993–94 season but was moved to football development officer after the club's narrow escape from relegation. He said hello to an elderly gent sitting next to me. Shortly afterwards, Ipswich player–coach John Wark wandered past. 'How are you?' he asked the man. I was curious. Who was he?

It turned out that he was the father of club secretary David Rose. Everyone seemed to know him, players and officials alike. He looked much younger than his 85 years. 'It must be the East Anglian air,' I said. He smiled and nodded in agreement. He couldn't exactly remember his first match at Portman Road, though it was before the Second World War. He hadn't played football as a lad and wasn't even that interested in sport back then, but Ipswich Town was in his blood. He lived in town and came regularly.

He said the stadium had improved beyond all recognition from the old days and was now much more comfortable. 'I can remember when there were just wooden bleachers along one side of the ground,' he told me. The bleachers were removed in 1952, when the Pioneer, or West, Stand was built and permanently separated the inside of the stadium from the practice pitch behind. The practice pitch was still there and lit by floodlights tonight.

'I met Alf Ramsey here once,' he told me. 'A nice man, Alf.' Ipswich had seen their best days under the shrewd guidance of the future England manager. He took over at Portman Road in August 1955, when the club was in the old Third Division. Two years later they were promoted and in 1960–61 they won the Second Division title. Remarkably, the following year they brought the League Championship to Suffolk, for the only time, in their first season in the top flight.

How things have changed. 'They were terrible last season,' said the club secretary's father. I recalled the halcyon days of the 1970s, when stars like Paul Mariner, John Wark and Mick Mills combined solid British play with the subtlety of Dutchmen Arnold Muhren and Frans Thijssen. The team shaped by another future England manager, Bobby Robson, won the FA Cup in 1978, beating Arsenal, and the UEFA Cup in 1981, defeating Dutch team AZ Alkmaar.

The only link between that team and the present side was the evergreen Scot John Wark, who was to play superbly once again tonight, scoring the equaliser against Norwich from the penalty spot after Rob Newman had put the Canaries ahead in the 14th minute. Wark's efforts would be in vain. But he was a mainstay at Portman Road. He'd twice left the club, once for the superb Liverpool team of the '80s, but he always returned to his spiritual home.

Wark would no doubt appear in the pictures taken that night by the press photographer sitting next to me in the Ipswich reception before the match. He was a young guy waiting for an extra press-pass for a colleague. He worked for Action Images and his photos would appear in some of the morning's newspapers as well as in the next Ipswich programme for the Coca-Cola Cup tie against Bolton on the following Wednesday night.

Despite taking the pictures for the Ipswich Matchday Programme, he had to bung a local resident £30 for the privilege of using their telephone line to send his images back to the company's head office, based just behind Tottenham's ground in North London. 'The club doesn't provide us with a phone,' he said.

'But you're taking pictures for the programme,' I replied in disbelief.

'It doesn't seem to make any difference,' he replied.

He had to send his pictures back at half-time, to make the early newspaper editions, and at full-time, for the later ones. He had the equipment to develop the film and scan it into a computer which could transmit the photos down the telephone line to a screen in Action Images London office. His pictures might get picked up by the national newspapers. Whether they were used depended on how good they were.

His beat covered the Midlands and the North-West, but he could be sent anywhere in the country. 'The boss tends to pick the games closest to the office for himself, which means Arsenal and Tottenham, mostly. Me. I cover Ipswich, Manchester United and lots of other teams.' Wherever he went he had to find someone who would let him use their phone. The £30 payment seemed to open enough doors, literally.

I grabbed a jumbo hotdog and a cup of coffee (my diet was deteriorating fast) and went to find my seat in the Pioneer Stand, named after the Ipswich sponsors at the time it was built. The stand cost £1.4 million in 1982 and was built on top of the old West Stand. To my right was the Churchman's Stand, named after a former Ipswich player whose tobacco factory stood behind it. It cost £300,000 to rebuild in 1977, when old timber footings – which once caught fire during a match – were replaced.

Opposite, in Portman Road, was the Portman Stand. Along the front was a string of executive boxes, partly financed by the club's FA Cup win in 1978. It was opened in 1971 by Sir Alf. The stand now contains a restaurant and the club shop. When it was completed in 1975, just over 38,000 turned up for an FA Cup match against Leeds. That's still the record attendance at Portman Road.

The auntie next to me (I didn't catch her name but we'll call her Beryl – just so my parody of the Bacardi ad used for the introduction to this chapter works!) said Ipswich manager John Lyall would be in the Portman Stand directors' box. 'He never sits in the dugout,' she said disapprovingly. Below me was Norwich manager John Deehan alongside substitutes Efan Ekoku and Scott Howie. The Ipswich subs, Bulgarian World Cup star Boncho Guentchev and 21-year-old Mauricio Taricco, an Argentine utility player, sat in the dugout alongside.

How a team like Ipswich could leave out a member of Bulgaria's World Cup semi-finalists, conquerors of World Champions Germany no less, and an Under-23 international, after such a dismal start to the season, beat me. It's not like World Cup stars are ten-a-penny in East Anglia, though they're fast becoming so in the rest of the country. Guentchev was to get his chance but, despite a lively performance, it was too late to save Ipswich from defeat.

Taricco was not used at all on the night but, alongside Ipswich's other new signing, Uruguayan international Adrian Paz, would soon add a South American flavour to the proceedings at Portman Road. Paz was ineligible tonight because of enduring work-permit delays. He should have enlisted the support of Bryan Robson at Middlesbrough, who had his own views on Home Office procedures. (Paz was cleared to play later that week and made his début versus Manchester United on the Saturday.)

'This is the most adventurous deal I've ever done,' said Ipswich manager John Lyall. 'It is testimony as to how much the World Cup has broadened people's horizons in this country, and it also shows the status the Premiership enjoys overseas.' The deal was overseen by Marcello Houseman, brother of ex-Argentine international Rene, who represented both Paz and Taricco.

'Obviously we are taking a risk, as they are, but I think they have the quality to succeed,' said Lyall. 'It won't take Adrian long to settle and with Mauricio, who is that bit younger, we have just got to be sensible. He will know when he is ready and that will show through in training.'

Taricco was an attacking midfielder who could operate on either flank. His desire to join Ipswich was so strong that he cut short his honeymoon with new wife Evangelina so that he could fly to England and sign for the club!

Taricco was eligible to play for Ipswich immediately, for his father Piero, who himself played for Juventus and Torino, held an Italian passport and his son therefore automatically qualified for a permit under European Community law. Taricco's English was better than his new South American team-mate's, but they hoped to help each other settle in their new surroundings. They would spend at least one hour a day learning English.

Ipswich saw the capture of Paz as a major coup. A powerful striker who is comfortable operating down either flank or playing straight through the middle, the 26-year-old had already gained 24 caps playing for Uruguay. He had told supporters: 'English football is respected throughout the world and I am looking forward to the challenge.' Ipswich had competition from an old friend in their bid to sign Paz. Bobby Robson had shown interest in taking the former Penarol striker to Porto in Portugal.

'Adrian took one look at the pitch here at Portman Road and said that if he couldn't play on that, then he couldn't play anywhere,' said Town manager John Lyall. The Portman Road pitch has a reputation as being one of the best in the country and tonight it looked lush and green under the floodlights.

The teams were already warming up as I took my seat. I wondered what had happened to the Sky Sports dancing girls and was reliably informed by Auntie Beryl that they didn't appear before matches anymore.

'Why not?' I asked.

'It's just not a tradition in this country like in the States,' she said.

I discovered later that she was the auntie of the boy sitting next to her. His father sat in the row in front taking a barrage of abuse about the Ipswich players, notably Ian Marshall, bought from Oldham.

'He's too slow,' the woman said every time Marshall lost the ball.

Actually, Marshall was having a good match. At least he was giving 100 per cent, unlike some of the Ipswich team. 'He's a trier,' said the father.

Behind me in the press-box was my old friend from the Millwall game at the New Den the week before, former Spurs and Fulham star Alan Mullery. He was almost as omnipotent (or should I say peripatetic) as David Pleat, the Luton manager, who was also giving a colourful commentary for one of the radio stations. 'He should concentrate on his own team,' said one Ipswich fan. 'They need all the help they can get.'

The match itself was full of passion. Norwich had much the better of the first half and deserved more than the 1–1 scoreline they took to their dressing-room at half-time. They had dominated the first 45 minutes and only a dubious penalty on the stroke of half-time denied them the lead at the interval.

The penalty came after Marshall had just carried the ball into the Norwich area when he fell under a challenge from Jon Newsome, Norwich's record £1 million summer signing from Leeds. The 18-yard line had almost been washed away by the rain, but the referee pointed to the spot. The home fans went wild and up stepped John Wark to equalise.

Norwich again made most of the running in the second half and twice hit the woodwork before Carl Bradshaw, the former Sheffield United player, scored at the second attempt, after his penalty was blocked by Ipswich keeper Craig Forrest.

It was a controversial penalty decision. Simon Milton brought down Ian Crook and the referee gave a free-kick just outside the box. He then consulted his linesman and gave a penalty. The home fans went wild again, but this time it was a completely different emotion.

Interviewed after the match, Norwich manager John Deehan was questioned on the penalties and asked about the evidence given by the television cameras. He said there was too much frame-by-frame analysis and that the referee's split-second decisions should just be accepted. Interview over, the Norwich boss wasted no time asking commentator Ian Darke if the cameras showed that Ian Crook's shot had crossed the goal-line after coming off the bar and therefore should have counted!

At 2–1, and with Norwich in control of the match, their supporters began to really enjoy themselves. 'Down with the Walker, you're going down with the Walker,' was the refrain – a reference to the problems of former Norwich manager Mike Walker (now back at Carrow Road), whose Everton team propped up the Premier League. The Ipswich fans were not amused.

After the match I made my way back through town getting soggier with every step. The rain, which had been coming down in sheets during the match, was still drizzling. I checked into the Golden Lion Hotel, the longest-established business in the town. The guy at reception told me the hotel was pretty full. 'Norwich City fans?' I enquired.

'No, journalists,' he said. 'The bar will be busy tonight.'

After a cup of tea and a lie down I ventured into the bar. There were quite a few Ipswich fans there talking about their team's woeful performance.

'We've got Manchester United Saturday, haven't we?' said one.

'Yeh, and I daren't think about what will happen when we play Newcastle. They'll probably beat our record defeat.'

There was then some debate before they recalled that the most goals anyone had put past Ipswich was in a 10–1 defeat by Fulham. I'd read my *Rothmans Football Yearbook* and knew that it was a match in the old First Division in 1963. Quite remarkable when you recall that Ipswich had played in the European Cup the season before!

I slept in the following morning despite the ear shattering noise coming from what sounded like a compressor. I thought I was sleeping outside a council rubbish tip, but on looking out of my windows at about nine o'clock there was nothing I could identify as being responsible for waking me up. I made some tea and crawled back into bed.

At breakfast I was reading the match report from the *East Anglian Times* when I noticed another guy eating alone. He was a reporter with one of the tabloids.

'What did you think of the match?' I asked.

'Norwich were all over them really, they should have won by at least four,' he replied.

He was off to Lincoln City that night for a Coca-Cola Cup tie, but first had to complete a feature on a woman sky diver. 'It fills in the time between matches,' he said. His beat was the Midlands and the North-West but, like the photographer from Action Images, he could be sent anywhere. He was from Norwich, so tonight's game had a particular poignancy.

Never good enough to be a professional footballer, or a professional at any other sport, he decided at a young age that if he couldn't get paid to play, then he would like to earn a living by writing about sport. He appreciated his lifestyle, though the travelling could be a little tiresome. 'Do you know the way to Lincoln?' he asked. I didn't. On Wednesday he'd be back in Ipswich for the Coca-Cola Cup match against Bolton, which Ipswich were to lose 3–0.

Reporting on a football match was a difficult job. He had to file reports continuously during the game to meet the various regional editions. He'd concentrated so much on getting his updates out that he'd missed four of the six bookings in the game. A fellow journalist in the press-box had to fill him in on the others so that he could complete the list, which was closely followed for his paper's dream-team competition. 'You lose two points if one of your players gets booked,' he explained.

Ironically, the edition of the paper that hit the streets of East Anglia contained only his half-time report plus a couple of updates covering the second half goal. The London editions, which carried a much smaller report, would be more up-to-date.

Tabloid journalists have their own code of ethics and they never let the truth get in the way of a good story. He was grateful to Millwall chairman Reg Burr for off-the-cuff remarks which could be turned into eye-catching headlines. Like the time Burr blamed the black Derby striker Paul Williams for causing trouble at a play-off match at the New Den. Just the sort of seemingly racist remark the papers crave.

The tabloid journalist had been frozen out by Millwall after a story saying that their manager Mick McCarthy wanted to leave the club following their play-off defeat against Derby. 'I spoke to some of the Millwall players and they said they thought he might have had enough. I interviewed McCarthy three times but I just couldn't get him to say he wanted to leave. So I wrote the story anyway. He wasn't very happy.' Hardly surprising.

SUSSEX IN ESSEX

Southend United v Bolton Wanderers – Roots Hall, 24 September 1994

A day at the seaside. Well, not quite. In fact, I didn't see the sea – famous as an attraction for East End day-trippers. They still come even today. Southend United probably wish a few more would make their way to Roots Hall to support the local football team. With gates averaging less than 4,000 they could do with the extra ticket sales.

The south end of the old village of Prittlewell, near the mouth of the River Thames, grew into the resort of Southend-on-Sea, from which the club takes its name. It owes its existence to the Prince Regent who, in 1809, decided that Prittlewell, now a suburb of Southend, would provide a healthier climate for his wife, Princess Caroline. She stayed at the south end of the village and that became the town's official name.

Southend's population of 150,000 is spread across most of the nearby towns along a seven-mile stretch of sand and stones facing south to the Thames Estuary. The football club's nickname, the Shrimpers, therefore requires little explanation. At the old cockle sheds in nearby Leigh-on-Sea you can eat a plate of shrimps as well as cockles (the local delicacy), mussels, whelks or crabs. Visitors either take home the fruits of the sea for their tea or eat them by the water with a pint of beer.

They are also attracted by the Kursaal amusement park (where Southend United once played), the crazy golf and the world's longest pier. You can walk or take a train to the end of the one-and-a-half-mile pier – not that there's much to see when you get there. Along the seafront Kiss Me Quick hats vie with pink candyfloss. Fortune-tellers predict your future. The tacky bright lights of endless amusement arcades line the Eastern Esplanade. The culinary choice is mainly fish and chips or bangers and mash.

The classier part of the town is along the Georgian Royal Terrace, with its wrought-iron verandas, which runs along the embankment above the seafront. Princess Caroline stayed in two of the houses during her rest there. Nearby is the Royal Hotel – the resort's social centre during the nineteenth century. Nowadays, the socialising goes on in the restaurants and pubs dotted around the town.

Money finds its way to Southend, but not a lot goes to the local football club. Southend United rely on commercial activities to boost their takings, like the £400,000 earned each year from the use of the main car park outside the stadium as a market. The members' bar, decorated like an Essex pub, also brings in much-needed revenue, along with the main restaurant.

Like all clubs, Southend are desperate for funds to develop their ground, named Roots Hall after the house which once stood on the site. The supporters originally bought the ground and the club moved back there in the late 1950s, after leaving the Southend greyhound stadium. Parts of the ground had been closed but it's all open again now, including the new £1.5 million South Stand.

Former West Ham star Brian Dear was on hand to serve meals before the match. Nice as it was to see Brian looking so well, it was rather sad that a former professional footballer was waiting on tables. There should be a fund for old players to ensure they don't fade and die like the bubbles in the Hammers theme song.

One player who hadn't yet faded or died was former Liverpool star Ronnie Whelan, recently arrived on a free transfer. Southend's form had begun to improve since his arrival. A win against Bristol City was a glimmer of hope after thrashings by Wolves and Stoke. Today's visitors were Bolton, fresh from a 3–0 Coca-Cola Cup win against Ipswich at Portman Road. They were tough opponents, but Southend showed they had spirit in an entertaining match.

Before the game I was introduced to the Southend manager Peter Taylor, a former England international who played for Crystal Palace, Spurs and Orient before moving into management. He joined Southend from Watford, where he was assistant to former Tottenham team-mate Steve Perryman.

Taylor liked his sides to play attractive football and, on their day, Southend had the players to perform. The exciting touchline trickery of Ricky Otto and the strength and aerial power up front of Dave Regis, a new arrival from Birmingham along with Roger Willis, in a deal which took Gary Poole and Jon Hunt to St Andrews.

Unfortunately, Nigerian international Dominic Iorfa, known as the Lion of Lagos, was sidelined with a medial ligament injury picked up against Luton. As we sat in one of Southend's executive boxes to watch the match I asked him how long he would be out of action. 'I'm hoping to be back for Nigeria's match against England at Wembley on November the sixteenth.' His team-mates thought he was being hopelessly optimistic. He was.

Iorfa was well built, though not as stocky as Nigerian team-mate Daniel Amokachi, Everton's £2 million signing. He'd spoken to Amokachi the previous Thursday to see how he was settling in. Everything was fine except for Everton's form. They couldn't win a match.

Iorfa joined Southend from Peterborough after a spell in Turkey with Galatasaray, conquerors of Manchester United in the 1993 European Cup, and, before that, at Queens Park Rangers. I asked why he left Galatasaray. 'Well, the money was good. I was on a two-year contract worth $200,000 a year. But my wife was unhappy. She wanted to come back to England. I didn't have much choice.'

He was doubtless earning less at Southend, where the players could expect to pick up about £500 a week, or £25,000 a year. Salaries varied widely between First Division clubs, but the average weekly wage was just under a grand. Those backed by rich chairmen, like Derby, could pay a lot more. Southend were not so fortunate. 'It's a living, but you can't save much for the future,' said Andy Sussex, the Shrimpers' 30-year-old midfield schemer and penalty-taker. 'It's only top players that can secure their future outside the game.'

Sussex had been at the club for four seasons. He had worked his way up the League ladder after an apprenticeship at Leyton Orient and a spell at Crewe. Sussex planned to learn the 'knowledge' so that he had something to fall back on when his football career was over. He was out of the side today with a calf injury but had to report to the ground at 11.30 for treatment.

At Orient he played alongside Southend manager Peter Taylor. Sussex was a young apprentice whereas Taylor was in the twilight of his career. 'I used to go down the betting shop at ten to three to put the bets on the horses for Stan Bowles,' he recalled. 'Mervyn Day [the former West Ham, Leeds and Carlisle keeper] was there as well. They'd all be watching the racing in the dressing-room just before going out onto the pitch.'

I'd met up with Sussex in Southend's restaurant, where we tucked into a full English breakfast for lunch! He was eating with a young player just signed from Tottenham. No doubt it was difficult for any apprentice to make the grade at a club like Spurs, where internationals were ten-a-million. He'd come to Southend because there would be more opportunities.

He seemed like a model professional. Sharply dressed in shirt and tie; well spoken; dedicated. He was ribbed by the other players because he wasn't sure he would be going out on the town that night. A cup of cocoa and *Match of the Day* seemed more likely. He was also out through injury and would join us in an executive box later.

I asked the players about the changes in football since Lord Justice Taylor's report. 'It has improved the game a lot,' said Sussex. 'The stadiums all needed modernising and that is happening.' The worst ground he'd ever played at was the Shay at Halifax – no longer members of the Football League and fighting to survive.

Sussex's fondest memory was putting Crewe in front against Liverpool at Anfield in the Milk Cup. They lost 5–1! He also scored in the second leg, which they lost 4–1! His best season in the goalscoring stakes was 16, two coming from the penalty spot. Sussex's approach to the game obviously engendered loyalty among supporters. He was amazed to discover that the guy who sponsored his kit at Orient stayed loyal when he was transferred to Crewe. But he didn't follow Sussex to Southend, where the intriguing Lieutenant-Colonel J. Boorman had taken over as his sponsor.

After a few beers in the members' bar it was time to take up our positions in one of the club's executive boxes. It was like being in the treatment room; for I was surrounded by Southend players on the injury list along with some of the reserves. Their comments during the game were as colourful as they were revealing.

Footballers do not like to watch football. They are trained to play and that is what they do best. But it must be good experience for a job in management to have to watch the team rather than orchestrate the proceedings from the middle of the park. When Southend were awarded a penalty early in the first half, Andy Thomson stepped up to take the spot kick. 'I don't fancy him taking this,' said Andy Sussex. His hunch was right. Thomson missed.

Thomson was later to redeem himself with the winning goal after an opportunist headed equaliser from mercurial winger Ricky Otto, the subject of much transfer speculation involving Premier League clubs. (He said he was happy to stay at Southend, but he would be sold to Birmingham later in the season.) Earlier, a stunning 25-yard drive from Bolton's Richard Sneekes had put the away side ahead.

As the match moved into the last few minutes Southend's players became increasingly nervous. Iorfa stood up, teetering unsteadily on his plastered left leg. 'Come on, we need this one badly,' he said. He knew what it was like to struggle from his time at Peterborough and didn't fancy the experience again.

I looked across at Southend chairman Vic Jobson in the executive box next door. He was pensive, brow furrowed, concentration intense. The club desperately needed three points to move up the table. Otto took the ball over to the far touchline near the corner flag at the Bolton end. Foot on the ball, he hopped and twisted, trying to keep possession while the Bolton defenders attempted to get the ball off him.

Finally, the whistle went and everyone breathed a sigh of relief. We watched the results of the other matches coming through on *Grandstand* in the executive box before heading for the players' bar. That week's results proved again that, as Jimmy Greaves would say, 'It's a funny old game.' On Wednesday night Bolton had beaten Ipswich 3–0. Today Southend beat Bolton 2–1. And Ipswich? They beat Premier League champions Manchester United 3–2!

Few of the Southend team came into the players' bar after the game. Many of them preferred to mix with the fans in the members' bar. Others were exhausted and just wanted to go home after their day's work. One player who did emerge was Southend full-back Mark Hone.

'You look tired,' said his wife as he joined her and their two sons.

'I'm completely knackered,' said Hone, as he sat back in his chair puffing. The game had taken its toll.

His small boys had been watching the highlights of the game on the TV in the bar. 'Look there's dad,' said the older one.

'There he is again,' said the smaller one. They were excited to see him on television, though he had to compete with crisps and cola for their attention.

The players' bar was an extension of the pub-like atmosphere in the members' lounge. The trophies on the wall were a real mixture. One from the early 1980s, presented to the club's top goalscorer, stood beside a bowl given to every club by the Football League in 1963 to celebrate its 75th anniversary. A few of the pieces had been glued back together. It had clearly seen better days.

I was non-plussed by the figure of a man with a gun. It was given to the winner of a clay pigeon shooting championship. A former player perhaps? I was also intrigued by the cup awarded to Southend as runners-up in a match against the Sri Lankan President's XI. 'Cricket?' Sussex suggested.

Above the bar hung pennants given to Southend by famous European teams like Borussia Moenchengladbach. The contrast with the old framed fixture list hanging from the wall was striking. It included matches against teams like Rochester just up the road. Southend had certainly seen the highs and the lows since their first match at Roots Hall in September 1906.

The team's only major honour is the Fourth Division Championship they won in 1981 – a season in which they set 17 club records, including 30 wins and 985 minutes without letting in a goal. Even England's World Cup-winning captain Bobby Moore couldn't help the Shrimpers land a major trophy when he took over as manager in February 1984. Peter Taylor was never likely to bring any silverware to the club. Nobody really expected him to. The best that players like Andy Sussex could hope for was a good cup run or at least a plum tie.

GUNNED DOWN

West Ham United v Arsenal – Upton Park, 25 September 1994

West Ham v. Arsenal. East London against north London. Poor against Rich. And it showed. The Hammers just couldn't match the Gunners. Not that they tried very hard. With the exception of the exceptional John Moncur they lacked artistry and determination. Arsenal were efficient rather than spectacular. Two headed goals from captain Tony Adams and Ian 'Wright, Wright, Wright' were enough to secure the win.

I'd parked near East Ham underground station on the District Line and taken the tube one stop to Upton Park. Away supporters often get confused about the tube stops, because West Ham is not the closest station to the ground. That explains the signs at the Upton Park tube which tell you to get off there for West Ham United Football Club. I walked along Green Street and picked up a copy of the fanzine *On a Mission from God*.

Lots of handy pocket-sized fixture lists with 'Kick Racism Out of Soccer' plastered over the front were being given away. The campaign may have been having some effect, but it hadn't registered with all Hammers fans. One season ticket holder had returned his book of tickets to the club in protest at the anti-racism campaign! The ethnic mix runs thick in the Upton Park area and obviously caused tensions. The local papers often reported racial attacks from both sides of the black and white divide.

I didn't have a ticket for the match, which was all-ticket. I'd called the ground to be told that it was a sell-out despite being Sky's Super Sunday game. I'd decided to take a chance and try to buy a ticket at the match. I wandered around the West Ham Supporters' Club and noticed a group of Arsenal fans in red and white replica shirts standing in the corner by the bar. I couldn't believe they were allowed into the members' club. It wasn't as if you could mistake them for Hammers supporters! Maybe it was a sign of the improved atmosphere at football. I couldn't imagine it happening in the '70s or early '80s without sparking a whole lot of trouble.

I bought my ticket from a bloke called Bob, a tall, gangling chap with thinning hair combed across his head like the Baldie Man on television. He was milling around outside the Supporters' Club looking for a punter without a ticket. His mate couldn't come to the game and he just wanted face value. Bob was a football fanatic. He'd got divorced about a year ago and I sensed this had freed him to do what he loved best: watching football. Not just the Premier League, but non-League too. Bob explained that he'd used his new-found freedom to see matches at four grounds over one weekend: Walsall, Birmingham, West Brom and Coventry.

Funny, isn't it? Women and football just don't seem to mix. Some women like football. But not that many. And those who do probably go to see the dishy-looking centre-forward with the sexy legs. How many women would have adored Gary Lineker if he was a bald, bespectacled beanpole with skinny pins? Did they watch him because he was the greatest goalscorer in English football since Bobby Charlton? What do you think?

Sky Sports isn't just another channel. It's man's revenge. Germaine Greer eat your heart out. Men may change their homes, their jobs, even their women. But their football team, never. It's in-bred. If you change your club, you cannot claim to be a serious supporter. You're a casual. A floating fan. If you care about football, you care about your team. And it's your team. No matter that you have to share it with a few hundred, a few thousand, or, in the case of Manchester United, forty-five thousand at Old Trafford and possibly millions of fans across the globe.

As if to make the point about the relationship between women and football, the West Ham programme contained the results of a survey sponsored by Carling and conducted by Leicester University. It found that females were 'under-represented' at Upton Park. Only 9.6 per cent of the crowd was female, compared to the national average of 12.7 per cent. But that national average is itself a small percentage, though a growing one. Now there are even a few female football presenters (no commentators yet, though). But progress is very slow.

And even if a woman does like football, it doesn't mean your problems are over. Nick Hornby in *Fever Pitch* tells how his girlfriend loved watching Arsenal and he thought he'd struck lucky – until they started thinking about kids and she said they'd have to take it in turns to see home matches.

As Bob and I passed through the main gate to the West Stand I saw Brian Dear, the former West Ham star I'd been introduced to at Southend the previous day. Brian played under Ron Greenwood at Upton Park. But West Ham has been a breeding-ground for managers over the years, with Frank O'Farrell, Malcolm Allison, Dave Sexton, Noel Cantwell, Jimmy Bloomfield, John Bond and Ken Brown among the star-studded list of successful football brains from the Hammers Academy. The club has had only nine managers in its history. Brian signed my programme and I made my way, with Bob, to the turnstiles.

The West Stand had little character from the outside, but from previous visits I knew that inside it was quite an imposing structure. A little further along Green Street is Castle Street, which has a sweet little chapel on the corner – a reminder that the ground stands on what was once all church land. On the next corner is the Boleyn pub on Barking Road. Most football fans believe West Ham play at Upton Park rather than the Boleyn Ground, but Upton Park is the name of the district in which the ground stands rather than the name of the stadium itself.

The name Boleyn Ground comes from a house which stood next to the ground on Green Street until the 1950s. Built in 1544, the house had two turrets and was known as the Boleyn Castle, taking its name from King Henry VIII's wife Anne Boleyn.

The house was used as a reformatory, a priory and as the headquarters of a bowling club. When West Ham built a new main entrance to the ground in 1958, following promotion from the Second Division, the last remaining turret of the Boleyn Castle was demolished. The house was falling apart, but it still seems sad that it could not be preserved given its historical significance. The school behind the South Bank on Castle Street now stands on the site of the Boleyn Castle.

I grew up a bus ride away from Upton Park in Dagenham, home of then-England coach Terry Venables and the England and West Ham captain Bobby Moore. I'd seen West Ham play at Upton Park many times in my younger days. All my school-friends were keen Hammers fans, but as a Spurs supporter my spiritual home was White Hart Lane.

Meanwhile, at this afternoon's match against Arsenal a man dressed as a hammer was wandering around the pitch entertaining the crowd. To my left I could see the half-finished North Bank. Its predecessor had been demolished over the summer and builders Robert McAlpine were putting up a brand-new construction similar to the new 7,600-seater Bobby Moore Stand rapidly filling up on my right.

The late West Ham and England captain would have been proud of his stand. Moore is the only one of the club's famed World Cup winners to have a stand named after him at Upton Park. The North Bank would be called the Centenary Stand – at the suggestion of a supporter – since it was completed during the Hammers' 100th year. It would be opened by Labour Party Deputy Leader John Prescott before the match against Everton the following February to cheers from 3,500 local schoolchildren allowed in free to watch hundreds of claret and blue balloons drift into the evening sky.

The Bobby Moore Stand – a two-tier construction with 20 executive boxes, modern kiosks, betting booths, toilets, club offices and the prestigious '66 Club' on the upper tier – contained a bust of the great man inside the main entrance. Fans were peering through the glass doors to see the sculpture before the match. On the wall to the right was a replica of the famous number six shirt worn with distinction by England's World Cup winning captain. Who could forget Moore lifting the Jules Rimet Trophy on that glorious summer's day back in 1966? All our yesterdays. I watched the final in my uncle's flat on a small black and white television, amazed that grown adults were jumping and dancing around the living-room over a football match. I was six years old.

There were 'innovative concourse areas' in the Bobby Moore Stand, popular with fans who came early to watch the closed circuit televisions the club were linking up around the ground. 'When I think of the old South Bank facilities – awful toilets, one kiosk and a shed as a bar – I'm delighted with the improvements we've made,' said Peter Storrie, West Ham's managing director.

Once the North Bank was finished at Christmas the ground was supposed to hold 26,001. 'The architects told me the capacity would be 25,999. I asked them to find me one extra seat, and they came up with two!' said Storrie. When I returned to Upton Park in February to see the official opening of the new North Bank, the capacity was given as 26,014 – it seemed the architects had managed to find an extra 16 seats in all!

West Ham, their tightly packed ground tucked away in a small corner of east London, had spent £11.5 million modernising Upton Park and had no plans to expand the stadium. Perhaps the club likes the fact that its fans are so close to the pitch that they almost breathe down the necks of their opponents. In fact, the West Ham pitch is 8,064 square yards – the eleventh smallest in the League. However, somewhat surprisingly, it's larger than the pitches of north London rivals Arsenal and Tottenham. In fact, Highbury has the smallest pitch in the League.

'There's no room to extend the East Stand because of the flats behind,' said Storrie. 'We could redevelop the West Stand, but if we closed that for a year the capacity would drop to around 18,000. We could try to join up the corners, but that would cause all sorts of problems because the stands are different heights. It would cost us a lot more money without providing many more seats. If you look at our gates over the last few years, though, we've rarely needed a capacity of much more than 25,000.'

The cost of a new West Stand works out at £500 a seat. Fifteen thousand seats equals £7.5 million or one Dennis Bergkamp, depending on how you look at it. The West Stand was built in 1925 after West Ham's success in 1923, when they were promoted to the First Division and also played in the first Wembley FA Cup final, losing 2–0 to Bolton. They joined Bolton, Barnsley, Huddersfield and Wolves as Second Division clubs which had been beaten in the Cup final. But the Hammers were to enjoy success as a Second Division team in the 1980 Cup final.

West Ham's first major honour was the Second Division Championship of 1958. They were to grace the First Division for the next 20 years. In 1965 West Ham emulated Tottenham's achievement a couple of years earlier by winning the European Cup-Winners' Cup. And in 1966 the crowning glory was the World Cup as England beat West Germany 4–2 with three goals from Hurst – the only man to score a hat-trick in a World Cup Final – and an enormous contribution from

Moore, as captain, and Peters, who scored the other goal. Hurst was such an all-round sportsman that he found the time to play cricket for Essex as well!

In 1969 the club spent £170,000 on a new East Stand. That was towards the end of a decade which saw the name of West Ham United etched on the country's mind for ever. The triumvirate of Bobby Moore, Martin Peters and Geoff Hurst brought a huge amount of success and fame to the homely East End club.

Tottenham pop up again in West Ham's history, for in October 1970 they were the opposition when the club's official attendance record of 42,322 was set for a First Division match.

In 1975 West Ham won the FA Cup again, beating Fulham in the final. It was the club's first trophy for ten years. Ironically, former idol Bobby Moore was wearing the white shirt of Fulham in that match. How strange he must have felt playing against his old club. West Ham triumphed 2–0 with both goals coming from Alan Taylor, a £40,000 buy from Rochdale. I remember watching the match with my dad and a noisy bunch of friends at a flat in north London. Amidst the beers and cigarettes it was a disappointing final, I recall, with the Fulham goalkeeper, Peter Mellor, allowing Taylor to squeeze the ball through his legs for one of the goals.

In 1980, they returned to Wembley as a Second Division team and beat Arsenal 1–0 in the third all-London Cup final with a rare headed goal from Trevor Brooking and an appearance from Paul Allen – the second-youngest player ever to appear in a Wembley FA Cup final. That was the last trophy the Hammers lifted, though in 1983 they registered their record victory with the 10–0 defeat of Bury in the second leg of a second round League Cup match.

West Ham have never been a club to splash out large sums for players. But the club set two transfer records just before and after the First World War: in 1912 they sold Danny Shea to Blackburn Rovers in the first £2,000 transfer; and in 1922 they sold Syd Puddefoot to Falkirk in the first £5,000 deal. Much later, in 1970, the club sold their World Cup hero Martin Peters to London rivals Tottenham for £200,000 in the first transfer of that size.

After the club received its record transfer fee of £2 million from Everton for Tony Cottee in July 1988, they had enough money in the bank to pay Celtic £1.25 million to bring Frank McAvennie back to Upton Park in March 1989. Cottee and McAvennie were brilliant when they played together and had helped West Ham challenge for the Championship in the 1985–86 season. Apart, they weren't so effective. When McAvennie broke his leg during his second spell at West Ham, the writing was on the wall and he would never be the same player again

Peter Storrie is the man who greets the match and club sponsors for a tour of the ground. (West Ham, to their credit, are one of the few clubs who give ordinary supporters a free tour if you arrange it in advance.) He takes you up a flight of stairs towards the West Stand. At the top, on the wall to the right of the Ron Greenwood Suite, hangs a picture of Bubbles – a pretty little girl with curly blonde hair who used to star in Lux soap adverts. I wondered how many Hammers fans knew the origins of the Bubbles song which reverberates so often around Upton Park.

Once in the West Stand you're invited to sit in the directors' box to hear about the club's past, present and future. My tour was conducted against a backdrop of torrential rain which threatened to drown out Storrie's pre-match pep talk. At this point Wally, a Chas 'n' Dave sort of character, took over as our guide and led us into the dressing-rooms underneath the West Stand. Those dressing-room walls must have heard some stories over the years.

The players' shirts were hung on pegs around the walls. MARTIN, DICKS, MONCUR, MIKLOSKO. Stars on parade. Bobby Moore's famous number six shirt always hung beneath the clock on the back wall. 'He was immaculate,' said Wally. 'Bobby didn't leave his kit here for the laundry to wash. He took it home and washed it himself. He'd even take his laces out of his boots and wash them. People said he was smarter when he left the ground than when he'd arrived.'

Wally showed us the showers and the bath. 'We used to put the water on in the second half, but then Julian (Dicks) started playing for us and we had to turn it on at quarter to three,' said Wally, referring to the full-back's reputation of being sent for an early bath. 'But he's a reformed character now since he came back to us from Liverpool and we don't have to do that anymore.'

Wally's next story was apocryphal – I think. He told us about the Arsenal player who'd always struggled to score goals. He said the striker had notched up only three goals in 68 matches. The player had always been a Hammers supporter and had therefore asked his relatives to make sure that when he died his ashes were spread over the West Ham pitch. His wish was granted and the ashes were spread on the turf just outside the penalty area. 'You'll never guess what happened,' said Wally. 'A gust of wind came along and blew them over the bar!'

I spotted a cabinet in the corner of the lounge which contained a few trophies and mementoes – testimony to West Ham's travels in Europe. On the wall was an old print of a ship built at the Thames Ironworks, where the team was founded. West Ham's origins in London's East End docks explain where the nickname 'The Hammers' comes from; hammers symbolise the tools used by shipyard workers.

West Ham were formed in 1895 by Arnold F. Hills, owner of the largest surviving shipyard at the time – the famous East London shipbuilding company called the Thames Ironworks. The players helped to build HMS *Warrior*, the first ironclad warship.

The Arsenal match was a scrappy affair. The visitors always looked the more composed and were dangerous on the break. Paul Merson linked up well with Alan Smith and Ian 'Wright, Wright, Wright', the darling of the Arsenal supporters (later to become a West Ham favourite, too). The first goal saw Smith nod on to Adams, who had the simple task of beating Ludek Miklosko in the Hammers goal from the edge of the six-yard box. In the second half Wright sent an acutely angled header into the top right-hand corner beyond Miklosko's flailing arms.

At 2–0 the Arsenal fans behind me in the top left-hand corner of the West Stand gave full voice to their Ian Wright repertoire. The West Ham fans responded in kind with their own version: Ian 'Wank, Wank, Wank'. It was hardly original. Their sense of humour came out, however, when the Hammers fans in the South Stand began to sing 'We're going to win the League.' The Arsenal fans responded with 'We all agree West Ham are better than Tottenham,' which wasn't saying much given Tottenham's form.

SUICIDE

West Bromwich Albion v Portsmouth – The Hawthorns, 28 September 1994

Suicide. No, not the West Bromwich Albion defence, though they committed it enough times in the opening 15 minutes to have been at least three goals behind. That they went in at half-time only one goal down was a miracle. Sadly, miracles were not to hand when my Birmingham-bound train from London was delayed by a suicide.

'Does it always take this long to get to Birmingham?' I asked the staff who came through my train compartment serving drinks and food.

'No, not usually. But someone threw themselves under the train at Harrow. Didn't you see the mess?'

'Er, no.' I said, trying desperately hard not to conjure up a mental picture of what that mess might look like. All I knew was that I wouldn't get to the Hawthorns for my tour of the ground.

Why tonight? Strange how the actions of one so desperate can affect others, albeit in a minor way. It was sad. I suppose being delayed and not being able to tag along with the sponsors of tonight's rearranged Endsleigh League match against Portsmouth paled into insignificance beside someone taking their own life. But I wasn't happy about missing the tour or the reason why.

You often hear passengers on the London Underground complaining about suicide victims being inconsiderate. 'Typical. If they want to kill themselves why can't they do it somewhere else? I mean it's the bloody rush hour for Christ's sake.'

I finally got to Birmingham New Street station at 6.30 – one hour late, and I still had to catch a bus to reach the Hawthorns. At the first bus stop, two West Brom fans got on wearing bright green and yellow striped away shirts. At least I'd know where to get off.

The bus made its way slowly through Birmingham town centre towards the ground. Two things struck me on the short journey. The first was a mural memorial to US President John Kennedy. He was surrounded by Brummies reaching out to him. Very odd. The second was an advertising board which read: 'A SMOOTH RIDE FROM HOUSTON TO D'ARBY We've got your music at HEART. 100.7 FM'. The Houston in question was Whitney and the D'arby was Terence Trent – both pictured in the ad.

The bus passed through the district of Handsworth, and then the two West Brom fans stood up to get off. I followed. The ground was just ahead of us and the part I could see looked like the metal supports beneath a giant roller-coaster. This was the unfinished Birmingham Road End stand.

To get to it, I had to pass the Woodman Inn pub, with its hanging sign showing a woodman in a peaked green hat, axe across his shoulder. Supporters were queuing up to get in the pub, but I couldn't tell why. The obvious answer was that it must have been full and the landlord wouldn't let anyone else in until someone left. The usual weekend scene outside a disco in London. But it didn't seem to be full from the outside.

The Birmingham Road End stand was the last piece in Albion's ground rebuilding jigsaw. The sign outside said it was due for completion by August 1994. Since it was now late September, it seemed that the construction company had missed its deadline. The ground would hold 27,500 – all-seated – when it was finished.

The stand was a futuristic criss-cross of white struts, like a real-life version of the computer simulations you often see on television. The basic structure had gone up over the summer, but the concrete steps had only been laid in the upper tier. The lower tier still looked like a building site, complete with mechanical diggers and lots of earth and sand.

The Smethwick End stand at the other end of the stadium had itself only just been finished. The 'can you believe it?' story doing the rounds among supporters concerned the word ALBION, picked out in white from the background of blue seats which covered most of the stand. When the club photographer came along to take the annual pre-season picture of the Albion squad, using the Smethwick End as the backdrop, he noticed something odd. The word he saw was ABION. They had left out the L – and nobody had noticed! The opening of the stand was delayed while the seats were speedily removed and repositioned to spare the club the ultimate embarrassment.

The other problem with the £2 million stand, used for the first time in a friendly against Kilmarnock in September 1994, was finding the way out. The signs the fans had to follow for the exit said Vomitories – though they had nothing to do with throwing up. The word, which means an opening, was written on the original plans by the architects and the club, not wishing to seem uneducated in these matters, put the signs up around the stand. 'As for their supporters, they will probably still be inside come Christmas trying to find the exits,' according to Martin Smith of *The Daily Telegraph*.

As I made my way towards the main entrance I heard 'Get your Baggies, Get your Baggies here.' No, it wasn't an attempt to sell me the latest fashion in men's jeans, but sellers of the club newspaper called *The Baggies* – West Brom's nickname. I grabbed a copy of *Grorty Dick* 'WBA's oldest and bestselling fanzine' wondering whether the title referred to a dodgy part of the anatomy. I was later to learn that it was a variation on Groarty Pudding, a traditional Black Country stew. Thank God for that!

I went into the club shop to find Diane Ashton, the chairman's secretary, whose office was behind the advance ticket sales desk. West Brom were doing a brisk trade in tickets for the upcoming matches away at Stoke on the Sunday and at Tranmere in a few weeks' time. In the display cabinet in the corner of the shop was a picture of former idol and current Middlesbrough player–manager, Bryan Robson, in his days at the Hawthorns. The £1.5 million received from selling him to Manchester United in October 1981 smashed the British transfer record and still stood as the record transfer fee received by the club. There was also a picture of a young Jeff Astle, both arms in the air, after one of his many goals for the Baggies. The team which included Astle, Tony Brown and John Wile lives on in the fans' memories. And for good reason.

In 1965 West Brom made a belated entry into the League Cup – and won the competition in which they were also finalists in 1967 and 1970. In between, they enjoyed their greatest triumph of recent times by beating Everton in the 1968 FA Cup final. It was their fifth FA Cup success, though it was 14 years since they had last lifted the trophy and would be even longer before they reached the final again.

I apologised to the chairman's secretary for my late arrival and she confirmed that I'd missed the night's tour. I still managed to get a quick look behind the scenes, though. On her office walls hung pennants from West Brom's various European matches. One commemorated a match against a Limassol XI at the Tsirion stadium. There was also a plaster block with the club's crest modelled on the front. I guessed it had formed part of the stadium before the recent redevelopment.

She took me up a flight of stairs to the directors' lounge to see some of the trophies in the cabinet at the centre of the room. One item immediately caught my eye. It was an antique jug called the Loving Cup and had been presented by the Friends of Albion in the City of Stoke to commemorate the club's 1888 FA Cup win against Preston. It's a tradition among the West Brom directors to drink champagne from the jug on the anniversary of that Cup success more than a century ago.

The trophy cabinet contained two other items celebrating anniversaries. A bowl commemorating the 75th anniversary of the Football League, which I'd seen before at Roots Hall, the home of Southend, was one. The difference was that Albion's copy was in perfect condition – no repair job had been necessary here. The other was a mini replica of the FA Cup to mark the 100th anniversary of the competition, which began in 1882. The centenary final was a classic encounter between Spurs and Manchester City, won, after a replay, by possibly the greatest goal ever scored in a final. Who could forget the way the bearded Argentine, Ricky Villa, beat what seemed like half the City team before sliding the ball under Joe Corrigan for the winning goal?

We couldn't take a peek in the boardroom because the directors had already assembled for the pre-match get-together with their counterparts from tonight's opponents, Portsmouth. Instead, we made our way out to the pitch. I didn't get a cheer but I felt privileged to tread the well-worn path taken by the Albion greats of the past – Astle, Brown, Wile, Cantello, Regis, Statham, Robson.

The match programme was running a series called 'A is for Albion' and tonight it was the turn of the Cs in the alphabet guide to the club's history. And C is for . . . Cantello. Sadly, the biopic informed me, Len's playing days were over, and he was now working in a Manchester fashion store. He was still scouting for several clubs and had tried his hand in management at Radcliffe Borough after a spell as assistant to former West Brom star Asa Hartford at Stockport County. Len left Albion for a club record £350,000 in 1979, when he joined Bolton a month after his testimonial.

I thanked Diane Ashton for her lightning tour and returned to the streets outside the ground. I stopped en route to my seat to pick up the obligatory pastie and a cup of tea. I now knew I should have bought shares in Maxpax.

The stadium's capacity had been reduced to about 17,000 because of the rebuilding of the Birmingham Road End stand. But, in any case, it was not full tonight, partly because Manchester United's European Champions League grudge match against Galatasaray of Turkey was live on TV.

Before the match the local press were looking to 21-year-old Albion winger Lee Ashcroft to cast a magic spell on Portsmouth, his 'lucky' club. Ashcroft had turned in two of his best performances against Pompey to help West Brom complete a double which saved them from relegation. The £250,000 signing from Preston spearheaded a 4–1 home win against the south-coast side and then scored the goal that kept Albion up, in a 1–0 win at Fratton Park on the last day of the season.

The Ashcroft magic was missing tonight as Portsmouth dominated the opening exchanges. Left-winger Ray Daniel missed a golden opportunity to score when, unmarked and just inside the 18-yard box, he fluffed his shot. But it wasn't long before the visitors went ahead through 23-year-old full-back Robbie Pethick, his first goal for the club.

A break down the right resulted in a Gerry Creaney cross to Pethick, whose half-hit shot still had enough power to beat Stuart Naylor in the Albion goal. The small band of Pompey fans in the corner of the – wait for it – West Bromwich Albion Building Society Family Stand, erupted. They gave a quick rendition of that old favourite 'Play up Pompey, Play-Up'. There weren't many of them but they sure made a lot of noise.

West Brom steadied themselves after that and created a few chances. But Portsmouth always looked dangerous on the break. The match then moved into a period of stalemate, the only excitement being generated by a lone trumpeter in the Smethwick End stand. I couldn't make out anything he played and, unlike at other grounds, the crowd didn't follow his cue with a song. Maybe they didn't know any of his tunes either. I figured that perhaps the Hawthorns was the only place he could practise!

There then followed a minor scuffle between the police and a young Albion fan who was ejected for refusing to sit down. Of course, the crowd were on his side and a large section of them in the Smethwick End stand got to their feet and burst into a quick round of 'Standing Up, Standing Up, Standing Up'. This was followed by 'Come On, You Baggies' and then the most curious chant of all. At the time, I thought they were shouting 'oink, oink, Baggies, Baggies' as a derogatory reference to the police while they jumped up and down in the pogo-style beloved of punk rockers in the 1980s. I was later corrected by former youth-team player Andy Hughes, now a trader at Glencore International in London's financial district. He was at the Albion in the glory days of Statham, Regis and Laurie Cunningham. 'The chant you heard from the Baggies fans was in fact "Boing, Boing – Baggies, Baggies" and not "oink, oink",' he told me. One theory is that the chant originated at an away game when some Albion fans were sitting on a bench. Whenever those seated at one end jumped up and down, those at the other end were catapulted into the air! Amid the fun and games they began to sing 'Boing, Boing – Baggies, Baggies'.

The West Brom players were booed off the pitch at half-time as their dismal start to the season continued. 'Things Can Only Get Better' sang D-Ream at the interval. Tonight, though, they would get worse for both teams. Shortly after the break, the lively Paul Hall, substitute for injured Bjorn Kristensen, put Portsmouth further ahead after a dreadful error by Albion defender Scott Darton.

Then Portsmouth ran into a spell of bad luck when former England Under-21 international defender Andy Awford was carried off with a suspected broken leg after a full-blooded clash with Albion's former West Ham defender Gary

Strodder. Awford had broken his leg in four places after it snapped under Strodder's challenge. He would be out of action for the rest of the season, though manager Jim Smith cleared Strodder of any blame.

In the dying minutes another Pompey defender, Tony Dobson, also left the field when he was sent off for swearing at a linesman. Smith was still fuming about the incident after the match and planned to fine Dobson. 'We were five minutes into injury time, 2–0 up and he was arguing with a linesman.' Some players never learn.

MEMORIES OF LEEDS

Colchester United v Bury – Layer Road, 1 October 1994

The first I saw of Colchester's stadium, after driving through the Essex countryside in the rain, was the set of floodlights looming up ahead like those at Stalag 14 in that old black and white film about the German prisoner-of-war camp. They're huge great things which overshadow Layer Road, the ground and just about everything else.

Today I was the guest of Colchester's Match Day Club for kids. Being a big kid myself, I felt perfectly at home. I was the guest of Micky Cook, the club's Community Officer and a member of the squad on that illustrious day back in 1971 when Colchester United did the unthinkable by knocking the mighty Leeds United out of the FA Cup in the fifth round. At the time, that result was sensational and is still talked about today.

Micky did a sterling job coaching and organising children's football at the club and in local schools. A seasoned pro who spent 16 years at Colchester as a player, and holds the club record for number of League appearances (613 between 1969 and 1984), he commanded the kids' respect. They looked up to him and with good reason. He seemed disciplined but fair. Just the sort of defensive midfielder you'd want in your side.

Most of the kids had already arrived at the Soccer Centre for their day out. By the end of it they would have had a tour of the club, a question-and-answer session with some of the Colchester players who were not in the first team for today's match, a coaching session, a six-a-side game on the Layer Road pitch before the main match and lots of chocolate, coke and crisps. Above all, they would have had a whole lot of fun.

The boys sat there with anticipation etched across their faces. They were all Colchester supporters but you wouldn't have known it from the kits they wore. The assortment included both Manchester clubs, Spurs, West Ham, and only one or two Colchester shirts. The talk around the tables was not about the visit of Third Division pacemakers Bury, but about Old Trafford, Stamford Bridge and Selhurst Park. Even the Colchester players who politely answered the kids' questions supported other teams.

I tagged along behind the kids and their dads for a tour of the ground as we were taken around the perimeter of the pitch from the Popular Stand to the Main

Stand. 'Look at that pitch,' said Micky. 'It's like a snooker table. The ball will stay nice and true and consistent. So if I'm going to support someone and they roll it back to me, I've got every chance of hitting it first time into the box.

'Now on a lot of pitches, I may get that situation, it comes back, takes a bobble and I end up putting it up there,' said Micky, pointing towards the seats at the top of the Main Stand. 'Some say that I found the stand a few times when I was playing as a pro. But it's a lovely pitch to play on.' The dads around me laughed at Micky's reference to his playing days. Many had seen him play for Colchester and some remembered coming to the Leeds game as small boys to watch their local heroes topple the country's best.

We climbed the terrace steps towards the sponsors' lounges and directors' room at the top of the Main Stand, past the groundsman who had earlier been praised for his pristine pitch.

'Stadium manager you mean,' one of the dads corrected Micky with a laugh.

'That's right, stadium manager,' said the groundsman.

The sponsors' lounge was newly decorated and very smart, though a bit small. 'If you look at Premier Division clubs and the facilities that they have, all these lovely boxes and everything else, well this is our equivalent,' said Micky, surveying the sponsors' lounge with its bar and freshly made sandwiches. There was no sign of an executive box anywhere, but that may come one day. The club has been talking for years about moving to a new purpose-built stadium. It hasn't happened yet, but you never know.

Leaflets headed 'U's on the Move' were prominently placed in the Soccer Centre, inviting supporters to become members of a scheme which offered a guaranteed top prize of £500 in a weekly draw. The rationale behind the scheme was clear. 'When the U's leave the Layer Road ground . . . to develop a new stadium we need to raise a substantial amount of money. We hope to provide excellent facilities . . . for our supporters and the local community. We're also hoping the new scheme will help to purchase new players and develop and expand our youth team policy.' Lofty ambitions indeed!

I thought that the club must have adopted the motto that it's better to live in hope than die in despair. I was surprised they didn't plan to use funds from the scheme to purchase Romario for their forward line as well. Until those vast sums came rolling in they had to make do with buying players like centre-forward Steve Whitton. He was brought to Layer Road just before the previous season's transfer deadline for a five-figure sum (£10,000) from northerly neighbours Ipswich Town.

'It costs a lot of money to run a pro club. We're no exception to that, so we have to generate as much income as we can. So we rely on businessmen to come and watch our games and have a bite to eat and they sponsor the games and footballs,' Micky explained to the boys. More sponsors would no doubt be welcome at Colchester and most other clubs. Only two companies – Techni-Flo Services Ltd Coggeshall and Roger Dicker, Tokyo UFO – were listed as players' kit sponsors in the programme

I'm not sure that the under-tens took on board the full extent of the cash crisis facing most clubs in the 1990s, but they listened politely. They would be more interested in our next stop: the directors' room, which doubled as a trophy room. The trophies stood on the sort of sideboard that most people have in their front room. There wasn't a lot of silverware on show, but the club were proud of their modest achievements.

'We're not Manchester United, we're Colchester United, obviously; but what you see here are a few of our success stories over the years and we're very proud of what you're looking at there,' said Micky. One of the kids at the front said he wanted a trophy to take home. Which kid wouldn't?

One of Micky's favourites was the FA Trophy won by Colchester in 1992, when they beat Whitton 3–1 at Wembley. 'We had about 25,000 people who went down the A12 to see the match. What was nice about that was that it tells you that if we can be successful, there is the support in the town. And it also tells you that it's a successful product that people want to come and watch. It was great.'

He then pointed to a bronze football boot on top of a ball: a replica of the GM Vauxhall Conference Championship trophy. Micky asked the kids whether they would rather win the FA Trophy or the GM Vauxhall Conference trophy. Their decision was unanimous; they all wanted to play on the hallowed turf in a cup final at Wembley.

Micky had other ideas. 'From a footballer's point of view, this is the trophy they will cherish the most,' he said, holding up the Conference trophy. 'The reason is that this trophy represents 42 games of football. Every game that we played was equivalent to a cup final because we were a Football League club, we dropped down out of the League, and every Vauxhall Conference club was saving their best game for Colchester United. They thought, "We'll show that old pro's team." So they had to serve up a good level of performance game-in, game-out for 42 games over six to seven months. But in their hearts somewhere will be a special place for that Wembley appearance.'

Micky then ran through the trophies won by Colchester's impressive youth team both abroad and in domestic competitions against Blackburn, Fulham and Crystal Palace. 'Because we're a small club, we need to have youngsters come here and want to play for Colchester United. And you, young man,' said Micky pointing to the kid at the front who wanted a trophy to take home, 'may be our first-million pound player. And if you were . . . we'd be in good shape as a pro club.'

'But I'm rubbish,' said the kid to roars of laughter from the dads.

'If you practise, you might be surprised,' said Micky, offering encouragement.

One of Colchester's greatest triumphs was their victory over First Division West Brom in the 1971 final of the Watney Cup – the League's first sponsored tournament. They won the match 4–3 on penalties after a 4–4 draw in what was the first-ever penalty shoot-out. The Watney Cup was a pre-season competition for the two highest-scoring clubs in each division other than those promoted or in Europe. There was a photograph of the trophy next to the Giant Killer's Cup, which Colchester also won that year to mark their win over the Baggies.

'We built up over the years a good reputation for giant-killing. And I go around the schools a lot and we talk to the kids and they think giant-killing,' said Micky. 'When the FA Cup comes round there's always a little air of expectancy. You think who have we got now, who are we likely to take on. We've had some great games; of course, there's Leeds, but it goes back further than that, to Blackpool in 1948. We got thumped 5–0 but they had a very good side.'

Indeed, Colchester first made an impact in that 1948 FA Cup competition through an amazing sequence of giant-killing acts. They were still members of the Southern League when they knocked out Huddersfield Town and Bradford, who themselves had beaten Arsenal, before eventually losing to Blackpool in the fifth round. Their manager at the time was Ted Fenton, who later took West Ham back to the old First Division.

The publicity surrounding that impressive cup run and a further run of good performances resulted in Colchester being elected to the Football League in 1950. Twenty years later Leeds United came to Layer Road. That Leeds team had won the Championship two seasons before and were runners-up in 1969–70. The side was packed with internationals in all positions bar one. Colchester's side was known as Grandad's Army, since seven of their players were over 30.

Leeds were then at their peak with the most feared team in the country. 'Everybody thinks of Leeds,' said Micky:

> I was on the subs' bench that day. Ironically, when you talk about how you progress in football, I'd just broken into the first team and I played in all the League games and we went to Rochdale. We were losing 3–1 and the guvnor gave me the call and said come and sit with me (on the bench) and another guy went on and we drew 3–3.
>
> We brought them back here and he kept the same team. There were a lot of old heads in the side in those days, and we thumped Rochdale 4–0. And then we went into three League matches, and I played in all three. Then Leeds came out of the hat, so there was a buzz of expectancy. And he gave me a nudge and said 'Micky' – no actually he didn't say 'Micky', we weren't that close – 'you're on the subs' bench, son, I'm going for experience.' You didn't argue with him and I said, 'Thank you, boss.'
>
> There were 16,000 out there. We doubled up on the revenue, so we had a big pay-day at the equivalent of 32,000 people effectively.

Colchester burst into an astounding 3–0 lead and eventually won 3–2 to join the ranks of the greatest giant-killers of all time. Unfortunately, they lost 5–0 to Everton in the quarter-finals. Never mind. They had savoured their moment of glory.

Each group of Colchester's Match Day Club boys in twos and threes were given a minder for the afternoon as they made their way to the family enclosure to see today's match. I made a quick detour to pick up a jumbo hotdog (good value at £1.60; Chelsea charged £2.50 for the same delectable cuisine at Stamford Bridge the following day) before joining the youngsters on the terraces.

The crowd were warming up with sophisticated chants like 'Shit on Bury. We're gonna shit on Bury.' Well, it is pretty rural in the wilds of Essex. Behind me were a group of locals who obviously attended all the home matches together. They had broad Essex accents and were all in need of a decent haircut, not that they had much to cut between them. These were the bread-and-butter fans of football teams like Colchester. They would come rain or shine, whether the team was brilliant or rubbish, in good times and in bad. They were real characters and the game would be lost without them.

Colchester had given some meaning to their nickname, the U's, with their performances in the Endsleigh League's lowest division. They lost their first six games but were unbeaten in their last six. According to manager George Burley (now at Ipswich), a replacement for Roy McDonough after he was sacked by his father-in-law, there was no magical reason for the change. They simply persevered with their short-passing game.

It was hard to imagine Colchester playing with any style, for Gus Caesar – the Arsenal defender held responsible by many fans for the north London team's defeat in the 1988 League Cup final and the man immortalised in Nick Hornby's *Fever Pitch* – was the bedrock of the U's defence. As it turned out, he played okay. He even picked up the knack of scoring goals later in the season to defy his critics. Fancy running into him at Layer Road. It was a shock, I must admit. I thought he'd been consigned to the depths of the Scottish League for ever. Arsenal fans must be shuddering with the memories.

Towards the end of the first half against Bury, Colchester's Mark Kinsella left the pitch to get some stitches in a head wound. He returned, heavily bandaged like a modern-day Terry Butcher, to a round of applause. But as soon as he made his way towards the centre circle the referee blew his whistle for half-time. The crowd fell about laughing as Kinsella did an about-turn and made his way back to the dressing-rooms.

Each issue of the club programme features a question-and-answer profile on a Colchester player. When Kinsella is featured and asked to 'Tell us about a funny moment at Colchester United', I'm sure he will recount his short-lived return against Bury. In the second half, he was joined by one of the Bury players who also had his head bandaged. It was beginning to look like a hospital out there on the pitch.

The deadlock was broken in the second half by the tallest player on the pitch, defender Peter Cawley. Colchester were awarded a free-kick about 25 yards out. The supporters around me were calling for Cawley to step up and take the kick. He duly obliged, thumping the ball into the top right-hand corner of Kelly's goal.

Alyson Rudd's match report in *The Times* on the Monday after the game said Colchester would be pushing for promotion if they avoided injuries. No doubt, Bury would also be up there at the end of the season. They could have done with the presence of former Bolton and Everton star Peter Reid, now the manager at Sunderland, but then a summer capture from Notts County. But his pay-as-you-play contract was proving to be as unrewarding as this trip to Layer Road: he had managed only six minutes all season.

CZECH IT OUT

Chelsea v West Ham United – Stamford Bridge, 2 October 1994

It has to be said that of all the League clubs in Britain, Chelsea is the most glamorous. It's not just memories of the late '60s and early '70s, when the likes of trendy, fashion-conscious players like Peter Osgood, Alan Hudson and Ian Hutchison delighted the crowds with their exciting brand of fast-flowing, attacking football. It's not just the celebrities, ranging from Prime Minister John

Major to David Mellor and from Sebastian Coe to David Baddiel, who regularly come to the Bridge. It's also the place. Chelsea is in the heart of one of the most fashionable parts of London. The area oozes class from the King's Road, famous as the fashion-centre of the world in the Swinging Sixties, to the imposing three-storey Edwardian houses which cost millions to buy and house many of the rich and famous living in London. It's against this backdrop that Stamford Bridge plays host to Chelsea Football Club.

The ground is named after the bridge by the main entrance which once crossed a canal but now spans the railway. The London Athletic Club had first occupied the site when their new running track opened in April 1877, almost 30 years before the football team was formed. Before that, the area had been covered by an orchard and a market garden.

The London Athletic Club's Fred Parker got together with brothers Gus and Joe Mears and they planned to turn Stamford Bridge into a stadium which would rival Crystal Palace, venue for the 1895 FA Cup final. But the owner didn't want to sell and it wasn't until 1904, two years after the owner's death, that Gus Mears could purchase the ground.

Mears wanted to build a complex for cycling and athletics as well as football, and he tried to rent the ground to west London's best-known club Fulham who were about to face a court hearing over their Main Stand. But Fulham, director Henry Norris, who later joined Woolwich Arsenal, was against the idea. Mears gave up his plans for a stadium and decided to sell the ground to the Great Western Railway, which wanted to use the site as a coal yard.

Fred Parker was not very happy to hear that Mears was accepting the Great Western offer, since he desperately wanted to see a stadium built at Stamford Bridge. As the two men discussed the issue on a walk one Sunday Mears' dog bit Parker's leg. Although Parker was bleeding, he found the incident amusing and began laughing. Mears thought Parker's good-natured reaction showed him to be a man he could trust and his desire to see a stadium at the Bridge was probably based on sound judgement. So it was that the ground was built and Chelsea Football Club was formed.

Soil and clay from the tube tunnel being dug by the Mears' building company at Kingsway, and from the construction of the Piccadilly underground in central London, were brought up the River Thames on barges and used to build oval-shaped banking around the athletic track. The next step was to form a football club, which Mears and Parker duly did in May 1905, adopting Parker's suggested name of Chelsea. When the Blues' application to join the Southern League was turned down, they gained immediate entry into the Second Division of the Football League. Chelsea bought top players from other clubs, including William 'Fatty' Foulke. And they became known as the Pensioners, because the ground was close to the Royal Hospital which served as a refuge for old and disabled soldiers (who were given special dispensation to attend matches at the Bridge).

I'd arrived at Fulham Broadway station, west of Stamford Bridge, on a bright Sunday afternoon to meet up with a colleague called Iain Rodger at a nearby café. A mad Chelsea fan, he ranked meeting Dennis Wise as one of the highlights of his life. Iain was a regular on the Shed who was coming to terms with the many changes going on at the Bridge. We met at a trendy outdoor café near the ground along with Iain's current flame, a blonde from Denmark. A former girlfriend was ever grateful to him for her love of the Blues. After introducing her to the delights of Saturday afternoons at the Bridge, Iain was amazed to discover that not only did she like football but she wanted to watch the lads play away as well. Midweek trips to Birmingham on cold Tuesday nights became commonplace. Their relationship may have ended, but her love of Chelsea burned as brightly as ever.

We made our way from the café along the Fulham Road past the houses, flats, pubs, souvenir shops and take-aways. The Blues were today playing West Ham at a stadium in transition. There are three entrances to Stamford Bridge: Britannia Gate, Bovril Gate and Stamford Gate. We passed through Stamford Gate, the main entrance, and immediately could see that the Bridge was being almost totally redeveloped, not least because the Shed was being demolished to make way for a brand new stand. Not before time, according to some fans; but others lamented the passing of a landmark.

The Shed was where you stood if you wanted to prove you were hard enough to fight (literally) for the Chelsea cause. Many a good kicking had taken place in the Shed, particularly during the mad, bad days of the '70s, when the Blues' favourite victims on the terraces were the 'Yids' from White Hart Lane. The Chelsea Headhunters were feared throughout the game in those days.

Now all those 'good' times were a fading memory as the club prepared for the '90s and a reshaped Stamford Bridge. Our seats for the game were in a temporary stand which was much closer to the pitch than the Shed had been. Once in my seat I turned to see the bulldozers standing amidst remains of the South Stand terracing. It seemed to be miles away from the pitch. I'd stood there with Iain and that former girlfriend for a game against Liverpool the season before and remembered how far back from the pitch we were – not unlike being at Wembley.

The plan now – as part of Ken Bates's Chelsea Village scheme to redevelop the Bridge, first hatched in 1985 – was to build an underground car park for 220 cars, which would cost £3.4 million, and above it a three-star hotel with 160 beds, which would be part of a development incorporating a new £20–25 million South Stand. But that was the future. For now, the Chelsea faithful would have to put up with temporary, uncovered seats at the south end of the ground. Not that the atmosphere had suffered. In fact, since the stand was now so close to the pitch, the temporary stand had intensified the matchday atmosphere. Once the new North Stand opened, the noise would be even louder.

The contrast between the south and north ends of the ground was striking. The North Stand, the first phase of the redevelopment plan, was nearly ready and set to open in a few weeks, on 26 November for the match against Everton. The entrance was all glass and steel, with a spiral staircase leading up to Chelsea's first members' club and banqueting suites. The members' club was called Drake's after Ted, the only manager to lead the team to the League title, which they won in 1955 with a squad of young players dubbed Drake's Ducklings. It was extravagantly decorated like a nightclub or one of the top sports bars which have been springing up around the capital. The banqueting suites were called Tambling's and Dixon's after the club's top scorers Bobby and Kerry (though Tambling holds the scoring record with 164 goals between 1958 and 1970).

There were four bars behind the rows of blue seats, each of which had many of the clubs all-time greats decorating the walls. Strikers had pictures of Roy Bentley, Barry Bridges, Hughie Gallacher, Jimmy Greaves, George Hilsdon,

Tommy Lawton and Osgood. The Halfway Line sported Ken Armstrong, Frank Blunstone, Charlie Cooke, Pat Nevin, Ray Wilkins, Andy Wilson and Dennis Wise. The Back Four showed Steve Clarke, Paul Elliot, John Harris, Joey Jones, Eddie McCreadie, Colin Pates and Dave Webb. And Keepers had action shots of Dave Beasant, Peter Bonetti, Willie Foulke, Dmitri Kharine, Harry Medhurst, Eddie Niedwiecki and Vic Woodley.

Chelsea Broadway, an area for exhibitions, was on the lower concourse. The club hoped the bars would be kept busy by early arrivals, who'd be able to relax in comfortable surroundings. A specialist design consultancy firm was brought in to make sure the lighting and colours mixed well with the signs to create an attractive ambience. The televisions dotted around the stand would broadcast programmes from Channel Chelsea, the club's own service. That famous football architect Archibald Leitch must have been turning in his grave!

According to the match programme, the new North Stand encapsulates what many 'middle-aged' supporters will feel is special. 'Sitting in the Upper Tier near the East Stand, you get a very special feeling like the old days in the double decker North Stand. Remember them? Feet banging on the trembling wooden floor when Jimmy Greaves or Bobby Tambling trotted over to take a wicked inswinging corner, the stadium reverberating to the noise. Now there will be no greyhound track between the stand and the pitch as there was then. There will be no open spaces around the touchline. It will be like touching distance.'

One of Chelsea's modern-day heroes, the Norwegian Erland Johnsen, who'd been signed from Bayern Munich, could already feel the difference out on the pitch. 'It hasn't felt that windy since the new stand has gone up,' he said. ' . . . The whole atmosphere is better. Stamford Bridge has definitely been one of the worst grounds for wind in the past.' The North Stand was being built in two phases. The first phase, which also included some work on the East Stand, car parking and the approach to the ground, cost £8.5 million. The second phase would cover the north-west corner of the stand and cost almost £2.5 million.

The towering East Stand was across to my right. It was a significant structure; the largest stand ever built at a British football club, at a cost of £2 million, had nearly put the club out of existence. The stand seats 11,500 fans in its three tiers and was originally supposed to be phase one of a £5.5 million development to provide Chelsea with a 60,000-capacity stadium. Work had begun in 1972, when the old Main Stand, built by Archibald Leitch, was demolished. A weather-vane, put on the stand's gable in 1932 and which sports the image of a player believed to be George Hilsdon, who played for the club in the early part of the nineteenth century, was taken down. Chelsea fans had long thought it would be bad luck if the vane was ever removed from the top of the Main Stand.

The club had indeed suffered a run of bad luck, but much of it was due to the cost of the East Stand rather than any divine intervention. In 1979 the club's debts and the ground were put under the control of a holding company called SB Property (SBP). New chairman Ken Bates arrived on the scene in April 1982 and the following August signed a seven-year lease with SBP which gave Chelsea an option to buy the ground. In September 1983 the Mears family sold out to Marler Estates for £1.25 million and Chelsea's situation took a turn for the worse.

Marler wanted to redevelop Stamford Bridge with flats, offices and a supermarket – but no football ground. Under the terms of the lease the company had to find Chelsea an alternative home within 15 miles of the Bridge. Selhurst Park was the favourite until Charlton moved in after leaving the Valley. Then in May 1986 Marler bought Craven Cottage for £9 million. Their intentions were obvious. But Marler's plans for Chelsea and Fulham to share were blocked when a new Labour council adopted a policy that football should be preserved at all three clubs in the borough. Undeterred, Marler bought the other club in the borough, QPR, for £6 million and announced that they'd merge with Fulham and become Fulham Park Rangers, while also hinting that Chelsea could share Loftus Road. But after the council had thrown down the gauntlet, the Football League stepped in to block a merger.

The plot thickened when Cabra Estates bought out Marler for £82 million. Chelsea's lease duly expired in August 1989, but Bates used the courts to buy time for the club. Meanwhile, Chelsea built a third dressing-room to accommodate Fulham, who'd been promised £5 million by Cabra if they left the Cottage and moved in with Chelsea. This, despite the council's policy and the fact that planning consent for Bates's own redevelopment plans for the Bridge specifically ruled out ground-sharing. But neither Fulham nor Chelsea need have worried about the fate of Cabra, because both clubs finally escaped the clutches of property developers when Cabra collapsed, along with the property market, in November 1992. (By then the weather-vane had been put back on the top of a stand, only this time it was on the West Stand.) The Royal Bank of Scotland took over the freehold and on 15 December 1992 granted Chelsea a 20-year lease with an option to buy the Bridge for £16.5 million.

Matthew Harding was the next protagonist in the unfolding saga. He'd put up £5 million for the new North Stand in the form of loan stock, enabling him to convert the loan into shares at the end of the 15-year agreement, plus £2.5 million for new players; and he had joined the board. From inside Stamford Bridge on a bright Sunday afternoon it was impossible not to notice the difference that Harding's money had made to the club. The evidence, in the form of the gleaming new North Stand and the redevelopment of the South Stand, was there for all to see. The West Stand still needed to be replaced, but surely that was just a matter of time. The important thing was that the ground was now taking shape.

Chelsea's performances on the pitch had been improving in line with the stadium. Having been trounced 4–0 in the previous season's FA Cup final by double-winning Manchester United, they at least had the consolation of playing in Europe in the Cup-Winners' Cup while the Reds entered the more prestigious European Champions League. Chelsea had just disposed of Viktoria Zizkov of the Czech Republic in the first round the previous Thursday, drawing 0–0 in the away leg after a 4–2 win at home. One of the supporters in front of me had been to the match and was wearing a Russian-style fur hat which, he joked, he'd got from Chelsea keeper Dmitri Kharine.

Injuries and restrictions on the use of foreign players at the time meant the Blues had to draft in former Arsenal midfield star and youth-team coach Graham Rix for the away leg, after he came on briefly as a substitute in the first game. His appearance at Stamford Bridge made him the oldest player ever to make his début for Chelsea, a distinction held by Bryan 'Pop' Robson for more than 12 years. Rix had played more than thirty European games and manager Glenn Hoddle had no doubts about naming his good friend and former rival as one of the five substitutes. Rix and Hoddle had enjoyed many battles during their numerous north London derbies at both Highbury and White Hart Lane. But now they were on the same side.

Rix had kept himself fit by playing in the six- and eight-a-sides in training as well as making the occasional appearance for the reserves. 'Glenn forewarned me a couple of weeks before the game that I might be needed,' said Rix:

> First of all I was chuffed even to be considered for the squad, not having played at that level for more than a year. I trained with the first-team lads on the Wednesday, after which Glenn told me I was on the bench. The lads were great. There was the usual banter about having an old man in the squad, but they all said they hoped I got on the following night. I was so excited when I woke up on the Thursday morning. I turned to my wife and said: 'Today I'm a player again. I'm not a youth-team coach, I'm a player. I'm going to train a little bit in the morning, have my pasta, go to bed in the afternoon, get to the ground, my kit's going to be laid out for me, I'm going to be a player today.'

In the first leg Rix came on as an 89th-minute substitute for another former Arsenal midfielder, David Rocastle.

> Obviously, I was delighted to get on but that was incidental. The fact was I was involved and part of it. I love it. One of my big sayings to the lads is: 'Influence the game.' You know, do something. I went on and, yes, I did misplace a couple of passes. I appreciate that. But I did affect the game. I got a few tackles in, I body-checked one of their lads, I did something that was going to help my team. I got a great reception from the crowd, which gave me a hell of a boost. It's not easy for a nearly 37-year-old going on for his début in a European Cup tie. There's not many have done that.

Rix was asked if he could have played longer: 'I could have lasted another two or three minutes I suppose! I must have been the only person in the ground that didn't want the referee to blow.'

Rix had not totally ruled out reviving his playing career, though he realised how difficult it was to come back into a game which was getting quicker all the time. 'To be fair, the game is played at such a hectic pace these days that 90 minutes away to Manchester United might be asking a bit too much for me. But if I'm needed, I'll give it my best shot. Whether I'll be able to walk two or three days after I don't know. But I do know I'll enjoy it.' It wouldn't be long before he found out. The same injuries and foreign-player restrictions which hit Chelsea for the first leg were still there when the second leg came around two weeks later. This time Rix was asked to play a full 90 minutes.

The travelling Chelsea fans had to find their way to the Czech city of Jablonec. There was only one road into town and road blocks would ensure that fans without special tickets would be sent back to the airport. 'Troublemakers could be in for a nasty shock,' said Chairman Ken Bates. 'Dixon of Dock Green has no part in Czech Police culture.' Chelsea were taking no chances with their team either. They took their own food and their own chef to cook it!

The ageing Rix gave a good account of himself in a hard-fought 0–0 draw. Glenn Hoddle knew the value of having someone with Rix's experience to draw on. In his programme notes 'Glenn's View' he gave him a special mention. 'He's not played a full 90 minutes in a long time, especially at that level. He may yet be needed again.'

The fans were also 'magnificent . . . and properly conducted' in the words of Dennis Wise. Unfortunately Wise himself was booked for time-wasting. The Chelsea captain was also impressed with Rix's contribution. 'Special congratulations to Rixy, who I've never seen go so long without a cigar. Ninety minutes! You were a credit, Rixy.'

It wasn't only the playing squad and the fans who were under pressure as a result of Chelsea's European campaign. Managing director Colin Hutchinson got back around midnight on the Thursday after the match in the Czech Republic and had to be on the first plane to Geneva to attend the draw for the next round and to make arrangements for those two matches. He then returned to Heathrow on the Friday night and had just 24 hours to finalise the arrangements for today's match against West Ham.

It was like a throwback to the early '70s when the Blues last competed in the Cup-Winners' Cup, after winning the FA Cup by overcoming Leeds 2–1 in a thrilling replay at Old Trafford – the first time the final had gone to a replay since 1912. Chelsea went on to lift the Cup-Winners' Cup after a victory over Real Madrid in another replayed final – this time in Athens. The following year they reached their third successive final, but lost to Stoke in the League Cup final at Wembley. Back in 1965 they'd been the first London club to win the League Cup under Tommy Doherty, who also guided them to the FA Cup final in 1967, when they lost to arch-rivals Tottenham in the first all-London final. Later that year Dave Sexton arrived and the rest is history.

Chelsea's pensioners are old enough to have lived through a lot of the club's ups and downs. They can always be seen at home matches wearing their distinctive dark-blue uniforms (they wear scarlet in the summer). There were quite a few of them in the East Stand for the West Ham match and they must have enjoyed it since Chelsea won 2–1. A victory over Chelsea's east London rivals was always something to savour – even in the twilight of your life!

AN ACT OF GOD

Southampton v Everton – The Dell, 8 October 1994

Matt Le Tissier arrived at the Dell just after 1 p.m. As the England midfielder got out of his car he was surrounded by young supporters clamouring for his autograph. Matty, as he is affectionately known to fans and team-mates alike, patiently signed everything thrust before him: programmes, autograph books, even shirts bearing his number seven with the word GOD sacrilegiously printed above. 'Thank you very much,' he said after signing each autograph. Modesty personified.

To say that Le Tissier was worshipped by the fans on the south coast is an understatement. His name was on everyone's lips before the match. 'Good luck on Wednesday, Matt,' said one passing fan decked out in red and white. 'He'll have to pick you now.' The references were to the England coach Terry Venables and the goals scored by Matty in the Coca-Cola Cup second round second leg tie at the Dell the previous Wednesday night. Le Tissier had destroyed Huddersfield almost single-handedly, scoring all four goals in the Saints' comfortable victory.

Le Tissier's arrival had electrified the waiting fans in the main car park outside the ground. Bruce Grobbelaar, Southampton's close-season signing from Liverpool, was also besieged by supporters as he made his way towards the players' entrance.

'I suppose it takes you longer to sign autographs than other players because your name's so long,' I said as Bruce tried to move on without appearing rude to the fans.

'Don't blame me, blame my father. It's his fault,' he said in a soft Zimbabwean drawl.

Everton fans were also milling around outside the stadium among the home supporters. All were hoping to get a ticket for the match. With the Dell's capacity reduced to 15,000 by the Taylor Report's requirements for all-seater stadia, tickets were in short supply. They were sold out a couple of hours before the match, leaving many Evertonians stranded a long way from home. One family, complete with tiny tot dressed in NEC embossed Everton shirt, shorts and socks plus the tiniest football boots I'd ever seen, asked if I had a spare ticket. Unfortunately I hadn't.

Some of the Everton fans were returning to the south coast for the second time in a week, following their team's 1–1 draw with Portsmouth the previous Wednesday night in the Coca-Cola Cup. That result, which followed a 3–2 defeat at Goodison in the first leg, ended their involvement in the first of the season's major cup competitions. A dismal run of results had also left them without a win in the Premier League after eight matches. The pressure on the players and manager Mike Walker was already building. They needed to get something from today's game.

The outlook couldn't have been brighter for former England World Cup winner and Southampton manager Alan Ball. He had turned up before the players in his yellow Mercedes. As he took his gear from the boot the fans gathered around. Ball patiently signed autographs and I asked him if he had mixed emotions about playing against Everton. 'Yeah, sure I do,' he said. Ball had spent some of the best years of his playing career at Goodison before moving to Arsenal.

Some of the Evertonians remembered the white football boots Ball had pioneered in the 1970s. I told the man himself about their recollections. He just smiled. Perhaps the memory was too embarrassing. Maybe he had his mind on other things – like today's match. There was no time for sentiment. His heart was with Southampton and only one result would keep him happy this afternoon.

Alongside Lawrie McMenemy, a long-time favourite at the Dell and now the director of football, Ball had turned the club from no-hopers into genuine contenders for a European place. They were relegation certainties at the back end of the previous season, but a win today would put them seventh – their best position in more than four years.

Much of the credit for the club's survival in the previous campaign and their healthy start to the current season rested with Le Tissier. Here was a midfield artist in the Glenn Hoddle mould who could score goals. His touch was exquisite. 'He can do things with a ball which surprise even his team-mates as well as me and Alan,' said McMenemy. So why was he still playing for Southampton when the glamour clubs were queuing up to sign him? What was the attraction of the Dell?

'Matt's ambition is to play for his country and he can achieve his ambition by staying at Southampton,' said McMenemy:

> Some people have suggested he needs to move to a big club, like Manchester United, but that is simply not true. Just look at the people who have come before Matthew at Southampton – Alan Shearer, Danny Wallace, Steve Williams and even Alan Ball, Kevin Keegan and Mick Channon. This is a very professional club, very homely. And there has been a procession of big names here.
>
> Matt is happy here. Sure, he can get higher wages elsewhere, but he gets regular Premiership football playing a good style. Manchester United have got their Le Tissier in Cantona and they are both exceptional talents. I have to say I'd rather have Matt, because I know him better and he is more placid. But they both do something special, something that no other players can achieve, yet it comes naturally to them. They do not find it difficult. People pay their money just to see the likes of Le Tissier and Cantona and they get value for money because they get entertainment and excitement.
>
> Matt just does amazing things. Peter Osgood was like him. He could do things the Brazilians could and Matt is the same. He can ping balls around 40 or 50 yards with no effort. He also has great balance over the ball and is very nimble for a big man. And he brings out the best in the players around him.

Praise indeed from a man who has worked with some of the biggest names in the game at both domestic and international level. There was no doubt that Le Tissier was happy at Southampton. Over the summer he had been linked with most of the top Premier League sides including Manchester United, where a fee of £6 million was mooted. But Le Tiss liked his roots. And his roots liked him. He was clearly in good form. Against Everton Le Tissier made one goal and scored the other in a 2–0 win which sank the Toffeemen just as effectively as the iceberg which downed the Titanic in 1912 on her maiden voyage from Southampton.

After the match, one Saints fan put Le Tissier's case for an England call-up to a journalist who had just emerged from the press-box. 'He should be given a chance after performing like that,' said the grey-haired Southampton supporter.

'Read all about it in the *Express* tomorrow,' said the newspaper's reporter. The week after the match against Everton the likeable Guernsey star was picked to play for England against Romania.

McMenemy recalled the day Alan Ball rushed into his office to tell him about the exciting talent in their midst. 'Alan came back from training and said: "You won't believe what I've just seen." He then told me how Le Tissier had a free-kick rolled back to him, had flicked the ball into the air and then volleyed it over the wall and into the top corner of the net. What staggered Alan was that Le Tissier didn't just do it once, he tried it five times and scored five out of five.'

Ball was just as fulsome in his praise of Matty as the avuncular McMenemy. 'He is the best player in the country. And I've got him. I wouldn't swap him for anybody else. I'm a lucky man. From the first moment I walked into this club it was easy to recognise the boy's outstanding ability. I told the other players: "Look, whether you like it or not, he's the best player we've got – and now we've got to get the best out of him."

'It's taken a while to get Matty in areas where he can deliver. That's what we've worked on from the first day I came here,' said Ball. 'Now there's two of them [Le Tissier and Danish international Ronnie Ekelund – a recent capture from Barcelona] in areas where they can cause people problems providing we can get the ball to them. In the right areas, they both can deliver. Matty's shooting is so good, we're shocked when he misses.' Between them, they opened up Everton's defence repeatedly as Southampton coasted to victory in the second half.

I was sitting in the West Stand to the left of a man who managed an Australian football team which drew most of its players from the Italian community. 'If you're ever in Oz stop by and see us,' he told me. 'If the football's no good, at least we can guarantee you a nice cappuccino!' He gave me his card.

To his right sat a mother and her son – a dyed-in-the-wool Saints fan. The young boy kept looking round at the men in the seats behind me. One of them was former West Ham and Spurs star Paul Allen. He was presently injured but even when he was fit had struggled to get a regular place. I would come across him again at Luton where he was to play on-loan from the Saints. His days at the Dell seemed to be numbered.

But despite being out-of-favour, Allen, the second-youngest player ever to appear in a Cup final when he played against Arsenal in 1980, was clearly idolised by the youngster on my right.

'Would you like Paul's autograph?' I asked the boy.

'Yes, please,' he said eagerly. His mum passed me the match programme and I asked Allen if he'd oblige.

'No problem,' he said.

The teams came out onto the pitch from the dressing-rooms in the south corner of the West Stand down to my right. There's not a tunnel at the Dell, so the players have to walk down a flight of stairs! But it was worth it. Red and white balloons mixed with the blue of Everton as confetti rained down from the terraces. Grobbelaar was up to his usual tricks juggling a ball as he walked, while Le Tissier accepted the cheers from the home supporters in a dignified manner, ever the gentleman.

Throughout the match Paul Allen had been discussing his form and the game. 'Samways started well but he's faded,' said the guy next to him.

'Same old Vinny,' said Allen, recalling his days playing alongside Everton's new £2.3 million summer signing. They'd appeared together in the Tottenham team which won the 1991 FA Cup final against Nottingham Forest.

Same old Le Tissier capped a fine Saints performance with a super sidefooted goal which gave Neville Southall no chance and the Saints a commanding 2–0 lead. He ran across to salute the crowd. God had spoken. The fans responded with their 'We're not worthy' routine borrowed from *Wayne's World*. If Le Tissier ever left the Dell, their world would fall apart. There's a huge responsibility on his shoulders. Handle it? He seemed to thrive on it. King Canute is supposed to have told the waves to go back at Southampton; if Le Tissier had gone down to the beach and given the order, few Saints' fans would have bet against the ocean beating a hasty retreat!

Playing at the Dell was pure pleasure for Le Tissier. I wondered whether he knew the ground had been a charming beauty spot around a large pond when one George Thomas paid £10,000 to develop it into a football ground in the late 1890s. Probably not. Thomas had to turn the pond into a series of underground streams before he could build stands and terracing to accommodate an initial capacity of 24,000 supporters.

Southampton were formed before the Dell even became a football ground by players from Deanery FC, a club that was founded in 1880. Most of the team were members of St Mary's Young Men's Christian Association (YMCA) – hence the nickname the 'Saints' – and they formed a new club called Southampton St Mary's. The curate of St Mary's was their first president. Southampton St Mary's won the Southern League in 1897 before giving up their formal link to the Church and becoming a limited company under the name of plain old Southampton.

With gates rising to 12,000 the Saints looked for another ground (they were then playing at the County Cricket Ground on Northlands Road) and found the Dell. It was opened on 3 September 1898 for a Southern League match against Brighton United.

Southampton reached the FA Cup final in 1900 and 1902 but didn't join the League until 1920, when they became founder members of Division Three. By the 1925–26 season they'd reached the Second Division, where they would remain for 30 years, and that success enabled the club to sell some of its star players. The transfer fees, along with a loan and funds raised by the fans, were used to buy the ground from George Thomas's widow for £26,000 in 1926. The club had enough money left over to build the double-decker West Stand, a design which was virtually copied on the other side of the ground after a fire destroyed the original East Stand in 1929.

More damage was done to the Dell during the Second World War – not because the Germans had anything against the Saints' style of football, but due to the strategic importance of the nearby docks. The city stands on a triangular peninsula formed at the point where the rivers Itchen and Test flow into Southampton water, an eight-mile inlet from the Solent. The area also enjoys what's known as 'double tides' – a prolonged period of high water as the Channel swirls first up the westerly side of the Solent, then, a couple of hours later, backs up round the Isle of Wight past Portsmouth. This allows very large ships to dock at the city's ports, either in the Eastern Docks at the tip of the promontory or in the Western Docks stretching up the Test estuary, which has the largest commercial dry dock in England.

Since the Dell is only a mile from the main docks, it was almost inevitable that the ground would be hit when the Luftwaffe began bombing the area heavily during the Blitz. So it was that in November 1940 a bomb landed on the ground at the Milton Road End, breaking an underground water culvert and flooding the pitch. Southampton, or the Scummers as they're known by Portsmouth fans, had to do the unthinkable and temporarily use Pompey's Fratton Park for home games.

The intense rivalry between the two south-coast clubs apparently has its roots in a strike at the respective ports. After several weeks of solidarity the strike was broken by the workers from Southampton. The name of the Southampton-based union was the Southampton Company Union Men or SCUM. The acronym led to the Saints becoming known by Pompey fans as the Scummers.

Back at the Dell, Southampton were one of the first clubs of the modern era to install floodlights, after playing under lights on a foreign tour. In fact, after the Football Association lifted its ban on floodlit games, the Dell became the first ground in England to stage a competitive match between two League teams under lights when the Saints played Tottenham reserves before a crowd of more than 13,500 on 1 October 1951. It took another four years for Kidderminster to become the first club to stage a competitive floodlit match when they took on Brierley Hill in September 1955.

I'd arrived at the ground from Southampton docks after driving down from London early that morning with my mum and dad. They were leaving on a cruise around the Mediterranean aboard the P&O luxury cruise liner *Sea Princess*. While they prepared for a tour of the ship I headed for a tour of Southampton's stadium, the once beautiful Dell.

On arrival at the main entrance I was met by two very smart doormen dressed in dapper red suit jackets and pristine white shirts. One of them was to be my tour guide. He took me first into the boardroom, where various trophies were proudly displayed including a silver tea kettle from one of the club's foreign matches. Ladies weren't allowed in the inner sanctum; it was, as at so many other clubs, a traditional male enclave. Chauvinism was the order of the day down on the south coast, it seemed.

An adjoining room contained a long polished wooden table, not unlike those seen in boardrooms of large companies in the City of London. Mounted on the wall was a series of wooden plaques on which was inscribed the names of all the players who had represented their countries whilst playing in the red and white stripes of Southampton. The roll-call stretched back across the decades and was impressive: Alf Ramsey, Terry Paine, Ron Davies, Mike Channon, Peter Shilton (the club's most-capped player with 49 England appearances under his belt whilst playing between the sticks at the Dell).

Paine and Channon were joined by Martin Chivers in the Southampton side that reached the First Division for the first time in the club's history in 1966. They stayed there until 1974 when, under Lawrie McMenemy, they were relegated alongside Manchester United. It was ironic in a way, since United had attracted the Saints' record crowd of just over 31,000 for a League match in 1969.

But Southampton went on to produce one of the biggest shocks in FA Cup history in 1976, when a solitary goal by Bobby Stokes beat red-hot favourites Manchester United. Southampton's name went on the Cup for the first time as they became only the third Second Division side to win the trophy at Wembley. West Bromwich Albion (1931) and Sunderland (1973) were the others at the time. The side included such great players as former Chelsea star Peter Osgood and Sheffield Wednesday idol Jim McCalliog.

In July 1977, Manchester City paid a record fee for a Saints player when they took Mick Channon to Maine Road for £300,000. But despite losing the wily striker, Southampton bounced back to the First Division in 1978 before losing the

League Cup final the following year. Their best performance in the League came in 1984, when a new generation of old stars, including Alan Ball, Kevin Keegan and Peter Shilton, led them to runners-up spot.

I left the memories behind in the boardroom and went to find my seat in the stadium. The Dell is the smallest ground in the Premier League. The East Stand is hemmed in by houses and a church hall, while the height of the West Stand is limited by the surrounding houses.

I was fortunate enough to have a ticket for the West Stand. To my right was the Milton Road End, once famous for the so-called Chocolate Box enclosures – three concrete platforms on stilts above the terracing. According to Simon Inglis in *The Football Grounds of Britain,* they were the only uncovered upper tiers of terracing at any British ground. Sadly, the chocolate boxes came down in 1981. In fact, Southampton had just built a new Milton Road End stand the previous summer, although limited space behind the ground meant the seats still sloped down from right to left a third of the way across the stand so that there are fewer seats in each row the higher you go.

The Milton Road Stand overhangs the back wall of the ground because there's such a small amount of space around the stadium. The Dell is wedged between two roads which cut across the back of each end stand at an angle. In fact, the roads are only a few yards from the goals at either end. To the left of the Milton Road Stand are the strategically important docks and, much further away, the New Forest.

Southampton had been trying to escape the confines of the Dell for years, but their efforts had gone unrewarded. To meet the requirements of the Taylor Report they thus had to invest in the Dell. In 1993 the club built a new 1,300-seater stand at the Archer's Road End and the following year they developed the Milton Road End. The remodelling of both ends cost £1.6 million.

THROUGH THE LOOKING GLASS

Coventry City v Ipswich Town – Highfield Road, 10 October 1994

This was football Through The Looking Glass. The Premier Club, Highfield Road. Monday night. The visitors, Ipswich Town. Both teams struggling at the bottom of the Premier League and desperate to pick up points as the spectre of relegation already hung over managers Phil Neal and John Lyall. The Sky cameras were here to bring an early-season dogfight to your screens. Pressure, what pressure?

I arrived just before kick-off as the last trickle of supporters made their way through the dimly lit streets of back-to-back houses which snuggled up to the ground. I had a seat in Coventry's new Premier Club, opened at the start of the season. For £1,000 per double membership you could watch all first-team home League and Cup matches in the comfort of 'luxurious theatre-style seating in warm and comfortable surroundings'.

There were plenty of spare seats for tonight's match, both in the Premier Club and in the real world outside. In fact, the Sky Blues were playing in front of only

9,526 – their lowest crowd of the season so far. The locals had either decided that Ipswich weren't an attraction or they were sitting at home by the fire with a cup of hot chocolate watching the game on TV. They could have joined me in the Premier Club for £40 a seat.

It was like a cross between a hotel and a cinema. I was welcomed at reception like a hotel guest on a weekend break. 'Could you give me your name please?' said the receptionist. 'Thank you. Here's your ticket, sir.' It was so civilised. Hard to imagine I was about to watch 90 minutes of blood and thunder Premier League football. Still, an interesting concept. And not at all surprising that Coventry were at the forefront of new innovations.

The club was formed in 1883 by workers at the Singers' bicycle factory and first played as Singers' FC. The name was changed to Coventry in 1898 and the following year they settled at Highfield Road. They joined the League in 1919 as members of the Second Division and moved between there and the Third Division. Then, in 1958, when they were relegated to the old Fourth Division for the one and only time, a certain James W.T. Hill, recently retired from playing the game, became manager. What followed was nothing short of a revolution and the period is still called the 'Sky Blue era'. Under Hill's guidance City went from the Third Division to the First in six years. They became the only club to have played in six divisions of the Football League (Third Division North and South plus all four of the mainstream divisions). The team played in a new sky-blue strip, which is how they got their nickname.

But it wasn't just success on the pitch which attracted attention to the Sky Blues. The off-the-pitch changes were equally remarkable. The Thackhall Street Stand on the north side of the ground was replaced in the early '60s with a revolutionary new pre-fabricated construction known as the Sky Blue Stand. This futuristic concept was put together by a company called Banbury Grandstands. It was like something out of Marks & Spencer: made to fit any size. The cost: £120,000.

The next innovation was an electric scoreboard given to the club by the *Coventry Evening Telegraph*. The League's first executive club was launched in the Main Stand with a membership at 100 guineas a year. Radio Sky Blue kept fans entertained before matches alongside the dog-handling displays, pop concerts and netball matches! And the club began to televise away games on large screens at Highfield Road.

After promotion as Second Division champions in 1967 a double-decker West Stand was built for £85,000. Coventry had clinched the title in a Championship decider, against Wolves before a record crowd of over 51,000. The club also launched the Sky Blue Match Day Magazine, just a little ahead of its time. It took most other League clubs some 20 years to realise what a good idea such a broad publication was.

In 1968 the Main Stand was destroyed by fire along with the Second Division Championship trophy. City immediately replaced the stand with a large version of the Sky Blue Stand – only this one had a restaurant on the first floor.

But the most dramatic innovation, and again an idea ahead of its time, was the decision in 1981 to turn Highfield Road into the country's first all-seater stadium. The conversion required an extra 8,000 seats and cost £400,000. It reduced the capacity from 38,500 to 20,616 (present capacity is 22,600). The main aim of this momentous undertaking was to tackle hooliganism, which the club believed had undermined the family atmosphere.

The club's proudest moment came in 1987 when they beat Spurs 3–2 in extra-time to win the FA Cup for the only time under manager John Sillett and his assistant George Curtis, the club's former centre-half. Since then Coventry have built a new stand at the Kop End and extended the roof to the Sky Blue Stand at a cost of £6 million. In 1994, the new 5,000 all-seater East Stand was built.

But what of today's innovative approach to professional football at Highfield Road? Mark Jones, director of sales and marketing, was planning Coventry's version of air miles for supporters buying goods in the club shops, or spending money in the Premier Club, with a club card. 'Football Miles' would be redeemed for merchandise or match tickets. Great idea.

But that was the future. Tonight I'd experience the luxury of the Premier Club. Soft, royal-blue padded seats. Plate-glass window separating well-heeled supporters from the fans outside. Crowd noise piped in through speakers embedded in the ceiling, like skylights. The atmosphere was almost surreal.

'It's a totally different game from in here,' said a bald-headed man with a greying moustache and glasses who was sitting next to me.

'Sure is,' said his bearded friend.

The speakers were turned off before the match and at half-time so as not to disturb the diners in the Premier Club restaurant. When I arrived they were tucking into a selection from the matchday menu – basically a carvery. If you didn't want to leave the restaurant, it was possible to see the whole match from your table. All the comforts of home. But is this any way to watch football? Coventry had so far sold more than half of the Premier Club memberships, so the demand seemed to be there.

Outside, the game had started. Midway through the first half Coventry's Paul Cook swung in a corner, which was headed down by Roy Wegerle, bringing a good save from Ipswich keeper Craig Forrest. Outside, the 'real' fans reacted with an 'Ooooohhh'. Inside, the patrons of the Premier Club clapped politely as if they were registering their appreciation for a movement at a symphony concert or the finish of a crescendo at the opera. There was about as much passion as afternoon tea at the Ritz.

I could see the lights of the carvery reflected in the plate-glass separating me from the majority of the Coventry supporters. Staff in royal-blue bow-ties and white shirts with royal-blue waistcoats scurried around behind me preparing for the half-time refreshments. The supervisor was decked out very smartly in a sky-blue two-piece suit. Just before half-time the chef made an appearance in his tall hat. The bulk of his work was over for the evening. He could relax now.

The four men in the front row ahead of me had decided to give Coventry defender David Rennie a bit of stick.

'You're so mobile, Rennie,' said one.

'Come on, Rennie, let's see what you can do now,' said the other sarcastically. As Coventry began to get on top the criticism became more muted. Just before half-time, they scored. Julian Darby broke down the right and Ipswich captain John Wark, making a desperate attempt to block the cross, only succeeded in stabbing the ball into his own net.

'Johnny Wark, Johnny Wark, Johnny Wark,' rang out from the Coventry fans as the two teams left the field at half-time to be replaced by Sky's dancing girls. So they did still exist. Auntie Beryl at Ipswich had told me they'd been dropped from this year's Sky repertoire, but there they were. Resplendent in their sky-blue leotards with matching pompoms. I wished I had binoculars to get a closer look!

The Warwickshire cricket team paraded around the pitch at half-time with the four trophies they'd picked up from their wonderfully successful season: three winners trophies and one runners-up. They received a warm reception from the home crowd.

Inside the Premier Club, the punters were tucking into tea and biscuits as they watched Alan Parry on the television monitors beaming Sky Sports' Monday Night Football to all corners of the suite. I took a cup of coffee and returned to my comfy chair to watch the second half. Expensive cigar smoke wafted over my head from the front row. The atmosphere was like a posh London men's club.

Coventry keeper Steve Ogrizovic saw more action in the second half and came to the rescue four times. He snatched the ball from the head of Chris Kiwomya, dived at the feet of Claus Thomsen and Stuart Slater, and then stopped a close-range header from Steve Sedgeley. 'Oggie, Oggie, Oggie,' chanted the crowd. (I knew that's what they were chanting because of the speaker positioned just above my head.)

One of the liveliest players on the pitch was American World Cup star Cobi Jones. His dreadlocks flowed all over the pitch as he jinked and twisted and turned his way into space. His lightning pace was unsettling the Ipswich defence, leaving gaps for Coventry's other American international, Wegerle, and £2 million summer signing Dion Dublin. The former Manchester United star had scored six goals in six games since his arrival at Highfield Road, but Dublin did not add to that tally tonight.

'Pass it to Cobi,' said a young lad in the front row. 'Give it to Cobi,' he repeated, as if the young American was his best friend.

Jones had arrived at Highfield Road for a £500,000 fee, but his contract would come up for discussion at the end of the season. One official thought he'd leave to join America's new Major League Soccer (he did). 'He's pretty homesick here,' she said. Jones was still living in a hotel. 'But he's also overwhelmed to be playing in the Premiership before thousands of people every week.'

The supporters next to me were discussing the cost of advertising on the club scoreboard. 'They rang me and asked if I'd like to advertise,' said the bearded one, obviously a local businessman. 'They wanted £150 to flash an ad on the scoreboard at every home game up to Christmas.'

'You wouldn't get an ad in the *Evening Telegraph* for that,' said the bald man. 'That sounds cheap to me.'

Not cheap enough. 'The trouble is the fans aren't watching the scoreboard, they're looking at the football. That's why I didn't have it in the end. Mind you, I've heard people say they've seen my ad at the match. I had it last year. It cost me £150 for the season.' He might have had a chance of selling them something from the scoreboard tonight. The football being served up was distinctly less appetising than the carvery.

One of the few flashes of brilliance came from Ipswich keeper Craig Forrest, who denied Wegerle after 68 minutes. But it was only a matter of time before Coventry scored again. It came from a Paul Cook penalty after Wegerle was bundled over by Gavin Johnson.

Towards the end of the match a cheer went up for substitute Peter Ndlovu as he began to warm up. Surprisingly, manager Phil Neal took off Cobi Jones. Ndlovu's arrival, after a long lay-off with injury, cheered the home fans. 'Down with the Leicester, you're going down with the Leicester,' rang out across Highfield Road. A couple of weeks before, the Ipswich players had been serenaded by supporters from Norwich who sang 'Down with the Walker, you're going down with the Walker.' Different companions, but the same message. Ipswich were in deep trouble.

The match over, I grabbed a drink from the bar and asked an official to call me a cab. After half an hour she'd had no luck. I said I might take the advice of the taxi driver who'd dropped me outside the ground and walk into the city centre to hail a cab there. 'I wouldn't walk through the back streets at night on your own,' said the official. 'It's not too safe around here on your own at night. The stadium is on the border of the Hillfields district of Coventry, an area of town notorious for crime.'

Perhaps crime is the result of the depressed and downbeat atmosphere in the city since its car industry, first established in the 1890s, had suffered badly. Or maybe it's because Coventry is plagued by some of the ugliest urban planning in England, including the shopping precinct and inner ring road, which resulted from the rebuilding of the city after bombing raids in 1940. The Germans destroyed the armaments factories and devastated much of the old town, including Highfield Road, which took three direct hits and was closed for 18 months.

As I was leaving the ground one of the club's security guards added credence to the warnings I'd been given about the safety of the area. When the Coventry official, smartly dressed in a sky-blue two-piece suit, offered me a lift to the station I gratefully accepted.

FAREWELL TO THE COUNTY GROUND – AGAIN

Northampton Town v Mansfield Town – The County Ground,
11 October 1994

'The lights will go out at the County Ground tonight,' said the local *Northampton Chronicle & Echo* under the headline 'End of an Era'. 'Tonight signals a landmark for Northampton Town Football Club,' said the Cobblers manager John Barnwell. It was billed as one of the most exciting and eventful weeks in the club's history. After nearly 100 years Northampton were leaving the County Ground and moving across town to the new £5.2 million Sixfields Stadium. Mansfield would be the ground's last visitors.

Of course, the fans had seen it all before. 'Last Game II – The Sequel' was being shown at the County Ground tonight by virtue of the fact that the first 'last game', if you see what I mean, was supposed to have been played against Chester the previous season. The Cobblers won that match before more than 6,000 fans on an emotional 'final' day at the ground they'd shared with the cricket and bowls club for 97 years. However, their new 7,646-capacity all-seater stadium wasn't finished on time, bringing yet another curtain call.

I'd arrived in Northampton earlier that afternoon to soak up the atmosphere in the town on this historic day. As I checked into the Moat House Hotel near the station, a white concrete 1960s monstrosity with about as much warmth as the Arctic Circle, there were no signs that this was a special day for the people of Northampton. No banners to greet me at the station. No posters advertising 'The End of An Era'. Only the local paper had made any effort to drum up excitement about the move in this pretty sleepy town best known for its shoe industry; hence the club's nickname, the Cobblers.

As the night began to draw in I left my hotel and walked through the town square past the market stalls and the paved shopping area towards the Northampton Town Football Club and County Cricket Ground. Young fans were already making their way to the stadium to bid the old ground farewell. Mind you, judging by the *Chronicle & Echo*'s special report on the last game it didn't sound as if many people would miss the club's old home. 'Tonight the curtain comes down at the tatty, three-sided County Ground – a joke venue for football fans over several years – and this time there will be no encores.'

At least it had the distinction of being the only three-sided ground in the Football League! Ironically, that accolade was bestowed on the Cobblers after Sheffield United built over their cricket pitch in 1974. United's Bramall Lane had recently returned to its former prominence of having only three sides by virtue of ground redevelopment resulting in the demolition of one of the main stands. But that was a transitionary phase and didn't really count.

The local Northampton paper's back page *Sports Chronicle* section echoed the feelings expressed in the special report. 'Sixfields, in all its splendour, is lying in wait in Northampton's west end. And the boys from the soccer slums will be kicking their last ball in the ramshackle hovel that has been home for far too long.' It wasn't for nothing that the ground's 'temporary' Main Stand was known as the Meccano Stand. It looked as if a group of young kids had been let loose for an afternoon with their nuts and spanners.

As I turned into Roseholme Road, past the Abington Park Brewery Co. on the corner, I could see the County Ground floodlights. They'd replaced the old-style lights a decade ago, after they blew a fuse during their final appearance, causing a match to be abandoned. I wondered if the same thing could happen again tonight. The *Sports Chronicle*, then as now, had almost prophesied the disaster with their statement that, 'The lights will go out at the County Ground tonight.' They certainly did that night.

The back of the ground displayed a sign which said, 'Northamptonshire County Cricket Club' in gold relief letters on a maroon background either side of the entrance. Signs inside the cricket ground entrance said, 'Dr Martens Air Wair Welcomes You to the County Ground'. There were tiny turnstiles to the left and right. All seemed to be decorated in gold and maroon – except for the Mansfield team coach parked over to my left in a corner of the tiny car park.

The eight-and-a-half-acre site started out as farmland before being converted into a cricket pitch in the 1880s. The football club used the cricket pavilion on the condition that they would not play before 1 September or after 1 May – a condition that remained in force until the Cobblers left for their new stadium in the autumn of 1994.

I soon realised that the main ticket office was on the other side of the ground, on Abington Avenue, and not at the entrance to the cricket ground, even though it was used by football fans who wanted to stand on the touchline across from the Meccano Stand. I backtracked and walked around to the front of the stadium. Suddenl, the atmosphere began to fill me with excitement and anticipation. There were thousands of people queuing outside the Hotel End in a long line stretching halfway up the road.

'There'll be 6,000 here tonight,' said one fan who passed by me among the rush of supporters heading for the main entrance on Abington Avenue. The maroon-coloured Main Stand was now half its original height; the club had lopped off the top section in November 1985 because some of the steel roof girders were deemed to be unsafe and it was too expensive to replace them.

Maroon balloons decorated the directors' entrance in the middle of the Main Stand. Paper sellers were flogging special editions of the *Chronicle & Echo*. 'Farewell County Ground – Picture Special' was stamped on billboards displayed around the ground. Fans in the club shop were enquiring about tickets for County's opening match at the new Sixfields Stadium, against Barnet on the coming Saturday.

Camera crews were milling around outside the ground to film the line of supporters waiting to get in at the Hotel End – so-called because of the County Tavern pub on the corner between that end and the Main Stand. The pub was packed and the fans inside were in good voice. I joined the queue to get in to the Main Stand, if you could call it that. An attractive young woman was selling newspapers alongside a billboard which read: 'County Ground Special: End of an Era'.

'What's your most memorable visit to the County Ground?' one television reporter asked an elderly grey-haired man in the queue.

'He hasn't got one,' interrupted the fan in front of me.

The old man thought for a moment. 'When we beat the Arsenal,' he replied.

'That was in 1958 wasn't it?' said the reporter.

'Aye. The glory years,' said the old man.

'I must have missed those,' quipped the man in front of him.

'Oh yes, I remember, when we kept a clean sheet against Bradford.' The supporters around him laughed. It's tough at the bottom.

And that's where Northampton were – almost. An unbeaten run of five matches had pulled the Cobblers from 92nd place into 90th position in the League's basement division. Things could only get better. Manager John Barnwell certainly hoped so. 'Of course, we're all looking forward to the move to Sixfields. After such a long wait for a new ground, it's a dream come true for everyone involved with the club, and it will be a big asset. The players trained on the pitch on Tuesday and they loved it. I'm sure that the club can now realise their full potential at such a ground.'

The first match at the County Ground was in September 1897 against Earls Barton from the Northants League in a pre-season friendly. The Cobblers secured their first win in their first competitive home game, a 3–1 victory over Rushden

Reserves. The gate receipts were nine shillings and fourpence, about 47 pence. Tonight's match against Mansfield was expected to net £30,000 from the fans.

Northampton progressed from the Northants League (now the United Counties League) through the Midland League (1899–1901) and the Southern League (1901–20). Their first success was as Southern League champions in 1909 under the great Herbert Chapman, who was later to guide Huddersfield and Arsenal to First Division titles. Town became a founder member of Football League Division Three in 1920, but the Southern League was their only trophy until they won the Third Division Championship in 1963.

And that's where they were now, though today it's effectively the old Fourth Division. In between, they had scaled the lofty heights of the old First Division in the 1965–66 season, after enjoying a dramatic rise with promotion from the Fourth Division in 1961; progress into the Second in 1963; and finally, from the Second in 1965. They were the first team to rise from the Fourth to the First Division and they did it in a remarkable five years. But they lasted only one season in the top grade before being relegated in front of a record crowd of 24,523 in a game versus Fulham. Their final home match was against Sunderland.

By 1969 they were back in the Fourth Division and even had to apply for re-election in 1972. One of their most famous matches was in the fifth round of the FA Cup in 1970 when Manchester United were the visitors. Georgie Best scored six goals as the Reds slaughtered the Cobblers 8–2 in a game shown on *Match of the Day*. It was one of Best's virtuoso performances. Who could forget the goal he scored after beating seemingly the entire Town defence before dummying the keeper and nonchalantly knocking the ball into the back of the net and then raising his arm in triumph? It was one of football's magical moments.

The game was the only one in the County Ground's history watched by supporters in stands all around the ground, for a temporary stand had been put up along the cricket pitch side. That's why it grossed record receipts at the time of £17,000. Those who turned up had seen a genius at work in the shape of Georgie Best. They'd never see anyone like him again. And certainly not tonight against Mansfield.

The crowd was warming up with chants of 'Come on, you Cobblers'. The atmosphere was beginning to build up as the kick-off approached. At the Hotel End I could see a few fans watching from the top windows of the pub, beers in hand, as the teams came onto the pitch.

On the opposite side of the ground a handful of people lined up a few yards back from the touchline behind a rope which separated the pitch from the rest of the cricket ground. I could see the cricket pavilion in the distance, with the scoreboard on the left. The football and cricket pitches overlapped by about 20 yards and, during the summer, the football pitch was used by cricket fans as a car park.

To my left was the temporary Meccano Stand. It was the strangest-looking stand I'd see all season and basically looked like a lot of scaffolding. It was almost as if Northampton were in the process of building a new stand, except that they weren't. Barnet manager Ray Clemence and David Pleat stood in the Meccano Stand near the touchline with their hands in their pockets on what was a chilly night. Northampton would play Barnet in their first match at the new Sixfields

Stadium the following Saturday. Clemence had come to check out the opposition.

To my far left was the Spion Kop – a name used at many grounds around the country but never applied to such a strange end as the one at the County Ground. The Kop didn't quite reach the far corner of that end of the ground, ending near the edge of the penalty area. From the Kop you could see the bowling green off to the left behind the cricket pitch. The far touchline cut across the outer edge of the cricket field as it marked out the football pitch – the longest in the League at 120 x 75 yards.

The local fans were now filling the ground. Mums and dads with their kids; a father and son wrapped in claret and blue scarves; three young girls on a night out; a group of lads standing behind me; and behind them the old guard, the die-hard supporters who'd seen the best and the worst of times at the County Ground but who still came back out of habit and a sense of loyalty to their local team, even if the football was sometimes dire.

At least it was better than the food. 'Simply the Best' said the sign advertising caterer Tony Ansell's fare. I was sure they could have been done under the Trade Descriptions Act. 'Simply the Worst' was more like it . The cheeseburger I bought from 'The Family Cabin' refreshment hut, served up by a woman who looked just like a farmer's wife, was the worst I'd ever tasted, and by now I'd tasted quite a few. 'Where's the Beef?' I wondered. I had some good advice for the young couple queuing behind me. 'Try the pasties,' I told them, 'they can't possibly be worse than the hamburgers.' Could they?

The ground was getting full by now, though there was still room on the terraces in the Family Stand and on the Spion Kop, where the travelling Mansfield supporters had gathered to cheer on their team. The Hotel End was a different story. It was packed to the rafters now. The Family Stand terrace was filled with kids along the front, standing on two reverse steps made of chipboard and constructed so that the little tykes could see the match. The back of the stand was also full because the view was good.

Two young Northampton apprentices wandered through the crowd before the kick-off raffling a signed football. The draw would be made at half-time. I bought a ticket. Number 59. Would I be lucky? What do you think?

Midway through the first half, smoke drifted over the Main Stand. The home supporters thought it might be ceremonial.

'Maybe they're cremating the stand,' said one fan.

'Or the directors,' said his mate wearing gold-rimmed glasses a check lumberjack shirt and quilted tank-top jacket.

The game started and the ball soon came over to the near touchline. Mansfield's Kevin Noteman shouted 'Fucking hell' after tussling for the ball. The crowd complained at him and he suddenly realised there were lots of kids lined up along the front of the terraces. He held up his hand to apologise.

Town manager John Barnwell hoped his team could bid the ground farewell with a win. 'It's sure to be an emotional night in many ways, and it would be nice to sign off with a victory.' But, as so often happens on these occasions, Mansfield spoiled the party by taking the lead after 20 minutes when centre-forward Steve Wilkinson scored with a shot which went in off the post. Northampton pressed for an equaliser, but it never came.

The fans were asked to stay off the pitch at the end of the match, but there was little chance of that happening tonight. When the referee blew the final whistle, the fans at the Hotel End swarmed onto the pitch, joined by the young lads at the front of the Main Stand. The celebrations were finally broken up by police on horseback – a bit extreme, since it was very good natured and there was not a hint of trouble.

So that was that. The end of an era. Town manager John Barnwell was certainly looking forward to the move to a new stadium, but he was also sad to see the club move from their old home. 'History is history and I'm sure a lot of fans will have fond memories of the ground. For example, the teams associated with Dave Bowen and Graham Carr certainly served up their fair share of memories.' But Barnwell also had a word of warning. 'I've said before that supporters won't pay to watch a new stand, or a new ground. It's all about what happens on the field.'

After the match I walked back around the ground, passing a group of young lads carrying part of an advertising hoarding and a sign – mementoes of the last game at the County Ground. They could show their grandchildren and tell them they were there the night the curtain came down.

I finally reached the station to catch my train to London. There were only a few fans on the platform, but one middle-aged man appeared smarter than the rest. He wore a blazer with a Mansfield Town club tie. His name was Sandy Whetton and he was a Stags director. In fact, tonight he was the only Mansfield director at the match. We started talking about the game and football in general. My journey home would be fascinating.

Sandy lives in London and works for a publishing company but he still manages to watch about 35 Mansfield games a year. His wife is very understanding and goes to many matches with him. Sandy is, like myself, a football fanatic. His passion for the game was clear. 'I was that archetypal little kid kicking a ball against the wall in my back garden,' said Sandy. Lacking the talent of a Georgie Best or Rodney Marsh, Sandy had settled for a career as a Mansfield Town supporter.

After following the Stags all over the country as a fan, he got to know the players, manager and directors. Eventually, his commitment to the cause confirmed, he was invited to join the board. When the club reached the Freight Rover Trophy final in 1987, Sandy was so emotional that he cried when the teams walked out onto the Wembley turf. 'I got control of myself, but then the national anthem started and I was bawling my eyes out again,' he told me as our train trundled towards London.

One of the highlights of Sandy's football supporting career was Mansfield's 3–0 fifth round FA Cup win over West Ham in February 1969. The Third Division side astounded the football world that day by beating a Hammers team including their three World Cup stars Bobby Moore, Geoff Hurst and Martin Peters and a young Trevor Brooking. Brooking later described the defeat as one of the worst of his career.

Sandy had moved to Putney in west London, within walking distance of Fulham's ground at Craven Cottage. One day, as he left his house early in the morning to go to work, he noticed a fair-haired man walking his dog. It was Bobby Moore. They exchanged good mornings and then, just as Sandy was about to drive off, the England World Cup captain motioned to him to open the car window.

'Is that your Mansfield sticker on the window?' enquired Moore.

'Yes,' said Sandy. Moore looked at him with a glint in his eye. 'You mean I've got to walk past that every bloody morning!'

A more recent giant-killing in the Cup – this time the Coca-Cola version – resulted in Sandy acquiring one of his prize possessions. Mansfield recorded one of the biggest upsets of the 1994–95 season by knocking out Leeds 1–0. After the match, the sponsors couldn't decide who to nominate as Man of the Match. The players also refused to vote for one player. Nobody was chosen and the Coca-Cola jacket, usually given to the best player, complete with Man of the Match logo embroidered on one side and the Coca-Cola logo on the back, was instead awarded to Sandy in recognition of his services as a Stags director. He cherishes it to this day.

Sandy's one remaining ambition was too see his team play in Europe. 'That would top everything off nicely, travelling abroad with Mansfield.' He had hopes of a match in the Anglo-Italian Cup some day, but was realistic enough to realise that he might have to settle for a pre-season trip to Majorca! Where would football be without the passion and commitment of people like Sandy Whetton? Now here was a director whose love of the game was total. The Alan Sugars and Barry Hearns may have the money, but the Sandy Whettons have the loyalty and the heart.

THE GODFATHER

Leeds United v Tottenham Hotspur – Elland Road, 15 October 1994

On the morning of the match I woke up to hear alarming headlines on the radio: 'Twenty-two policemen have been hurt in clashes with youths on the rampage in Leeds,' said the announcer. 'Cars have been overturned and set alight and 26 police vehicles have been damaged in the Chapeltown area of the city.' Great, I thought, just the time to be travelling north to watch United play Spurs.

Leeds fans have not had the best reputation over the years and rioting in the city was hardly the prelude I needed for my first game at Elland Road. Apparently the trouble started when two policewomen were attacked by a 20-strong mob as the officers tried to arrest a youth. The rioters' number had grown to nearer 200 by the time they began stoning police and other vehicles.

'The incident in Chapeltown was totally unprovoked and at one time clearly co-ordinated by a hard core of youths intent on causing as much trouble and injury to police as they could. The vast majority of people in this area are law-abiding and supportive of police. But there is a hard core of youths who have no respect for authority whatsoever.'

Those statements from Inspector Stuart Cuthbert could have been used to describe the football fans who once followed Leeds United on an orgy of violence across Britain and Europe. But not today. The fans at the Tottenham game were impeccably behaved. It wasn't the friendliest ground I'd visited (Doncaster took that accolade); nevertheless, the atmosphere was friendly and not at all hostile, unless you were one of the players on the pitch wearing the navy-blue change strip of Tottenham Hotspur.

I'd driven to Leeds from London – an easy task, since the M62 passes within 100 yards of Elland Road. But anyone arriving at Leeds City station by train will be welcomed by Joshua Tetley. Not personally, of course, but his name is on the station's welcome sign. Tetley's Brewery stands on Hamlet Road and, according to one local guide, the beer is to Yorkshire what Guinness is to Ireland. There's a special visitors centre on Dock Street and twice-daily tours of the brewery itself. Supporters probably know as much about the local beer as they do about the football team.

In 1847 Charles Dickens called Leeds 'the beastliest place, one of the nastiest I know'. Much has changed since then. The city has been cleaned up and urban renewal is the buzzword. Leeds is today one of the fastest-growing cities in Britain. The city, built across a basin of the River Aire, was traditionally a centre of the textile industry. The main industries, including engineering, are concentrated on flat ground south of the river, whereas the suburbs stand on the heights that ring the city to the north.

The Leeds markets area, on the east side, is impressive, particularly the Kirgate Market, the largest in the north and a descendant of the medieval woollen markets that made Leeds the focus of the region's textile industry. The outdoor market is where Michael Marks set up his stall in 1884 with the slogan 'Don't ask the price, it's a penny.' It was the forerunner of Marks and Spencer. Leeds is also the home of Harry Ramsden's famous fish and chips – now being franchised all over England. I was to enjoy Harry's fare, but not at Leeds. I would have to wait for my visit to Blackpool.

But Leeds is probably more famous for its football team than anything else, especially the great Leeds side of the '60s and early '70s which included stars like Billy Bremner, Johnny Giles, Jack Charlton and Allan Clarke. Their all-white strip was adopted under the management of the legendary Don Revie, nicknamed the Godfather, who wanted his team to look, and play, like Real Madrid. Revie, an England international and Footballer of the Year in 1955, took over as player–manager in 1961, when Leeds were in the Second Division. They won the title and promotion in 1964.

Revie's team captured their first major trophies in 1968, when they collected the League Cup and the European Fairs Cup. The following season they were First Division champions with a record 67 points (teams got two points for a win back then), many of which were chalked up during a run of 34 matches without defeat. In 1970 they were on track to record a remarkable treble of European Cup, FA Cup and League Championship, but lost in the European Cup semi-final, in the FA Cup final against Chelsea and came runners-up to Everton in the League.

But the team's strength of character ensured further successes and in 1971 they won a second Fairs Cup, followed by the FA Cup in 1972 (1–0 against Arsenal with an Allan Clarke strike) and a second League Championship in 1974. They became only the third British team to reach the European Cup final the following year, but lost 2–0 to Bayern Munich and were banned for three years from European competition because of a riot by their supporters after the match in Paris.

That was the swansong for the great Leeds team built by Revie, though he'd left by then to take over as England manager. He quit the England job in 1977 amid controversy following secret negotiations to take over as manager of the Arab Emirates national team. But he'll always be remembered as the manager of one of the greatest club sides ever assembled. It's remarkable that they reached the final stages of 17 competitions but only won six major honours during Revie's reign.

Three times they came close to the double (1965, 1970 and 1972), but defeat in the FA Cup final snatched it away on the first two occasions and, when they eventually won the Cup in 1972, they could only manage runners-up spot in the League. The FA Cup was also a competition in which Leeds were often the fall guys to a giant-killing. Odd-goal defeats from Fourth Division Colchester in 1971 (see Colchester United v Bury); Second Division Sunderland in 1973; Bristol City, another Second Division team, in 1974; and Third Division Crystal Palace in 1976 had embarrassed the team that Revie had built throughout their glory years.

Success on the pitch led to changes at the ground: Elland Road. The road from which the ground takes its name runs west to the town of Elland, near Huddersfield, whereas Leeds Road (the name of Huddersfield's ground before they moved into the futuristic McAlpine Stadium – see Huddersfield v Hull) brings you east to Leeds.

A new West Stand had already been opened in 1957, after a fire destroyed the Main Stand. It cost £150,000 – an enormous sum at the time. But it was the rising attendances, and soaring gate receipts, accompanying the Revie revolution that heralded further changes at Elland Road. The open Kop End on Geldard Road was replaced by a £250,000 covered terrace in 1968. (The North Stand, as it was called, was made all-seater at the end of the 1993–94 season for just over £1 million). A new South Stand replaced the small scratching shed at the Elland Road End in 1974 for £400,000 and executive boxes, the first at any club in Yorkshire, were installed at the back of the stand in 1983.

More recent developments include a family stand and executive boxes, costing £500,000, built during the 1989–90 season; a new south-east corner, constructed before the 1991–92 campaign for £820,000; and a £1.3 million banqueting suite, built later that season. The most recent development is the new £6.5 million 17,000 all-seater East Stand, which replaced the Lowfields Road Stand. It has the largest cantilever roof span of any ground in Europe.

So impressive is the new Elland Road that it was chosen as a venue for the 1996 European Championships. The capacity is around 40,000, but the number of tickets available to the public for the European Championships was in the region of 25,000. The rest went to the participating countries, VIPs, television people etc. Leeds were therefore urging supporters to buy tickets early to avoid disappointment. United chairman Leslie Silver made a presentation before the Spurs game to the first season-ticket holder to secure his Elland Road seat for Euro '96.

The day after the Tottenham game the club honoured their legendary former manager with the official opening of the North Stand under its new title of the Revie Stand. Don's widow, Elsie, unveiled a plaque in her husband's honour alongside the entire Revie family, United players past and present, the backroom staff associated with the Revie years and 200 supporters lucky enough to have bought a special programme distributed at Leeds' last home match against Manchester City.

'The stand and the plaque will stand as a fitting testament to the work and success that Don Revie brought not only to Leeds United but the city,' said general manager Alan Roberts. 'The chairman and directors sanctioned that it should be called the Revie Stand and I think most supporters will appreciate that – and certainly the Revie family will. There will also be a memorial wall in the stand with pictures, newspaper cuttings highlighting Don Revie's success and achievements.'

One player from the Revie era, who'd regularly struck fear into the hearts of strikers, had today returned to the scene of his greatest crunching tackles to provide commentary for radio on the Spurs game. Norman 'Bites Yer Legs' Hunter looked the picture of health as he made his way to the main entrance, signing autographs as he went. He was still famous here and recognised by most of the crowd around me. Hunter's looks had fared well over the years. He was a little greyer, but that's all.

Hunter had strong views about the new FIFA rules outlawing tackles from behind – an art form he'd perfected. 'Obviously, it's right to outlaw the sort of tackle in which the defender just clatters into the back of his opponent – the one that let's him know you're there, as we'd have said in my day. But what about the tackle in which you're genuinely going for the ball? Say it's your first tackle of the game, and you've only got to mistime it slightly and you could be sent off. That can't be right. And you have to remember the pace the game is played at nowadays. Mistakes are bound to happen. Tackling is an art form – just as much a part of the game as any of the other skills. And I think that if the physical side of the game gets lost, then you really are in trouble. Football is a physical game. There's nothing better than a good challenge, a good 50:50 ball. You have to have that sort of competitive edge or the game loses something vital.'

Norman should know. He was one of the fiercest tacklers the game had seen and won the first Player of the Year award in 1973. Leeds and England trainer Les Cocker recalled: 'Norman Hunter phoned me once to say that he'd gone home with a broken leg. I asked him, "Whose leg is it?"'

Inside the ground Spurs chairman Alan Sugar sat behind me up in the directors' box. He had a glowering look about him, as if he thought he was surrounded by enemies waiting for the chance to stab him in the back. I wondered if he'd seen Terry Venables in the crowd. Sugar's serious demeanour remained with him throughout the match, even when Tottenham scored. At half-time he was asked for his autograph by a young girl and duly obliged after straining to hear her over the front of the directors' box.

Sugar was flanked by Tony Berry, the longest-serving member of the Spurs board who'd survived from the regime of Irving Scholar, Tottenham's previous chairman. Berry's picture was splashed across the next morning's *Sunday Times* following the withdrawal of a Department of Trade and Industry investigation into his role in the so-called Blue Arrow affair. The story alongside reported that Amstrad, Sugar's electronics company, was expected to report a loss of £5 million. That would be substantially lower than the previous year and a good few million short of his investment of more than £8 million in Tottenham Hotspur Football Club.

The Leeds supporters next to me in the old West Stand looked round at Sugar after each incident in the match to gauge his reaction. Before his joint bid with Venables for a controlling stake in Spurs he was known to only a handful of football supporters. Now, he was a household name. I assumed he craved the attention, though judging by his face he didn't seem to be enjoying the match.

Spurs dominated the opening exchanges and went a goal up through Teddy Sheringham. The Romanian midfielder Ilie Dumitrescu cut back a precise pass after his shot was parried by Leeds keeper John Lukic and the England striker carefully sidefooted the ball into the top corner from the edge of the 18-yard box. Tottenham then created two super chances to tie up the match – and missed them both. Nick Barmby and Gica Popescu were the culprits.

The second half was to be a different story. Dumitrescu was the first out onto the pitch after the half-time break; or, more precisely, during the interval. He re-emerged a full ten minutes before his colleagues. The Romanian international squatted near the centre circle either to soak up the atmosphere or perhaps to escape the half-time team talk. The Spurs manager Ossie Ardiles surely wasn't screaming abuse at his players; after all, they were 1–0 up.

As the match went on, the home fans became more impatient. 'There's a joke going around about Brian Deane,' said the Leeds fan from Derby via Devon sitting next to me. 'They say Brian Deane can turn like an articulated lorry.' At first, I wasn't sure if the joke had finished. But it had.

Unable to drum up enough enthusiasm to laugh I responded with a joke I'd heard about Everton's Nigerian international striker Daniel Amokachi. 'Why is Amokachi like a taxi? Because he's big, black and carrying a load of passengers.' It went down better than the one about the articulated lorry!

As the second half unfolded, Leeds began to pile on the pressure. Spurs keeper Ian Walker was playing out of his skin, spurred on, no doubt, by the fact that Erik Thorstvedt was sitting on the substitutes bench waiting for his chance to return to first-team action after injury. Walker had made three blinding saves in the first half and was equally impressive in the second. He was finally beaten by Deane in the 62nd minute.

The football over I walked past the home fans in their blue and white scarves who were spilling out of the ground and returned to my car. My next stop was the village of Haworth in Brontë country to the west of Leeds and Bradford. The bustling village sits on the very edge of the Pennine moors like a gritstone fortress. The moors had changed little since the time of the Brontë sisters. There were crumbling drystone walls, a few old farms and lots of sheep. The grass and heather are still buffeted by the wind and rain. There was mile after mile of awe-inspiring, yet forbidding, emptiness.

More than a century ago, when the Reverend Patrick Brontë came to be minister at Haworth Parish Church, the village was little more than a collection of stone-built weavers' cottages huddled together for protection from the harsh winter winds. But within a few decades, a series of books, including *Wuthering Heights* and *Jane Eyre*, caused this obscure Yorkshire village to become a major centre for literary pilgrims.

All six of the Brontë children died from illness while still young, but during their short and sad lives the three youngest sisters – Charlotte, Emily and Anne – spent long hours writing in secret, leaving a priceless legacy of novels. Thousands of visitors now come to Haworth to see the sites and buildings which provided the inspiration for the sisters' books and to experience the atmosphere of the surrounding moors. Three miles outside Haworth stood a ruined farmhouse in a remote moorland spot called Top Withens, which is thought to have been the inspiration for Wuthering Heights.

The steep Main Street, lined with shops, cafés and galleries, led down to one of Britain's best-preserved railways, the Keighley & Worth Valley Steam Railway, where films like *The Railway Children* and *Yanks* were made. The Main Street, paved with stone setts, looked as if it had come straight out of a Hovis ad. I stayed at a small guest house on Main Street called Heather Cottage. It was formerly two weavers' cottages built about 260 years ago.

The next morning I went for a walk around the village. As I looked up the hill on Main Street I could imagine a young lad cycling down with a loaf of bread under his arm. At the top of the hill was the Black Bull Hotel and the Druggists Store – a deadly combination for the Brontës' brother Branwell, who died from a deadly concoction of drink from the pub and opium from the druggists. Strange to think that drink and drugs were now a problem facing the nation's wealthy footballers.

THE LION OF VIENNA

Bolton Wanderers v Oldham Athletic – Burnden Park, 16 October 1994

My next stop was a famous old club whose President was an England star of the 1950s known as the Lion of Vienna. Bolton Wanderers' centre-forward Nat Lofthouse still worked as a miner down the pits after making his début for the Trotters in 1939. He'd get up at four o'clock in the morning and work an eight-hour shift before playing for Bolton in the afternoon. He was aggressive, yet courageous, and thought nothing of knocking goalkeepers into the back of the net with the ball.

Lofthouse came from the same town as that other legendary centre-forward Tommy Lawton, a star with Everton and Chelsea, and followed him into the England team in 1950. Lofthouse was voted Footballer of the Year in 1953, after scoring in every round of the FA Cup, including the final when Bolton played Blackpool in one of the most famous domestic matches ever staged at Wembley. The game is remembered as the 'Matthews Final' after Sir Stan's achievement in gaining his first winner's medal; but Lofthouse also stamped his name on the record books with his goal, a game record.

Mind you, with 20 minutes to go and Bolton leading 3–1, it didn't look as if Stan would emerge clutching that treasured medal of victory. Of course, Blackpool fought back to win 4–3 (see Blackpool v. Birmingham). And their manager? Joe Smith, Bolton's record-holder for most League goals scored in a season (38 in 1920–21). Lofthouse emulated Smith by becoming the club's top scorer in the First Division in 1956 and he captained Bolton to victory over a depleted

Manchester United team, following the tragic Munich air crash (see Manchester United v. Tottenham Hotspur) in the 1958 Cup final.

His role in that '58 final was particularly controversial because he forced the keeper over the line with the ball for his second goal, which won the match. Lofthouse also scored the last of his 30 international goals in 33 appearances – a club record – in 1958. He retired in 1960, because of injury, with a career total of 285 goals in 485 matches.

I'd driven across the Yorkshire moors from the village of Haworth to reach Bolton a couple of hours before the game against rivals Oldham to the south-east. Bolton, a city of almost 150,000 people, is surrounded by other football towns like Blackburn to the north, Wigan to the south-west, Bury and Rochdale to the east and the two Manchester clubs (United and City) plus Stockport to the south. There must be more League clubs concentrated in Greater Manchester than any other part of Britain.

Bolton itself was a textile manufacturing centre specialising in wool and, later, cotton. Nowadays engineering and chemicals have taken over as the main industries. The football club was formed in 1874 by boys from Christ Church Sunday School in Blackburn Street, led by their master Thomas Ogden, and was called the Wanderers because in the early years the team had no particular home ground. Their peripatetic state also accounts for the club nickname, the Trotters.

In 1877 they broke away from the Church after a dispute with the vicar, changed their name to Bolton Wanderers and became founder members of the Football League. They lost their first FA Cup final at Goodison Park in 1894. They reached their second Cup final in 1904, when they became the first Second Division team to lose in the final, in a match played at Crystal Palace. Some of the money earned from that Cup run was used to start building the first section of Burnden Park's Main Stand, on Manchester Road, at a cost of £3,500.

Starting with the White Horse final at Wembley in 1923, Bolton won the Cup three times in six years without conceding a goal. They beat West Ham in 1923 (2–0), Manchester City in 1926 (1–0) and Portsmouth in 1929 (2–0). Bolton were to get their hands on the Cup again in that 1958 final remembered for Lofthouse's second goal.

Bolton have never won the League Championship but as long ago as 1905 they came runners-up to Liverpool. They have won the Second Division title, in 1909, but finished bottom of the First and were relegated once more in 1910. After gaining promotion again in 1911 Bolton stayed in the top flight for 22 years. Some years further on, in 1987, they escaped from the Third Division – into the Fourth for the first time in their history!

That relegation promoted them to equal third in the list of Most Relegated Football League Clubs in history – a distinction they share with Birmingham and Grimsby (only Notts County and Preston have been relegated more often). They bounced back and by 1992 were securing promotion to the Second Division. That is how they ended up back in the First Division. Did you all follow that?

Bolton's most recent cup success was in 1989, when the club won the prestigious Sherpa Van Trophy (which has absolutely nothing to do with sherpas or vans, though there is a trophy for the winners!) Among the club's famous players are strikers Frank Worthington and Francis Lee. When Lee made his début at 15 on the right wing he scored a goal, was booked and was in tears, comforted by Lofthouse.

The Lion of Vienna was Bolton's manager between 1968 and 1970 and again in 1971, when he resigned. He took over again briefly in 1985 and the following year accepted the post of club president. The memory of Lofthouse permeated Bolton's Burnden Park ground on the Manchester Road. Pride of place in the club trophy room went to the shirt he wore in the 1958 FA Cup final. Lofthouse says he's done everything at the Wanderers from making the tea to scoring Cup final goals.

Other features of the trophy room were a huge photograph of the 1923 White Horse final and a mini FA Cup in the trophy cabinet to mark Bolton's 2–1 win over West Ham in the first final at Wembley. One of the Wanderers' goals was scored after the Hammers full-back ran into the crowd which was lined up along the side of the pitch after chasing a ball. He couldn't get back on the field and in the meantime Bolton took the throw-in and scored.

Bolton's oldest fan, 105-year-old James Bradley, whose father played for the club, remembered that 1923 final. He would be at Wembley in early April to see the Wanderers in the Coca-Cola Cup final against Liverpool 72 years after that first FA Cup final at the venue of legends. Sadly, Bolton would lose the match 2–1.

Bolton's ground was less impressive than I'd imagined. The main entrance was in the Manchester Road Stand. It was almost hidden behind the club's offices, social clubs and executive facilities along the front. The car park and the back of the stand were painted by Lowry in his work 'Going to the Match,' complete with matchstalk men and matchstalk cats and dogs. The original painting is in private hands but would fetch about £100,000 at auction. Limited edition prints signed in pencil by Lowry cost about £1,000 but they are rarely for sale. Football supporters are also art collectors, it seems! The wooden stand was typical of those built in the early 1900s.

A group of teenage girls were waiting in the car park for the Bolton stars to arrive. They were on the lookout for their idols Alan Stubbs and Jason McAteer. McAteer, now at Liverpool, was then being chased by all the big Premier League clubs, after his stirring performances for the Republic of Ireland in the World Cup finals in America – as well as his teenage fans. One problem for the girls clamouring for his autograph was that he had a steady girlfriend. They arrived together but McAteer, looking very smart in a trendy black trenchcoat, was still happy to sign autographs outside the ground.

Bolton originally moved to Burnden Park in 1895, when the site was a complete mess. One end backed onto a railway and the land itself was a stagnant mixture of chemicals from the nearby works and dumped refuse. The pitch was apparently built up on old barrels and cotton bales and had the most cambered surface in the League.

Bolton played their first game at the ground in September 1895 with a benefit match against Preston. In 1901 the ground staged the FA Cup final replay between Tottenham and Sheffield United. The first game at Crystal Palace had attracted 114,815 – England's first six figure attendance. But the Burnden Park replay was watched by an official gate of only 20,740. And even though the actual attendance was higher, perhaps as many as 30,000, this is still the lowest crowd at an FA Cup final this century.

In 1915 the Main Stand had an extra wing added at the Southern End. In 1928 Bolton began to build the Burnden Stand, which cost £20,000 and should not have been beyond the means of a successful club which had just played in two packed

Wembley finals. However, there was uproar when cup-winning hero David Jack was sold to Arsenal in October 1928 for a record fee of £10,340.

The ground was taken over by the government during the Second World War; the pitch was used by the education authorities and the stands by the Ministry of Supply. The Burnden Stand was still full of food when an event which was to stand out in the history of football ground tragedies took place on 9 March 1946. It was the precursor to Ibrox, Valley Parade and Hillsborough – the Bolton Disaster.

The match itself was unusual because in the season immediately after the War all cup ties up to the semis were over two legs. The extra games helped to compensate clubs, for League matches did not begin on a proper basis until September 1946. Bolton won the first leg of this quarter-final tie at Stoke 2–0. An estimated 85,000 squeezed into Burnden Park for the second leg. Most of them knew nothing about the tragic events unfolding at the Railway End.

The disaster was the first inflicted by a crowd upon itself. Thirty-three people died, including seven from Bolton. The accident occurred in the Railway Enclosure, so-called because it was formed on the embankment supporting the main LMS Yorkshire to Bolton line.

Pressure began to build up outside the turnstiles at twenty past two and by two thirty some people in the crush were already trying to move away from the turnstiles. Five minutes later it was impossible for people coming through the turnstiles to pass along the terraces. Shortly afterwards police began to help spectators out of the north-west corner onto the perimeter track. People then began to force their way into the ground over the railway line fence and at the eastern end of the enclosure. The crowd continued to clamber over walls and force open doors. A father who wanted to get his small son out of the ground picked the padlock of the exit gate next to the boys' entrance and people rushed in there.

So many people were packed into the ground, some with tickets and some who had forced entry, that when the teams came onto the pitch at five to three the crowd swayed and the spectators in the north-west corner of the terrace were thrown down into the bottom corner. The crush barriers either bent or collapsed as the crowd seemed to sink. People began to pile up and were trodden underfoot. Many were asphyxiated. As the match kicked off hundreds of fans spilled out onto the pitch. Just after ten past three bodies were brought out and the referee was told there had been fatalities. The players left the pitch and the 33 bodies were laid out on it before being taken away to mortuaries. First aid was given to about 500 people.

Hardly anybody who wasn't in the north-west corner of the Railway Enclosure realised how serious the disaster was. The *Manchester Evening News* commented on the fact that so many people broke into the ground, many of them servicemen. 'Possibly the war has left some people with less respect for law than they used to have.'

Afterwards, questions were raised which were to result in lower capacities at every ground in the country. After the government report, which did not blame Bolton specifically, the club spent £5,500 modernising the Railway End, improving the turnstiles and gates, and fencing off the railway line.

From my seat in the Main Stand on the Manchester Road I could see the Railway End to my left. In 1986 the 16,000-capacity terrace was cut in half when a superstore was built on the land flattened behind. The famous embankment with its haunting memories and railway at the back was gone for ever. The Normid End, as it was now called after the supermarket, was a source of great amusement to away fans and an embarrassment for Bolton supporters. But the change did mean that access to the Burnden Stand and the back of the terrace was improved by the building of a road, car park and new turnstiles along the route of the former railway.

It was from here that Burnden Park featured in Arthur Askey's 1954 film *Love Match* in which a train-driver stops to watch a match played before a packed crowd wearing cloth caps and smoking Woodbines. Today you can't see the pitch at all from there. A few years after that film Bolton's new floodlights were switched on for a friendly against Hearts in October 1957. It was said at the time that they had enough power to light the streets from Burnden to Blackpool!

To my right was the Great Lever Stand, named after the district nearby which I assumed was itself named after Lord Leverhulme, the soap magnate who lived in Bolton between 1851 and 1925. And behind the Burnden Stand opposite the Manchester Road was a modern sports hall and a floodlit artificial playing surface, which cost £150,000 in October 1986 when it first opened.

The crowd were in full voice for the match against Oldham and were ecstatic when Bolton took a two-goal lead. When their Finnish star Mixu Paatelainen scored they sang: 'Mixu, Mixu Mixu, Mixu Mixu, Mixu Paatelainen' to the tune of 'No Limit'. McAteer was pulling the strings in midfield, David Lee was making surging runs down the wing and John McGinlay looked dangerous up front. Unfortunately the defence let Oldham back in and they scored twice in the second half to square the match at 2–2. The atmosphere changed from joy to despair, optimism to pessimism. The new mood reflected the view of the fans about how the club was being run off the pitch.

After years of fending off complaints from the Burnden Park faithful about the lack of money spent on the ground's facilities, the powers that be had finally decided to move. However, there weren't any plans to relocate within the town, but to a place called Red Moss, a large expanse of muddy industrial wasteland in Horwich, to the north of Bolton. Simon Jones of the 'Keep Wanderers in Bolton' campaign vented his feelings about the planned relocation in *When Saturday Comes*:

> For many fans the club might as well be thinking of moving to the other side of the moon.
>
> The news that's filtered out . . . from the *Bolton Evening News* has already mentioned 'secret negotiations' with the council and various consortia. The only merits that we can see in the club's backing for this Lancashire San Siro is that it shows that they're ambitious and have a desire to regain the lofty heights we have not seen since Frank Worthington last graced the Burnden Park turf with a full head of hair.
>
> In the opinion of many Bolton fans, however, the move is ill conceived, ill advised and, sadly, a prime example of the gulf of communication that exists between the boardroom and the terraces. Financial gain and commercial interests look like triumphing over tradition and loyalty once again at Bolton.

A reference to the Railway End and its Normid supermarket? I wondered.

COLLYMORE FOR ENGLAND

Nottingham Forest v Wimbledon – The City Ground, 17 October 1994

Stan the man. Pure Magic. Collymore for England. The night belonged to Forest star Stan Collymore, who scored a spectacular second goal to reinforce his claims to be considered for the England team. 'He's not so much Stan the Man – as Superman,' trumpeted the *Nottingham Evening Post*. Liverpool obviously thought so, after spending £8.5 million to take him to Anfield. Aston Villa must have faith in him following their £7 million purchase. But really the jury is still out on Stan.

Since his arrival from Southend Stan had notched up 34 goals in 43 games for Forest. England coach Terry Venables had sent scouts Ted Buxton and Don Howe to spy on Collymore, but so far Stan had not been called on to serve his country. Competition for places was hot with Ian Wright, Teddy Sheringham and Les Ferdinand all ahead of the man in the queue to partner Alan Shearer.

After Forest had demolished Wimbledon 3–1 (they could have scored five) I went along to the post-match press conference. Former Forest full-back, then manager, Frank Clark, was the first to appear before the assembled hacks. Surprisingly, while acknowledging the quality of Stan's 30-yard strike to put Forest two up, he was not full of praise for the striker. There were still many things he had to learn.

'He needs to get in the six-yard box more often. And I have told him before how he can get better and areas he can improve. There are times when he just stands still when we're building attacks. I'd like to see him charging into the penalty area. That's where strikers should be, getting on the end of things. I think he feels scoring tap-ins in the six-yard box are perhaps beneath him a little bit. He does score them, but he likes to do the ambitious thing. So there is more to come from Stan really. There's room for improvement in certain areas, but you can't take away his individualism.'

Actually, he was probably right. Collymore grabbed the headlines because of that one flash of brilliance. He picked up the ball in his own half and ran at the Wimbledon defence. A burst of speed and good close control took him between Alan Reeves and Warren Barton as he ran across the 18-yard box past Peter Fear before unleashing a stinging drive that took Wimbledon keeper Hans Segers completely by surprise. 'His goal was brilliant, totally out of the blue and that's a special quality. I don't think you ever get used to it. It's a goal out of nothing,' said Clark, dishing out some praise.

That goal sewed up the match for a Forest team which had struggled to break down their south London opponents in a dour first half. They'd taken the lead through Lars Bohinen – the Norwegian whose spectacular second-half strike for Norway in Oslo virtually ended England's chances of qualifying for the 1994

World Cup Finals. Graham Taylor, at the City Ground as summariser for a radio station, must have watched Bohinen with mixed emotions as he struck the first Forest goal. Ian Woan put the Reds three ahead before Marcus Gayle pulled one back for Wimbledon in the 81st minute. It was a consolation goal. The Dons had been outclassed.

The pace and skill of this buoyant Forest team meant they were already being compared with the Championship side of the late '70s. That team had won seven, drawn two and lost one of their first ten matches. This year's vintage had also won seven but had drawn three and lost none of their first ten games. They didn't suffer by comparison with the team of Trevor Francis, Peter Shilton, Viv Anderson, Tony Woodcock, Peter Withe, Larry Lloyd, John McGovern, Ian Bowyer and Frank Clark.

After the reporters had run out of questions, Clark handed over to Kinnear. 'I'll leave it to you, Joe,' he told the Wimbledon boss. 'I haven't said anything nasty about you.'

The former Spurs star laughed: 'You must be one of the only clubs that haven't.' Kinnear was more upbeat than I expected. At first, he said he wasn't disappointed with his team's performance, but later admitted he was, in so far as he felt they should have scored first. They did have a couple of chances but anything less than a Forest win would have been a travesty.

Kinnear, looking tired but relaxed, was in good humour. He was a solid manager. His efforts had been rewarded with the Managers' Manager of the Year award earlier in the year after a hat-trick of Manager of the Month awards the previous season as he led Wimbledon to their best ever finish of sixth in the Premiership. Kinnear had become the Dons' third manager in 13 months when he replaced former Forest striker Peter Withe in January 1992 after spells in the Middle East, Malaysia and at Doncaster.

'I'm not that disappointed, to be honest,' said Kinnear. 'Sometimes you don't get what you deserve in football.' Joe's grumbles, delivered in a hoarse voice which clearly revealed his vocal involvement in the match, were connected with the Dons' growing injury list rather than sour grapes about whether Forest deserved their win.

Wimbledon were without striker Dean Holdsworth – who spent the evening giving his views on the match as a guest of Sky Sports – Alan Kimble, Roger Joseph, Robbie Earle, Brian McAllister and Dean Blackwell. Over the summer John Fashanu had gone to Aston Villa and John Scales had joined Liverpool. Kinnear had brought back Andy Thorn, a free transfer from Crystal Palace, and brought in Efan Ekoku from Norwich. But the depleted squad was struggling. 'It probably hits us a bit harder. You need a little bit of experience to bring them [the younger players] through,' said Kinnear.

The economics of football were clearly hard felt at Selhurst Park, the ground Wimbledon now shared with Crystal Palace after their move from Plough Lane. 'You need a lot of money to keep a club going,' said Kinnear. 'We have got a big wage bill that needs to be covered weekly.' There had been speculation that Barton and Holdsworth would soon be sold, but Kinnear ruled that out. 'We couldn't even think about letting people like Barton and Holdsworth go at the moment.' The emphasis was on 'the moment'.

Before the match I'd heard the Wimbledon players warming up. As I wandered down the passageway behind the team dressing-rooms on a tour of the ground I could hear rap music blaring out of a ghetto blaster. It was the Dons psyching themselves up for the battle ahead. I headed through the tunnel and out onto the Forest pitch past former Liverpool defender Jim Beglin, another ex-professional earning a living as a colour commentator on radio. He was chatting to the groundsman about the grass the club had used to resurface the pitch over the summer. The Forest pitch measured 115 yards by 78 and was one of the largest in the Premier or Football League – bigger even than Wembley. It used to be 79 yards wide but for some reason Brian Clough had its width reduced by a yard.

Former Aston Villa, Wolves and Everton striker Andy Gray, now more famous as a commentator on Sky, was reading through the Forest team sheet to see who would be starring in tonight's Monday Night Football. As he emerged from the tunnel a group of middle-aged women clamoured for his autograph.

'Do you remember this one, Andy?' said a lady with permed hair and glasses as she handed Gray a picture from his playing days. 'Aye,' said the balding star. 'You looked younger then.'

'I was,' replied Gray as he turned to make his way towards the commentary box.

The tour guide was showing a group of sponsors around the City Ground and I tagged along. He told us the original Main Stand at Forest burnt down on 24 August 1968 during a game against Leeds. The fire started near the players' dressing-rooms and spread to the wooden parts of the stand. The fans ran onto the pitch to escape the flames and, fortunately, nobody was seriously hurt. The guide told us there was a joke going round at the time concerning star centre-forward Joe Baker. After the blaze each player had to submit an estimate of the value of any personal possessions lost in the fire. There was a lot of speculation about how much each of them put in for. One player being teased about the size of his claim replied, 'You think my insurance claim was big; you should have seen Joe Baker's.' After the fire Forest had to share Notts County's ground at Meadow Lane for six games (all of which they lost).

It was time to take my place in the Main Stand. I sat in front of a young boy who'd come along with his mother and grandmother. They seemed to know everyone around them and were clearly regulars. All three were wrapped up in red and white Forest scarves. The boy was eagerly awaiting the appearance of his idols, especially Stan Collymore and Brian Roy.

I looked around the stadium. The face of the City Ground was changing and Forest were in the process of spending between £5.7 million and £7 million pounds on a new 7,500 all-seater stand at the Trent End. The cost of building football grounds was rising, though the quality was also going up. Does that explain the rise in ticket prices? Maybe partly. Besides, a lot of the fans actually liked the old stand on the riverbank. Not that they had any choice. When Forest celebrated promotion to the Premier League in May 1994, it was the last opportunity for fans to stand on the Trent End terrace.

The finishing touches to the new Trent End stand were still being applied at the time of my visit. The basic structure was up and the seats were being installed on the upper tier, spelling out the name of the stand. It was impressive. The white stand, supported by a red goalpost frame, was a striking statement that Forest were headed for the twenty-first century in style. Seventy feet high and built from

650 tons of concrete, the A frame alone weighed 70 tons. It had two floors with lifts to carry supporters between levels.

There was a huge glass screen running along the back of the stand, slightly curved to follow the river's natural bend. When the stand was finally open, it would include 550 exclusive seats in the so-called Castle Club on match days, complete with piped in-crowd noise for that authentic Saturday afternoon at the City Ground feel. Pre-match meals would be available at the American-style Pitch Sports Diner, sponsored by Canadian brewers Labatts. The brewery had plans for a giant TV screen and 100 monitors, including some in the toilets so that you wouldn't miss any action even when nature called. Pool tables, darts, video games and a merchandising outlet would complete the experience along with memorabilia from the world of football including a signed Pelé shirt and various Forest mementoes collected by the club over the years.

When Forest weren't playing, the executive facility would be open to the public as a sports bar and diner and would be able to hold 750 people in total. Most Forest away games would also be shown live so that fans could follow the team without leaving the city. And if the game was dull, there was always the view of the River Trent, the windmill at Sneinton, Nottingham castle and, just across the river, the ground of rivals Notts County. The stadiums are so close it seems you can almost touch Meadow Lane from the City Ground. It's hard to believe the city can support both of them. But it does.

Part of the reason is that, with a population of over 270,000, Nottingham is one of England's big cities. It's a manufacturing centre for bikes, cigarettes, pharmaceuticals and lace but is probably best-known for its connection with the legendary thirteenth-century outlaw Robin Hood. Sadly, the lair of Hood's bitter rival the Sheriff of Nottingham is nowhere to be seen today, although you can visit the Robin Hood Experience in the city which includes a reconstructed ride through the streets of Nottingham in Hood's day complete with the thirteenth century sights and sounds.

The Saxon town of Nottingham was built on one of a pair of sandstone hills whose 130-foot cliffs look out across the valley. The town was important because it controlled a strategic crossing over the River Trent. In 1068 William the Conqueror built a castle on the other hill and the Saxons and Normans bought and sold their goods in the Market Square in the valley below. The castle was a military stronghold and royal palace rivalling the great castles of Windsor and Dover. Every medieval king of England frequently visited it. Later in history, in 1642, Charles I rode out of the castle to start the Civil War. But although he raised his standard four days running, the locals weren't exactly enthusiastic and hardly anybody joined his crusade. If only Brian Clough was around in those days, the response would have been much greater.

After the Civil War, Parliamentarians sacked the castle. In the 1670s the ruins were cleared and the Duke of Newcastle set about building a palace. You can see the castle from Forest's City Ground, which affords views across a city once described by Daniel Defoe as 'one of the most beautiful towns in England'. The same can't be said today, unfortunately, because of the post-war development, including the all-too-familiar tower blocks and the obligatory ring road.

The town was originally transformed in the second half of the eighteenth century by the expansion of the lace and hosiery industries, which turned much of the place into a slum. The population rose five-fold from 10,000 and the conditions fostered a radical movement which came to the surface during a recession in the early 1800s. The workers, calling themselves Luddites after an apprentice called Ned Ludlam, went on strike and set about destroying the knitting machines they blamed for taking their jobs.

But Robin Hood and Brian Clough are probably the most famous of Nottingham's citizens. And the rivalry between Forest and County is almost as intense as that between the Sheriff of Nottingham and Robin Hood. 'It's friendly though,' I was told by the taxi driver who drove me the short distance from the station to the City Ground before the match. I was dropped off outside the main entrance and walked along Pavilion Road to the Main Stand past the club shop and a mix-and-match of offices and lounges at the back of the stand. I was to join the sponsors of tonight's match for a tour of the ground, the highlight of which was a look at Forest's huge trophy cabinet.

Forest have picked up quite a few trophies since they were formed in 1865 at a meeting in the Clinton Arms. By that time rivals Notts County, the oldest football club in the world, were already up and running, having been founded three years earlier. The Forest club's members had first come together to play a form of hockey called 'shinney', which was popular in the North before they switched to football in 1865. The club took its name from the Forest Recreation Ground where they first played.

Forest are one of only three professional clubs whose names are taken from their original grounds. (The others are Crystal Palace and Queen's Park in Scotland.) It consisted of a number of pitches in the middle of a hippodrome-shaped racecourse. The ground still exists and hosts the annual Nottingham Goose Fair. It witnessed a number of landmark events in the history of football. In 1874 Forest's England international Sam Widdowson was the first player to wear shinpads. Then, in 1878, a referee used a whistle for the first time in the game between Forest and Sheffield Norfolk, instead of signalling with a handkerchief as had been the custom.

Not only have Forest and County been rivals for more than 130 years, they've also played at many of the same grounds. When Forest moved from the Recreation Ground in 1879 they went to the Meadows, County's home from 1864 to 1877. Forest stayed for just a year during which they reached two cup semi-finals. Their success encouraged them to move to the most modern stadium in Nottingham: the Trent Bridge Cricket Ground. But the cricket club preferred hosting County's games and Forest's days were numbered.

Forest left Trent Bridge after two years and moved out to a ground called Parkside in Lenton. Three years later they went to the nearby Gregory Ground where they turned professional in 1889. But Lenton was too far from the city and Forest's gates were only around 3,000–4,000. So, in 1890, they moved to the Town Ground near Trent Bridge.

On Monday, 12 January 1891 the Town Ground hosted a representative match between the North and the South which saw goalnets used for the first time. They'd been designed by J.A. Brodie, the City Engineer of Liverpool, where they'd first been on trial. The 4,000 crowd, including all of football's leading officials, watched Nottingham-born goalkeeper Fred Geary, who played for Everton, test them out first. Just over a year later the FA finally approved their use in professional football. The same year saw Forest set a record victory when they beat Clapton 14–0, a record number of goals for an away game in English professional football.

County couldn't use Trent Bridge at the start and end of each season because cricket was played there, so Forest let them use the Town Ground. In return, County supported Forest's application to join the Football League in 1892, but there was a price: County could choose the dates for five home games before the selected clubs could meet Forest at the Town Ground. The deal struck, Forest were duly elected to the First Division and drew 2–2 against Everton in their first match at Goodison.

Six years later Forest changed grounds yet again. It was to be their last move. They decided a more spacious site across the river would best suit their needs and they left the Town Ground in the City of Nottingham for the City Ground in the town of West Bridgford. Their new home was just a couple of hundred yards across the river from the Town Ground and next to Trent Bridge. At the end of their first season at the City Ground Forest won the FA Cup for the first time.

They were relegated for the first time in 1906, but bounced straight back by winning the Second Division title at the first attempt. In 1909 they were again close to relegation but incredibly managed a 12–0 win over Leicester Fosse. Their victory was such a shock that an inquiry was held to look into the circumstances and found several of the Leicester players had taken part in the wedding celebrations of one of their team-mates the day before the match! The result is still the record for a win in the First Division (or Premier League), but not Forest's record score, which was that victory by two more goals over Clapton in 1891.

Two years later Forest were relegated and this time it took them 11 years to regain their top flight status. They returned as Second Division champions in 1922, the year when they achieved another first by using the rounded goalposts presented to the club by the Standard Goals company of Nottingham. Forest survived only three seasons in the First Division before being relegated again, in 1925. They wouldn't play First Division football again for more than 30 years.

During the Second World War German planes only caused £75 worth of damage to the City Ground, which meant the club got off lightly compared to some stadiums. But a much bigger post-war disaster was waiting in the wings. In March 1947 the River Trent overflowed and flooded the City Ground. The water was so high it reached the crossbars and swans swam across the pitch. Forest turned to their old friends and rivals County, who offered them the temporary use of Meadow Lane.

In 1949 Forest experienced their darkest hour when they went down to the Third Division (South). They'd never played outside the top two divisions. But they won the Third Division (South) in 1951, a year after Notts County, and were runners-up in Division Two in 1957 under manager Billy Walker. He'd been in charge since 1939 and after 18 years had finally got Forest back to the top. Their return was celebrated with a new £40,000 East Stand. But floodlights had to wait until 1961 when they were the second from last First Division club to have them.

In 1964 Forest did a shrewd bit of business with the Nottingham City Council by signing a 50-year lease for the 11-acre City Ground for just £750 a year. Had the City Council, which owns the land even though it's in Rushcliffe, known the next decade was to propel Forest to the very top they would certainly have asked for more.

In 1972 Forest returned to the Second Division, but it was only when a young man named Brian Clough arrived in 1975 that the club was to head for unparalleled success. He'd begun his playing career with Middlesbrough in 1952 and won the first of two England caps in 1959. Cloughie was already an established goalscorer by the time he joined Sunderland in 1961. His 254 League goals for the clubs was a post-war record.

Clough's career was sadly cut short after a serious knee injury and he was forced to retire in 1964. He has always regretted having to give up playing. 'No matter what I do in life I will never find anything to match scoring goals,' he said. 'I fed on goals. Every time I put the ball into the net it was ecstasy. Goals were like a drug.' Those sentiments were to be echoed down the years by players like Jimmy Greaves, Gary Lineker and Alan Shearer.

Clough couldn't stay away from football, however, and in 1965 he became manager of Hartlepool. 'I know I am better than the 500 or so managers sacked since the war,' said Clough. 'If they had known anything about the game, they wouldn't have been sacked.' It was at the Pool's Victoria Ground that Clough formed what was to become a close and successful partnership with Peter Taylor.

But Hartlepool were a struggling Fourth Division side when Clough took over from Geoff Twentyman. Things got so bad that he had to work for nothing for a while and even drive the team bus. But the dedication of Clough and Taylor, combined with a flaunting showmanship, made the football fraternity sit up and take notice. In 1967 they moved to Derby, where their magic potion took immediate effect with the League title coming to the Baseball Ground in 1972. The dynamic duo controversially quit the following year amid a storm of protest from the fans, to join Brighton. Then Cloughie spent an unhappy 44 days at Leeds on his own before moving to Forest, where Taylor rejoined him.

Forest won promotion in 1977 and the following season lifted the League Cup and – more importantly – the Championship for the only time in their history, after a run of 42 consecutive First Division games without defeat. Clough had become the only manager apart from Herbert Chapman to win the title with two clubs.

In February 1979 Forest made Trevor Francis the first million-pound footballer in Britain when Clough paid Birmingham £1,180,000 for his services. Three months later Francis repaid his manager's faith by scoring the goal that beat Malmo in the European Cup final in Munich.

Forest started the new decade by beating Barcelona to win the European Super Cup. They then matched Liverpool's 1978 achievement of retaining the European Cup. Forest beat a Kevin Keegan-led Hamburg team 1–0 in Madrid before a 50,000 crowd, John Robertson scoring the all-important goal. They also retained the League Cup.

Forest's success gave them the means to improve the City Ground. In August 1980 Clough opened the new £2.5 million East, or Executive, Stand, complete with 8,500 seats and 36 executive boxes. It replaced the old East Stand, which had cost £2.46 million less in 1957. The Executive Stand was directly opposite my seat in the Main Stand. As I looked up I could see the Forest name, spelt out in white seats against a background of red ones in the upper tier. It was so big that the name could be seen from the centre of Nottingham.

Forest seemed to have a love affair with the League Cup, winning it again in consecutive years in 1989 and 1990. Sadly, Taylor died in the year of that second League Cup triumph and Clough was unable to recapture the glory days. But Forest continued to work on developing the City Ground and the year after their League Cup triumph turned their attentions to the Trent End. Unfortunately, they needed to build over a strip of land behind the stand which was owned by the council. Having undercharged Forest for their lease on the City Ground, the council demanded a lot more for the extra land. The two sides eventually agreed on a rent of £22,000.

Forest's hopes of staging matches during the 1996 European Championships rested on having an all-seated capacity of 30,000; they also had to meet the Taylor Report deadline of August 1994. So they switched their attention to the Bridgford End. But they faced problems here too because the southern corner of the stand backed onto houses. They therefore had to have a lower seating tier in that corner. That accounts for the strange shape of the stand and, like at Southampton, shows the problem of being in a residential area.

The £4.6 million Bridgford Stand opened in late 1992 after which Forest focused on sorting out the Trent End. Meanwhile, Clough retired in 1993, when Forest were relegated from the Premier League. But Cloughie had made his mark. Forest may never be that successful again. A sobering thought for the City Ground faithful. But while the best manager they'd ever had departed, the club had to carry on. Improving the City Ground was something Clough applauded, though spending money on the ground that could have been used to buy players wouldn't have found favour.

Stan Collymore was one of Forest's recent signings and he'd proved there was no substitute for class with a peach of a goal. Wimbledon would return to south London nursing their wounds. Forest looked forward to the rest of the season. The crowd of just over 20,000 had enjoyed their night out by the riverside. A couple of hours earlier the teams had entered the ground to the original version of 'Robin Hood, Robin Hood riding through the Glen'. But Forest were in no mood to be generous. Tonight it was the rich who robbed the poor.

I left the ground and sleepily made my way back to the Greenwood Lodge guest house I'd booked into for the night. I was exhausted, having got up at 5 a.m. and worked my shift before catching the train to Nottingham. It was as much as I could do to drag myself up to my room and collapse for the night. The following morning I was awoken by a knock on the door. My host was worried that I would miss breakfast and was concerned in case I had to be at work. The place was usually filled with businessmen.

I explained that I had a day off, so I wasn't in a hurry. However, breakfast was a different matter. That was something I didn't want to miss. I threw my clothes on and scrambled down the steep stairs to the dining-room. The host kindly agreed to cook me an English fry-up while I talked to her husband about Nottingham and the game the night before at the City Ground. It was one of the best breakfasts I'd ever had.

I'd woken up to a beautiful sunny day in Nottingham and I was keen to explore the city. I walked up to the castle and took a tour bus around the city. It was full of pensioners and tourists enjoying a day out. The mini-bus took us around the Old Market Square, still the heart of the city, and through the Lace Market with its narrow lanes and alleys. I was also fascinated to be told about a maze of ancient man-made caves that honeycomb the sandstone rock beneath the castle, but unfortunately didn't have the time to explore them because there was one other place I had to go.

No visit to Nottingham would have been complete without a look around the Robin Hood Experience. There's no true story of Robin Hood's life and the earliest reference to him, in Langland's *Piers Plowman* of 1377, treats Hood as fiction. But to the balladeers of fifteenth-century England he was a symbol of yeoman decency, a semi-mythological opponent of corrupt clergymen and evil officers of the law. Hood also made the occasional appearance in folk drama and contemporary chronicles.

The early folklore invented by the balladeers place his exploits in Yorkshire and Cumberland as well as Sherwood Forest. He became firmly linked with Nottinghamshire only in later centuries when efforts were made to find a historical basis for the legend. In the earliest references to Hood he showed little sympathy for peasants and had a good deal of respect for noblemen – there was no mention of robbing the rich to give to the poor. These elements of the story, along with the existence of Maid Marian and Friar Tuck, were introduced much later.

Joseph Ritson, who published the first collection of the Robin Hood ballads in 1795, identified him as Robert Fitz-Ooth, born at Locksley in 1160 and reputed to be the Earl of Huntingdon – doubtful claims which have frequently been challenged. Scott's *Ivanhoe* (1819) and Thomas Love Peacock's *Maid Marian* (1822) consolidated the romantic image of the outlaw and his merry men. One could imagine future tales of Brian Clough becoming almost as legendary, especially as his well-known support for the Labour Party would cast him in the role of robber of the rich and giver to the poor.

A CLASSIC

Manchester City v Tottenham Hotspur – Maine Road, 22 October 1994

'The finest display of attacking football from both sides that I've seen in many years' was how BBC *Match of the Day* commentator John Motson described the events at Maine Road, Manchester, on a sunny autumn Saturday in October. The game between Manchester City and Tottenham Hotspur had everything: world-class internationals from Germany, Romania, England and the Republic of Ireland; seven goals; an almighty downpour; and some of the most exciting football I'd ever seen.

City manager Brian Horton's programme notes were prophetic. Under the headline 'This could well be a classic', he wrote: 'A visit by Tottenham Hotspur to Maine Road always promises to be one of the highlights of the season. Ossie [Ardiles] plays the game the way spectators love football to be played, and with his recent overseas signings he has been able to produce some marvellous attacking soccer this season.'

I'd arranged to travel with the Manchester City London Supporters Club – MCLSC to the initiated – thanks to a former colleague. He'd followed City as a boy and usually took his mother, now in her eighties to most home games. She'd been afraid to go alone since the late '70s after being mugged by City fans who ran off with her handbag. Such things were, hopefully, less likely to happen today, but she'd still only go with her son. Some scars take a long time to heal. After the match he'd usually catch the bus to Manchester Piccadilly and a train to London, while his mother went home in a taxi.

I arrived at London's Euston station just after nine o'clock to catch the 9.50 to Manchester. Small groups of football fans in their team colours were dotted around the main concourse. The red and white of Liverpool alongside the blue and gold of Wimbledon. They were playing at Anfield. The sky-blue and white of Manchester City could be seen at intervals in the long queue for the train to Manchester. It wound its way like a snake from the platform entrance towards the centre of the station. The match at Maine Road was a sell-out, though: because of the rebuilding of the Kippax Stand, the ground held only just over 25,000 compared to an eventual total of 40,000.

The MCLSC had close links with the other supporters clubs in London and we'd be joined today by Plymouth, Stoke and Bolton fans for the journey north. Plymouth were playing Stockport, Stoke were at Oldham and Bolton had a match at Port Vale – all stops along the way. It was cheaper to travel in large numbers, but each supporters club needed at least ten fans to get a discount. City were the only team to reach that magical figure today, hence the link up with the other clubs.

The presence of fans from around the League made for a colourful spectacle. There were scarves and hats of all colours: the green and black of Plymouth, the red and white of Stoke and the white and black of Bolton. There were also badges, bags and shirts in team colours. Harmony at last among football supporters. The recurring theme throughout my journey around the country was that the bad old days of football violence were past. Even if occasionally there might be an incident or two, we'd not returned to the full-scale war mentality that reigned when I watched football as a boy.

There was one shirt – blue and white – which I couldn't recognise. It wasn't until the journey home after the match that I discovered from the Plymouth supporters that it belonged to a Gillingham fan. I grabbed my copy of the famous *Manchester Evening News* sports supplement *The Pink* to find out who they were playing and why this fan had travelled north for the day. Table-topping Bury was the answer. I wondered whether Gills fan Brian Moore, the ITV commentator, was also at the match.

We walked towards the centre of Manchester to catch a bus to Maine Road in Rusholme, on Moss Side – a community that has repeatedly been near breaking point, partly owing to a high crime rate and the presence of drug dealers. The *Rough Guide to England* noted that 'an outsider's view of Manchester is all too often negative, conditioned by stories of inner-city mayhem in Moss Side, where crack-related crime brought a dozen shootings during two months in 1993.'

When City moved to Moss Side from their old ground at Hyde Road in 1923, they were closer to Old Trafford, which lies only three miles to the west. But there were advantages in settling on Moss Side. The main one was that there was a large population in the suburb and people were moving to the huge new council development. This gave City a large catchment area, it was easy to reach Maine Road from the city centre and South Manchester.

'Traditional images of shabby back-to-back houses, their slate roofs and cobbled streets glistening in the ever-present rain, tend to be reinforced by the suburbs flanking most routes into the city . . .' according to the *Rough Guide*. 'But this place is very much alive, especially when the country's largest student population is in town, and although the so-called "Madchester" youth culture scene may have peaked, the city still boasts the north's most vibrant nightlife.'

The docks and the cotton mills, once the main source of employment in the area, have now gone and the city is a mixture of bleak modern architecture, built to fill the gaps caused by German carpet bombing during the Second World War, and Victorian buildings. Manchester's campaigns to host the Olympic Games have helped to clean up the city, but much still needs to be done to finish the job.

The image presented by *Coronation Street* still prevails in many parts of the city, even though much of the programme is now shot elsewhere. Still, you can see the original set if you take the Granada Studios Tour, along with the other three-quarters of a million people who troop through the studios' doors each year to see the sets for Britain's longest-running soap opera. That's almost as many people as file through the turnstiles at Maine Road each year to see the Blues.

As we waited for a number 99 bus from the city centre I noticed lots of posters of Manchester United's star players on sale in a nearby shop – but there was not a City player in sight. A Norwegian football fan asked if he was queuing at the right stop for Maine Road. He was. He'd come over for a week's holiday with his two friends to hit the football grounds and the nightclubs. And his wife let him!

The Norwegians were at Old Trafford for United's European Champions League game against Barcelona on the Wednesday night, a thrilling 2–2 draw, and would travel to Ewood Park the next day, Sunday, for the Reds' Premier League match against Blackburn. This little jaunt was an annual event. They just loved watching English football.

At Maine Road I picked up my ticket from the main reception, where I saw the BBC's Mottie talking to former Blues' stars Mike Summerbee and Francis Lee. Motson looked very smart in a dark-pink jacket. City had turned things around since Lee became chairman and, with the other member of the famous City triumvirate, Colin Bell, now head of the Social Club, it was surely only a matter of time before they started filling the trophy room. Wasn't it?

The famous Bell, Lee, Summerbee trio had spearheaded City's quest for honours in the '60s and early '70s. The golden era began in 1965, when Joe Mercer became manager and Malcolm Allison was coach. Over the next five years the club won the Second Division Championship (1966), the First Division (1968), the FA Cup (1969) – a Neil Young goal beating relegated Leicester City – the League Cup and the European Cup-Winners' Cup (both 1970).

FA Cup success had been City's before, in 1904, 1934 and 1956. The future managers of two of City's rivals played for the Blues in the last two of those games. Matt Busby actually lifted the Cup as City captain in 1934 and Don Revie was centre-forward in 1956. Revie was featured as part of the 'City Post-War A–Z' in the match programme: 'The early years with City were a struggle until the inception of what became known as "The Revie Plan" . . . a version of the Hungarian national team's soccer tactics.'

Malcolm Allison returned to Maine Road in January 1979 and, over the next 15 months, £7.5 million changed hands in the transfer market as Big Mal bought ten players for £4.5 million and sold 13 for £3 million. The £1.5 million paid to Wolves for Steve Daley is widely regarded as one of the worst deals ever struck. The other million-pound man, Kevin Reeves, was a better purchase at £1.25 million. Under Allison's successor John Bond, City reached the 100th FA Cup final in 1981 but lost 3–2 in a replay to a stunning Ricky Villa goal. Since then, City had failed to deliver and divided their time between the top two divisions.

The fans were hoping that Frannie Lee's arrival was the start of a new golden era. The link with the past was there on the pitch as well as in the boardroom. Mike Summerbee's son, Nicky, was on the right wing against Tottenham today. He bore an uncanny resemblance to his dad, with his shirt outside his shorts and his stooped running style. Summerbee junior tore Spurs apart down the right wing, while on the other side of the park an inspired Peter Beagrie ran Spurs ragged down the left wing.

The centre of the Tottenham defence was softer than those famous chocolates. You can imagine the half-time team talk in the Spurs dressing-room.

Ossie: 'We have to defend in the second half.'

The players: 'What does defend mean?'

They desperately needed O.J. Simpson's lawyer. I was later to learn that Ardiles, desperately looking for help, had asked Spurs' Norwegian international goalkeeper Erik Thorsvedt how Norway defended. Certainly better than Tottenham I can tell you!

Having said all that, Tottenham played some delightful football and should have scored at least five goals themselves. In the event, they could manage only two and that soft-centred defence let in five. City's Paul Walsh, the former Portsmouth, Spurs, Liverpool and Luton striker, was outstanding. He scored two goals, helped create the other three and generally caused chaos in the Tottenham defence. Ossie's diamond formation was flawed. His famous five undermined by his flat-footed back four.

The City fans were happy. Their anthem 'Blue Moon', the Rodgers and Hart song borrowed from Crewe, rang out across Maine Road. The City and Spurs fans in the Kippax Stand opposite were getting soaked, despite the white plastic macs City had generously handed out before the game to help keep some of the water off them. It was like a gathering of the Ku Klux Klan. And Spurs were being burned at the stake.

The new Kippax Stand followed the opening of the club's new Umbro Stand in 1993, which replaced the old Platt Lane Stand. (Confusingly, Kippax Street is actually behind the North Stand whereas Platt Lane is a few streets away). Unfortunately City fans invaded the pitch the day the stand was opened for an FA Cup quarter-final against Spurs, resulting in 60 supporters being banned. The disturbances haven't helped City's hopes of being a big-match venue and the ground wasn't chosen for Euro '96.

Maine Road was originally a claypit for brick-making and had to be levelled when City first took it over. But when it was ready, at the huge cost of £200,000, it could hold more than 80,000. In those days there was just one Main Stand. Today there is the new Umbro Stand, the rebuilt Kippax Stand, the Main Stand and the North Stand.

The North Stand, which used to be called the Scoreboard End, was rebuilt and covered with a smart cantilever stand during City's halcyon days in the '60s. The Main Stand was also covered by a huge white roof supported by a large steel cross beam. The roof's plastic panels can apparently withstand up to seven feet of snow. Is the weather ever that bad up north during the winter?

Maine Road's use for big matches hasn't been helped by its closeness to Old Trafford, Anfield and Hillsborough. But, ironically, Manchester United's record attendance was not for a game at Old Trafford, but a match at Maine Road against Arsenal in January 1948, when the Reds shared the ground because of bomb damage to Old Trafford in the war. The crowd of 82,950 was the largest ever to watch a League match.

City's record attendance, the highest for any English club match except a Cup final, was 84,569 for a sixth round FA Cup tie against Stoke in 1934, when the Blues were on their way to a second Cup success. The 80,407 fans who packed Maine Road for an FA Cup semi-final replay in 1946 was the highest ever for a midweek game. The following season 2.25 million people saw City and United, plus a Cup semi-final and the Northern Rugby League Cup final, at Maine Road, a record for a League ground.

The crowd today was only 25,473, but that was mainly because of the ground redevelopment. It was City's biggest crowd of the season so far and they could have attracted thousands more for a pulsating encounter. 'We played well, we entertained. But the object of the exercise is to win matches,' said Ardiles after the match. 'We are not defending properly. It's as simple as that. We should have done something to cut out their crosses into the area but we didn't compete hard enough to do that.'

Match of the Day and the tabloids were full of praise for the philosophy of attacking football. But the little Argentine's days were numbered. Bob Cass in the *Mail on Sunday* summed up the way most people viewed his approach to the game. 'Ardiles seems prepared to go to his managerial doom presenting the smiling face of football. If unemployment is to be the Spurs manager's ultimate fate, it will be a tragedy for entertainment and a triumph for those who insist that results are everything.' It was.

PLAY UP POMPEY

Portsmouth v Middlesbrough – Fratton Park, 23 October 1994

The entrance to Portsmouth's Fratton Park is unlike any other in the country. The approach along Frogmore Road leads to a cul-de-sac at the end of which is a magnificent grand pavilion in the shape of a cottage. Its mock Tudor design comes complete with a half-timbered gable window in the centre over a large gate which happens to serve as the classiest main entrance to a stadium I ever saw.

To the right of the cottage stands another mock Tudor building which used to be a pub called the Pompey, with a sign showing a footballer in action. It was now home to the club shop. On the left were Pompey's offices. The grand entrance was built in 1905, when Portsmouth were doing well in the Southern League. Unfortunately the pavilion flatters to deceive, since the rest of the ground fails to live up to its splendour. 'Set amongst terraced back streets . . . Fratton is no palace from the outside,' is how *Total Football* describes the stadium. ' . . . the ground is circa 1920s and in need of repair.' They could say that again – it was badly in need of being completely modernised.

Portsmouth began life at Fratton in 1898, after a local solicitor called Alderman J.E. Pink and five of his business colleagues bought what was a market garden for just under £5,000 and set up a limited company to run a professional club. A team of professionals was signed up and the club entered the Southern League in time for the 1899 season. This all came to pass after the city's leading club, Royal Artillery, were suspended by the FA for breaching amateur regulations. At that time Fratton was ideally placed: near the railway station and close to a large residential area.

I'd travelled to Portsmouth by car on a bright Sunday morning with a friend and Pompey fanatic called Simon Denyer and his girlfriend Sarah. Known as Britain's main naval station, Portsmouth occupies most of the peninsula of Portsea Island, flanked by Langstone Harbour to the east and the magnificent Portsmouth Harbour to the west.

Her Majesty's Naval Base covers 300 acres and is almost a town in itself. There are 15 dry docks, 62 acres of fitting and repairing basins, 6,000 yards of wharfage, ten miles of railways and elegant eighteenth-century houses, including a Navigation School and Admiralty House which serves as the office of the Commander-in-Chief of the navy.

The Romans built a fortress on the northern edge of the inlet and a small port developed during the Norman era. But the city wasn't fully exploited until Tudor times, when Henry VII established the world's first dry dock and declared Portsmouth a Royal dockyard and garrison town. Since then it has become a large industrial city with a busy harbour crammed with naval frigates, ferries headed for the continent or the Isle of Wight and innumerable dredgers and tugs. The city's quaint Georgian streets huddle behind a fifteenth-century wall at the mouth of the harbour in Old Portsmouth, which also contains the historic dockyards to the north.

HMS *Victory* set sail from Portsmouth on 14 September 1805, almost 190 years before I set foot inside Fratton Park to see Pompey take on Middlesbrough. Three months later the ship returned, victorious from Trafalgar, with the body of Admiral Nelson on board. The great ship sailed for another 20 years before being retired to dry dock. You can visit the restored and newly fitted-out ship in the Old or King Charles's dock; stand where Nelson was killed by a sniper; and see the cockpit where he died.

But probably the most famous vessel is the oldest of all, the flagship *Mary Rose*, pride of Henry VIII's navy, which capsized in Portsmouth harbour in 1545 on her maiden voyage. 'In 1982 a massive conservation project raised the ship from the seabed and painstakingly eased the brine from its fragile timbers,' recalled the *Rough Guide to England*. Pompey hoped Manager Jim Smith could mount a similar rescue operation at Fratton.

Smith joined Pompey in 1991, when they reclaimed their place in the First Division. Since then the closest they'd come to getting back to the top flight was in the 1993–94 season. In fact, my only previous visit to the ground was with my friend Simon and his brother for the play-off match that season against Leicester, which Portsmouth drew 2–2 before a packed crowd. Unfortunately they failed to progress over two legs, though they had far more League points than the other play-off contenders. This gross injustice was felt deeply by the Fratton faithful, who have moaned about it ever since.

We were given a tour of the ground before the game against Bryan Robson's high-flying Middlesbrough. The highlight was a look around the Pompey trophy room, which consisted of a small oak cabinet containing a mini replica of the FA Cup, which the Football Association presented to every Cup-winning team in 1981 to celebrate the 100th anniversary of the competition.

Portsmouth won the last FA Cup final before the Second World War, in 1939, with a surprise victory over Wolves. Manager Jack Tinn became famous during that Cup run for wearing a pair of lucky white spats to every match. He insisted they were fastened by winger Fred Worrall, who eventually got tired of the tradition, though he himself carried a lucky sixpence and a miniature horseshoe onto the pitch. The war gave Portsmouth a record they're unlikely to lose: they've held the FA Cup for more consecutive years than any other team. By coincidence, Field Marshal Viscount Montgomery of Alamein, who distinguished himself in that war, was once president of the club.

After the war Pompey had their most successful period to date. They won the Championship in 1949 and 1950 and crowds soared to an average of 37,000. In February 1949 more than 50,000, the club's highest gate ever, saw a Cup-tie against Derby. The trophy room contained mementoes of those back-to-back titles. At the time Portsmouth were only the eighth club to successfully defend their First Division crown. They were also the first former Third Division side to win the Championship. They've never come close to winning the title since, let alone in successive seasons.

On 22 February 1956 the first League match under floodlights took place at Fratton when Newcastle were the visitors. Unfortunately the lights failed an hour before the scheduled kick-off and the players had to use candles to change by. The lights were eventually fixed and the match kicked off only ten minutes late.

Pompey have had many great players over the years, including Mark Hateley and Guy Whittingham, the club's highest scorer in a season with 42 goals in 1992–93. But the real stars in the eyes of the older fans are the players who brought glory to the club in their halcyon days starting with that 1939 Cup win. Among the legends are half-backs Jimmy Scoular, Reg Flewin and Jimmy Dickinson along with wingers Jack Froggatt and Peter Harris, who holds the record for the most goals in Pompey's colours having scored 194 between 1946 and 1960. But Dickinson was probably the best known. Between 1946 and 1965 he set a British record with 764 appearances for Portsmouth and won 48 England caps in post-war internationals.

Sadly, the glory days faded and Portsmouth were relegated to the Second Division in 1959 and to the Third two years later. But they bounced straight back by winning the Third Division title in 1962. By the mid-'70s they were struggling again. In 1976 they slipped back into the Third Division with former Liverpool star and current television presenter Ian St John at the helm. Two years later came their darkest hour when they dropped to the Fourth Division for the first time in their history, ironically under manager Jimmy Dickinson. He'd brought the club the best and the worst of times.

In 1983 they won the Third Division title for the second time under former Everton, Arsenal and Southampton star Alan Ball, but that's the only major success they've had in recent times apart from an FA Cup semi-final appearance in 1992. On that occasion Pompey – inspired by Darren Anderton, their record sale to Tottenham at £2 million – were desperately unlucky to lose to Liverpool on penalties after a replay.

In one corner of the trophy room stood a computer which ran the electronic crowd tracking system. At a glance officials could see how many fans were entering the ground and in which areas. As the supporters began to arrive it was time for us to take our seats in the South Stand. Our guide took us back through the club offices, selling us each a Pompey lottery ticket along the way and giving us our tickets for the match.

We thanked him and wandered through the blue wooden gates of the mock-Tudor entrance to take our seats in the South Stand. Inside the stadium the pavilion is obscured by a steel stairway, not that this ruins what is actually a very plain building on this side. We made our way underneath a patchwork of corridors and stairs, passing a brass plaque commemorating the start of work on the £12,000 stand on 17 June 1925. It was opened just over ten weeks later by League President John McKenna.

The Stand was designed by the famed football architect Archibald Leitch and included his trademark criss-cross steelwork in blue on a white background. Nowadays, though, the steelwork is covered by advertising hoardings. Although Leitch was a revered architect, he certainly hadn't left much legroom for the fans. The seats were very uncomfortable and my increasing discomfort wasn't helped by one of the most boring games I'd seen all season – though of course Leitch couldn't be blamed for that.

To the right was the Milton End, named after the nearby district. It was separated from the houses behind by a narrow road called Specks Lane. In the north-east corner is an area nicknamed the 'Boilermakers Hump' after the local shipyard workers who used to stand there to watch Pompey in the days when the dockyards were thriving.

Opposite was the North Stand, which stood on stilts above the narrow Milton Lane, which separates the stand from the industrial estate behind. It was built during the 1934–35 season, after Pompey had been promoted to the First Division in 1927 as Division Two runners-up (with a goal average that was marginally better than Manchester City's), and lost in the FA Cup finals of 1929 and 1934. Despite that second Wembley defeat, the club ran up profits of £10,000 from the '34 Cup run and received a similar amount from the sale of Jimmy Allen to Aston Villa. The North Stand was even known as the Jimmy Allen Stand because his transfer had contributed so much towards the cost.

To our left was the Fratton End. A two-tier stand was built in 1956, but the concrete structure deteriorated so quickly that in 1988 the top tier was taken down for safety reasons. All that remained was part of the lower terrace, which held less than 4,000 fans. The removal of the upper tier meant that the famous Pompey Chimes, 'Play Up, Pompey, Play Up' sung to the tune of a chiming clock, often drifted away into the sky. Portsmouth's connection with chiming clocks has been linked to the clock in the dockyards, but it may in fact result from confusion over the local name for the beaches, which are known as the Portsmouth Chines. As usual, the fans would chant the Pompey Chimes again today to encourage the players against Middlesbrough.

Fratton Park is clearly not suitable for a modern-day football club, given the limited space around the stadium for development. But after years of fruitlessly searching for an alternative site, Portsmouth have been left with little option but to redevelop Fratton. Having received two extensions to the Taylor Report deadline for all-seater Premier and First Division grounds, Portsmouth clearly had to take action to improve Fratton Park and provide enough seats for the fans.

As part of a £4.5 million refurbishment the club planned to build a new single-tier Fratton Stand in 1996, complete with 16 executive boxes and a restaurant. There would be parking for 150 cars, a new club shop and a new entrance at the north-east corner of the ground from Anson Road, which had been cut off from Milton Road.

The club also planned to build a new stand at the Milton End and seat the paddocks on both sides of the ground for an eventual capacity of 19,000. That would have been more than big enough to accommodate the sort of crowds they'd been getting. The biggest so far in the 1984–85 season was just over 13,500 for a second round Coca-Cola Cup tie against Everton which Pompey drew 1–1 after a 3–2 victory at Goodison.

At least staying put was better than sharing a ground with arch-rivals Southampton. There was once talk of a new stadium halfway between Fratton and the Dell, which would have enraged the supporters of both clubs. Pompey captain Kit Symons made his feelings clear to *90 Minutes*: 'I'd rather sit on a red hot poker than share with Southampton,' he told the magazine. (I'm not sure that would be my preference.) The rivalry with Southampton, or the Scummers as they're known on the Fratton terraces, runs deep. Being a Spurs fan, I'd always associated the Scum with Arsenal, but here was a variation used no less vehemently.

One well-known Pompey fan, Docker Hughes, once ran in a by-election for the 6.57 Party, whose manifesto included moving Southampton out of Hampshire. His wife once claimed he loved Pompey more than her! Former Portsmouth player Ian Baird, local TV presenter David Bobin and former Southampton manager and director of football Lawrie McMenemy have also come in for abuse from the Pompey faithful over the years.

If they continued to dish up the sort of football on show against Middlesbrough, it surely wouldn't be long before the Pompey players came under fire from the home fans. I was very tired, having travelled to Manchester the day before, but that wasn't the only reason I began to fall asleep towards the end of a dull first half. The most exciting thing on display all afternoon was the Pompey cheerleaders performing their routines before the match. I was almost tempted to strike up a chord of 'When the Saints go marching in' just to gee up the Pompey players and the crowd a bit.

At half-time the famous Portsmouth sailor walked around the pitch with his Play Up Pompey sign. He seemed to get more abuse from the home fans than the travelling Middlesbrough supporters at the Milton Road End. The away fans had been known to taunt the Pompey faithful with chants of 'Where's your home end gone? (Where's your home end gone?)' to the tune of 'Chirpie Chirpie Cheep Cheep', but the Fratton faithful were spared the embarrassment today. The red and white army were too focused on the need for precious promotion points.

MAJOR TRIBUTE

Fulham v Carlisle United – Craven Cottage, 29 October 1994

It was a cloudy Saturday afternoon in south-west London. In this fashionable part of the capital it's unusually hard to find a parking space among the rows of expensive cars that line the back streets off the Fulham Palace Road. Lights glowed through the stained-glass windows of posh Edwardian houses as the fans made their way to the home of Fulham Football Club on the banks of the River Thames.

Craven Cottage is a stadium once graced by Johnny Haynes, Britain's first £100-a-week footballer. The contrast with the workmanlike former Millwall idol Terry Hurlock, signed from Southampton, could not have been greater.

Even Prime Minister John Major admitted in the match programme that he coveted the skills of the midfield maestro in his younger days. Major's tribute to Haynes, believed to be the first time a Prime Minister had supplied an article for a Football League club programme, was penned to mark the 60th birthday of the Fulham legend.

'Although my footballing loyalties rested with Chelsea from an early age, I remember as a schoolboy casting covetous eyes across West London to Craven Cottage, where a player with the uncanny gift of being able to unlock any defence with a pinpoint pass was regularly winning rave reviews for his performances,' wrote Major. 'That player was Johnny Haynes, and how I wished he would exchange Fulham's colours for those of Chelsea!'

Haynes played a record 594 times for Fulham between 1952 and 1970, gaining 56 England caps, 22 as captain. He never won any major domestic honours, although Fulham did reach the FA Cup semi-final in 1958 and 1962. What Haynes made of the present Fulham team I didn't know. The idea that he'd turn up for his 60th birthday celebrations to watch a team languishing in the lower half of the Third Division would have seemed a ludicrous notion when he was at his peak.

And it wasn't only the team that was under attack. The ground had also been the subject of controversy for as long as most supporters could remember. The Craven Cottage saga began in 1985, when chairman Ernie Clay bought the ground from the Church Commissioners for £940,000 and sparked a crisis by selling it to property development company Marler Estates for £9 million, about £4.5 million of which was for Clay's 75 per cent shareholding. The deal triggered a period in which the club's fate was in the hands of a series of property companies. There was talk of moving to Chelsea and plans to merge with Queens Park Rangers. Fulham have been on the brink of closure more than once.

Chairman and former player Jimmy Hill had incurred the wrath of the fans in 1990, when a deal with property firm Cabra, who'd bought out Marler, could have forced Fulham to ground-share with rivals Chelsea at Stamford Bridge. You can imagine how the supporters felt about playing in what one fan described as 'the shadow of hell'. After Cabra collapsed, the Royal Bank of Scotland became involved – which was probably the best thing that could have happened.

The bank, which had been Cabra's main creditor, now owned the ground and had given Fulham the option to buy it if the club could raise £7.5 million by 2003. The only snag was that if the club didn't raise the money by June 1996, the rent would then rise from a modest sum to something between a half and three-quarters of a million pounds. The most any other clubs paid was £100,000. Clearly, the bank was not in the mood to hang around, because it had already suffered a big loss from Cabra's collapse and wanted to sort the problem out quickly. Owning Craven Cottage was not a priority in terms of its planned portfolio of property assets.

Fulham wanted to redevelop the stadium with a scheme which was attractive to a property developer and met the requirements of Hammersmith and Fulham Council, while preserving the Cottage as the home of Fulham Football Club.

That explained the Fulham 2000 campaign fund-raising leaflets being distributed outside the ground before the match against Carlisle. The campaign aimed to secure the club's future at Craven Cottage. It had so far raised £220,000 for the Craven Cottage Fund, launched the previous March with Haynes, George Best and disc jockey David Hamilton as the patrons.

Actor Hugh Grant was also backing the campaign. He'd revealed his allegiance to the Cottagers as a guest on the BBC's *Desert Island Discs* with Sue Lawley. He chose 'Viva El Fulham' as the record he'd take with him on his desert island. Sounds like the best place for what is a truly awful record. The actor, whose favourite player is keeper Jim Stannard, urged listeners to send money to the Fulham 2000 campaign.

Among the celebrities the club hoped to tap for money and/or support were tennis star Stefan Edberg, who lives in Fulham; Aston Villa's most famous supporter Nigel Kennedy, the violinist who was apparently once a Fulham fan (he's not alone); and even Pope John Paul who is supposed to have been a regular at the Cottage whilst studying at a local seminary (and if you believe that . . .).

The ground is in the middle of an area which was once poor but is now very affluent. It stands on the banks of the Thames in a charming riverside spot next to the delightful Bishop's Park. Staging Third Division football amid this abundance of wealth somehow seems out of place with the surroundings. On gates of less than 5,000 the club would have found it hard to survive unless a suitable development scheme was found. Hill envisaged a 15,000 all-seater stadium incorporating a refurbished Cottage and Stevenage Road Stand, three narrow stands and 142 flats.

There was no doubt about the determination of the dwindling band of committed supporters to a future at the Cottage. As one pointed out, 'For supporters of little clubs, the ground is almost more important than anything else'. In Fulham's case, Craven Cottage was worth fighting for. The Edwardian architecture and famous cottage give it an old-fashioned warmth and nostalgia which the fans are understandably sentimental about. Even the tea ladies serving home-made scones in the press-room were a throwback to the past. It must be the only club where children are allowed to play cards in the press tea-room during the match.

The original Cottage was built in 1780 by the sixth Baron Craven in woods which were once part of Anne Boleyn's hunting-grounds. Hence the name Craven Cottage and Fulham's nickname of the Cottagers. At that time it really was a cottage, complete with thatched roof and latticed windows. George IV used it as a hunting lodge before a moneylender called Charles King bought it in 1834. The statesman Edward Bulwer-Lytton took over the Cottage in 1839 and wrote at least two of his popular novels there, though his most famous *The Last Days of Pompeii* was probably not one of them.

Sir Ralph Howard was the next resident and among his guests were Disraeli, Prince Louis Napoleon and the Prince of Wales. The next owner was an American called W. Bentley Woodbury, who sold the Cottage to a farmer from Surrey, who rented it to a retired policeman. While he was living there a fire broke out on 8 May 1888 and the Cottage was burned down. After that, the site was neglected and became overgrown.

Fulham struck a deal with the owner of the land, a Mr Tod Heatley, under which they would clear the area and lay out a ground if the club could keep half of the gate money. The Mears building firm, which went on to build Stamford Bridge and found Chelsea ten years later, prepared the land for Fulham to play on. It took two years to complete the job; the ground was finally ready for the opening fixture on 10 October 1896!

Excavations from the nearby Shepherd's Bush tube line were brought to Craven Cottage to raise the ground level. This was necessary to avoid flooding, for the land was on the banks of the River Thames and there was a creek running across the middle. The Borough Council provided road sweepings used to build banking on three sides of the pitch, while the remains of the burned down Cottage, which stood somewhere near the south end of where the Main Stand is now, were put at the Putney End. Mysteriously, one building worker, clearing what was left of the Cottage, fell into the hidden entrance of what was claimed to be a secret underground tunnel leading to a wharf in Barnes on the opposite side of the Thames. If only the fans knew where it was they could have used it to make a quick escape from the dreadful football Fulham had been playing at the Cottage!

I came across the present Cottage in the south-east corner of the ground between the Stevenage Road Stand and the uncovered Putney End. I'd walked along the Fulham Palace Road and through Bishop's Park before emerging on Stevenage Road. The away coaches which had brought the Carlisle fans to the ground were parked just outside the wrought-iron railings of the park. As I walked towards the ground I could see the Cottage on my left with the name Fulham picked out in white against a black background on the side wall. The sight of a Cottage inside a football ground is an odd one but it's not the only striking feature of Fulham's ground. The red-brick entrance to the Main Stand is also a sight to behold and oozes class. The only other ground with such an impressive red-brick facade is Villa Park, which I'd see later in the season. The Stevenage Road Stand looked more like a municipal building and I half-expected local authority office workers in suits and ties to appear rather than fans wrapped up in black and white scarves and hats.

The present-day Cottage was built by the famous football-ground architect Archibald Leitch, who also built the Main Stand in his familiar red-brick style.

The new Cottage was ready on 2 September 1905, just two days before the opening of Stamford Bridge. That 1905–06 season was the only time Fulham have consistently had bigger crowd's than Chelsea. In March 1907 Craven Cottage became the first club ground, apart from that at Crystal Palace, to be used for an international match, when England played Wales.

The Cottage has a small gable on the slated roof with chimneys on either side. The building contains dressing-rooms on the ground floor and an ornate wrought-iron balcony on the second floor supported by columns. For the Carlisle match I could see a number of privileged visitors sitting on the balcony sipping tea as they watched the game from what was perhaps the strangest vantage point I'd see all year. The Cottage also contains offices, a boardroom and a small apartment for the staff or players.

The new Main Stand was one of the first of Leitch's designs featuring an upper tier of seats with a paddock in front and a pitched roof with a pedimented gable in the middle. But the most distinguished part of the stand is at the back, where the red-brick fits in nicely with the surrounding terraced houses. Simon Inglis describes the facade well in his book *The Football Grounds of Great Britain*:

> Fulham's red brick frontage is split into bays and divided horizontally into three levels. The lower and upper floor windows are arched, the centre ones rectangular, with stone lintels, mullions and decorative sills. Between the windows are mouldings with the letters FFC, and, erroneously, 'Est. 1880'. Along the parapet are three dutch gables. Plain brickwork can be seen at each end . . .

Fulham were in fact established by churchgoers as Fulham St Andrew's Church Sunday School FC in 1879. The club adopted the name Fulham in 1888, the year the Football League was introduced, and turned professional in 1898. They joined the Second Division in 1907 and have spent most of their history there with a few years in both the Third and First Divisions. Their best position ever was tenth place in the old First Division in the 1959–60 season, the year after they were promoted as runners-up in Division Two. Star players at the time included Haynes, George Cohen, who would star for England in their World Cup victory at Wembley in 1966, and the future Tottenham captain Alan Mullery. Later the great Daley Thompson, who went on to become the World and Olympic decathlete champion, was rejected by Fulham. He obviously got the better of the deal.

But Fulham's tag as 'London's friendliest club' has over the years applied as much to their inept performances on the pitch as to the welcome awaiting supporters at the Cottage. They bucked the trend in 1975, when they reached the FA Cup final for the first time after losing four semi-finals. Their Cup success owed much to the signings of Alan Mullery from Tottenham, who was voted Footballer of the Year, and Bobby Moore from West Ham for only £25,000. A year after joining Fulham Moore was leading his new club out onto the lush Wembley turf to play against his old club in the world's oldest cup competition. Unfortunately, a less-than-spectacular performance by keeper Peter Mellor allowed the Hammers' Alan Taylor to score twice, once through Mellor's legs, and that was that.

But Fulham do have the distinction of being the only club to beat a team in the

FA Cup who then went on to reach the final. That was in the first season after the war when the early rounds of the competition were played over two legs. On 7 January 1946, Fulham beat Charlton 2–1 in a second-leg tie but still went out on the aggregate score. And they are also the only London club to host the great Pelé when he played at the Cottage in 1973 in a friendly against Fulham with his club Santos.

The players wearing the black and white of Fulham may come and go (other famous stars over the years include George Best, Rodney Marsh, Bobby Robson, Ron Greenwood and Jimmy Hill), but the Stevenage Road Stand remains and is likely to do so for the foreseeable future given its Grade Two listed building status. The Stand does need upgrading, though: the gloomy concourse, and I use the term loosely, underneath looks like something out of the Dark Ages. Indeed, it's so outdated that it was used as a set for the 1986 movie *Shanghai Surprise* starring Madonna and Sean Penn. Hard as it is to believe, they both appeared at the Cottage in a scene in which the dark recesses of the Main Stand were supposed to resemble the Shanghai racecourse.

I arrived at the ground with my Anglo-Norwegian girlfriend Anne-Lise. It must have been true love for her to come with me to watch Fulham. She'd never been to a football match and I knew she'd never seen anything like Craven Cottage on a bright autumn afternoon. But Anne-Lise insisted on joining me, so I got her a ticket in the Stevenage Road Stand from the Main Office. Once inside we had tea and scones from the quaint, old-fashioned press-room and then took our seats in the press-box. She wasn't really supposed to sit there, but the place was hardly heaving with Fleet Street's finest. The days of big crowds and glamorous celebrities visiting the Cottage were long gone, although actress Honor Blackman and singer Alan Price are fans of the Cottagers – along with the aforementioned Hugh 'Viva El Fulham' Grant, Nigel Kennedy (sort of), Stefan Edberg (probably) and the Pope (supposedly).

We sat on wooden seats inside a wooden area reserved for the Press. Light was streaming in from the arched windows at the top of the stand. To our right was the Hammersmith End, described by Simon Inglis as 'one of the last great end terraces', though Sunderland's appeared far more impressive to me when I visited Roker Park later in the season. To our left a small band of Carlisle supporters were clustered on the uncovered terraces of the Putney End. The rear section, which had been fenced off, contained what was left of the club's electronic scoreboard. It hadn't worked since it broke down during a game against Manchester City in 1984, when Fulham scored five times. Air-raid shelters could still be seen half-covered by the terracing. There was a tree in the corner of the Putney End near the River Thames which was protected by a preservation order after the efforts of a fan to save it.

Opposite our prime seats in the Main Stand was the Riverside Stand, formerly known as the Eric Miller Stand. Miller was a businessman and board member, who proposed building the stand in 1972 and later shot himself when his business was investigated. The stand cost £334,000 to build and was opened in February 1972, when Fulham played Benfica in a friendly. It replaced the Thames-side terrace which allowed fans to walk all around the ground if they wished. Craven Cottage used to be opened early on Boat Race day so that supporters could watch the Oxford–Cambridge boat race from the top steps of the stand, but that view was blocked when the Miller Stand went up. The crest of the Borough of Fulham and Hammersmith can be seen on the front of the roof and the club's name is in one corner.

The metal and concrete used to construct the stand made it seem oddly modern in a ground which had changed little from the early 1900s, apart from Mr Miller's development. Views across the Thames towards leafy Barnes were blocked by frosted glass along the rear wall. The only views came with possession of one of the executive boxes which lined the back of the stand. Meanwhile, it looked as if the club hadn't quite completed the building work, for there were blocks of terracing without any seats. I later learned they couldn't afford to replace any broken seats and, in any case, didn't need to, for attendances at the Cottage were nowadays so low. Fulham decided, instead, to remove whole sections of seating.

Today's visitors, Carlisle, also played in an unfinished stadium. But they were second in the table thanks partly to their own headline-grabbing chairman Michael Knighton. After running down the pitch at Manchester United juggling a ball, he challenged other chairmen to match his skills. Jimmy Hill recalled his reaction when a journalist asked whether he was ready to take up the challenge: 'Blimey, no! I couldn't even do that when I was playing!' Now we know why his expert analysis for the BBC's *Match of the Day* is often so wide of the mark.

Anyone who could juggle the ball like Knighton could have walked straight into the Fulham team. The lumbering Hurlock looked very overweight, though a journalist from the Press Association told me at half-time that Fulham's midfield schemer had actually lost weight since he arrived at the club. Former Newcastle forward Gary Brazil displayed some nice touches but failed to penetrate a solid Carlisle defence, bolstered by former Everton, Aston Villa and Wolves star Derek Mountfield.

By half-time Fulham were 2–0 down to goals from David Reeves and Mountfield. In the second half Carlisle added a third through Paul Conway and should have scored at least three more before allowing the home side to pull one back through captain Simon Morgan.

The frustration of the home supporters was encapsulated by one fan who ran onto the pitch wagging his finger at the referee after he'd failed to award Fulham a free-kick at the start of the move which led to Carlisle's third goal. The stewards just stood and watched as the incensed supporter made a bee-line for the man in black to make his point before crossing to the other side of the pitch. He then calmly walked around the perimeter to take his place in the Stevenage Road Stand.

Belatedly, a steward from the Putney End ran after the supporter and just managed to grab him round the waist as he was climbing over the low wall to his seat. But the other fans surged forward to pull him into the crowd before pelting the steward with cans and other objects. The police eventually arrived but seemed non-plussed. They couldn't find the fan and stood around hands on hips wondering what to do. The mobile phone bill must have been huge as stewards tried to co-ordinate their movements in an attempt to apprehend the miscreant.

Back on the pitch Fulham remained underwhelming. 'He doesn't look much like Robbie Fowler,' said a hardened season ticket holder sitting behind the press-box as he watched Fulham's centre-forward.

'He doesn't even look like Harry Fowler,' quipped his cynical sidekick. These guys had suffered all the humiliation you could imagine as season ticket holders. They'd earned the right to criticise the players, manager, linesman, referee and supporters and they were going to use it to the full. Nobody was spared from the abuse they showered on everyone and everything.

Ian Branfoot, recently sacked by Southampton, was not a popular choice as manager. The fans complained that there were too many old players in the team, like former Wimbledon and Sheffield United striker Alan Cork. Branfoot disagreed. 'The older players have been our saving grace. Without them you'd have a team full of innocents. You'd get slaughtered.' The problem with older players, and a problem readily acknowledged by Branfoot, is that they get injured more often and for longer periods.

A growing list of injuries to experienced players had robbed Fulham of their momentum. 'Thirteen games into the season and I have not yet been able to select a team from anywhere near a full squad of players,' complained Branfoot. Without them Fulham would struggle. 'I'm always a supreme optimist. But . . . you know that in some departments we're not good enough.' He described the club's two young full-backs as 'incredibly naïve'. That would have been an apt description of the performance against a supremely confident Carlisle team.

Branfoot's sympathy for his players ran deep. He'd seen enough to convince him that a footballer's life was not all wine and roses. Injuries could take their toll on the fittest players. 'Two games almost every week give little respite or recovery time and most players will play in many games while carrying an injury. One of the few plusses when you retire is being able to wake up on a Sunday morning without the ever-present aches, strains and pain.'

Branfoot went on, 'Some people will say that footballers are overpaid prima donnas, but those people normally sit behind a desk and incur no pain and little discomfort during their careers. The aftermath of a career in soccer is another thirty or forty years of severe arthritis and constant pain, and any money earned does not compensate for that.' He had a point. It made me wonder what shape Paul Gascoigne would be in when he finished. His body already contained more plates than a Harrods sale.

With little to console them on the pitch the Fulham fans were left to wallow in their own graveyard humour. 'Like the bloke who goes with his dog to the game, and when Fulham score the dog jumps up and claps. The man next to him says, 'Does he do that every time Fulham score?' and the first man replies, 'Well, I don't know, he's only been coming three seasons!'

After the final whistle we returned to the dark recesses beneath the Stevenage Road Stand. The small band of journalists covering the match had already raced to the bank of wooden telephone boxes next to the press-room to phone in their match reports and full-time scores. The bank of phones was not unlike the one in the film *Airplane* and I half-expected them all to fall over like they do in the movie. But this was real life and whilst dry rot and woodworm were no doubt eating away at the wooden structure it still had a few years left in it yet. The same could probably not be said for the whole stand. (The fans had to leave the stand during a match in April 1990 when council officers raised concerns about its safety!)

We left the ground and made our way across to the River Thames where a few boats were making their way up the river. A group of kids were playing football in Bishop's Park no doubt pretending they were Ryan Giggs or Alan Shearer. It was hardly likely they'd have wanted to emulate any of the Fulham players who'd just been outplayed by Carlisle. I wondered if they ever watched the Cottagers play or even knew the names of the players. It wasn't like that in the '60s. Back then they'd have all wanted to be Johnny Haynes.

STILL CRAZY AFTER ALL THESE YEARS

Wimbledon v Norwich City – Selhurst Park, 30 October 1994

I woke up on a bright Sunday morning with one thought in my head: the Crazy Gang. I'd heard so much about the antics of Wimbledon's self-styled nutters that a trip to their temporary home at Selhurst Park was something I'd been looking forward to since I'd started my football odyssey a couple of months back up at Carlisle.

There's no other team quite like Wimbledon. Their nickname was borrowed from the eccentric comedy team of the 1940s and was based on the club's unorthodox management style and non-League approach to the game. They brought the fun back into football and, as the underdogs, made sure they always had a good time.

Originally based at Plough Lane, the Dons were as far removed from the manicured grass courts and strawberries and cream of the All England Lawn Tennis Club (a mere mile to the west) as could possibly be imagined. Almost as strange as Uncle Bulgaria and the rest of his Wombles on Wimbledon Common, the Dons had upheld a tradition of craziness as far back as their Southern League days.

One man more than any other was responsible for preserving their nutty reputation: former hod-carrier Vinnie Jones. He summed up the club's willingness to battle against all the odds under any circumstances. Vinnie had joined the Dons from Wealdstone in 1986 and began to establish a reputation as one of football's hard men.

He came recommended when Wimbledon signed him. 'He's incredibly loyal,' said the Wealdstone physio Arnie Reed. 'Ask him to jump off the stand roof and he'd do it. But he's as thick as two short planks. He always grabbed the quiz book on our coach trips so that he could ask the questions. That way he didn't have to answer.'

Jones's notoriety at Wimbledon was built on incidents such as the time he grabbed Paul Gascoigne by the balls in Gazza's Newcastle days. Gazza sent Jones a lavatory brush and received a red rose in return. He was also reported as saying that he'd tear Kenny Dalglish's ear off and spit in the hole. 'I like to upset anybody I play against,' he said.

After being sent off six times in six years Vinnie was fined a hefty £20,000 by the FA in 1993 and given a six-month ban suspended over three years for bringing the game into disrepute. His crime was to star in a video called *Soccer's Hard Men* in which he showed how to commit professional fouls. Nice bloke, our Vinnie.

When Jones wasn't picked as the new Wimbledon captain in 1988, he responded: 'I have been a great ambassador for this club.' He left the following year to join Leeds and moved on to Sheffield United in 1991 before returning to the Dons after a short spell at Chelsea. Turning out for Wales was yet another example of how unorthodox he was and it reflected the sense that nothing was ever impossible with Wimbledon.

The club began life in 1889, when old boys from Central School formed the Wimbledon Old Centrals. They were really just a parks team who played at first on Wimbledon Common, home of the characters in the children's television show *The Wombles*, and changed in a local pub. After moving around the local parks they begged the council for a pitch, but got nowhere, and in 1910 the club disbanded.

Several of the players and officials joined Wimbledon Borough which, by a twist of fate, had been formed by council workers. Borough formally merged with the old Wimbledon team in 1912 and moved a few hundred yards down Plough Lane from the Wimbledon Greyhound Stadium to a new ground. It had been swamp land used as a rubbish dump before the Dons took up residence.

Wimbledon played in several leading amateur leagues for more than 70 years. Between 1958 and 1963 Plough Lane was developed under chairman Sydney Black and the Dons began to dominate the Isthmian League. They also reached three successive Amateur Cup finals, finally winning the trophy by beating Sutton at Wembley in 1963. A year later they turned professional and joined the Southern League.

At the end of that first season in the Southern League they cheekily applied to join the Football League. It was the first of what was to become an annual bid to join the ranks of the professionals. But it was the FA Cup, rather than the Football League, which first brought Wimbledon into the limelight and turned the players into celebrities overnight.

The Dons captured the public's imagination in 1975, when they were drawn against First Division Burnley in the third round. Burnley, managed by Jimmy Adamson, captain against Spurs in the 1962 FA Cup final, were seventh and their 45 goals made them top scorers in Division One. Wimbledon were third in the Southern League.

Burnley watched Wimbledon play three times before the Cup-tie and the Dons had lost twice. The manager of the Plough Lane side, Allen Batsford, was meanwhile preparing his own dossier on Burnley. The major finding was that most of their goals were made by Welsh international winger Leighton James.

On the morning of the match Batsford and his coach Brian Hall stayed up until two in the morning 'scrapping and reconsidering ideas' on how they could beat their illustrious opponents. Later that morning they put their theories into practice with the players on a Burnley sports ground before the big match.

The Wimbledon team included Dave Bassett, who, just a year earlier, helped Walton & Hersham thrash Brighton 4–0. Bassett, of course, would go on to manage the Dons. But it was goalkeeper Dickie Guy who was to be the most important man on the pitch. Having failed to make the grade at a League club, Guy worked as a tally clerk at the London docks. He'd played every first-team match over the past four years.

With Guy in inspirational form and full-back Bob Stockley keeping Leighton

James under wraps with back-up from his team-mates, the Dons survived the first half without conceding a goal. Then just four minutes after the break bank clerk Ian Cooke shot and the ball ran loose to Roger Connell. He miscued to Mickey Mahon who struck a sweet left-foot drive into the net. Turf Moor fell silent and the Wimbledon players celebrated. 'I will never forget the look on the faces of the Burnley players when we scored,' said Mahon, who'd starred in Colchester's 3–1 giant-killing of Leeds in 1971.

It was the only goal of the match and the Dons had arrived. They became the first non-League team to win away to a First Division side since Darlington back in 1920. 'I don't think they realised we could play so well,' said Dons manager Allen Batsford after the match. 'It might have been different if Bob Stockley had been skinned three times by Leighton James in the first ten minutes, but he wasn't.'

Wimbledon nearly caused an even bigger upset in the fourth round when they held Leeds to a goalless draw at Elland Road thanks to Guy, who saved a Peter Lorimer penalty. Unfortunately they lost the replay 1–0 at Plough Lane with the Leeds goal deflected off Dave Bassett!

The Dons followed their Cup exploits by achieving League status in 1977 thanks in no small part to the forceful personality of new chairman Ron Noades. Wimbledon became London's 12th League club when they replaced Workington Town in the Fourth Division after winning the Southern League for three years in a row.

But they weren't ready to begin their meteoric rise up the divisions just yet. At the start of the 1978–79 season they were thrashed 8–0 by Everton in the second round of the League Cup. It's still their record defeat. Their League form was also patchy and they were promoted and relegated in successive seasons between 1979 and 1982.

Finally, after winning the Fourth Division Championship as top scorers in the country in 1983 they not only avoided an immediate return to the League's bottom division but managed to climb straight up to the Second Division as runners-up to Oxford. Striker Alan Cork was responsible for Wimbledon's goal-rush in that 1983–84 season with a tally of 32, after missing most of the previous two seasons because of a broken leg.

The speed of the Dons' rise through the divisions – they'd reached Division Two only seven years after leaving the Southern League – meant that they'd held onto the sort of team spirit which was rarely seen in top-class football. 'It's a bit like being at school with your mates,' said Cork who, along with the other players was still expected to wash his own kit, bring his own towel and clean his own boots.

Unfortunately, despite their amazing success, Wimbledon were drawing crowds of less than 4,000. Their best in that 1983–84 season was the 7,500 who showed up to see them outplay Nottingham Forest 2–0 in the second round of the Milk Cup (once the League Cup). Nevertheless, the success story continued and in 1986 the Dons reached the First Division behind today's opponents, Norwich, and Charlton. They finished a remarkable sixth in their first season and there was immediate talk of the club moving from Plough Lane. After considering alternative sites the Dons decided to stay put.

But even promotion to the top flight and lucrative home matches against the likes of Liverpool, Manchester United and Arsenal wasn't enough to push average gates above the 10,000 mark. The club was pulling in about 8,000 fans per game and its debts rose to £600,000. There were rumours of a merger with Crystal Palace, whose new chairman Ron Noades, the former Wimbledon chairman, had long harboured plans for a South London United team.

Meanwhile, the fairy story on the pitch was complete in 1988, when Wimbledon beat hot favourites Liverpool 1–0 in the Cup final. They must have had the most basic ground of any FA Cup-holders in the modern era. Plough Lane was a typical non-League stadium with few attractive features. In the summer, away fans on the East Terrace were blinded by the sun; in winter their only refuge was the temporary toilets.

The Main Stand on the north side, built in 1958, was cramped and journalists were none-too-impressed with the press-box, which many described as more like a bird's nest. After games, players and directors had to rub shoulders with the fans in the very basic lounge, since there were no other facilities available. No wonder they were crazy.

But they weren't crazy enough to invest in Plough Lane. The restricted site offered little scope for expansion and would have cost a fortune to redevelop. If the location was more appropriate, they could have demolished the stadium and started again, but that wasn't an option. In fact, the club had wanted to move for some time. 'We have to live in the real world, not in fairy tales,' chairman Sam Hammam told the fans.

There had been plans for a new 20,000 all-seater stadium on a disused sewage works in the Wandle Valley, just a few hundred yards from Plough Lane, but after spending £600,000 over seven years preparing for a move, the council changed from Conservative to Labour and the site became a public park.

There were reports of plans for a new £17 million stadium on part of a 2,000-acre site at Beddington Lane on the border of Merton and Croydon. The Borough pushed the club to consider Beddington, but in September 1991 the council ruled it out! There was also an audacious bid to use Twickenham, which was turned down by the Rugby Football Union in February 1991, and unsuccessful talks to share Loftus Road.

By now Wimbledon were getting desperate, for there was no hope of Plough Lane being ready for the August 1994 all-seater deadline imposed by the Taylor Report. Their only option was to ground-share. Against all the current thinking of other clubs they struck a deal with their former chairman Ron Noades to share Selhurst Park.

As Michael Heatley and Daniel Ford remark in *British Football Grounds: Then and Now*, it was certainly a palace after the largely underdeveloped Plough Lane. The climb from non-League to the First Division and FA Cup winners in just ten years is unlikely to be repeated and, although money was spent on improvements, Plough Lane paid for that success.

The last first-team game at Plough Lane in May 1991 was, ironically, against Crystal Palace. Just a few months earlier the Dons had attracted a post-war record low First Division crowd of just 3,981 for the visit of Coventry. Nowadays the gates at Plough Lane don't come anywhere near that level, since the ground is used for reserve and youth team games and only the Main Stand is open.

Wimbledon didn't get off to the best of starts at Selhurst Park when their first scheduled match was called off because work being carried out over the summer had not been completed in time for the new season. But they attracted higher average gates at their temporary home, although a new post-war record low First Division (now Premier League) crowd of 3,121 was established with the visit of Sheffield Wednesday in October 1991.

Shortly after the move, in January 1992, Joe Kinnear was appointed as the Dons' new manager. The former Tottenham right-back had a strong pedigree and played in two very notable Cup finals. He won an FA Cup-winners' medal in 1967, when Spurs beat Chelsea 2–1 in the first all-London final – and a UEFA Cup-winners' medal in 1972 after playing in a two-legged victory over Wolves in the first all-British European final.

Big Joe had done as much as anyone to foster the Crazy Gang spirit at Wimbledon. He seemed happier leading his players to the pub than taking them on a gruelling run. I'd seen him once with Graeme Souness in London's popular Dover Street Wine Bar in – believe it or not – Dover Street. He seemed as comfortable there as he was playing for Spurs or managing Wimbledon. While Souness spent the whole evening sitting at a table with his girlfriend Big Joe boogied the night away on the dance floor.

During the 1991–92 season Kinnear asked the players to vote for the worst Wimbledon performer in each game. The winner, or loser depending on how you look at it, was sent to see Chekhov's play *Uncle Vanya* at the National Theatre. That may seem like a reward, until you know that it was described as 'the most boring play in London'.

Meanwhile, the club remained successful on the pitch and season-ticket sales doubled to 2,500 as the average home gate rose by some 30 per cent to more than 10,000. (By the 1996–97 season crowds had risen 115 per cent since the move from Plough Lane). Nevertheless, Selhurst Park was still seven miles from Plough Lane and the fans had to take a 40-minute train journey across South London for 'home' games.

Many times chairman Sam Hammam has justifiably given up the idea of Wimbledon ever returning home. After the council ruled out the Beddington site in 1991, he wrote in the club programme: 'It's over. I'm finished with Merton Council. They've destroyed my dream and it's divorce.'

The following year the Greyhound Racing Association offered the club the chance to redevelop their old home at the Wimbledon Greyhound Stadium on Plough Lane into a 15,000-seater stadium for dog racing and football. Merton Council were in favour of the scheme. But in August 1994 the borough once again dashed Wimbledon's hopes by refusing permission for a Safeway supermarket to be built at Plough Lane in a deal which could have netted the club £10 million at a time when it was losing some £5,000 a week.

Hammam was furious. 'We are not going back to Wimbledon,' he said. 'Never. It is all over. We have crossed the Rubicon. We have gone on the river of no return.' But while the chairman may have reached the end of his tether, the fans still hoped for a return home. The day before my visit many fans had turned up at Merton Civic Centre to protest to the council by handing in a petition signed by 3,500 supporters.

'A petition of this size is a credit to all of us and certainly makes it very clear to Merton Council that our club has a lot of local support,' said the Dons

Supporters Club. The fans gave the Leader of the Council, Tony Colman, letters from David Mellor and other MPs including the Shadow Minister for Sport Tom Pendry. The campaign was also backed by Gordon Taylor, Chief Executive of the Professional Footballers' Association, and the FA's Chief Executive Graham Kelly.

The council leader had been a great supporter of the club's campaign to return to a new home in Merton and had recommended that the Safeway plan should be accepted. 'We are grateful to him for his efforts on our behalf and for accepting the petition,' said the Supporters Club. '[But] the campaign hasn't finished there . . . We are still a long way from home.' Indeed they were and unfortunately still are.

The council's rejection of the Safeway plan was upheld on appeal to the Department of the Environment in 1995 and strengthened Hammam's determination to find the club a new home outside the borough of Merton. He has spoken to other London boroughs and even entertained the idea of moving Wimbledon to another city altogether, including Dublin, which offered to play host. Now that really would be crazy.

By 1997 Sam Hammam favoured a move to a site on land next to a David Lloyd tennis and fitness centre in Raynes Park; the site had a good access road and is only two miles from Wimbledon town centre. Merton Council, on the other hand, has been conducting a feasibility study for a sports complex on the Wimbledon Greyhound Stadium site with the football club as its centrepiece. But Hammam says the Dons will never play in a stadium where the fans have to watch from behind glass and a greyhound track. He's also against paying rent to the Wembley Stadium company, which owns the site.

Many long-standing Dons fans said they'd rather watch Third Division football with a club in their own stadium in the borough of Merton than carry on as Premier League nomads with little chance of a return home. The reality, though, is that until Wimbledon find a new home they'll have to soldier on at Selhurst Park.

The ground-share arrangement means watching their team in a ground painted in their landlord's home colours of blue and red, stewarded by Palace fans. The club shop next to the Sainsbury's supermarket at the entrance to Selhurst Park sells Wimbledon souvenirs which look as if they've been put on display by mistake. And the fans have to drink in a bar called Crystals – there's no Dons bar in sight. They even have to share a trophy cabinet which has Palace's cups and mementoes on one side and Wimbledon's on the other, including the 1988 Liverpool Cup final programme.

The Cup win came before Joe Kinnear's time at the club, but his approach had reaped dividends. Nevertheless, when I went to watch Wimbledon play Norwich in a match screened on Sky Sports on a Sunday afternoon in October, they were having a rough time and had slipped to fourth from bottom of the Premier League.

The players had suffered from injuries and illness and Kinnear was having to change the team virtually every week. He had already used an incredible 21 players in just 11 League games and three Cup matches. Among the casualties were top goalscorer Dean Holdsworth and midfield linchpin Robbie Earle. So was Big Joe a worried man? Not on your life. He remembered much tougher times with the Dons in his early days:

The one thing I want to make crystal clear from the start is that there is no panic here, no crisis, just a determination to get moving in the right direction again. It has been a pretty miserable time for us all so far this season both on and off the field, with our run of successive defeats [four] perhaps putting us under the microscope more than we would like.

It never ceases to amaze me just how quick and eager some people are to say that the Crazy Gang bubble has burst, that it's all doom and gloom and despair here. Sorry, chaps, but you've got it all wrong. We have had a bit of a bumpy ride but we will get back on the right track again – have no doubt about that.

When I took over from Peter Withe, Wimbledon were rock bottom in terms of results and morale, hadn't won in 18 games yet still finished mid-table. There is no way that the bunch of lads I've got here are going to go that length of time without a win. I won't allow it and they certainly don't want to wait. The season is still barely a quarter of the way through with another 90 points to play for, so I think those who are putting the boot in already are going to look mighty foolish come May 1995.

I took my seat in the Main Stand for the match against Norwich – the team Wimbledon had played the most times since joining the Football League. They had met twice in the old Second Division, a dozen times in the old first Division and on four occasions in the Premier League. The Dons had won ten of those meetings with four draws and only three defeats of which just one came at home. The omens looked good.

Sitting behind me was the Southampton manager Alan Ball and his son. Ball was looking to strengthen his squad and had come to observe someone in particular. I asked who he was watching. 'One of the players,' Ball replied cryptically. He wasn't letting on as to who it was. I assumed he was worried that if anyone found out, then the price might be somewhat affected when he made initial enquiries.

After a 1–0 Wimbledon win that eased the club's early-season relegation worries, I wandered into the players' lounge, where a *Sun* reporter I'd met at Ipswich was propping up the bar. Wimbledon's recent signing Efan Ekoku was also there with his family and seemed happy enough to sign autographs for the young fans. He even posed for photos with one of them, giving the sort of smile that confirmed the Dons had won.

TO THE MANOR BORN

Oxford United v Blackpool – The Manor Ground, 1 November 1994

As the taxi from Oxford station passed through the University town, with its historic spires and steeples, it was hard to imagine I was going to a football match. Even when I left the town behind to enter the leafy suburbs surrounding the aptly-named Manor Ground it seemed an unlikely setting for an Endsleigh League match.

But all of a sudden, up ahead, I could see the floodlights glowing through the light haze of a fine autumn night. Floodlights are famous at Oxford since, in their days as Headington United, they were the first professional club to install them at their ground. They were mounted in twos on 18 wooden poles, and believed to have come from various Oxford buildings whose facades were lit up at night.

The first floodlit match at the Manor Ground was a charity match between Headington and a local team called Banbury Spencer on 18 December 1950 to raise money for local hospitals. The experiment almost ended in disaster when rain caused some of the lights to blow out. But the rain stopped and that first use of lights opened up the whole question of staging floodlit matches, bringing forward the day when such games were officially sanctioned.

It took time, though. When Headington drew against Millwall in the FA Cup at the Den in 1954, Oxford asked the FA if the replay could be under floodlights. The answer was no, but the request attracted national press coverage and legendary Liverpool manager Bill Shankly joined the debate. 'Good luck to little Headington for having the pluck to ask a very, very important question and arouse interest which could be a portent for the future,' said Shanks.

Headington were formed in 1893 by a doctor and a vicar at the Britannia Inn, which still exists opposite the Manor Ground's London Road entrance. United was added three years later. But they didn't turn professional until 1949. In 1960 the name was changed to Oxford United (the same as a previous club who played in the early years of the twentieth century) and won the Southern League in 1961 and 1962. They were elected to the Fourth Division in place of the once great Accrington Stanley, who resigned in March 1962. They lost their first League game 3–2 away to Barrow but more than avenged that defeat two years later, when they recorded their record win by thrashing them 7–0.

That December win was followed by an impressive FA Cup run in which Oxford became the first Fourth Division side to reach the sixth round. A record crowd of almost 23,000 crammed into the Manor Ground and its temporary stands to watch the Cup-tie against Preston in the February. Under manager Arthur Tanner and led by captain Ron Atkinson, later more famous as a manager and pundit, Oxford were promoted to the Second Division for the first time in 1968. Another Atkinson, Graham, was well on the way to becoming the club's all-time leading goalscorer during this period and eventually tallied 77 goals between 1962 and 1977.

Oxford's troubles began when they were relegated in 1976. Five years later the club was saved from bankruptcy when millionaire publisher Robert Maxwell took control. He made good use of the Manor Ground as a landing pad for his helicopter! But in the spring of 1983 he announced that Oxford and Reading were to be merged into one club to be known as the Thames Valley Royals and that they'd play midway between the respective grounds, in Didcot. The news sparked protest marches in Oxford and sit-ins at the Manor Ground, as well as fierce resistance from Reading, and resulted in a boardroom coup. Fortunately, both clubs retained their identities in the end.

After Jim Smith took over as manager from Ian Greaves in 1992, the U's fortunes began to take a turn for the better on the pitch as well. During the

1983–84 season they pushed for promotion and enjoyed two long runs in the domestic cup competitions. In the Milk Cup they beat Bristol City, Newcastle, Leeds and, after two replays, Manchester United – before losing a fifth-round replay away at Everton. Oxford shrewdly increased ticket prices round-by-round and smashed their gate receipts record at five successive home ties. They also reached the FA Cup fifth round.

When all the cup excitement was over, Smith got his players back to the business of winning promotion as Third Division champions. The following season they won the Second Division title to reach the dizzy heights of the First Division for the first time. Oxford won the League Cup in 1986 with a 3–0 victory over Queens Park Rangers, but that was also the year they suffered their worst defeat when they lost 6–0 to Liverpool. Two years later they slipped back to the Second Division.

Meanwhile, Smith's fame had taken a while to spread in sleepy Oxford. Jim Smith explained: 'It took me weeks to convince the man on the gate that I was the manager. He always gave me the third degree before they let me in,' complained the U's boss. Smith is the only manager to have taken teams to every ground in the Premier and Football League.

Oxford have spawned a host of talent in recent years, including Republic of Ireland international John Aldridge, their highest League scorer with 30 goals in the Second Division campaign of 1984–85, and Welsh star Dean Saunders, who they sold to Derby in 1988 for £1.2 million – the most Oxford have ever received for a player. Aldridge's Republic of Ireland team-mate Ray Houghton was also an Oxford player at one time.

Oxford were relegated to the Second Division in 1994 and at the time of my visit for the game against Blackpool were joint second. Tonight's visitors would provide a severe test of the U's 16-game unbeaten home record, for Oxford were missing several key players including former Sunderland and Celtic defender Anton Rogan and captain Mike Ford, better known as Fordy to team-mates and supporters alike.

But Oxford manager Denis Smith was optimistic. 'We've still got [Paul] Moody and [John] Byrne, who will terrorise most defences in this League, and, remember, we've got a very, very good home record in the League this season. Blackpool will be well aware of that,' he said before the match.

I'd arrived outside Oxford's small (less than four acres) Manor Ground just in time for the kick-off. The main gate was on London Road, opposite the Britannia pub, and this led along a private road to a small office building behind the London Road End. However, to reach the back of the Main Stand I had to make my way quickly along a quiet, suburban street called Beech Road. The turnstiles were only a short distance from the front of some very nice houses. I imagined the residents weren't exactly overjoyed to be living so close to the ground. Not that there was trouble at Oxford.

The area on which the Manor Ground stood was used as a recreation ground by several amateur village clubs as well as for grazing horses and sheep during the week. Headington used the ground intermittently before and after the First World War until their final move there in 1925, after it had been laid out by the Headington Sports Ground Company for football, bowls, cricket and tennis.

The present ground developed after the Second World War by which time

Headington was no longer a village but an Oxford suburb. The formation of a supporters club in 1946 was the catalyst for the development of the ground, because the fans raised £250,000 towards ground improvements over the years. The first stand went up in 1946 and terracing was laid two years later.

United became the sole tenants in 1949 after the cricket club moved out because the pitch became too enclosed. They applied to develop the ground but were given only temporary permission lasting ten years. Still, professionalism brought rapid development and the club spent £4,000 on new stands, terracing and dressing-rooms as they raised the capacity to 12,000 by 1950. Four years later the council agreed that the ground could be developed permanently despite opposition from local residents.

Five years later United bought the site for £10,000 with money raised by the supporters club and the club continued to build new stands and other facilities before joining the League in 1962. My seat was in a small 145-seater stand in the left-hand corner of the Beech Road side, which had been built as part of a £4,000 upgrading of the stadium as long ago as 1949. The Manor Club, for members only, was underneath the stand; its bar and televisions offered comfort for some fans before, during and after a match. Next to this small stand was another one – seating just over 100 people, mainly guests, club staff and junior players – on the corner of the Cuckoo Lane End.

To get into the ground at this end, supporters had to walk along the narrow Cuckoo Lane behind the terrace alongside playing fields and the John Radcliffe Hospital. The Cuckoo Lane End was a strange uncovered terrace shaped like a wedge of cheese. It had been built between 1962 and 1965 after Oxford entered the Football League. The terrace rose to a peak at the Osler Road corner and was quite colourful with its yellow barriers. There was a high but narrow box at the back for the announcer. The visiting Blackpool fans were perched on the Cuckoo Lane End terrace, enclosed by a fence along the front and with closed circuit cameras watching their every move.

The Main Stand had cost the grand total of just under £30,000 when it was built in the mid-'50s and paid for by the supporters club. It was unremarkable and only stretched along 50 yards of the pitch, but at least its yellow walls trimmed in blue added a splash of colour. There was a seated family section on half of the stand.

The opposite Osler Road side had two small stands, seating less than 500 each, which were put up as part of a £1 million refit inspired by Oxford's successive promotions in 1984 and 1985, when the late Robert Maxwell was providing the funds. The other half of that side of the ground had also been upgraded in 1985. There was a bowls club behind the stand which had originally been part of the Manor Sports Ground in 1925.

The Manor Ground pitch is notorious for its slope, which is seven feet from the Cuckoo Lane/Osler Road corner to the opposite corner and four feet from Osler Road to Beech Road. The pitch sits on natural sand, which is why it drains well, and Oxford have learned to live with the slope. After going a goal behind in the first few minutes against Blackpool, they began to take control of the match. Centre-back Matt Elliott equalised and then John Byrne popped up to knock in a second from a fine left-wing cross by Alex Dyer. Byrne was well known for the goals he scored in Sunderland's 1992 Cup run, which ended in a 2–0 defeat by Liverpool in the final.

The Oxford fans greeted Byrne's strike with the refrain from Gary Glitter's 'Leader of the Gang' – you know the bit that goes: 'Come on, come on, come on, come on, come on, come on, come on . . . Oxford'. But their joy was short-lived when Blackpool equalised in controversial circumstances through Andy Watson. The linesman flagged for what the crowd thought was offside and the referee made a hasty backwards retreat towards the halfway line pursued by Blackpool players. He then signalled a goal to the disbelief of the Oxford team and the home supporters. The crowd roared their disapproval but, after consulting his linesman, the goal was allowed to stand. Cue mega abuse from the Oxford faithful at the London Road End.

After the usual expletives had failed to reverse the decision (as if they would), the die-hards began to seek divine intervention by chanting, 'You'll never go to heaven, you'll never go to heaven'. At least it was original. At one point even the executive supporters in the Manor Club, situated in the south-east corner of the ground, and those in the main Osler Road stand joined in by clapping along with the London Road End after they'd teased them into a demonstration with: 'If you think the referee's a wanker clap your hands'. Such passion from an Oxford crowd. Whatever next?

But the referee was to earn a reprieve when Oxford scored the winner in the dying minutes. An inspired substitution by manager Denis Smith saw number 12 David Rush steal in behind the Blackpool defence to send the U's fans home happy. At the Cuckoo Lane End the Tangerine army couldn't believe it. Seconds from a useful away point and it was gone. They had a long trip back to the North with nothing to show for their committed support except the memories of a very exciting and entertaining match. It was the best game I'd seen outside the Premier League – so far.

In the executive lounge the Manor Club members were queuing at the bar for their post-match refreshments. They were also watching the second round UEFA Cup match between Aston Villa and Trabsonspor of Turkey. Their interest wasn't only based on the fact that Villa were an English side competing in Europe. There were also two former Oxford stars on show: Ray Houghton and Dean Saunders. And of course Villa boss Big Ron was fondly remembered at the Manor Ground. The big cheer that went up in the Manor Club bar when Villa snatched a goal through Atkinson (Dalien not Ron) to level the aggregate score after 70 minutes testified to the links between the two clubs.

I'd arranged for a cab to pick me outside the ground and take me to the station after the match so that I could catch the 10.04 train to Paddington. The driver was late, caught up in a traffic jam along the main road, but by coincidence the cab I hailed as I walked in desperation towards the bus stop was the one I'd booked. 'Here, take a look at the match,' said the driver as he handed me a portable TV plugged into the cab's lighter so that I could watch the end of the Villa game.

Sadly, with just a few minutes to go, Trabsonspor drew level on the night for a 2–1 aggregate lead. Villa pulled one back shortly afterwards through Atkinson to bring the score level on aggregate, but it was too late to save the game with the Turkish side's away goal counting double. The following morning I discovered that Newcastle, the other English team in the UEFA Cup, had also gone out on the away-goals rule to Athletic Bilbao after a 1–0 defeat in Spain following

United's 1–0 win at St James's Park. It was a bad night for English football on the European stage.

With Villa's match over I asked the cabbie whether Oxford was his team. It was. He didn't go to games very often because 'money is tight' and he had to work most evenings. In the Stadium Update column in the programme Oxford managing director Keith Cox said the club could be in a new ground by August 1996. Was that likely? The cabbie said it was something the club had talked about for years but, so far, that was all it amounted to: talk.

In 1984 the council had proposed that the club build a new 15,000 all-seater stadium on Watlington Road between the Blackbird Leys estate and Rose Hill on the outskirts of town. Oxford pursued other sites but in 1988, with Kevin Maxwell now the chairman after his dad had left to take over Derby, they considered moving to Watlington Road after all. South Oxfordshire District Council rejected the proposal.

After Robert Maxwell died at sea, United were taken over by a local company called Biomass Recycling and they pledged to create an environmentally friendly stadium. At the time of my visit there were rumours that Oxford might move to another site on Sandy Lane between Blackbird Leys and the ring road, but neither of the cab drivers thought it was a good idea. 'The lads in those two neighbourhoods don't get along too well. It would be asking for trouble,' said the driver who'd taken me to the ground. I'd never thought of Oxford as a divided city. Tesco, who owned a nearby superstore, objected about road access to the site and Oxford had to look for new pastures.

Three months after the U's were relegated in 1994 the council put forward a plan for a new ground at Minchery Farm on the south-west border of Blackbird Leys. After my visit on 7 June 1995 there was a breakthrough. In the words of Simon Inglis in *The Football Grounds of Great Britain*: 'After some 30 different sites considered since 1949 and a dozen different planning applications, Oxford City Council finally resolved to grant permission for a new stadium for Oxford United.'

Minchery Farm was not an ideal location, however: 'Access to the site could only be provided if the council paid for a link road. The adjacent Minchery farmhouse was a listed building. Part of the land, a former sewage works, was contaminated. There was a possibility of archaeological artefacts on the site. Even worse, two footpaths were in the way.'

But in its favour, the site was adjacent to a prestigious new university science park, with the possibility of a rail halt nearby. Best of all, the stadium could act as a catalyst for leisure and employment opportunities, tying in with new housing in the area, which is partly why the council eventually agreed to build the vital link road out of public funds.

In February 1996 United signed a £15.3 million contract with builders Taylor Woodrow for a 15,000-seat stadium with three two-tier stands and a single-tier stand along the North side. The corners could be filled in at a later date to take the capacity up to 20,000. There are plans for a fast-food outlet, a conference suite in the Main Stand and an astroturf pitch for local use. Unfortunately, at the time of writing Oxford have run out of money because Taylor Woodrow are ahead of schedule and work has been virtually at a standstill since the beginning of 1997.

The club's directors have been trying to raise £6 million to cover the work already completed and Taylor Woodrow have threatened to pull out of the project unless United can guarantee a future payments schedule. Enter Italian football club Juventus of Turin and Italian clothing company Benetton. They have been considering a cash injection, Juventus looking to use Oxford as a training centre to develop young players. When the new stadium finally opens, it will be the club's seventh ground and the first away from Headington, where it all began. Seventh heaven, perhaps.

THE BRADY BUNCH

Brighton v Bournemouth – The Goldstone Ground, 2 November 1994

You may not believe this but the Goldstone Ground, originally called Goldstone Bottom, takes its name from a stone supposed to have been placed by Druids on the site which is now occupied by the pitch. A local farmer got fed up with archaeologists coming to see the stone and in 1834 had it buried. In 1900 the stone was dug up and put in Hove Park across the road from the ground. It was a pity the legend far outshone the football served up on a cold Wednesday night.

It was one of the worst games I'd endured so far: a 0–0 draw. Even the substitute of one veteran, 38-year-old Frank Stapleton, for another, Steve Foster, failed to light the sparks that were barely flickering on the pitch in the run-up to Guy Fawkes night. Former Arsenal and Manchester United star Stapleton was, however, by far the best player on view and his contribution grew during the match. He'd already done his homework on opponents Bournemouth by watching them play their previous match as a spy for Brighton manager and former Arsenal and Eire maestro Liam Brady.

The Hove in Brighton & Hove Albion is an independent borough of 90,000 people west of Brighton, where the seafront begins along a seven-mile stretch beyond Rottingdean in the east. Brighton, mentioned in the Domesday Book as Brighthelmston or Brithelmeston after a mythical Bishop of Selsey, is the largest town and most famous resort in southern England and is nicknamed 'London by the Sea'. At the centre of town is the Old Steine, believed to be named after the stone on which fishermen used to dry their nets. It's an open area with gardens dominated by the Royal Pavilion – the palace built by George IV for himself.

Brighton first became a prosperous town in the mid-1700s, when its air and sea-bathing was recommended by doctors. And it grew rapidly after the decadent Prince Regent began visiting the town in the 1770s with his mistress, giving it notoriety as a destination for the typical 'dirty weekend'. The *Rough Guide* calls it 'Brighton's major contribution to the English collective consciousness.'

His Pavilion, a mixture of Indian, Chinese and Gothic architecture, is the most famous building in Brighton. The minarets and balconies are oriental in the loosest sense, but it looks like it came straight out of Bombay or New Delhi. 'That's some Indian restaurant,' said a pal of mine once on passing the building in a mini-bus full of footballers on a stag weekend in Brighton.

Today Brighton tries to play down its reputation as the town to come to for a dirty weekend and prefers to focus on its Georgian charm, shopping, and thriving conferences. It's a fascinating town, partly owing to the mix of people from tourists through to the students who fill its many language schools, the art college and its two universities.

I'd arrived in Brighton on a train from London after work. The weather was cold, so I was glad the station was only a short walk to the ground. I went into the main entrance and found a copy of a painting of the 1961 FA Cup final between Tottenham and Burnley on the wall. It was not the first time I would cast eyes on the scene. Many clubs have a copy. On the floor was a blue and white mat decorated with Brighton's club crest – a seagull. I rang the bell on the front desk and was taken to the Seagull Lounge for a cup of tea.

The match officials had already arrived. They were chatting over a cup of coffee and, strangely, the conversation had turned to football. Referee Mike Pierce was making his first appearance of the season at the Goldstone Ground. It was his fifth season as a League referee after moving up through the Hampshire League, the Football Combination and the Football League. Outside football he enjoyed cricket and most other sports. He also worked as an electrician during the day.

Pierce and his linesmen, plus back-up referee, were pondering the new FIFA regulations requiring players to be cautioned immediately for a serious infringement. The balance of opinion seemed to favour the new interpretation of the law, though there was concern that some of the other changes, such as players not being given offside when running back from an attacking position, had made their job more difficult.

Pierce usually refereed two games a week. He mostly handled games in the south. The farthest he'd travelled was to Wolverhampton from Portsmouth to take charge of a game at Molineux. 'A wonderful stadium and a fine venue for football.' The financial rewards were improving. Pierce could claim £102 mileage for tonight's game and was paid £82.50 for refereeing the match. A Premier League referee gets £300 a match. Not bad for doing something you enjoy.

I asked if a referee had to put in much training. 'If you've got two games a week, you don't really need to train. But in the summer I go running every other morning. You have to pass a fitness test at the beginning of the season. If you fail they give you two weeks to get into better shape and allow you to take the test again. If you don't pass that, they kick you out. So 20-odd years of refereeing could be out of the window just like that.'

The physical demands of the job are quite high, hence the fitness test. 'The League give you a stamina test involving sets of sprints between two cones twenty metres apart. The sprints increase in speed as the test progresses. You have to get to level ten point five, which is five shuttles at level ten, to pass. We do one other physical test. You have three cones, ten metres apart and do sixty-metre shuttle sprints with thirty seconds in between. We do six of them within a set time.'

The League also check the officials to make sure they're fit and healthy enough to do the job by testing their haemoglobin, heart, cholesterol, weight, blood sugar and blood pressure. 'It's a good thing for referees to be seen to be in shape. At least you know you're in reasonable condition,' said Pierce.

He welcomed the FIFA rule changes but said it would be hard to improve on the dedication and professionalism of English referees. The back-up referee agreed. 'You take Italy where they have professional referees. I don't think the standard is any higher than it is here. They make mistakes too.'

Did Pierce resent any abuse shouted at him when he'd made a decision the crowd didn't like? 'They pay their money and they can say what they like, within reason,' he said. Was he always aware of the fans barracking him during a match? 'You tend to hear it if there aren't many in the ground. If there's quite a few then it's just a mass of noise. But you know when you've made a mistake or something's wrong. You'll soon be told. But you try not to take any notice of it. If you took notice of everybody, you just wouldn't get on with the job.'

The only downside to the FIFA changes seemed to be the lowering of the retirement age. They're now looking at an upper limit of 40 to 45 and the aim is to bring it down to 40, which would exclude a number of top class referees. 'You take George Courtney,' said the back-up ref. 'He's probably one of the best referees the country has ever had, but he can't do the job any more under the new regulations and that's a loss to the game.' The silver lining is that younger referees are finding their way onto the League list much sooner than they would have done. 'This will speed everybody up. At 32 or 33 a referee from the amateur game could be on the League line.'

Talk then turned to the sacking of Spurs boss Ossie Ardiles, announced the previous day. There was sympathy all round for a nice guy who, like a bad lawyer, just couldn't sort out his defence. 'I suppose he had to go,' said one of the linesmen. 'Inevitable really.' At which point he himself had to go, to prepare for his night's work.

The Seagull Lounge was starting to fill up as the kick-off approached. Former Crystal Palace goalkeeper John Jackson, now Brighton's goalkeeping trainer, appeared at the tea and coffee bar. It was run by two of the sweetest old girls you could wish to meet. They told me they didn't get to see much of the match when Brighton played at home (and I doubted they travelled to away games at their age); but they did run outside the lounge whenever Brighton scored, to find out who was the goalscorer and to soak up the atmosphere. They could save their breath tonight.

The tea ladies went to Wembley in May 1983 for Brighton's only FA Cup final appearance, against Manchester United. 'We had a lovely day then,' said the one who'd been at the club since 1977.

'And Smith must score . . .' I reminded them of the BBC commentary when Gordon Smith had the chance to win the Cup for Brighton in the dying minutes. He missed and, after battling to a 2–2 draw in the first game – a feat which had manager Jimmy Melia dancing a soft-shoe shuffle in celebration – the Seagulls were outclassed 4–0 in the replay. Even Ray Wilkins scored when he deceived the entire Brighton team by curling the ball into the top corner instead of playing his customary square pass to Bryan Robson. You couldn't blame the defence. Who'd have expected 'the crab' to shoot?

In the boardroom, once graced by the presence of comedian Norman Wisdom when he was a director, stood the trophy cabinet. There was a faded programme from that great day at Wembley in 1983, but no trophy. 'The players got medals, of course, but I don't think the club received anything to mark the occasion,' said the official who gave me a lightning tour before the sponsors arrived for tea and sandwiches. He must have been wrong. On a later visit to Tottenham I saw a Football Association pennant marking the occasion of Spurs' 3–2 defeat against Coventry in the 1987 Cup final. Brighton must have had one somewhere.

There was also no sign of any silverware to mark Brighton's Third Division (South) title in 1958, the Fourth Division Championship of 1965 or the Charity Shield win over Aston Villa in 1910. There was, however, a plate on the wall presented to Brighton by Arsenal to mark the Seagulls' first League match in the old Division One in 1979. The Gunners won 4–0. There was also a clock engraved with the Arsenal crest to mark their meeting in the FA Cup in the '80s. The Gunners won 2–1.

I left the boardroom with its trophies, long wooden table and bar to look around the rest of the ground. The changing-rooms were empty but the players' kit was neatly folded ready for the team to get ready for the task ahead. On top of each kit was a match programme and a packet of Wrigley's chewing gum. 'Liam doesn't let anybody near the dressing-rooms on a match day,' said the club official. I was privileged.

Brady, the mercurial genius loved by Arsenal fans in the '70s, guided the Gunners to FA Cup success in a thrilling final against Manchester United. They won 3–2 after a stirring United comeback from 2–0 down. The Reds were beaten in the dying moments by an Alan Sunderland goal fashioned by 'Chippy', as he was known to Gunners fans. The Irishman had joined the south-coast club after a dismal spell as manager of Celtic which had ended in the sack. Happier years had come as a player in Italy at Juventus, Sampdoria, Inter Milan and Ascoli before he returned home to join West Ham.

The tradition of colourful managers at the Goldstone Ground had been upheld by the likes of George Curtis, Alan Mullery, Brian Clough, Mike Bailey and Jimmy Melia. So what did Brady bring to the job? 'The first task was to get a bit of confidence back,' said Brady. 'We worked on getting the players to play in an entertaining way. That got everybody's enthusiasm going again.' Trying to instil a flair for entertaining football was just one part of Brady's job. The other was to operate on a tight budget. 'We have got money for wages, but not for transfer fees,' he said. His main close-season signings were two free transfers from Tottenham, Jeff Minton and Junior McDougal.

The official then took me out onto the pitch. Along with Doncaster Rovers' Belle Vue it was probably one of the most run-down stadiums I'd see all season. It was no surprise to hear at the end of the season that the club planned to leave and temporarily share Portsmouth's Fratton Park ground, 50 miles along the south coast, from the start of the 1996–97 season. The club hoped to build a new 30,000 all-seater multi-purpose stadium.

The problem with ground-sharing was the distance Seagulls' fans would have to travel to watch home games. 'It will be the end of Brighton as we know it. Who is going to travel to Portsmouth on a wet Tuesday to watch them play someone like Crewe?' said one fan. The supporters were also sceptical that the club could ever afford a new stadium. Brighton planned to sell the Goldstone Ground to pay off debts 'which they cannot contain'.

I took my seat in the Main Stand next to Preston manager John Beck. He was under pressure at Deepdale after a bad start to the season. I wondered which player he was checking on tonight. Opposite was the open East Side of the ground. I was surprised to see rows of houses overlooking the pitch behind the terraces. They should have sold season tickets to the residents! The terracing began to drop away towards the South Stand on my right so that there were only a few steps by the corner flag.

Brady's Brighton team had a blend of youth and experience. Players with potential like Junior McDougal and Kurt Nogan, nurtured along by elder statesmen such as 40-year-old player–coach Jimmy Case, the former Liverpool, Southampton and Bournemouth midfielder. Case, the oldest outfield player in England, had just had a testimonial against Liverpool. His Albion XI included Matt Le Tissier.

Case started out at his home-town club, Liverpool, 21 seasons and almost 800 matches ago. His experience had helped Brady, for he was a 'real presence on the field'. He was sceptical about players who retired early, saying they wanted to get out at the top:

> That's a load of nonsense. They say they would not enjoy playing at a lower level. But, for me, that's where your enthusiasm for the game comes in. I played at Sittingbourne. Not for money – there's not much around at the lower levels – but because I just love the game.
>
> When I started at Liverpool, the older pro was Tommy Smith. I would learn off him. If all the older pros packed in at 30, at the top, who's going to learn anything? If you have a team full of 22-year-olds there are certain parts of the game that they have no knowledge about, like concentrating at the end. The older pro is there to protect the younger ones.

So how long could Case continue to defy Father Time?

> There is nothing in my head saying this week, or this season, I will stop. I know I can't go on forever. [Brady] will be looking to replace me, if he gets a person who's better than me. That's always been the case. At Southampton Chris Nicholl used to buy a midfield player every year, but I was still there at the end of the season, still playing up to 37. If I was playing for Wimbledon, I wouldn't be playing now. Not because I wouldn't enjoy it, but because there would be too much running. I can't keep up but I have other attributes.

So does Case do anything special to keep in shape?

> Not really. I didn't look after myself that much in my younger days. But when you are younger and fitter you can cope better with the knocks, whether from football or life. But when you get a little bit older, and get a bit more responsibility, you think, 'If I don't settle down here, I'll end up on the moon.'
>
> I used to drink a fair bit. But then a few years ago at Southampton I just said I'd pack all that in. Not necessarily to extend my career, it was just

getting in the way with certain things, whether it be home life or whatever. No real big incident, I'd just had enough. Everyone should take stock at some point. I didn't have any alcohol for two and a half years. Now I just have a shandy. In the past, the drinking would start straight after games. At no other times, just then.

We believe you, Jim!

WALKER'S MILLIONS

Blackburn Rovers v Tottenham Hotspur – Ewood Park, 5 November 1994

'He wasn't anything special at school,' said Jack Aspin referring to his school chum and namesake Jack Walker. But he was certainly something special now. 'Nobody would have dreamed he'd take over Blackburn. But football is about money and Jack Walker has it,' said Aspin after another Rovers victory on their way to the Premier League title – their first major trophy since their FA Cup win back in 1928. 'Every team would like a fairy godmother. We've got one,' beamed Aspin.

Jack Walker, owner of Blackburn Rovers Football Club, was the richest man in British sport. A survey by *Business Age* magazine estimated his personal wealth at £345 million. Some estimates put the figure nearer £400 million – and said even that might be conservative. However, unlike most of his fellows among the very rich, Walker's wealth is diminishing – and Blackburn is the main reason why.

Walker had spent more than £50 million to ensure Rovers would win the Premier League title. Jack Aspin, who attended the same school as Walker between 1941 and 1944, told me he'd put £50 million into a trust for the club so that they'd never have to worry about money again. 'He looks upon it as his participation in Blackburn Rovers and in the town,' said Blackburn chairman Dick Coar.

Combined with his other hobby, Jersey European Airways, the fairy godmother had invested £100 million in two of the biggest financial black holes known to man – a football club and an airline. Blackburn alone made trading losses of £14.5 million over the previous two years. But Walker clearly wasn't in it for the money. As Martin Luther King might have put it: He had a dream.

His dream was built on the millions he'd acquired from selling the family steel business. His father started out with a sheet metal business, while Jack began with a couple of textile mills acquired with government grants. In 1989 British Steel bought the business for £330 million but, according to Aspin, Walker still owned the largest steel stock warehouse in Europe, which he rented out to British Steel for £100,000 a week.

That brought in £5 million a year, or one Chris Sutton. But Aspin reckoned

Walker's interest earnings had paid for his investment in Blackburn Rovers. Walker lived in Jersey, but he flew in for every match. His exile meant he could come into England for only 90 days a year, but the days he flew in and out to watch Rovers didn't count. It was a good job he owned the airline – he was saving a fortune in plane fares!

When Howard Kendall was manager of a cash-strapped Rovers in 1979–81, he was asked to economise by not using too much milk in the players' half-time tea and to send his mail second class. Ewood Park's old brickwork and turnstiles were the backdrop for a Hovis ad depicting the timeless traditions of northern England. But all that had changed now. The club even had a fanzine called *Loadsamoney* now that Jack was picking up the tab for multi-million-pound players and a refurbished stadium.

'Jack Walker's commitment is total,' said Dick Coar. 'Without his backing Blackburn's recent rise to prominence would not have been possible.' Paul Warhurst, Tim Flowers, David Batty, Graeme Le Saux and Chris Sutton had cost Walker £12.3 million. Manager Kenny Dalglish had been given a total of £27 million to play with. The wage bill in 1993 was £5.3 million and growing. The SAS (Shearer and Sutton) were each rumoured to be earning £15,000 a week.

When Liverpool won the title in the first season after the Second World War their team cost just £21,000, worth £420,000 today. Arsenal's League and Cup double-winning team in 1971 cost £165,000. And Manchester United's 1994 double-winners cost £15 million. Blackburn were the most expensive team ever to challenge for the title.

'My aim now is for Rovers to be not only the most successful club in the country but also in Europe,' said Walker. 'And there is no reason why we cannot achieve that. It may not happen overnight, but I would like to think it will happen sooner rather than later.' Baroness Margaret Thatcher of Kesteven, the club's honorary vice-president, no doubt firmly supported the ambitions of the entrepreneurial Walker.

Rovers had waited a long time for success. That 1928 FA Cup victory was a dim and distant memory, remembered by few. The match programme had a feature on the 'Tireless Kingpin' of that Cup-winning team, Harry Healless. He was the only Blackburn captain ever to lift the FA Cup at Wembley and for that alone was worthy of a place in Ewood Park's Hall of Fame. He was the only Blackburnian in the side.

When Rovers reached the Cup final again in 1960, Healless was one of the eight survivors of the 1928 team to go back to Wembley as official guests. Sadly, he didn't see the blue and whites lift the cup that day and died, aged 78, some 12 years later. Being a proud Blackburnian, Harry Healless would have been delighted to share his achievement with another Ewood captain.

The FA Cup had been the almost exclusive property of Blackburn Rovers in the late 1800s. They won the Cup in three successive years, 1884–86, and again in 1890 and 1891. Rovers were awarded a special shield to commemorate their hat-trick of FA Cup victories. It was displayed in the Ewood Park boardroom for those lucky enough to get a glimpse behind the scenes.

It was thirty-seven years after that 1891 triumph that Healless lifted the Cup at Wembley. And that was the last major trophy to find its way to the Ewood Park boardroom, if you exclude the Full Members' Cup in 1987. Jack Walker had waited a long time for success at the club he'd supported since he was a boy.

Rovers were original members of the Football League in 1888 and won the Championship in 1912 and 1914. In between, around the turn of the century, the club's namesake Fred Blackburn, who was born near the town, made 204 League and Cup appearances as a winger. His brother Arthur also had a spell with Rovers.

The club stayed in the First Division until 1936 and then spent most of their time in the Second Division. Their fortunes slumped to a new low in 1971 when they were relegated to the Third Division for the first time. The return to the big time started in 1980, when they regained their Second Division place.

Two of Rovers' most capped players since the Second World War – England winger Bryan Douglas and half-back Ronnie Clayton – were guests of the club today and were treated to a tour of the transformed Ewood Park. Douglas had appeared in 36 internationals and Clayton was just one cap behind. However, his 580 League appearances between 1950 and 1969 were still a club record.

The ground they saw had changed beyond recognition from the one they played in during the '50s and '60s. There were two new all-seater stands at the Blackburn and Darwen Ends, each holding 8,000, and the new Jack Walker Stand on Bolton Road, which had replaced the old Nuttal Street Stand. The only side not renewed was the Riverside Stand, now called the Walker Steel Stand after the company that Jack built. Its original name came from the narrow River Darwen, which runs behind the stand.

When Walker arrived, Ewood Park (which, like much of industrial Lancashire, was built in the late-Victorian period) had been desperately in need of modernisation. The main Nuttal Street Stand was built in 1906 for £24,000, a huge sum at the time, and opened on New Year's Day the following year against Preston. The double-decker Riverside Stand was built between the two League Championship years of 1912 and 1914.

The archetypal northern setting of Ewood Park, complete with cobbled streets, terraced houses, tramlines, mill and old-fashioned turnstiles, made it the ideal setting for Hovis ads in the '80s. Today the glass-fronted Main Stand would be more at home in an ad for Microsoft computers. Blackburn, with a population of just over 100,000 people, still looks like a mill town. But its football club is no longer in a backwater, struggling to keep up with its rivals to the south in Liverpool and Manchester.

Blackburn was once the greatest cotton-weaving centre in the world but, despite the mill buildings and chimneys, particularly by the Leeds and Liverpool canal, it now depends more on engineering than textiles. One of the fanzines, *4,000 Holes*, takes its title from the Beatles' song 'A Day in the Life', which includes the line '4,000 holes in Blackburn, Lancashire' in reference to the coal mines in the area. But it was Rovers, rather than the town's historic industrial might, that now put the place on the map.

'People forget how far we've come in the three years since Kenny Dalglish took over,' said the club's chairman, Dick Coar. 'In that time we have virtually trebled our average gate from 8,000 to the low twenty thousands.' The match programme confirmed the transformation. Ten years before, Rovers beat Brighton at Ewood in a Second Division encounter before a crowd of just 7,341. But 20 years ago nearly 14,000 turned up to see Rovers against Crystal Palace in a Third Division game. The progress was relative.

Incidentally, 40 years ago to within one day of the match against Spurs was a game for all Blackburn fans to remember and one which went down in history. It brought a record-breaking 9–0 victory over Middlesbrough. Eddie Quigley and Frank Mooney got hat-tricks and there were two goals for Eddie Crossan and one for Bobby Langton.

There was no chance of a repeat score against Spurs today, but the London side, with former captain Steve Perryman in temporary charge after the sacking of Ossie Ardiles earlier in the week, were clearly vulnerable. I feared the worst as I took my seat in the Darwen End, next to the away supporters. The stand was named after a small town four miles from Blackburn which had its own League club in the 1890s.

The noise from the travelling Spurs fans to my left was incredible. The chanting was sustained throughout the match, even when they'd gone 2–0 behind after goals from Jason Wilcox and an Alan Shearer penalty. They were hopeless optimists. Still, I suppose when you've driven from London to Blackburn, as I'd done earlier that morning, you've got to make it worthwhile even if your team is losing.

Basically, Spurs' new five-man defence performed as ineptly as the four-man defence, which superseded their three-man defence! Before the end of the season they'd probably have an 11-man defence and still concede goals!

The Blackburn fan next to me worked at the local Mercedes dealership. He told me that Kenny Dalglish and Alan Shearer had stopped by recently: Dalglish to pick up his dark blue 200 series Mercedes, registration number K7 KMD (the M is for his unusual middle name – though I still don't know what it is) and Shearer to purchase a dark purple 190 series Merc, registration number A9 ALS, for his missus. England's centre-forward drove a Rover himself – it was gratis, which explained the choice.

The Tottenham players had left their expensive cars back in London and had travelled up by coach. But Sol Campbell, the young Spurs and England Under-21 international defender, said he wished he'd driven to Blackburn. He told me he wasn't looking forward to the long journey home as I accompanied him through the main gates at Ewood Park towards the car park. Hands in pockets, head bowed, he was clearly bitterly disappointed at the way Tottenham were playing. 'I don't know what's going on,' he said dejectedly. 'We've just got to keep plugging away I suppose.'

After the match I browsed through my *Loadsamoney* fanzine as I waited for the Blackburn players to emerge from the main entrance. Under a feature called 'Back to Basics' the fanzine insisted it did not want to be accused of being ageist, sexist, racist or any other thing ending in 'ist' that's deemed to be derogatory to minority groups. It had therefore decided to rename various football teams:

> Sexism is the first issue to be addressed and the following changes will be effected as soon as possible: Motherwell becomes Parentwell, Queen of the South becomes Monarch of the South and Queens Park Rangers becomes Monarch Park Rangers. Mansfield Town becomes Personfield Town, and obviously Manchester City and United become Personchester City and United. Cowdenbeath become Bovine-quadruped-enbeath, whilst Peterborough will alternate with Petraborough on a strict rotation basis.
>
> Club nicknames will be alternatively sexed with Leicester City being

known as the Vixens, Derby becoming the Ewes, both changing week and week about, whilst Everton will be renamed the Toffeepeople. In order not to widen the north–south divide, Southampton and Northampton Town will in future be known as Hampton and Hampton Town, with Preston North End becoming Preston End. Middlesbrough will be called whatever you feel like at the time.

As we do not wish to offend vegetarians or people with special dietary needs, West Ham United become West Kosher United and Rotherham United will be known as Rotherlentil United. Religious bigotry will become a thing of the past as Falkirk rotate through a list featuring Falchapel, Falsynogogue, Faltemple and Falmission. Bishop's Stortford will similarly be Priest's Stortford or Gurus Stortford, dependent on where during the rota a particular game falls.

So as not to take sides in the anti-abortion debate, Bournemouth will be henceforth referred to as Conceivemouth. Finally, slang words for parts of the body will not be allowed to feature in club names. Arsenal will become Rectumnal, Bristol City and Rovers become Mammary City and Rovers, as it would be impolite to refer to the clubs as a nice pair of Bristols. And Scunthorpe United will be asked to resign from the League altogether!

Meanwhile, a large group of Rovers fans stood in the light rain, autograph books to hand, hoping some of Blackburn's stars would sign them or stop for photographs. The SAS appeared along with Flowers, the most expensive goalkeeper in the world. They were immediately surrounded by youngsters attracted like bees to honey.

The players signed and posed while their wives and girlfriends stood patiently by the smart four-wheel drives and executive cars their men drove around town. Trappings of the rich and famous.

One young fan approached Flowers. 'Could you sign this Chris?'

A bemused Flowers duly obliged. When the fan had left, he turned to the rest of us and said, 'He just said "thanks Chris." He thinks I'm Chris Sutton. Am I that ugly?'

I approached Sutton and told him what had happened. 'Tim said he wasn't too pleased about it,' I told him.

'I'm not too pleased about it either,' said Sutton.

As the supporters gradually drifted away and the rain continued to fall the women grew impatient. When the last photo had been snapped and the final autograph signed, Shearer, Sutton and Flowers were able to go home. Their women gave a look as if to say, 'at last', and they sped away into the night.

Most of the players had left by now, but a group of five young girls lingered around the exit from the ground.

'Who are you waiting for?' I enquired. 'Graeme,' they replied in reference to Rovers' England international full-back Graeme Le Saux. One of them had Le Saux's name on her blue and white halved Rovers shirt. Another had Shearer above the red number nine feared at Premier League grounds around the country.

After what seemed like an age the fresh-faced pin-up finally emerged from the splendour of Ewood Park. His fan club gathered around him as if he was a pop star.

'Graeme, Graeme could we take your picture?' they cried. Le Saux posed with his fans while I took a picture.

'Thanks Graeme,' said one.

'You were great today Graeme,' said another.

'You're a lucky man to have all these fans,' I said.

'Great,' said Le Saux, as if a mob of squeaky-voiced teenage girls was the last thing he needed.

Walker's school chum Jack Aspin had stood outside the main entrance to the new Ewood Park along with all the other fans hoping to get a glimpse of the most famous chairman in the Premier League. 'My daughter presented Walker with a picture of me and Jack playing snooker when we were young boys before a match in 1993,' said Aspin. 'And you know what Jack said? "Where have the years gone?"' It seems the King of Ewood Park has always enjoyed life. Blackburn Rovers have seen to that.

SAMBA COMES TO BOUNDARY PARK

Oldham Athletic v Tranmere Rovers – Boundary Park, 6 November 1994

On Sunday morning I slept in as late as possible. I was tired from the long journey to Blackburn and the beers I'd drunk the night before with the Leeds and Burnley fans at my hotel. I wandered down to breakfast just before 10 o'clock to enjoy a fry-up complete with black pudding. There was just me, a woman and her son. They'd been to a wedding nearby and were also suffering from the night's festivities.

The hotel was near Accrington and the woman told me she'd seen their last-ever match in the old Fourth Division in the 1950s. Her only other link to football was that her other son's girlfriend's sister had nursed Gary Lineker's son George, who was thankfully recovering from leukaemia. 'She [the nurse] was very discreet about it. She would never discuss the boy or talk about his problems.' I should think everyone in the country was concerned about the little lad's health when they heard of his illness. He has since recovered and the Lineker's have now added more children to their family.

It was a beautiful sunny morning. Just perfect for a drive through the countryside and an afternoon's football. I was headed for Boundary Park, the home of Oldham Athletic. Their success in the early 1980s, which culminated in the 1991 League Cup final (lost to Nottingham Forest) and the 1994 FA Cup semi-final (lost to Manchester United after a last-minute Mark Hughes goal secured the Reds a replay and eventual victory), had given way to relegation and the current struggle for promotion.

I didn't know it at the time, but Oldham manager Joe Royle, the longest-serving boss in the League after 12 years in charge at Boundary Park, would shortly be leaving to replace Mike Walker and try to turn things around at Everton, where he starred as a centre-forward in the 1970s.

Royle had taken Oldham as far as he could on limited resources. He needed a fresh challenge. Sorting out the mess at Goodison would require all his managerial skills, but Big Joe had already performed miracles at Boundary Park. Nothing was beyond him. Oldham, meanwhile, would have to battle on without their mentor. Royle was a hard act to follow.

I drove past an old mill, a reminder of the area's historic links to the cotton industry. The importance of King Cotton to the town is shown clearly by the fact that Oldham once boasted the largest number of spindles of any cotton town in the world. Nowadays there are only a few cotton mills still working, though there are lots of other textile mills. This was definitely the archetypal northern English mill town.

I parked in the club's huge car park behind the home supporters end. Oldham had plans to develop the car park into a rugby ground with the Main Stand backing onto the football stadium. The rugby and football clubs would share the same end stand, which would cater for about 12,000 football fans on one side and 8,000 rugby supporters on the other side.

I'd arranged to meet the club's public relations manager, Gordon Lawton, for a tour before the match. After wandering to various parts of the ground I eventually found him and he treated me to an extensive look behind the scenes. I was taken first into the directors' room, where one wall was covered with caricature drawings of the board of directors. This lot must have had a sense of humour. A glass case on one wall contained the silver spade used to cut the first piece of sod for the pitch in 1896.

I was taken through the dressing-rooms, noticing that the away facilities didn't include a bath. 'We try to make it as uncomfortable as possible,' joked Gordon. The Tranmere players' shirts were all in a line, hanging on pegs but, unlike most Premier League teams, they didn't carry the name of a sponsor or the players' squad numbers. John Aldridge's boots were laid out, but he played no part in the afternoon's proceedings owing to injury – much to Oldham's relief.

There were a couple of signed footballs in the Oldham dressing-room to be given away to two lucky television viewers in a competition on Granada. Some of the Oldham players were being treated in the physio's room. Sean McCarthy jumped off the physio's treatment table to replace Andy Ritchie in the starting line-up. Although McCarthy was receiving treatment, he felt fit enough to play and lasted the whole match. Joe Royle later explained why McCarthy played instead of a bitterly disappointed Ritchie, who was not even brought off the bench in the second half.

Next stop was the kit, or laundry, room, 'probably the busiest place in the club'. Gordon ran through the training kits and explained the significance of the different colours used by each team. 'Everybody has three kits, three training kits. Purple is for youth-team players, black is for the pros, blue is for the senior staff. 'Each kit was embossed with the player's club number, though Oldham had gone back to 1–11 on the pitch instead of the very confusing squad numbers used by most teams.

The executive boxes at Oldham may not be as big as those at Old Trafford, but Oldham pride themselves on their friendly service. 'We've had a lot of people in here who obviously, with being close, have gone to the Manchester Uniteds and the Liverpools. They've always said that our facilities may not be up to the size of those like, say, Leeds have got, but the actual service and the meal we give is better. We try to give that little bit more attention,' said the club official responsible for looking after the sponsors.

Among today's executive guests were a local bread manufacturer, and Invincible Double Glazing, one of the main match sponsors. They could look forward to a four-course meal with wine, a free bar before the match, at half-time and after the game, plus the chance to win a signed football or a bottle of champagne by guessing the attendance. The main sponsors were also allowed to pick their Man of the Match and could rub shoulders with the chosen one and a couple of his team-mates, who'd come up to see them after the game.

The boxes were a Portakabin-style construction, complete with speakers which piped in the crowd noise so that executive guests could soak up the big-match atmosphere in comfort. Unfortunately Oldham were now in the First Division after relegation at the end of the 1993–94 season, so there were few big matches for the crowd to get excited about. That, along with the development of Boundary Park into an all-seater stadium, had affected the atmosphere.

The club was so concerned about the subdued supporters that a Brazilian samba band had been invited along for today's match to stir them up with a Latin beat accompanied by whistles and drums. They certainly added an exotic touch to a brisk winter afternoon. The Oldham chairman was so enthusiastic he wanted to sign them up for every game.

'They did a trial run on Friday and the BBC filmed it and everything. The idea is to get the crowd going because it's gone so quiet,' explained Gordon. 'We thought there'd be five or six, maybe eight of them. But there's 52 of them. The manager's not very happy. The commercial manager had arranged it but when Joe Royle found out he wanted to cancel the whole thing.'

I ran into the band before the game as the musicians were taking up their positions. 'They don't sound very Brazilian,' I said after hearing their north-east accents. 'How much do they get paid?'

'They don't. They're doing it for nothing,' said Gordon. 'They're all Oldham fans.'

Granada were using 11 cameras to cover a match for the first time. Normally, they only used eight. There's one in each goal. One at the side of each goal. That's four. One at the side of the gantry, which is five. Two on the bottom gantry, seven. Two on the top, nine. One on the side, ten. And where's the eleventh? 'Oh, yes, the tunnel,' said Gordon. 'The referee's really going to get it today.'

We retraced our steps out through the main entrance and into the club shop. It was a busy little enterprise selling every article of merchandise you could imagine being associated with a football club, including a range of cosmetics called LATIQUE, after the club's nickname, the Latics from Athletic. There was also a lucrative travel business organising everything from trips to away games to fully-fledged holidays for supporters to places like Australia – a far cry from Oldham.

There was just time to meet Joe Royle in his office and grab a quick photograph with the big man before heading to the players' lounge for lunch. Royle is not quite as tall as me and he guessed correctly that I played centre-half. He was clearly pissed off by the presence of the Brazilian band, because he was still complaining about them under his breath as he left to get his players ready for the match.

I thanked Gordon for the tour and sat down in the players' lounge for lunch served in the best northern tradition: meat and potato pie, mushy peas and red cabbage washed down with strong tea. Former Manchester United star Lou Macari, the manager at Stoke, was Granada's match summariser. He sat talking to former Liverpool full-back Jim Beglin.

Norway's assistant manager and his wife were also having a drink in the players' lounge. They'd come to watch Gunnar Halle, Oldham's Norwegian full-back. He'd play an important role in the European Championships' qualifying tournament, which would lead to the 1996 finals in England. He told me that Ossie Ardiles had asked Spurs' Norwegian keeper Eric Thorsvedt how the national team organised their defence. Thorsvedt explained that in training Norway played twice as many attackers against their four defenders to put them under pressure. At his next training session Ardiles organised a practice match in the same way. The problem was he didn't ask how the Norwegians actually coached the defenders! At Tottenham, they seemed to train without the key ingredient: coaching. That explained a lot about Spurs' defensive problems. A few weeks later Ardiles was sacked.

The game itself was a bore-draw. One Latics fan offered £50 of his £800 half-time jackpot to the Oldham match-winner. The problem was, there wasn't one. 'He wouldn't have been in any danger if he had tendered the entire winnings of the National Lottery,' said *The Sun* the next day. Except for a brief spell at the beginning of the second half, when the home side laid siege to Tranmere keeper Eric Nixon's goal, the punter's money couldn't have been safer inside the Bank of England.

Royle was aware of the need for his team to get on the goal trail. 'We need a goal,' he said to reporters huddled together in a small ad-hoc press-box underneath the Main Stand. 'We have had four clean sheets in our last five games but have only scored once. We've got to start scoring again.' I wished they'd started against Tranmere!

GOODBYE VICARAGE ROAD

Watford v Southend United – Vicarage Road, 12 November 1994

Elton John's presence is everywhere at Watford. From the executive suite named after him, which hosts the match sponsors, through the photographs of the singer in action dotted around the walls, to the executive box he keeps so that local charities can enjoy a day out, the piano player extraordinaire looms large at Vicarage Road.

Elton's millions helped pay for the Sir Stanley Rous Stand and were one of the main factors behind Watford's dramatic rise from Fourth Division obscurity to runners-up spot in the old First Division and an appearance in the 1984 FA Cup final. 'He changed this club. Where would we be today without Elton,' said one of the smartly-dressed hostesses who look after the match sponsors in the Rous Stand.

If there's one man who ranks alongside Elton as a hero at Watford, it's former

England manager Graham Taylor. His long-ball game may have taken England to disaster when they failed to qualify for the 1994 World Cup finals in the USA, but at Vicarage Road his tactics are remembered for taking Watford to the most successful years in the club's history.

Taylor hasn't always been popular in north-west London, though. Watford's official photographer told me there was a time, after a bad run of defeats, when everyone was screaming for Taylor's head to roll. But he was supported by the players and never looked back. 'I always felt he should have been given more time, and he was. It was the right decision. Look what he went on to achieve.' At Watford maybe.

I'd arrived at the ground after a long drive through heavy traffic across London from the south-east to the north-west around the M25. But the most complex part of the journey was trying to negotiate the one-way system in Watford. Away fans must wonder how they'll ever navigate their way through the maze to the ground.

The location of grounds was a theme taken up in the match programme by Watford fan Olly Wicken, who posed the question: 'Do you know where Grimsby is?' His thesis was that football fans have a much better knowledge of the country's geography than those who don't follow the game. His wife hated football and he asked her where Southend was.

'Essex,' she told him with an air of satisfaction.

'Ah, but where's Sunderland?' he said.

'Up north, Lancashire somewhere – or Yorkshire maybe?' was her less assured reply. She also had no idea where to find Blackburn, Bolton, Stoke or Burnley.

'I couldn't believe such elementary knowledge was beyond her – or most non-football fans, male or female,' wrote Wicken.

Since the geographical knowledge of football fans is so comprehensive, he suggested we should include it on our CVs. 'And don't let anyone tell you that this knowledge has a limited lifespan. It's constantly being updated. In the wider scheme, getting relegated from the top flight six years ago was not a good thing – but look how much extra geographical knowledge we all have. We know that Tranmere is on Merseyside and Port Vale is in the Potteries . . . we get to know about the changing traffic systems on these away days. Hopefully, fans visiting Vicarage Road will also now have updated themselves on the Watford roadways – although my heart goes out to anyone caught on the ring-road without sight of our floodlights.' I knew exactly what he meant!

And it's not just your geography that is improved by being a football supporter, according to Wicken. 'My maths has been red hot ever since the days of goal averages. My Latin's pretty good as well – from poring over club crests in *Rothmans Football Yearbook*. And I'm getting good at modern languages too: I know from watching the football on Eurosport that the letter 'o' occurs 43 times in the Brazilian (Portuguese) word for goal. Nevertheless, it's geography where I get A-plus – I'm even good at recognising towns from their soccer grounds.'

But what real use is this fund of somewhat outré knowledge? 'Firstly, it brings us into our own when planning UK holiday routes – or getting that occasional football question on *Mastermind*. But, more importantly, it comes into play when we fans are being given stick for our football obsession. In my case, that happens when my wife thinks I'm a moron for following match scores on Teletext/Ceefax all evening. And she certainly thinks I've regressed when I lock myself in our bedroom after home defeats, particularly at the hands of Luton. But if she has a go at me, I know how to take the wind out of her sails. I just ask her where Hartlepool is.'

Having finally found Watford without being able to locate the Vicarage Road floodlights, I parked in the club car park next to Watford General Hospital and wandered around to the front of the ground. Part of the hospital was once a Union Work House until it was taken over by Shrodells (now Watford General) Hospital in the 1930s. The whole of Vicarage Road seems to be painted yellow and black – the club's colours since 1959. It's as if a family of bees own the place and have told the decorators to make sure the colour scheme matches their own outfits! The club shop was full of black and yellow merchandise including Watford's Blaupunkt-sponsored Hummel shirts.

I had a pass for an executive box and entered the West Stand, named after former club secretary Sir Stanley Rous, through the members' entrance beside the car park. As I climbed the stairs I could see pictures of the phases of development of the stand from the demolition of the old West Stand to the gradual construction of the new building. The pre-cast concrete stand cost £2.2 million to build and was financed with grants, pre-sales of executive boxes (£500,000) and a £1 million loan from Elton.

The Rous Stand was opened in October 1986 by the pop star himself, just a few months after Sir Stanley passed away at the age of 91. Rous had been one of the most influential people in recent football history. After a modest playing career he became a referee and developed the diagonal system of refereeing, which is still used today. Rous became FA Secretary in 1934 and was knighted for services to football in 1949 before being made President of FIFA in 1961, a post he held until 1974. He came up with the simplified set of 17 laws under which football is played and he campaigned for properly organised coaching.

At each end of the Rous Stand is the same quote from the great man: 'I don't want to look back instead of looking forward, but I do hope football never becomes anything more than a game.' Watford had taken his sentiments to heart and, while certainly looking to the future, the club's main concern was the welfare of the supporters. One of the ways in which Watford tried to create the right atmosphere was by developing the facilities at the ground so that the club was well prepared for the twenty-first century.

Indeed, Vicarage Road was fast becoming a very smart stadium. It was a far cry from the state of the ground in 1967, when Watford were given a 150-year lease by the Benskins Breweries. At that time the stadium – if you could call it that – was a hotchpotch of different structures thrown together over the years. 'Even ten to fifteen years ago the place was a tin shack,' admitted commercial manager Paul Burnett. Not any more.

At the time of my visit the old Rookery End, named after the silk mill which once stood on the site and was, at one time, occupied by the Watford Steam Laundry, had just been demolished and a new stand was rising in its place. As we stood outside one of the executive boxes surveying the ground Burnett told me the latest developments would soon make Vicarage Road a Premiership standard ground.

'The new stand replacing the Rookery will be a replica of the North, or Vicarage Road, End [built in 1993],' said Burnett. 'It's going to hold 7,000–7,500, compared to the North End, which holds just over 5,000.' (This new South Stand, still called the Rookery End by the fans, has since been completed.) The rear of the Rookery Stand was a mish-mash of vegetable plots and factories which away fans had to pass as they made their way north through the allotments beside the Watford General Hospital. The club had spent £1.5 million to replace the North End and £1.6 million to build the South Stand.

The East Stand was the last part of the ground still to be modernised. 'At the minute we meet the criteria of the Taylor Report,' said Burnett. 'The aim is to have a Premier standard ground and, when the South Stand is built, it will be of a Premier League standard.' A new East Stand was expected to cost £3–4 million. 'Just think how many players you could buy for that,' said Burnett. I asked how the club had paid for the South Stand. 'Paul Furlong,' he replied with an ironic laugh. I said it should be named after the striker who moved to Chelsea for £2.2 million in the summer of 1994.

Burnett outlined the sort of equation most smaller clubs, if they're lucky, have to solve. 'Basically, the criteria we set was that we could do three things: strengthen the squad, keep Paul Furlong or build a new stand. We could only do two of the three.' Watford had strengthened their squad as well but, as Burnett readily admitted, the team still needed a big centre-forward. 'At home we're all right, but on the road we've lost a few. A good solid position this year is what we expect. I'll be honest, if we scrape to the play-offs that will be a bonus. We were favourites to go down!'

The old East Stand opposite my executive box seat was once described as among the most modern in the country. But that was in 1922 when, as a former gravel pit, the ground had three sloping banks with a stand on the West Side brought across from the club's old ground at Cassio Road. The East Stand had changed little with the original section straddling the halfway line. At the back of the stand stood the press-box decorated with three cut-out trilby hats with press cards tucked into the hatband. The 1969 extension and an uncovered terrace with various temporary buildings behind completed the pot-pourri that was Watford's East Stand. Even the old cart track behind the stand, now called Occupation Road, was still much the same.

The summer after Watford attracted their largest-ever crowd of almost 35,000 for an FA Cup match against Manchester United, the club spent just under £50,000 on an East Stand extension. And in 1979 they added just over 2,000 seats to form one of the country's first family sections.

I watched the match against Southend from one of the 34 executive boxes in the Rous Stand. Unlike the false atmosphere at some clubs, Watford's boxes are designed so that the fans can sit outside if they want to brave the elements. Each box has sliding glass doors leading out to a double row of four seats for a perfect view of the match. From within, your every need is catered for by the staff, who were very friendly as you'd expect at Vicarage Road.

Watford haven't exactly won much in their history and there's even some doubt about the club's origins. The most accurate version seems to be that the present club's origins date back to 1881, when a team called Watford Rovers was founded. The name was changed to West Herts, who took over Watford St Mary's in 1898.

Watford moved to Vicarage Road in 1922 and their first match at the new ground was a goalless draw against Millwall Athletic in front of only 8,000. The ground was owned by the Benskins Brewery, which had bought it for £2,750 the previous year. Watford had been elected to the newly formed Third Division in 1920 and that's where they remained until relegation to the Fourth in 1958. After that they moved up to the Second Division and back to the Fourth between 1960 and 1978, a period which included the Third Division Championship in 1969 and the Fourth Division title in 1978. It was only when Elton John and Graham Taylor teamed up in 1977 as chairman and manager respectively that Watford really began to make progress.

Elton's credentials were impeccable. He was a former local resident who, as a teenager, had stood on the terraces in the corner of the ground between the old Rookery and Shrodells Stands on what used to be called the 'Bend'. His uncle, Roy Dwight, broke his leg playing for Nottingham Forest in the 1959 FA Cup final. Elton's involvement also drew a few wisecracks. 'Elton John decided to rename Watford. He wanted to call it Queen of the South,' said former Manchester United manager Tommy Doherty.

Elton invested a large sum from his personal wealth in the club and Taylor, working with former Arsenal manager Bertie Mee, used the money wisely to take Watford from the Fourth Division to the First in less than six years. The club gained a reputation for innovation, including extraordinary efforts to promote what they called 'family football'. The approach paid dividends both on and off the pitch during the early '80s.

Watford reached the League Cup semi-final in 1979 with players of the calibre of John Barnes, Luther Blissett and Steve Sims. But they were always on the look-out for players. The club even ran an advert in *The Times* in 1983, which read: 'Wanted: Professional footballers, men (or women) aged 18–80. Preference given to applicants with two arms and two legs in working order!'

Watford's able-bodied men played a bright, entertaining, go-for-goal, long-ball game and were rewarded by coming runners-up behind Liverpool in the old First Division in 1983. Luther Blissett scored 30 goals and was First Division joint top scorer with Liverpool's Ian Rush. In June 1983 he was surprisingly sold to AC Milan for £1 million. On arriving at the San Siro stadium in Milan he was reported to have said, 'The ground looks a bit different to Watford. Where's the dog track?' Blissett would return to Watford for just £550,000 the following year. He still holds the club's appearance record, having turned out for the Hornets 415 times in three spells at the club, as well as the overall club goalscoring record with 158.

Watford invested the proceeds from the sale of Blissett wisely, snapping up a young 20-year-old Scottish striker called Maurice Johnston from Partick Thistle for £200,000. Johnston was a scoring sensation, bagging a hat-trick in eight minutes away at Wolves. His goals helped the club to reach their first FA Cup final, in 1984, which they lost 2–0 to Everton. Sky Sports commentator Andy Gray scored with a controversial header, which Watford said should have been disallowed for a foul on keeper Steve Sherwood. When Graham Taylor left to join Aston Villa in 1987, the party was over; the following year Watford were relegated to the Second Division.

At the time of my visit Watford were still in the old Second Division, now called the First of course, and had lost only one of their last eight home games, whereas Southend were unbeaten in seven before a 5–0 thrashing at Port Vale the previous weekend. Today's match was one of only three League games being played owing to European Championship qualifiers and an England friendly against Nigeria at Wembley the following Wednesday. The only player at either club affected by the coming week's events was former Liverpool star Ronnie Whelan, who was plying his trade on the Essex coast (then as a player, now as manager). He was badly missed by Southend.

Before the match I wandered around the corridors behind the executive boxes and into the Elton John Suite. The walls were lined with some of Elton's Gold and Platinum discs on his Rocket label. Then I took my seat in a box used for guests. Tea and sandwiches were provided, but if I'd been a proper executive visitor, then a three-course meal and wine would have been the standard fare.

Watford dominated the match and should have had it sewn up long before they scored. They were denied when a fierce drive from captain Craig Rummage crashed against the bar, and former Millwall striker Jamie Moralee was guilty of a glaring miss when it would have been easier to score. It was left to in-form Lee Nogan to notch his eighth goal in ten games with a spectacular diving header from a cross by Rummage, which he powered into the corner of the net. It was the last action of an entertaining match.

The goal came five minutes into injury time much to the relief of the home fans. Southend manager Peter Taylor, since replaced by Whelan and now in charge of the England Under-21 team, was so incensed by the amount of time added on that he had to be restrained by Watford boss Glenn Roeder after the final whistle. The referee almost seemed to be waiting for Watford to score before ending the match. The game was over before Southend could kick off again. The few hundred travelling fans below me in the Rous Stand just stood in silence. They couldn't believe their team had succumbed to a last-gasp winner. But they had.

HOW SWEET IS MY VALLEY

Charlton Athletic v West Bromwich Albion – The Valley, 13 November 1994

Charlton had not won a live televised match since the 1947 FA Cup final, so the arrival of the London Weekend Television cameras for this Sunday afternoon game was greeted with apprehension by the home supporters. As they could have told you before the match, their team was again unable to break the sequence in a game they completely dominated. The die-hard fans know only too well the sense of self-delusion that takes over when they think Charlton have a game sewn up.

The teams ran out onto the pitch to the sound of that old Al Jolson classic 'When the Red, Red, Robin Goes Bob, Bob, Bobbing Along'. Charlton have a number of nicknames, one of them being the Robins owing to their red kit. Among the others are the Valiants, after their home ground, the Valley, and Haddicks or, more commonly, Addicks. The fishy tale is that the players once used a room above a chipshop in East Street as their base and the owner, a keen

Addicks fan, used to come to matches armed with a haddock nailed onto a piece of wood, which he waved about during games. Inspiration for the inflatable haddocks used at Grimsby?

The Charlton team certainly needed all the inspiration they could get. Cult hero Carl Leaburn had returned after recovering from knee and calf injuries, but had little impact on the match, and leading scorer David Whyte was still out of action and sorely missed. At least Kim Grant put the home side ahead after a long kick downfield by keeper Mike Ammann resulted in an attempted clearance by West Brom centre-half Paul Mardon, which hit Grant's shin and rebounded into the net.

The West Brom fans had turned up in large numbers and occupied at least half of the South End. Their team had given them little to cheer about after a disastrous start to the season, which had seen manager Keith Burkinshaw sacked and Alan Buckley recruited from Grimsby. West Brom were second from bottom of the Second Division at the start of the match. But the fans gave their team lots of encouragement even when, at one point, it seemed they'd gone 2–0 down before Mark Robson's goal was disallowed for offside.

Just after half-time the Baggies brought on substitute Carl Heggs and within two minutes he'd set up an equaliser for the prolific Bob Taylor, who volleyed past Ammann. Charlton's biggest crowd of the season – 10,876 – groaned all around me. They knew it was coming even in the first half when their team managed to miss eight good chances. The inevitability of an equaliser was there from the moment Charlton scored. The home fans had seen it all before.

It was a far cry from the Charlton team of the 1930s which became one of the top sides in the country under manager Jimmy Seed. They won the Third Division (South) in 1935, for the second time, and the following season went up to the First Division as runners-up. They went one better in 1937 when they were the second-best team in the country and, after coming second in the 1946 FA Cup final, they won the trophy in that televised 1947 final, beating Burnley – though Seed dropped the cup and broke the lid.

Charlton's most famous player of all time is probably their goalkeeper of that era, Sam Bartram, who many people believe is the greatest goalkeeper never to be picked for England. Sam was honoured at the Valley with the Sam Bartram Gate at the Main Entrance and the Sam Bartram Close. Jimmy Seed's contribution was recognised in 1981, when the club named the new South Stand after their former manager.

But a 'Hall of Fame' poll in the club's match programme, *Valley Review,* put striker Derek Hales, the club's top goalscorer with 168 strikes, just ahead of Bartram, whose 623 games for Charlton are a record. The race for third place was won by Robert Lee, now captain of Newcastle and an England international, but who made more than 350 appearances for the Addicks over an eight-year spell, scoring 60-odd goals.

Eddie Firmani, a former Charlton player and manager, and an Italian international, was fourth, just ahead of fellow South African Stuart Leary, whose 158 League goals are a club record. In sixth place was the man who had made more appearances for the club than anyone except Bartram, present reserve-team boss Keith Peacock, who played 591 senior games for Charlton over 17 years, many of them as captain. Keith was also one of only five players to score more than 100 goals for the club.

The Robins' most capped player and the third in terms of appearances (530),

John Hewie, came seventh in the poll. He also won 19 caps for Scotland. And last, but by no means least, was Allan Simonsen, who finished just ahead of Peter Shirtliff, Mike Flanagan and Colin Powell. Simonsen's Valley career was short, but the former European Footballer of the Year made quite an impact with nine goals in 17 games.

But while the present-day team may have faltered, the dedication of the supporters has never been in doubt. The club are now firmly re-established at the ground they called home for almost 66 years before being forced to leave and shack up with Crystal Palace at Selhurst Park on the other side of south London, and then West Ham at Upton Park in east London.

Memories of those dark days could be brought back on your VCR by purchasing the video of the 'last ever' match at the Valley on 21 September 1985 when almost 9,000 saw them bid farewell against Stoke City. At £11.99 it was a snip from the supporters club representatives in the VIP lounge.

Their club came back to the Valley in 1991 with promises to restore their old home ground after the damage caused by neglect and nature. The stadium re-opened on 5 December 1992, when Charlton beat Portsmouth 1–0.

The bitterness about the way the club was forced out of the Valley lingers on. The irony of their departure was that Charlton won that 'last ever' home match 2–0 and went on to gain promotion to the top flight. They stayed there for four years and it seems sad that this spell among the élite occurred at a time when they couldn't play at their spiritual home. Thankfully, the exile has ended, restoring to north Kent, one of the most densely populated areas in the south-east, its only League club.

The Valley sits in the middle of a chalk pit which was once in the centre of what was then known as Charlton Village. The pitch was levelled by an army of volunteers who built the terraces from rubble excavated from a nearby hospital. Apparently, there were a number of bones unearthed at the time, some of which made their way to the ground. It's obvious why it was named the Valley. From the Main Stand you have the sense of being in a large bowl with buildings above and around you. It was surprisingly windy given the natural shelter afforded by the steep banking.

It was hard to imagine that the stadium was once the largest club ground in Britain, with a capacity of probably close to 80,000, and that more than 75,000 fans packed the ground when Charlton played Aston Villa in the fifth round of the Cup in 1938. It was even considered as a venue for the FA Cup final.

The redevelopment which has transformed the ground into a smart modern venue, including the new 6,000 all-seater East Stand, also cut the capacity to 15,000. The atmosphere also suffered.

The development hasn't finished yet. Or at least, I hoped not, for the players changed in Portakabins behind the Main Stand and ran onto the pitch from the corner by the north end, which houses the more fervent home fans. 'We 'ate Millwall and we 'ate Millwall,' they sang in recognition of their south London rivals.

The fanzine *Voice of The Valley* gave its 'Optimist of the Month' award to defender Alan McLeary for thinking Charlton would do the double over the Lions. 'Most Charlton fans would settle for getting out of the New Den with all their body parts intact, but you can always hope.' Charlton seemed such a friendly club that I feared for the safety of their supporters if there was any trouble during their derby matches with their assailants from the Old Kent Road.

After the match one Baggies fan in a deep embrace with his girlfriend outside the ground attracted a crowd. It wasn't his Romeo act that was pulling in the punters, but his T-shirt which reflected the Midlands rivalry with the slogan, 'If you're a Wolves fan you must be very sad'. Maybe, but challenging for promotion beats the battle against relegation any day. Who would be laughing at the end of the season I wondered?

GREEN CARD

Sheffield United v Southend United – Bramall Lane, 26 November 1994

This match was all about a green card, and I don't mean the piece of paper which gives you the right to work in the States and was the title of the movie starring Gerard Depardieu and the gorgeous Andie Macdowell. This green card was the one held up by about 90 per cent of United's fans to protest against chairman Reg Brealey. The A5 slips of paper urged him to 'Go and go now'. Their main complaint was the lack of resources made available to strengthen the team.

Quite what the Southend supporters were doing joining in the protest is anyone's guess. I suppose supporters generally don't get on too well with football club chairmen whom they believe are not in it for the love of their team, though there are one or two exceptions like Jack Walker and Sir John Hall. Reg Brealey clearly felt he had more feeling for the club than the supporters. He'd arranged to meet the Independent Supporters Association on the morning of the match but pulled out more than a week before saying they didn't have the club's best interests at heart. Someone was wrong!

The Blades manager, Dave Bassett, had tried to sit on the fence throughout the dispute but was clearly angry that the team wasn't getting the support he felt they deserved after three straight home wins. 'If they roared their support for United while the game was on and kept their arguments with the board for before and after the game, it would be different; but people are beginning to take out their frustrations on the team when their frustrations lie elsewhere.'

Brealey had been involved in a long-standing run-in with the fans. But at least he said he knew what running a football club was all about. He certainly knew that there was no alternative to rebuilding the John Street Stand; it had been demolished over the summer leaving Bramall Lane with three sides, reminiscent of the days when United shared the ground with the Yorkshire county cricket club and only had three stands.

'Those who have responsibility for control must never forget that the club belongs to the supporters,' said Brealey. Funny that, since the fans were convinced it belonged to the chairman, the board, and the other shareholders. 'The shares might belong to individuals. But the ground is the home of the supporters and if I protect their "home", I protect their club,' insisted Brealey. He must have known his days were numbered, though, since he was determined to restore Bramall Lane to its rightful place in football before he departed. 'If that is the last thing I do for this club then I shall be satisfied, whatever the supporters may think.' Does that sound like someone on their way out?

I'd arrived in Sheffield by train from London, having passed through some of the most depressed industrial areas I'd ever seen. Sheffield is the fourth largest city in England, with a population of just over half a million, and the biggest city in Yorkshire. But some people refer to it as the county's second city after Leeds. No wonder there's such a great rivalry between the two Uniteds, not to mention Wednesday.

Sheffield stands at the foot of the Derbyshire hills, where the River Sheaf meets the River Don. It once prospered on steel, particularly cutlery, which explains United's nickname of the Blades. The city was renowned for its knives and fine blades from as early as the fourteenth century, and by the sixteenth century had about 60 hallmarks. It was famous for high-quality steel from the 1700s, when the crucible process was invented.

In 1742 Thomas Boulsover discovered that silver could be bonded to copper and then rolled into sheets, producing Old Sheffield Plate, the forerunner of electroplate. By the nineteenth century the great steel works stretched all along the Don valley to the north-east through the suburbs of Attercliffe, Brightside and Tinsley to Rotherham. The city's first football team doesn't quite go back that far but Sheffield FC, formed in 1857, is still the oldest club in the world.

Advances in steel production techniques soon turned the city into one of Britain's main centres of heavy and specialist engineering. It became a mixture of Victorian splendour and abject poverty. Falling demand for steel has, sadly, eroded Sheffield's industrial might. According to the *Rough Guide*: 'To approach the city by road or rail is to make a journey through some of the most dispiriting landscapes imaginable.' Nevertheless, it now claims the cleanest air of any manufacturing city in Europe and the city centre has been transformed by new developments in recent years, much like Bramall Lane.

The ground was originally used by the Sheffield Cricket Club, which was formed in 1854 and secured a 99-year lease from the Duke of Norfolk. Yorkshire County Cricket Club first played there in 1855 and Sheffield Football Club first set foot on the pitch in 1862. However, Bramall Lane's place in history was secured when the first game under floodlights was played there in October 1878. Two local teams played under four lights powered by two generators and equivalent to 30,000 candles. Although only 12,000 actually paid to see the match, there were about 20,000 people at the game.

The lucrative gate receipts from an FA Cup semi-final between Preston and West Brom persuaded the cricket club that football was a profitable business and Sheffield United was formed in 1889. In 1892 they joined the Second Division in the same year that Wednesday were elected to the First Division. United were promoted within a year and won their only League title in 1898. The following year they formed a limited liability company and bought Bramall Lane from the Duke of Norfolk for just over £10,000.

I'd arrived at the ground by taxi from Sheffield station and was dropped off at the entrance to the car park on Cherry Street in front of the South Stand. It was packed with posh vehicles of all kinds from Range Rovers to Mercedes, BMWs and the odd Roller. The South Stand, which cost £750,000 and opened in August 1975, is a full-length cantilever seating 8,000 with no posts to obstruct the view. It's certainly impressive from the outside with its announcement of Sheffield United FC in big white letters over the main entrance.

The car park covers what used to be the cricket pitch, used by Yorkshire until August 1973 when, after 150 years of cricket, the men in white flannels were forced to leave Bramall Lane. Northampton Town thus became the only League club in the country with a three-sided ground. They have since moved to their new Sixfields Stadium. The only clubs with three-sided grounds now are those awaiting further development such as Huddersfield's McAlpine Stadium and, ironically, Bramall Lane.

The demolition of the John Street Stand, built by Archibald Leitch in 1890, had left a clear view of much of the city including St Mary's church, built 50 years earlier, which is distinguished by its four Gothic pinnacles. The bulldozers had achieved what the Luftwaffe could not, for, despite being hit by German bombers in the Second World War which destroyed half the stand and its marvellous tall mock-Tudor gable, it was completely restored – even though it took eight years to complete the job.

United had already decided on the design of the new cantilevered John Street Stand, which would cost around £4.2 million and seat just over 6,500 fans. The club newspaper *Blades News* outlined the shape of things to come: 'The first tier is general seating; the second tier is a dining and lounge area with front rows of seats in the central area which will be behind a glass screen; the third tier consists of private boxes with external balcony seating. A feature . . . will be the return of the central clock, reminiscent of the past cricket era at the Lane.'

But that was the future. Today United's aim was to win three successive home games for the first time this season. A 2–0 win over Southend left them in the ironic position of doing so just as the protests against their chairman reached new heights. 'The players could have been forgiven for wondering just how important this victory had been in the context of what was going on around them,' said *The Yorkshire Post*. 'The reality is that they are doing their bit to keep United's season alive, but to expect them to do so indefinitely is unrealistic.' Or is it?

JORDAN RETURNS

Bristol City v Grimsby Town – Ashton Gate, 3 December 1994

I set out for Bristol in torrential rain. The downpour made driving very difficult and I could hardly see as I navigated my way around London's orbital M25 towards the M4 bound for Bristol. After what seemed like an endless journey I finally arrived in the town which has long been the most dynamic in the West Country. In recent years communications, computers and finance, developed in large part to support the aerospace industry, had given the city a high profile in the area of new technology. That reputation was helped enormously when Concorde was built in Bristol in 1969.

As I came up towards the River Avon I could see a speedboat approaching on the choppy water. The Avon was partly responsible for Bristol becoming one of

Britain's great inland ports, since it weaves its way through the centre of the town providing access to shipping. The river forms part of a system of waterways which has in the past been used to transport goods such as rum, tobacco and slaves. In fact, Bristol became the centre of the African slave trade in the eighteenth century. The city grew rich on trade with the Americas in the seventeenth and eighteenth centuries and still imports goods from across the Atlantic, though nowadays the bigger ships dock at Avonmouth. The City Docks had recently been regenerated as a leisure and recreation centre.

After I'd reached the city, the clouds at last disappeared, but I was still in something of a fog because I had yet to find the ground. I'd turned onto the dual carriageway and crossed the Clifton suspension bridge but then got lost in the city's one-way system and found myself returning to the bridge once more after circumnavigating the city looking for the floodlights of Ashton Gate. The bridge was designed by Isambard Kingdom Brunel, who'd laid the foundations of an engineering tradition in the city and had created the SS *Great Britain*, which you can visit. Indeed, Bristol City's chairman Harry Dolman was himself an engineer and had designed the club's first floodlights which were mounted on removable poles and had to be turned on one at a time.

The Clifton suspension bridge, Bristol's most famous symbol, is 702 feet long and stands 245 feet above high water. In 1829 Brunel won the competition to design a bridge held on the second round, but it wasn't until 1864, five years after his death, that it was finished. A shortage of funds meant the bridge never quite matched the original ambitious design, which included Egyptian-style towers topped by sphinxes at each end.

City were themselves certainly no strangers to financial difficulties. That was partly because their return to the First Division in 1976, after an absence of 65 years, was short-lived. In 1980 they were still in the top flight, but by 1982 they'd plummeted to the Fourth Division – a two-and-a-half year decline without parallel. City had the best ground of any club occupying the bottom spot in the Football League. But the club were by now in deep financial trouble. They were still paying First Division wages while attracting Fourth Division crowds. Saddled with £700,000 in debts, the club just had too many money problems. The only way out was for the company founded in 1897 to be wound up and a new one floated as 'Bristol City (1982)'.

In October 1983 a new era dawned when they appointed former Leeds and England full-back Terry Cooper as football's first player–manager–director. At 39 he was also the oldest player in the Football League, though most of his appearances were as substitute. Nevertheless, he led his team to promotion to Division Three in 1984.

Since then City had clawed themselves back into the First Division, though of course that was equivalent to the old Division Two, with the advent of the Premier League. The challenge now was to avoid relegation after their poor form had cost former Ipswich defender Russell Osman his job as manager.

The talk at Ashton Gate before the home game against Grimsby today was all about the return of Joe Jordan, once a towering colossus at the head of the Leeds and Manchester United attacks and installed again as the boss of Bristol City, the team he played for in the twilight of his career before taking over for his first spell as manager.

The image of Jordan which stuck in my mind came from a third round FA Cup tie at Old Trafford in 1981, when the Scottish striker clattered into Spurs keeper Milija Aleksic. 'Elastic', as he was known by the Tottenham fans, never recovered and was stretchered from the field to be replaced in goal by Glenn Hoddle. That challenge said everything about Jordan's style of play. He was uncompromising, and even when his head couldn't reach the ball, his elbows were almost certainly able to do some damage.

Nowadays his impact was restricted to picking the team and then jumping out of the dugout to urge on his players, remonstrate with the referee's decisions, or complain about a bad tackle on one of his men. Jordan's powers of motivation were desperately needed at Ashton Gate, which was why he'd been brought back to the club. But he was under no illusions about the size of the task ahead. ' . . . there is a great deal of hard work to be done if we are to move away from the bottom of the First Division,' said Jordan. 'Having said that, I have been encouraged by much of what I have seen since returning as manager. The players are capable of creating chances with good positive play and there is certainly something to build on. One of my first aims is to make the team strong at home and you supporters play a major role in creating the sort of atmosphere that helped so much against Swindon Town [in his first game back].'

City hadn't always struggled since they were formed in 1897, when the Bristol South End Club, founded three years earlier, turned professional and applied for admission to the Southern League. The historic meeting was held at the Albert Hall, Bedminster. City hired Sam Hollis from Woolwich Arsenal as manager and gave him £40 to buy players. In 1900 City merged with another leading Bristol club called Bedminster and both teams' home grounds, City's St John's Lane and Bedminster's Athletic Ground, were used alternately in a unique arrangement in League football.

When City joined the Football League in 1901, only one ground could be registered, so the club used St John's Lane for three seasons. But after a disagreement over the lease City returned to Bedminster's ground, which they now called Ashton Gate. (Bedminster's ground had first been used for cricket and the legendary batsman W.G. Grace played there in a Gloucester v. Somerset match in April 1897.)

In those early years City were quite successful: they took the Second Division title in 1906, after a record run of 14 wins in a row; were runners-up in the First Divison in 1907; and reached the FA Cup final two years later. Unfortunately they have never reached those heights since, though they did win the Welsh Cup in 1934 – without even being Welsh. They also got to the League Cup semi-final in 1971 and 1989, won the Anglo-Scottish Cup in 1978 and won the Freight Rover Trophy in 1986 before losing in the final the following year. They had seen better times, and far worse times, than now.

At least they'd managed to hold on to their ground, unlike their neighbours Bristol Rovers; it was a close call, though. In 1933 City offered to sell Ashton Gate to the local council for £16,000, but the council decided not to buy. Thus the club was spared the embarrassment faced by Rovers, who were hounded out of Eastville by their ground's owners. Ashton Gate is City's main asset and something both the club and its supporters can be proud of. Recent developments have made the stadium one of the best in the First Division.

When I finally found Ashton Gate, I parked my car in a side street and made my way to the club office to pick up my ticket. The ground looked like a factory or retail park with its scarlet and grey steel stands. It would have fitted in well with the warehouses and steelworks which surrounded the stadium. I half-expected to find a small manufacturing company inside rather than a football pitch.

The Main Stand and its counterpart are both named after Bristol City chairmen. The Main Stand was named after Des Williams in 1992, while the Dolman Stand, built in 1970, bears the name of Harry Dolman. There were two parts to the Williams Stand: the back half with wooden seats was the original stand, whereas the front section, with plastic seats and a new roof, had been extended towards the Covered End to my right. Previously both corners had been left open, but now it was only the left corner with its seats in front of the club shop that was still uncovered.

A famous Bristol landmark, Cabot Tower, stands on a hill due north across the River Avon to the left of the Dolman Stand opposite. The tower was built in 1897–98 to mark the quarter-centenary of an expedition by the Genoese-born navigator John Cabot and his son Sebastian in 1497. They set sail from the City Docks in their ship, the *Matthew*, discovered the mainland of America and claimed it for the English Crown. There's a memorial plaque to John Cabot at the southern end of what's known as the Centre, once an extension of the port but now the congested hub of the city.

From the Dolman Stand there was a great view, not only of the pitch, but of Bedminster Down and the bonded warehouses beyond the Winterstoke Road End to my left. (The warehouses were demolished in 1995.) The Dolman Stand was most remarkable for the bowling club underneath. I'd come across various facilities at the many grounds I'd been to, but this was the first bowling club.

Chairman Harry Dolman was a keen bowler and it was his enthusiasm for the game that led to City putting a long, low hall underneath the stand with two artificial flat greens which cost £20,000 to lay. The bowlers, including Dolman, paid £20,000 a year in rent, but City were still struggling to cope with the debts they'd taken on to build the stand. The final cost was £235,000 – more than four times the original estimate of £50,000! The Robins were in such a tight spot that they had to sell all the club's houses and seek support from the FA, sponsors and supporters to meet their obligations.

The bowling club explained the high brick wall I could see at the front of the Dolman Stand. There was a narrow terrace in front of the wall, though it wasn't open for supporters, and stairs leading up to the seats in the main part of the stand. Adverts for various local companies lined the front of the wall. Behind the Dolman Stand was Southbow House, a tall block of flats on the site of Bedminster's first pitch, which provided a great view of the games at Ashton Gate until the Dolman Stand was built. Before then the caretaker had even charged admission when City were playing at home!

The North Stand to my left had only been opened in August 1994. It was sponsored by Carling and named after the late John Atyeo, who played more than 700 games for the Robins between 1951 and 1966, including a club record 597 League appearances and another record haul of 314 League goals. He also scored 35 Cup goals and was capped by England. The City star died in 1993 and the new Atyeo Stand was a fitting tribute to one of the club's legends. The dressing-rooms were under the stand at this end of the ground and the players ran onto the pitch from a tunnel behind the goal like at Wembley, Blackpool and Burnley. You couldn't fail to realise you were at Ashton Gate when looking at the Atyeo Stand because BRISTOL CITY was picked out in white from the rest of the stand's red seats.

The Covered End to my right at the Winterstoke Road end of the ground had originally been built back in 1928 with the proceeds from the sale of two players, Keating and Bourton, to Blackburn for £3,650. The Covered End terrace was curiously some 30 feet longer on either side than the pitch was wide. It has since been made into an all-seater stand with the installation of backless tip-up seats. Since the Covered End was the only part of the ground not named after one of City's chairmen or former players, it seemed likely that the honour would go to City defender Billy Wedlock. He starred as a centre-half for the club between 1907 and 1912 and was the Robins most-capped player with 26 appearances for England.

Simon Inglis in *The Football Grounds of Great Britain* recalled that Wedlock's nickname was the 'India Rubber Man', which, wrote Inglis, 'might also be appropriate for those fans who must now strain and stretch from the seats cheaply installed at the Covered End. Apart from contending with columns, awkward corners and the quite unsettling lack of any backrests, the seats have been bolted onto one of the most irregularly raked terraces ever built, as can be seen from the undulating shape of the handrails.' Apart from that it was perfect!

Unfortunately for the City faithful it didn't really matter where you were in the ground because you would have still seen a poor performance from the Robins even in the best seats in the house. There were only a couple of hundred Grimsby fans at the away end but they were in full voice after their team went two goals ahead. '2–1 to the Mariners, 2–1 to the Mariners,' they sang. The Bristol City matchday magazine welcomed the Grimsby supporters who'd made the long trip south, a journey the City fans had themselves made in the opposite direction just six weeks before. City lost that match 1–0 'but at least we had the fish and chips to look forward to,' said the programme. The fish and chips may not have been as good in Bristol, but the Mariners had gone home with the points and that was probably a much better reward.

At half-time I popped into the social club for a swift half and a chat with some of the supporters. One of them was reminiscing about the goals scored by the club's record signing Andy Cole, bought from Arsenal for £500,000 in July 1992. 'He was a great player Andy. Lots of natural talent and an instinct for goals. We shouldn't have sold him but we needed the money. You could tell he was class the moment he arrived from Arsenal.' Unfortunately City had to sell him when Newcastle offered £1.75 million in March 1993. How they could have done with him against Grimsby Town today.

The match had given Jordan much to ponder. 'The story of success and failure in football is the story of chances at one end and stability at the other,' said the City manager. 'If you miss opportunities to score and also make errors at the back, you are not going to win matches.' Today he'd seen examples of both.

As I drove out of Bristol I then passed the floodlights of Rovers' old ground at Eastville beaming down on the market traders who now sold their goods where once the blue and white shirts of Bristol's other team had played on Saturday afternoons. City's plight was bad, but it could have been so much worse.

THE WANDERERS

Queens Park Rangers v West Ham United – Loftus Road,
4 December 1994

The day was overcast as I made my way through heavy traffic to QPR's ground in west London. Roadworks were holding everything up around what's officially known as the Rangers Stadium and it took an age to get close enough to park within walking distance of what most people in football know as Loftus Road.

It had taken Rangers some time to settle at their present home. Since they were formed in the 1880s by the merger of two west London teams, St Jude's Institute FC and Christchurch Rangers, they've had more grounds than any other League Club – twelve in all. And they've also played home games at two other stadiums.

The exact date of the club's formation is uncertain, but it's believed to be either 1885 or 1886. They retained the St Jude's name for a year before changing to Queens Park Rangers, because most of the players came from the Queens Park district. Ironically, the club has never played at the park from which it takes its name and which still exists. The fact that Rangers don't play at Queens Park has been a great source of confusion to away fans and casual supporters over the years; many take the tube to Queens Park station only to find that the ground isn't anywhere near the Bakerloo line.

Rangers first moved to Loftus Road in 1917, although they'd since left twice to try their luck at White City, the world's first purpose-built stadium which was designed for the 1908 Olympic Games. During their first spell at White City in the 1930s a record crowd of just over 41,000 watched QPR play Leeds.

Rangers bought the freehold at Loftus Road in 1948 but made one last effort to settle at White City in the 1962–63 season. As with earlier attempts they found that the crowds weren't big enough for them to stay. The small number of fans were lost in a stadium the size of White City and the players couldn't perform in such a hollow atmosphere.

Having parked my car in a side street, I made my way towards the Rangers Stadium to pick up my ticket. I noticed that many of the streets were named after Commonwealth countries, including South Africa Road where I found the main entrance to the ground. I later discovered that the names date back to the 1908 Olympics when the athletes' village was set up close to Loftus Road. The streets were named in honour of some of the Commonwealth countries competing at the Games.

As I walked along South Africa Road towards the ground I could see the name RANGERS STADIUM in big white letters on the blue metal sheeting above and to the left of the main entrance. I also passed the BBC's sparkling white headquarters, which had replaced part of the White City stadium after it was knocked down in 1985, and the Springbok pub.

I popped inside the ground to get my ticket for the match and a pass to the executive suite so that I could mix with some of west London's finest before, during and after the match. Inside the foyer there were glass showcases running along each side of a short corridor connected to the dressing-rooms and QPR's offices. They contained mementoes from some of Rangers opponents and pictures of the stars who'd donned the blue and white hooped shirts over the years. The most exciting were probably Rodney Marsh and Stan Bowles, but Rangers have had their share of other class players, including Frank McLintock, Terry Mancini, Don Givens, Gerry Francis, keeper Phil Parkes, Clive Allen, Paul Parker and player–manager Ray Wilkins.

As I waited for my ticket QPR's most famous fan came in waving a rattle and shouting for Rangers. He was decked out in royal-blue and white from head to toe, including a very tall top hat, scarf, rattle and, of course, replica shirt. 'He's well known here,' said one of the officials. 'He's almost as famous as the players. He's at every game, home and away. A real Rangers fanatic he is.' I had to admit he'd brightened up the atmosphere.

Having got my ticket, I left to find the executive suite. I was surprised to see some of the West Ham players sitting by the door as the wealthier Rangers fans and a few television personalities speculated on the outcome of the match. Among the Hammers stars who wouldn't play today were Alvin Martin, Martin Allen and Don Hutchison.

They sat around talking about football and today's game, clearly frustrated that they wouldn't be taking part in the afternoon's proceedings. I asked Martin Allen and Don Hutchison to sign the match programme for a young lad I knew and enquired about Allen's injury. 'I'll be out for a while,' he told me. 'It's very frustrating.' Allen had once played for Rangers and won England Under-21 caps while at Loftus Road as well as playing in the 1986 Milk Cup final, which QPR lost to Oxford at Wembley.

I left the executive suite to take my seat in the Main Stand and asked a steward about the street names I'd seen around the ground. 'It must sound strange,' she said, 'seeing the names of all those Commonwealth countries, but it dates back to the Olympics when the athletes all stayed in this area. The BBC's always had offices around here too,' she added. 'In fact, they still rent three storeys of this stand.'

My seat was in the two-tiered South Africa Road Stand. It was built in 1968 for £162,000 in time for QPR's first season in the top flight. The stand included 32 executive boxes so that the well-heeled fans I'd met in the executive suite before the match could sit and watch in comfort, gin and tonic in one hand, match programme in the other. The two worlds of football were as evident here as at most other grounds.

Opposite stood the Ellerslie Road Stand, which replaced the original Main Stand in 1972. It was a pretty simple single-tiered structure, backed by an outdoor concourse area which had been squeezed into the space between the stand and the gardens behind. The club crest stood proudly in the centre of the blue roof.

On my right was the two-tiered School End stand for away fans. It replaced open terracing in 1981 and was refurbished 12 years later. The stand had one major disadvantage for anyone not in the front row: you couldn't see the goal-line unless you stood up. So much for stewards enforcing the rule that all fans must sit down.

The Loftus Road End, or Loft as it's known to Rangers fans, was on my left. It was built in 1980 and was slightly bigger than the School End ,which helped the view. This end had the club's control room in the corner and the Terry Venables Bar, in honour of the former Rangers manager who'd fashioned a team including Tony Currie, Clive Allen and Terry Fenwick. Venables took them to the FA Cup final in 1982, when they lost to Spurs after a replay at Wembley courtesy of a Glenn Hoddle penalty.

QPR have had their share of the game's best managers over the years including Alec Stock, Bill Dodgin, Tommy Docherty, Gordon Jago, Dave Sexton, Jim Smith, Trevor Francis and Don Howe. The collective impact of that lot on the game had helped to shape British football in the post-war era despite their modest record at Rangers.

The best-ever QPR side was probably that built by Sexton in the mid- to late-'70s with the likes of Gerry Francis, Phil Parkes and Stan Bowles. The club were runners-up to Liverpool in the First Division in the 1975–76 season and went on to play in Europe for the first time in the UEFA Cup.

Francis and Bowles both gained England caps, but Parkes never made a lasting impression at international level, as he surely would have done if not for the presence of Ray Clemence and Peter Shilton. 'Then Joe Corrigan came along,' said Parkes. 'So in the end there were four of us virtually the same age. It really was a situation where, whoever got the manager's job at the time, would pick his favourite keeper. In the end I fell out with Don Revie completely.' After 344 appearances for Rangers Parkes joined West Ham for a world record fee for a goalkeeper of £565,000 and played exactly the same number of games for the Hammers.

QPR were now hoping for the sort of success they'd had when Parkes was between the sticks, as Ray Wilkins settled into the manager's job. His brother Dean played for Rangers in the early 1980s and there was clearly an affection for the club among the Wilkins family. Ray had accumulated years of experience after captaining Chelsea as an 18-year-old in the old First Division. He's since plied his trade at Manchester United, AC Milan, Paris St Germain and Glasgow Rangers. One of his first appointments at Loftus Road was his former United team-mate Frank Stapleton as reserve-team manager; he replaced Roger Cross, who'd joined Gerry Francis in his new job at Tottenham.

More than 17,000 turned up for Wilkins' first home match as manager and saw Rangers beat Leeds 3–2. His mother Win, who'd been very supportive throughout his career, was in the crowd that day to witness her son's début in the hot seat. She wasn't the only one delighted to see him chalk up a victory in front of a bumper crowd. Chairman Peter Ellis was also more than pleased with the near sell-out crowd. He felt that similar attendances on a consistent basis would help the club become more competitive in the transfer market: 'If we can fill the stadium week-in, week-out, a lot of our worries and the fans' worries will disappear or become minimised because it reduces the necessity of selling players. Of course, we can't say we're never going to sell a player, but we shall be buying and selling players with a little less pressure if we can fill the stadium every week.'

Ellis was responding in part to criticism levelled at the club, and its owner Richard Thompson, over the policy on selling players. Thompson Investments had taken over QPR in 1989 when the Thompson family bought the club from Marler Estates for £6.2 million. But their relationship with supporters had deteriorated. As well as concern about players, focused particularly on the endless rumours about the imminent departure of Les Ferdinand, the board was also under fire from both the supporters and fanzines, such as *In the Loft*, over the controversial departure of manager Gerry Francis.

Francis had left in a huff after the board tried to install former Rangers' idol Rodney Marsh as director of football. Francis hadn't been informed of the negotiations and clearly felt his authority as manager would be undermined if Marsh joined the staff. In the end Marsh felt unable to take the position he'd been offered given the circumstances, whereas for Francis there was no going back and he quit anyway. The whole affair was a complete fiasco which had been very badly managed.

The board tried to implement a damage-limitation exercise and Ellis drew attention in the Leeds programme to the fact that Rangers had spent £9.7 million on players since the Thompson take-over – a figure queried by many supporters. The club had responded by publishing a full list of every player purchased since 1989. The most expensive recruit was Andy Gray (not the Sky Sports version) at £425,000 from Crystal Palace.

New boss Ray Wilkins had firm convictions about how he'd use those players and the style he intended to impose at Loftus Road. 'I want the game to be played with the ball on the floor and being passed around,' said the man nicknamed 'the Crab' because of his tendency to play the ball sideways rather than forward.

To achieve his goals Wilkins had changed the training schedule: ' . . . we have to work harder with the ball. Therefore, I've introduced a lot of small-sided games in training. Also, we won't train for as long as we used to. Sessions will be short and sharp so that our players will be sharp when playing games.' The players must have been delighted with the new approach. Ninety minutes of training instead of two hours!

Wilkins had been only a player at Rangers until now and there were some adjustments to be made now he was the manager as well. Ray was no longer just one of the lads. So how would the players address him in his new role? 'The first team and reserves call me "Ray", as I know them well. And the youth team will call me "Boss",' he said.

The idea of being known as the Boss wasn't something that particularly appealed to Wilkins, but he'd noticed when playing in the north of England that respect carried through the clubs. 'It's a good policy for young players as they progress from the youth team to the higher level.' He'd been in the job just two weeks when I visited Loftus Road for the West Ham game and, although he'd worked under many great managers in the past, he'd found that actually being in the hot seat was a different proposition. 'I can tell you that being manager is nothing like I expected it to be,' he said.

Wilkins certainly had his work cut out to inspire the first team after they'd crashed to a 4–0 defeat at Blackburn's Ewood Park following their encouraging start at home against Leeds. They had some good young players like striker Kevin Gallen and exciting winger Trevor Sinclair. But the man they looked to for salvation was England international Les Ferdinand, who'd been banging in the goals, including two in the Leeds game, throughout the season. Big Les would answer the call again today with another couple against West Ham in a 2–1 win.

Despite being two goals down, the Hammers fans in the School End on my right showed they hadn't lost their east London sense of humour by singing, 'And now you're gonna believe us, we're gonna win the League' to which one Rangers fan responded, 'Yeah, the Endsleigh First Division next season'. West Ham did manage to pull a goal back but it was too little, too late and Rangers ran out winners.

The Loftus Road pitch was in excellent condition in the December sunshine and a far cry from the artificial turf the club installed in 1981. Back then their grass pitch was dreadful and the £350,000 Omniturf surface at least had grass all over it – even if it was artificial. QPR were the first British League club allowed to use an artificial pitch and, indeed, the first professional club in the world to use such a surface for competitive matches. It also enabled Rangers to stage other events such as concerts without ruining the pitch and seemed to offer a host of profit-making opportunities.

But the experiment proved to be nothing more than that and, although some other clubs such as Luton, Oldham and Preston followed in Rangers' footsteps, there was a lot of criticism from visiting teams. They had to arrive the day before the match to train on the pitch and get used to the surface and most didn't like the high bounces that the surface caused. There was nothing like real grass, it seemed. Thus, when Jim Gregory sold Rangers to Marler Estates for £5.5 million in February 1987, the new chairman, David Bulstrode, ordered a return to the real stuff.

After the West Ham match I returned to the executive suite where I'd met some of the Hammers' injured players before the match. Around the room there were glass cases containing some of the trophies and mementoes Rangers had picked up over the years. One item which stood out was a small black bust of Jim Gregory. Among the other souvenirs on display was a mini replica of the League Cup Rangers won in 1967.

The fans often look back on that season with more than a little nostalgia. QPR became the first team outside the top two divisions to win the League Cup in the first year it was played at Wembley. Their First Division opponents West Brom took a two-goal lead in the final before losing 3–2 in a thrilling encounter. Mike Keen, the father of former West Ham winger Kevin, proudly walked up the steps to the Royal Box to lift the club's first major trophy. But it wasn't just Cup success that made it such a memorable season. Rangers also won the Third Division title by 12 points under manager Alec Stock and were about to embark on a rapid rise up the divisions.

Shortly after that Wembley triumph goalkeeping brothers Ron and Peter Springett were involved in a unique £40,000 exchange deal with Peter moving from Rangers to Sheffield Wednesday and Ron going the other way to Rangers. But Peter found it difficult to follow in the footsteps of his older brother, who played 33 times for England. 'The most infuriating part was when people compared us,' said Peter, who was now working with the West Yorkshire Police and as the Sheffield United Supporters Liaison Officer. 'Any resemblance between our styles was just a coincidence.'

In fact, Peter was never influenced by his brother's success and might not have been a goalkeeper at all but for a twist of fate. Initially he played at centre-forward, representing West London Schools. But when the keeper failed to show up for a game, Peter volunteered to take his place and quickly impressed in goal.

Two other players who were influential for Rangers during their rapid ascent in the late '60s were identical twins Ian and Roger Morgan. 'I remember when Roger's cartilage went when Rangers were chasing promotion to Division One in 1968,' said Ian, who was now Assistant Sports Development Officer for Hackney Council. 'I went all strange inside just as though something had happened to me.' The twins were eventually parted when Roger was transferred. 'After Roger went to Spurs, little went right for either of us – we shared the frustration of an almost continual fight for fitness after a string of injuries.'

Promotion to the First Division in 1968 meant Rangers were only the second team, after Charlton in 1935 and 1936, to climb from the Third to the First Division in consecutive seasons. They'd come a long way since first joining the Football League as founder members of the Third Division in 1920.

Former Spurs double-winner Les Allen had been a key figure at Rangers during the 1966–67 season and the Allen connection with the club was to continue through his sons, Clive and Bradley, and nephew Martin. Bradley was the only member of the Allen clan still at Loftus Road when I visited the club. 'My dad is my fiercest critic and also my biggest fan,' he said. 'If it wasn't for him, I don't think I'd be where I am today. He's been a tremendous influence on my career and on Clive's as well.'

Les had always been there when Clive and Bradley needed him, notably when Clive left QPR for Arsenal in a record £1.25 million deal as a 19-year-old, in June 1980. Les had guided, encouraged and advised but never pushed his sons. 'If I had any problems at all, anything I was uncertain about, I knew my dad would help me sort them out,' said Clive, who's also played for Crystal Palace, Tottenham, West Ham and Millwall and is now a pundit on Sky Sports and was a kicker for the London Monarchs American Football team. 'But the final decision was always left to me,' he added.

After a few beers I left the ground and wandered down to the main entrance, where the West Ham coach was waiting to take the players the short distance across London to Upton Park. A cheer went up as Harry Redknapp and Frank Lampard emerged followed by the players including the diminutive Tony Cottee.

They clearly hadn't enjoyed their afternoon at the Rangers stadium and looked relieved to be leaving when the coach pulled away. A few half-hearted waves to the lingering West Ham fans was all they could muster before settling down to a game of cards to pass the time on the journey home. It's tough at the top!

AUTO CHAIRMAN

Reading v Middlesbrough – Elm Park, 6 December 1994

It's impossible to visit Reading's Elm Park stadium and not notice the advertising for *Auto Trader* magazine. It's there on a big board inside the ground; it's on the front of the matchday programme under the heading Club Sponsor; and it's plastered across the front of the team's royal-blue and white hooped shirts next to the car mag's logo.

The intervention of John Madejski, the owner of *Auto Trader*, at the request of a director, saved Reading from bankruptcy in 1990 after the collapse of then-chairman Robert Maxwell's publishing empire. At the time the club was losing £20,000 a week and the receivers were at the gates. But Madejski, who is 53 and calls himself Berkshire's oldest teenager, bought Maxwell's stake and now owns most of the shares.

'I was led to believe that the club would go under if I did not step in,' he says, though he's doubtful he was the only person who could have saved Reading. He's not a football fanatic, describing himself as 'just a supporter'. Fortunately he's a wealthy one, being the 85th richest man in Britain with a net worth of £200 million.

'I consider Reading as where I'm from,' he says. 'Having lived in California and travelled the world, I know what it's like to find a newspaper in a far-flung place and see the football results. Just to see the name of Reading in print, it's a reminder, it's like a suck of the thumb.' The comforter had so far cost him at least £2 million.

But Madejski is no Jack Walker or Sir John Hall. His commitment to Reading is more pragmatic than fanciful. His rescue package, including a £1.5 million loan and guarantee of the club's £600,000 overdraft, was designed to make Reading sound and to ensure its survival. If players were bought, others had to be sold.

'I haven't got vast sums to throw around, but even if I did, I don't intend to,' says Madejski. 'It's not my style. I don't like throwing money gratuitously at things. I think it's a bit vulgar just slinging £60 million at something. I have to remind people that unlike Jack Walker I haven't sold my business and I don't plan to. What he's done is somewhat grotesque. By fuelling expectations and salaries he makes it more difficult for existing clubs. We've seen stupid things happen in America like lock-outs and that would be the logical conclusion of what's happening here.'

Madejski certainly has the money to compete with the big boys if he wants to. He earned £11 million from his £200 million publishing empire between 1991 and 1994. Madejski owns 67 per cent of Hurst Publishing (a colleague called Paul Gibbons owns the rest), which employs more than 1,000 people and is estimated to be worth about £130 million. Hurst now publishes 12 regional *Auto Traders* and a host of 'free-ad' magazines. In 1994 alone, Madejski and Gibbons shared a £7.8 million pay-out.

Madejski's business spans the UK, Canada, and South Africa and generates a turnover of £77 million a year. In December 1993 he paid £5 million to buy 57 per cent of the loss-making quoted printing group Goodhead, appointed himself chief executive and the business now makes a profit. In 1994 he bought Car Trader, publisher of South Africa's *Auto Trader,* and would later expand his business to Italy. Madejski's success has allowed him to redesign and refurbish his house which sits at the top of Pangbourne Hill. There are signs of his eccentricity throughout the property. The door chimes welcome visitors with a rendition of Beethoven's 'Ode to Joy'. The entrance to the indoor pool, where he swims 20 lengths each morning, is via an innocent-looking wardrobe door in his bedroom. 'It's my favourite bit of the house,' he says. 'It reminds me of Alice in Wonderland.'

The walls are hung with paintings – one of his passions. A few years ago

Madejski fell in love with a large painting in a Mayfair gallery and gutted his house to turn three rooms into one big enough to show off the artwork. But his favourite piece is in the fully equipped gymnasium, where one entire wall acts as a huge picture frame. It lights up to display one of Madejski's three Ferraris mounted inside. 'It's the 328GTS – for me the most beautiful shape of all. I think of it as a particularly realistic hologram.'

His wealth had allowed him to nurture his love of classic cars. Thirty-two years after dreaming of a Jaguar XK140 drophead coupé he bought one. Madejski had other cars too. Three Ferraris, including the one on display in the gym, a 220 mph Jaguar XJ220 supercar, a Jaguar XK140, an AC Cobra which 'roars like a lion', and a Bentley Continental.

In the spring of 1996 Madejski was to meet Chelsea chairman Ken Bates at London's Savoy Hotel. The two exchanged pleasantries, doubtless discussing tactical formations and the cost of players' wages rather than commerce and fine wines. It was rare for them to come face-to-face, since their clubs are in different divisions. As they left, Madejski climbed into his large stretch Rolls-Royce, driven by a ravishing blonde chauffeuse, whereas Bates had to make do with a basic runabout Roller. The Chelsea chairman drew up alongside Madejski's motorised palace, wound down his window and called across: 'You may have a bigger car, but I've got a bigger football club!'

Madejski's investment in Reading clearly brings him something that purely material things cannot: a sense of community, of helping to put something back into the town he calls home. 'Reading has never been much of anything; it's too close to London for that. If you want to do something for the town you can help the hospital, but the football club really touches a lot of people. If you speak to medical people, they say everyone needs the feel-good factor. It's almost the ambrosia of the masses.'

Reading is the county town of Berkshire; it stands on the River Kennet and is cut off by the railway from the nearby Thames. A centre of the medieval cloth trade, it has become known for beer, bulbs and biscuits. One benefit of being so close to London is that many large companies have chosen to set up their headquarters in the town.

There's not much about Reading that stands out. King Henry I is buried in the grounds of the ruined Benedictine abbey which he founded in 1121; the author Jane Austen was once a pupil at the school which is now a heavily restored gatehouse at the Abbey; and Oscar Wilde wrote a book called *De Profoundis* in Reading jail in 1897.

I'd arrived at Reading on the train from London for this Tuesday night match and anticipated an exciting game given the Royals' well-known attacking philosophy under manager Mark McGhee. The team was spearheaded by that old striking war-horse and Irish international Jimmy Quinn, although he'd only managed four goals so far.

On arriving at Reading's British Rail station I followed the supporters decked out in their royal-blue and white scarves towards the Main Stand on Norfolk Road. It was covered in royal-blue corrugated sheeting, but apart from that architectural enhancement, was basically little changed from when it was built in 1926.

The original Main Stand was blown down in a gale in December 1925 and the present stand was built to replace it as Reading prepared for Second Division football. They'd originally joined the Third Division in 1920. The Stand was built by the London firm of Humphrey's but the opening was delayed until 13 November by the General Strike.

From the main office I picked up my standing ticket for the Tilehurst End, a ramshackle affair which highlighted the need for Reading to move to a new stadium. It was during the Main Stand's first season in 1926–27 that Elm Park hosted its largest-ever crowd of just over 33,000, for an FA Cup match against Brentford. Reading had their best-ever Cup run that year, when they went all the way to the semi-final, beating top-class teams like Manchester United and Portsmouth along the way.

Since Elm Park is built into the side of a hill, the pitch is actually some six feet higher than Norfolk Road. Reading originally spent £800 cutting a level pitch into the site's sloping ground, laying turf on the terraces and putting up fences. That explained why the players had to climb steps leading out of the dressing-rooms to get onto the pitch.

Middlesbrough's team included star names like Nigel Pearson, Robbie Mustoe, Craig Hignett and Jamie Pollock. Reading boasted Shaka Hislop in goal and Northern Ireland international Jimmy Quinn – the club's most capped player – up front, but there were few other stars in their team. Boro were eight points clear of the Royals at the top of the First Division and tonight's match gave Reading the opportunity to catch up.

The home fans created a noisy atmosphere which rose to a crescendo as the clock on the front of the Tilehurst Terrace struck 7.45 and the game began. That Reading still existed at all was something of a miracle. In April 1983, Robert Maxwell announced that he was merging his Oxford United team with Reading and calling the new club the Thames Valley Royals. He may have been bluffing to try to force Oxford City Council to find United a new ground, but, whatever his intentions, the result was a boardroom coup at Elm Park. Former Reading player Roger Smee, a 35-year old property tycoon, became chairman and the new board spiritedly fought off the proposed amalgamation.

Reading had just been relegated to the Fourth Division and crowds had slumped to less than 4,000. They had little choice but to sell striker Kerry Dixon, the Third Division's top scorer in the 1982–83 season, to Chelsea for a club record £150,000. They spent £35,000 of that money buying Trevor Senior from Portsmouth and his 36 League goals helped them win immediate promotion.

The new regime had brought instant success, and when Reading began the following season by winning their first 13 games, they set a new record which eclipsed the 11-game winning streak set by Spurs' double team at the beginning of the 1960–61 season. That start propelled Reading to the Third Division Championship – their second promotion in two seasons. The glory days had returned at last.

Elm Park was given a face-lift to bring the capacity up to 20,000 for the club's return to the Second Division. The work included the installation of executive boxes at the back of the Main Stand. The one major setback was that the groundsman, a former player who'd looked after the pitch for 20 years, sprayed the field with weedkiller by mistake! The result was a brown pitch, which undermined the attractions of Elm Park.

Despite modest improvements to the ground over the years, it was clear that

Reading needed a new stadium. Roger Smee raised the issue as soon as he took over, and proposals centred on an area of refuse tips at Smallmead on the southern outskirts of Reading, close to the M4. A greyhound and speedway stadium had been opened next to the site in 1975, the year after the Oxford Road stadium was closed.

Reading Borough Council were enthusiastic about the idea and included a new ground on the local plan for the area. The problem was money. Neither the council nor the greyhound promoter, who wanted Reading to share his stadium, could offer any financial help.

The 1980s came to an end with little progress on a new ground. But the Taylor Report began to force the issue, since, although Reading were in the Third Division in 1990, Elm Park could only accommodate a maximum of 12,000 seats and actually had a little under 2,500. The problem remained money: the club was £600,000 in debt.

In September 1990 Roger Smee faced financial problems of his own and resigned. Enter John Madejski. The rest, as they say, is history. (Reading were promoted as Second Division champions in 1994 and would come within a whisker of joining the Premier League the following season when they lost a closely contested play-off final to Bolton after being ahead.)

Madejski was to provide £10 million towards the cost of building the stadium, which was due to begin in April 1997. Funding for the rest of the scheme, including community sports facilities and 3,500 parking spaces, was to come from a retail park. The sale of Elm Park for residential development would contribute £2–3 million. 'We're building an audacious new stadium for £37 million, with room for 25,000 and a conference centre only half a mile from the M4,' says Madejski. 'I'll probably lose my shirt!' The complex is on the route of the new A33 relief road, which will connect the town centre with junction 11 of the M4.

Reading, like Middlesbrough, wanted to grace a new stadium as members of the Premier League. The omens looked good for Boro, if not quite so rosy for the Royals. The 1926–27 season had been the start of a curious sequence in which every time Middlesbrough had been in the same division as Reading they'd won promotion. 'It's happened four times before and who would bet against it happening again next May?' wrote Alan Sedunary in the Reading match programme.

Reading captain Adrian Williams was hoping the Royals would give Middlesbrough a run for their money, even though he was out of the side through injury. Boro manager Bryan Robson had been known as Captain Marvel during his playing career, but it was a label that could easily have been given to Williams. On 5 March 1994 he completed a record of playing in every shirt number for Reading when he wore the number ten against Wrexham. He'd even deputised for an injured goalkeeper two years earlier!

But neither Williams nor anyone else had brought that much success to Elm Park over the years. The only 'major' knock-out competition the club has ever won is the Simod Cup in 1988. They've spent most of their League history in the Third Division, including a 40-year spell between 1931 and 1971, with a couple of periods in the Second (now First) Division and frequent drops to the Fourth Division, the first and most embarrassing of which came in their centenary year of 1971.

They did win the Second Division Championship in 1994, the Third Division title in 1926 and 1986, and the Fourth Division in 1979. And they were once unbeaten at home in 55 consecutive matches between 1933 and 1936. Reading haven't done a whole lot to write home about. John Madejski hopes to change that.

FOOTBALL IS A RELIGION

Barnsley v Bristol City – Oakwell, 7 December 1994

Barnsley were founded in 1887 by the Reverend Tiverton Preedy, the curate of St Peters Church in Barnsley. The young preacher had resigned from the local rugby club, because they'd offended his principles by playing on Good Friday, and he decided instead to form a football team known as Barnsley St Peters.

It was fitting therefore that an Archdeacon should score the winner against Bristol City on a cold Wednesday night in South Yorkshire. Not that Owen Archdeacon, or 'Archie' to his mates, was a member of the clergy, even though most of the Oakwell congregation of just over 4,000 hardy souls who'd turned up for this First Division encounter were praying someone would hit the winner. Archdeacon answered their prayers five minutes from time.

The former Celtic player had only just returned to the side, in place of player–manager Danny Wilson, after an Achilles injury. There was a time when he thought he was never going to regain his place in the first team. 'But in only the third game of his comeback he scored a goal which typified Barnsley's constructive approach to an awkward game against Joe Jordan's strugglers on a bitter, windy night,' reported the *Yorkshire Post* the following morning. It was bitter, and it was windy. I could hardly feel my toes and the wind ran through me like an icy river.

Barnsley, a town of almost 75,000 people, sits in the middle of the depressed South Yorkshire coalfield area. To the north-east of the club's Oakwell ground is the industrial centre with its factories, glass works and coal mines. Barnsley are called the Tykes, the ancient dialect term for a native Yorkshireman. Its origins were far from flattering, being used as a reference to comic rustic characters, or as an insult from Old Norse meaning a dog or cur. But it hadn't stopped the club naming its bulldog mascot Tyke.

The Oakwell stadium is one of the few you can look down upon, which I did after parking my car at the top of a hill near the Metrodome, 'Yorkshire's Premier Indoor Swimming Pool Complex'. The leisure centre was impressive. 'Ride the surf and dive through the waves, lounge in the shallow lagoons or wander through the waterfalls,' said the brochure. It sounded more like a holiday in the tropics than Barnsley Metropolitan Borough Council's sports complex.

I could see the hazy glow of the floodlights shining ahead of me. The new East Stand, with its red tubular steel supports nestled on top of the roof, towered over the rest of the ground. It was all I could really make out between the floodlights, since rows of semi-detached houses partly obscured the rest of the stadium. The ground was a sea of red and white, but from the club's colours which decorated the stadium rather than an army of fans. Few of the locals would venture out tonight.

As I walked down towards the stadium a biting wind swept off the Pennine moor, swirling all around me. It was no surprise, at least to me, to learn that a gale blew down the club's first stand in 1895. Big white letters announcing Barnsley Football Club stood out on the back wall of the old Main Stand. The central section, which cost £600, was opened in 1904. The wings were added later.

The Pontefract Road End Stand to the right was built in 1900. It had been temporarily closed as Barnsley prepared to build a new all-seater stand to replace the terraces. Not that everyone was happy about the changes the club had to make to meet the new safety requirements. Supporter Richard Darn, writing in *When Saturday Comes*, called it: 'One of those injustices that convince Barnsley folk the world's against them. Not content with shutting the town's last remaining pit, the government also decided to close down Oakwell's terraces to force compliance with the Taylor Report.'

The new £2 million 4,500 all-seater Ora Stand, named after the sponsors Ora Electronics (the country's largest suppliers of mobile phone accessories) would be unveiled during the second week of the 1995–96 season. By then, Barnsley would have spent £5 million in two-and-a-half years to transform Oakwell. The ground would have more than 19,000 seats compared to just over 2,000 in 1993.

That development includes the impressive £2.5 million East Stand, made of brick, tinted glass and steel, which houses the Oakwell Executive Suite. There couldn't have been more of a contrast with the old Main Stand opposite, which had only been kept in half-decent condition with a regular lick of red paint. It must have seen some great players and had some stories to tell from across the years, though.

George Robledo, a Chilean-born forward, scored some magnificent goals at Oakwell before being sold to Newcastle. Danny Blanchflower, later to star with Aston Villa, Spurs and Northern Ireland, began his career with Barnsley in the late 1940s and even then looked something special. Tommy Taylor, Manchester United's magnificent centre-forward, so tragically killed in the Munich air disaster, began his career at Oakwell in the early 1950s, scoring a hat-trick in only his second game.

More recently, Allan 'Sniffer' Clarke and Norman Hunter, members of the great Leeds team of the '70s, had worn the Reds' shirt as player–managers. Surprisingly, given his rugged defensive skills, Hunter emphasised attacking play and received welcome praise from the Press for his team's entertaining brand of football! Barnsley seem to like player–managers. Current boss, Danny Wilson, had followed Viv Anderson into the hot seat. Not that any of the seats at Oakwell were hot tonight. Still, at least the match was not postponed. It had already been rearranged once because of international matches.

The fading red and white paint advertising the Spion Kop End of the ground was also a reminder of times past, not unlike the decaying surroundings I'd see at Blackpool's Bloomfield Road in the spring. Unusually, the Kop End at Barnsley was for away fans, who were also given part of the Main, or West, Stand. I assumed it was because of the rebuilding programme. Not that many had made the long journey up from Bristol on a freezing week night in the run-up to Christmas.

At least the City fans, and new manager Joe Jordan, could cheer a goal. The Barnsley defence tried to play offside but failed miserably to get it right, leaving Junior Bent to run onto a pass and drive a low shot into the Barnsley net. Bent, not renowned for his calm finishing, looked as surprised as anyone when the ball ended up in the back of the goal. That pulled City level after Andy Liddell had blasted a close-range shot into the roof of the net to give Barnsley the lead after half-an-hour.

And that would have been that without Archdeacon's divine intervention. Barnsley's manager would have looked up to the heavens in despair if that goal hadn't gone in. 'I would have been disappointed if we hadn't won. We didn't play particularly well, but we were the only side pushing for victory at the end.' Alas, it wasn't enough to propel Yorkshire's unfashionable club out of the Second Division – where they had spent more time than any other team. The fans would have to wait a while longer for a League visit to Old Trafford. But is was coming.

DOOMSDAY SCENARIO

Gillingham v Wigan Athletic – The Priestfield Stadium, 10 December 1994

> The fact is that Gillingham have once again failed to live up to the expectations of the support. Considering those expectations are about as high as an ant's testicles these days that is quite an achievement . . . If there is one single Gillingham fan out there who is not thoroughly fed up with the team then please get in touch – we'd like you to supply us with the same stuff you're on.

This was the verdict of the so-called 'Headitorial' in the imaginatively titled fanzine *Brian Moore's Head Looks Amazingly Like London Planetarium*. It's named after the Gills' most famous fan – the ITV commentator, not the rugby player. By coincidence, I would bump into him at Luton the following day.

There were plenty of match programmes on sale at the Priestfield Stadium for the visit of Wigan, but the latest issue of *BMH* (well, they had to have an acronym with a title as long as that) was sold out when I tried to catch up with its latest views on Gillingham Football Club.

I had to console myself with the previous issue of the fanzine, but I already knew that, while expectations among Gills fans may have sunk, they'd surely never been very high. There was little reason, then, for the club to live up to its nickname of the Shouting Men, since there wasn't much to shout about. (A display in the club offices explained that the nickname was taken from an ancient tribe who came from Gillingas – an area referred to in the Domesday Book as Gellingeham.)

Sure, Gillingham have produced players who've gone on to play at the top level – Tony Cascarino, Gavin Peacock, Peter Beadle – but their only major honour is the Fourth Division Championship of 1964. According to the otherwise excellent book *The Cassell Soccer Companion: History-Facts-Anecdotes,* this was achieved with an unbeaten run of 52 home games. Now, far be it for me to quibble over how Gillingham actually managed to play 52 home games in one season, but this record stood until 1981 when Liverpool were unbeaten at home for 85 matches.

If you've never heard of Peter Beadle (let's be honest, not many people have), he was signed by former England coach Terry Venables for a bargain £300,000 to bolster the Tottenham forward line. The fanzine gave me the impression that the Gills could do with a few quid, since, in an article headed 'Does This Mean We Get the Rest of the Money?' it raised the question of whether Gillingham deserved a cut from Beadle's subsequent transfer to Watford for the princely sum of £5,000.

Apparently, part of the deal with Spurs was that Gillingham would receive extra cash based on Beadle's appearances and even more money if he played for England. The total could have mounted up to £750,000. What *BMH* wanted to know was whether the terms of the deal still applied. If I were a Gills fan, I wouldn't hold my breath for that first England cap.

Money has been a constant source of worry for the Medway team; they dropped out of the Football League in 1938, to be replaced by Ipswich, and were not re-elected until 1950, when the League increased its membership from 88 to 92 by expanding the Third Divisions (North) and (South), as they were then called, from 22 to 24 teams.

The only 'star' players I knew in the Gillingham team today were Neil Smillie, formerly with Crystal Palace and Brighton, and substitute Gary Micklewhite, who played more than 100 games for QPR and over 200 for Derby before joining the Gills. He made a late appearance versus Wigan, but little difference.

According to Micklewhite, there were major differences between Division Three and the level of football at his former clubs. 'Obviously, the higher up you go the more quality players there are and, consequently, the better finishers they are and the better passers they are. There is a bigger gap between the Premier Division and Division One than there is between Division One or Two and then the gap between Division Two and Three is smaller.

'What I have found is that when I've been playing in higher leagues and when I've been playing wide, I've probably got more of the ball than I do now and that gets very frustrating – that's really why I now prefer playing in the middle of the pitch so that I can keep involved. That apart, I do believe that the quality of finishing is the biggest difference. In the lower divisons you get a good deal of young players learning the game and many of them are still naïve and with a great deal to learn.'

The only significant incident in the first half was the announcement over the PA for a Mr John Clarke to phone home. 'Your wife can't find the keys,' said the announcer. I was hoping one of the Gills players would find the keys to unlock the Wigan defence before half-time, but that was just wishful thinking. It would have been easier to steal the Crown Jewels from the Tower of London.

At half-time I popped behind the Main Stand for a cup of tea and started chatting to the guy in front of me, as you do.

'Do you come here often?' I asked, wondering if he'd think I wanted a quick twirl across the Priestfield pitch.

'No, I'm not a supporter, I'm a scout for Millwall,' he told me.

'Are you here to watch anyone in particular in the Gillingham team?'

'Actually, I've been asked to check out the Oldham seven.' I'd heard of the Guildford Four, but the Oldham Seven?

It turned out to be Ian Kilford, an ever-present in the Wigan team, who had spent two periods on loan from Nottingham Forest the previous season before signing on a permanent basis in the summer. He was Wigan's joint top scorer and word had spread that he was worth keeping an eye on. His talent wasn't immediately obvious to me, and if I'd been sending a report back to Millwall, I would have recommended Richard 'Chippie' Carpenter, the Gills midfield dynamo, who was outstanding and unlucky not to score with a 35-yard drive in the first half.

The Wigan centre-forward Mark Leonard won the match with a diving header inside the six-yard box in the 61st minute to send the hundred or so Wigan fans at the uncovered Gillingham End – yes, I know it's called the Gillingham End – home happy. They'd travelled a long way, but they'd savour the journey back to the north-west tonight. I left the Priestfield Stadium where the away fans were still standing behind a large white flag with a red cross. Their chants of 'Wigan, Wigan' were still ringing in my ears.

WELCOME TO THE KOHLERDOME

Luton Town v Derby County – Kenilworth Road, 11 December 1994

'Luton Chairman Ready for a Stretch Inside' was the headline in *The Sunday Times*. Yet another misdemeanour in the Season of Sleaze? One more bung in a brown paper bag at a motorway service station off the M25 uncovered at the 12th hour by the football authorities? Nothing of the sort. This was an article about what Luton Town's chairman calls the Kohlerdome.

The chairman in question is David Kohler and his 'dome' is the code name for a project to build a new multi-purpose indoor stadium near junction ten of the M1; the stadium will seat 20,000 and cost about £30 million. The key to his plans is a moveable grass pitch which would follow in the footsteps of the Pontiac Silverdome, the indoor stadium in Michigan touted as the wonder of USA '94 and an example of American ingenuity. It was the first, and so far only, World Cup venue to feature indoor soccer on real grass.

Laying a grass pitch inside the Silverdome was a major exercise. Two thousand hexagonal sections of grass were brought in by forklift trucks. It took three days to bring in and three days to take out. That's obviously far too long for a stadium to switch regularly between grass and other surfaces for different events. Under Kohler's plans the Luton pitch would be installed in five hours and removed in three, using hovercraft technology.

Basically, the playing surface is divided into nine large sections, each held on a steel tray weighing about 375 tonnes. These are moved by four small hovercraft, manoeuvred by four people, instead of the dozens needed at the Silverdome. The hovercraft are placed under the corners of each section, raising it up and floating it out of the stadium on a cushion of air. The grass therefore grows outside the stadium and must be stored in natural conditions until it's floated in. Luton thus need an extra area the size of a football pitch to store the grass.

The supporters seemed to favour the proposed Kohlerdome after rejecting plans for a move to Milton Keynes. The editorial in the fanzine *Mad as a Hatter* clearly gave the scheme it's backing. 'Some of those opposed to the new stadium are suggesting that the existing ground should be redeveloped. It is clear that these are people who have not stepped inside a football ground for many years, and have no appreciation of how poor our ground now looks in comparison with many others in the [First] Division. To improve the ground significantly would require the purchase of many houses around the ground and that process alone could take many years. The only way ahead is a new stadium, at a new location, and it will be up to us, the supporters, to give the proposals the backing they need to come to fruition.'

The club's reputation for innovation comes from the installation of an artificial pitch in 1985 and the controversial members-only scheme introduced the same year, partly in response to the chaos caused by rioting Millwall fans. Luton were banned from the fizzy drinks cup, then the Littlewoods Cup, in 1986 as a punishment for breaking the tournament's rules. The club got their revenge when they won the trophy by beating Arsenal 3–2 in 1988. They were also runners-up the following year.

News of the plans for a super stadium was first unveiled in October 1994, since when discussions have been taking place on a possible site. Kohler clearly has a vision: ' . . . we at Luton Town have a dream that one day we can move from Kenilworth Road, our home for the past 90 years, into a new stadium. The reasons for the move, apart from our lease running out in 1996, are obvious to all who have visited us.'

In fact, Luton have been trying to find a new home since the end of the Second World War. In the 1970s there was talk of moving to Milton Keynes, 23 miles up the M1. During the 1983–84 season the club announced that, because of road-building plans affecting the ground, they would be forced to move. Milton Keynes was again the planned location, but the supporters organised protest marches and it never happened.

I went to see the Hatters (Luton was once a straw hat-making centre) play Derby in a televised match screened live on a Sunday afternoon and the traffic was appalling. Queues of cars blocked the approach roads around the ground and the journey was one big headache. Clearly, improved access was impossible at Kenilworth Road.

I eventually arrived at the ground and was ushered into the Eric Morecambe suite. A portrait of the genial star of *The Morecambe & Wise Show* hangs on the wall. Morecambe was a Luton Town director from 1976 to 1983 and brought a lot of sunshine to the club and its supporters. The club played 'Bring Me Sunshine', the theme tune which used to bring the curtain down on the hit television show, when the Luton players run out. Sadly, they failed to deliver any rays at all.

I was in the Main Stand on Maple Road, built in the 1920s after a fire destroyed its predecessor. The centre section was bought from Kempton racecourse. A railway line runs parallel to the stand and its assortment of offices, social clubs and guest lounges. It only covers three-quarters of the length of the pitch, thanks to the presence of the railway line and the relief road which cuts across the south-east corner of the ground by the Kenilworth Road End.

Opposite was the North Stand on Beech Hill Path, which replaced the Bobbers Stand in 1986. It once cost a 'bob' (a shilling, or five new pence) to stand on the terraces, but today they've gone, replaced first by seats and now by executive boxes. Kenilworth Road is the only ground with boxes along the whole of one side of the pitch. Like those at Watford, box-holders and their guests can sit outside on a private balcony if they prefer to watch the match in the elements. Luton got the idea from Lord's Cricket Ground where sliding glass doors provide access to the seats outside.

To my left was the all-seater Oak Road End with its unusual three-tiered roof rising up to meet the roof of the Main Stand. Away fans are now allowed into Kenilworth Road now after the lifting of the club's ban imposed in 1986. I walked around the back of the stand before the match for a first-hand look at how cramped the ground is. The entrances actually run through terraced houses, along a pathway and up a flight of stairs looking over a row of back gardens.

The Middlesbrough fanzine *Fly Me to the Moon* summed up the attitude of away fans to this end of the ground. 'One thing I don't like is the fact that if the away end ever totally sells out then the front row is under pitch level and so far below the hoardings that you can't actually see the pitch. One thing I do like is climbing down the steps to the rear of the stand and being able to get a good insight into the kitchen and bathroom hygiene of the citizens of Beds.' Whatever turns you on!

The home fans were underwhelmed by Luton's display against Derby. The match ended goalless, though it was more exciting than the previous day's game at Gillingham. (After watching the Gills, even snooker player Steve Davis would have had me jumping out of my seat.) At least I got to see Marvin Johnson, the Luton number three who, according to the fanzine *Mad as a Hatter*, 'looks like a clown, defends like a Tottenham full-back and attacks like a Brazilian'. Nice combo.

The contrast between this performance and Luton's record win back in the 1930s couldn't have been sharper. One of the guest suites is dedicated to the hero of that game, Joe Payne. 'Ten Goal' was the nickname given to Luton's reserve wing-half who in 1936 scored a League record ten goals against Bristol Rovers in a 12–0 win. Payne had never previously played centre-forward. He described his afternoon's work as 'just one of those days'. Offers flooded in from other clubs, but he remained at Luton to score a record 55 goals the following season. He eventually left to join Chelsea, West Ham, and Millwall, earning an England cap along the way, before retiring in 1948.

Payne was a reminder of better days for Luton. The following year they were promoted from the Third Division as champions, though they had to wait until 1968 for their next taste of glory when they won the Fourth Division title. The Second Division Championship followed in 1982 and then a series of close encounters of the First Division relegation kind, including a last-gasp win over Manchester City at Maine Road in 1983 thanks to a goal from Raddy Antic in the closing minutes. Luton eventually ran out of luck and dropped down into the First Division (the new one) in 1992.

Perhaps a new super stadium will bring the good times back to the

Bedfordshire team. Kohler hopes so. 'On my office wall I have a picture of the proposed "Kohlerdome" with the words: If you will it, it is no dream.' He sounds like a cross between Martin Luther King and one of those flash foreign car ads and has yet to deliver his dream to the people of Luton. It doesn't look likely.

TED HOLDS COURT

Bournemouth v Wrexham – Dean Court, 16 December 1994

Four goals, the Bournemouth goalkeeper sent off and replaced by a YTS trainee, the South End Stand closed for safety reasons and the Wrexham fans singing 'You're going down with the Chester'. All in a night's work at Dean Court.

This was Friday Night Football in the run-up to Christmas. The stewards wore red Father Christmas hats with a white trim, the kids were given free fudge and the family room was packed with youngsters looking forward to seeing their heroes on the pitch. Not that there had been much to cheer about so far this season for Cherries fans.

Bournemouth itself dates from 1811, when a local squire built a summer house on the wild unpopulated heathland by the coast and planted the first of the pine trees that you now see all around the town and in the 2,000 acres of public parks and gardens. By the end of the 1800s Bournemouth's mild climate, sandy beaches and cliffs interrupted by beautiful 'chines', or ravines, had attracted 60,000 people.

Today the town, which stands at the mouth of the Bourne valley overlooking Poole Bay, is a major conference venue and full of language schools. The population has grown to almost 160,000 but only 2,000–3,000 of them regularly watch the local football team. The club's problem is that most people in the area are old – there's a geriatric nursing home around every corner.

Among the famous people associated with the town are Mary Shelley, author of *Frankenstein*, who is buried at the church of St Peter's, east of the town square; and Robert Louis Stevenson, who wrote *Kidnapped* and *Dr Jekyll and Mr Hyde* in Bournemouth, where he lived in a house called Skerryvor in the late 1800s. By the time the football club was formed in 1899 Shelley was long dead and Stevenson had left town. But a certain J.E. Cooper Dean was just coming onto the scene. In 1910 he let the club rent some wasteland in the suburb of Boscombe for a nominal rent. Dean Court was named after him and he later became club president.

Nevertheless, Bournemouth's most famous son is definitely Ted MacDougall, who chalked up an FA Cup record of nine goals in one match and a club record 42 in a season. Ted achieved his goalscoring feats in the 1970–71 season under John Bond, later the manager at Norwich and Manchester City. His nine goals came in an 11–0 first round win over Margate in 1971 – and only one was a penalty! His 42 goals helped the Cherries clinch promotion from Division Four as runners-up.

Black and white photos of the revered striker in action, including a celebration of one of the goals against Margate, adorn the walls at Dean Court. The fans still talk about him and apparently they haven't yet got over his transfer to Manchester United for a (then) club record £220,000 in September 1972.

'I was at school the day it happened,' said my tour guide, a lifelong Cherries fan. 'The teacher told us but I didn't believe him, or didn't want to. I remember rushing home to read the paper. I looked at the front page and there it was: MACDOUGALL JOINS UNITED. I could have cried. I was devastated. Even now it hurts to think that our star striker, our idol, was playing for someone else. It just didn't seem fair.'

The days of MacDougall's goalscoring feats are now long gone. The club's only honour since then, indeed ever, is the Third Division title captured in 1987. The glass Championship trophy with engraved frosted footballers stood proudly in the trophy cabinet in a corner of the boardroom along with the intriguing Uganda Cup.

Their one cup success is the 1984 Associate Members Cup which they lifted at Hull's Boothferry Park. They're the only club to win that version of the Cup, since its name was then changed to the Freight Rover Trophy. The supporters reckon they should have played the final at Wembley and say it shows the sort of luck Bournemouth have had since the glory days.

Dean Court is also showing signs of age. I arrived early for a tour and walked behind the Main Stand past the car park which backs onto King's Park with its fringe of tall trees. I was taken underneath the Main Stand, which looked the worse for wear. Indeed, the framework came from the British Empire Exhibition at Wembley, where it was first built in 1923 as a restaurant. Bournemouth bought it for £12,000 and opened it at the start of the 1927–28 season.

The South End Stand, opened in 1936, was closed tonight for safety reasons, though it was no longer half-boarded-up as it had been for some years. The name of the open Brighton Beach End opposite confuses many, since the rival seaside town is about 80 miles east along the coast. Even some home fans don't know its origins.

'Why is it called the Brighton Beach End?' I asked the lad next to me in the Main Stand.

'I haven't a clue,' he replied. 'Never thought about it really.'

The answer is that the terraces used to be a stony bank reminding the Bournemouth fans of Brighton beach!

The club was hoping for a change of fortune with their new chairman, Ken Gardiner. The way local football correspondent, Derek McGregor, described him he could have been a ringer for Ron Atkinson. 'With his chunky gold jewellery and eccentric ties, Gardiner gives the impression of being flash; a man with an ego who has acquired a media platform with his substantial stake in the Cherries.'

The *Evening Echo* reporter was himself a controversial character because of a long-running battle with former manager Tony Pulis which culminated in a telephone poll as to who was right about the team. (Who do you think got most votes?) McGregor is from Scotland and is a rare breed. A Celtic fan, he once worked for *Rangers News*!

The Cherries manager, former Bournemouth star Mel Machin, had taken over from Pulis at the beginning of September after a spell as manager of Manchester City and a more successful period as a player and coach at Norwich, where he won a League Cup winners' medal and helped the Canaries to their highest-ever League position of fifth.

Machin had inherited a struggling Bournmouth side which was still

177

floundering despite an almost complete change of playing staff. Former West Ham striker Steve Jones was a permanent signing after a loan period and spearheaded the attack alongside former Spurs forward Steve Robinson. The side also included midfielder Russell Beardsmore, once of Manchester United, but he failed to impress and was substituted.

Bournemouth had been stuck at the bottom of the Second Division for most of the season and desperately needed points. After taking the lead through an own goal by Bryan Hughes, who sent a spectacular diving header past his own goalkeeper, the Cherries had a hatful of chances to extend their lead but didn't take them. Wrexham equalised through Hughes who made up for his earlier error with a low drive into the corner before half-time.

In the second half Bournemouth keeper Neil Moss came out of his goal and brought down Steve Watkin. It was a professional foul and the referee held up the red card. The substitute goalkeeper was a 17-year-old YTS trainee who had little hope of holding out against the Wrexham forward line. Watkin and Gary Bennett scored the goals that sent the Welsh fans home happy.

For Bournemouth it would be a long, hard winter. They had nine points from 20 games and had conceded 43 goals whilst scoring only 14. The fans were already asking what life was like in the Third Division!

NICE ONE SIRREL

Notts County v Portsmouth – Meadow Lane, 17 December 1994

Notts County's Meadow Lane was the venue for the last match of my tour before Christmas. Things were so bad that the question on everyone's mind was whether the Magpies would be good enough to avoid the drop. Defeat at home to Portsmouth would leave County as the 'strongest' team in the First Division by virtue of holding all the others up. Getting stuffed at Christmas wasn't the ideal way to spend the holidays.

County were nothing if not inconsistent. They'd beaten Spurs 3–0 in the third round of the Coca-Cola Cup in a game which marked the end of Ossie Ardiles reign at White Hart Lane. The Magpies had also drawn against Ascoli, Atalanta and Venezia and beaten Lecce in the Anglo-Italian Cup. But when it came to the League, they were abysmal, winning just four of their 21 League matches, drawing six and losing eleven.

Notts County do not have a glorious history. In the early '60s they languished once again in the Fourth Division County and got into financial difficulty. County would probably have gone under without the financial support of chairman Bill Hopcroft in 1965. The arrival of Jack Dunnett, the one-time chairman of Brentford who'd become the local Labour MP, eventually turned the club's fortunes around. In November 1969 he brought Jimmy Sirrel north from his old club Brentford as County's new manager. It was an inspired choice and the start of a long association between Sirrel and the club which would see him enjoy three spells as manager.

Sirrel took County to two promotions in three years, starting with promotion from Division Four as Champions in 1971 followed by runners-up spot in the Third Division in 1973. The Magpies were sitting proudly on top of Division Two when Sirrel left in 1975 to join First Division Sheffield United. But things didn't work out at Bramall Lane with United relegated in 1976 and he returned to Meadow Lane.

The year Sirrel came back, 1978, the club demolished the tall but by now rickety Trent Bridge Stand. They realised that gates were unlikely to average more than about 12,000; so, instead of replacing the stand, they built an £800,000 sports complex called the Meadow Club. The only space available for supporters at that end was the executive boxes built on top of the wall which now backed onto the pitch.

Under Sirrel, County regained their place in the First Division after an absence of 55 seasons. In guiding them back to the top flight Sirrel had emulated the feats of Alan Ashman at Carlisle and Northampton's Dave Bowen to become only the third manager in history to take a club from the bottom division to the top. County splashed out almost half a million pounds on winger John Chiedozie from Orient as they tried to improve their chances of staying among the élite.

In 1982 Sirrel became general manager, handing control of team affairs to Howard Wilkinson. But County struggled to survive financially, even though they were in the top flight. Former Liverpool and Forest defender Larry Lloyd took over from Wilkinson, but with gates again falling below 6,000 in 1984 and debts of £1 million, relegation to Division Two was no surprise. Richie Barker replaced Lloyd but couldn't stop the rot, and in 1985 County were relegated to the Third Division.

By now, crowds of less than 5,000 were showing up at Meadow Lane. The chairman's exasperation was summed up when he said: 'Most of the people who can remember when we were a great club are dead.' Jimmy Sirrel returned for his third spell as manager, but more drastic action was needed to rescue County. It was time for change at the top and, fortunately, local businessman Derek Pavis was on hand to transform the fortunes of the oldest club in League Football.

A former Forest director who'd fallen out with Brian Clough in 1984, Pavis had made his money from the heating and plumbing industries. He turned down approaches from other Midlands clubs and took over at Meadow Lane. Less than 12 hours after Pavis arrived in 1987, Sirrel packed his bags and handed John Barnwell the keys to his office. Pavis wanted to make a clean start and Sirrel could see the writing on the wall. He moved aside without a hint of animosity towards the new owners of the club he loved.

Two weeks after taking over, Pavis sold his business and was able to give his time and £2 million to the Magpies. His arrival breathed new life into County, and they won promotion to the Second Division in 1991. The following November they paid a club record £685,000 for Sheffield United's Tony Agana, and he helped the Magpies win promotion to Division One. Their new-found success had the supporters returning to Meadow Lane, but it also raised the problem of meeting the Taylor Report deadline of August 1994 for Premier and First Divison clubs to have an all-seater stadium.

County had only 4,200 seats in their just-over-20,000-capacity ground. To make it all-seater in line with the Taylor Report would have cost £12 million. There was talk of sharing a new ground with Forest, who in fact weren't in favour of the idea, so County had to find a solution on their own. Fortunately Pavis was the director in charge of the building of Forest's Executive Stand in 1980 and had some experience.

When he announced the club's plans to transform Meadow Lane, many people doubted that there was enough time available and that it could be done for such a small amount of money. County proposed to build three impressive stands seating 13,500 for £3.2 million during the 1992 close season. If they could pull it off, the Magpies would have the best value-for-money redevelopment any League club had managed.

The night before the ground opened on 22 August, shattered building workers were found flat out in the stands by the officials making final checks that the ground was ready to open for business. It had taken just 17 weeks to complete and a crowd of just over 10,500 came along for the first game of the 1992–93 season. Pavis called it the 'ninth wonder of the world' and the supporters were stunned at the transformation.

The new County Road Stand seated just under 6,000 and, like the old stand, has a white gable with the club name and badge. When the directors were looking for candidates to take on the name of the County Road Stand, one name sprung immediately to mind: former manager Jimmy Sirrel. 'I was absolutely delighted when the chairman contacted me and explained what he and his colleagues wanted to do,' said Sirrel. 'It's a tremendous honour and although the Stand is going to carry my name, I see it as a tribute to all those I worked with in my time at Meadow Lane.'

Sirrel was talking about people like Jack Dunnett – 'a man of vision who picked the club up from its death-bed' – and Jack Wheeler – 'maybe you could find someone who worked as hard as him but you could never find anyone who worked harder. The strength of Notts County is that they have always employed people who are not in it for their own benefit, but because they have a genuine feeling for the club'.

The final phase in the redevelopment of Meadow Lane was the replacement of the Main Stand built in 1910. It was used for the last time on 30 April 1994 and in the early hours of the following morning fans were still stripping it for souvenirs. Some of the wood was used to make benches which sold for £95 each; one supporter even took away one of the urinals. It took just 19 weeks to build a new stand for £3 million.

The new stand was named after chairman Derek Pavis, the man who'd made it all happen, and took the overall cost of redeveloping Meadow Lane to £6.3 million. It has a capacity of 7,000, giving an all-seated stadium of 20,300. The total cost, including floodlights, fittings, lounges and so on, was getting on for £8 million. Pavis chipped in £1 million, almost £2 million was donated by the Football Trust and nearly £4 million was raised by selling Tommy Johnson and Craig Short to Derby.

As I approached the entrance to the shiny new stadium I could see two chestnut trees dating back to the early 1900s – all that was left of the ground from that period. The Main Stand has two brick towers at each end and a curved window at the front over the entrance trimmed in yellow. An electricity substation, put in the Main Stand by the local electricity board manager (a season ticket holder) in the 1930s, is hidden inside.

As it turned out, County didn't come anywhere near matching their impressive surroundings; Pompey took all three points with a 1–0 win and the Magpies were left to spend Christmas in last place. The club's plight saddened Jimmy Sirrel, who'd only just returned the previous September at the age of 72 to take up the position of chief scout after a spell in that job with Derby and Newcastle. Sirrel hoped to improve County's prospects by uncovering new talent who could bring glory to Meadow Lane.

County knew they could find nobody better than Jimmy when they made the appointment and he'd quickly made himself at home in the new surroundings. 'They say you should never go back but it didn't do me any harm the last time I returned to Meadow Lane and I can't imagine it will this time,' said Sirrel. Time would tell.

DEVON DERBY

Exeter City v Torquay United – St James Park, 26 December 1994

If anyone mentions St James you automatically think of Newcastle's home ground, right? But there's St James Park at the opposite end of the country in deepest Devon, where Exeter City play, and which couldn't be more different to the temple for Geordie worshippers who turn out in their black and white stripes to watch their beloved team. Apart from the fact that City play in stripes, there's no comparison.

This was the first of eight games I'd see in eight days over the holidays, including two in one day on three occasions. Apparently I wasn't alone, for the Exeter programme included a feature by Mike Blackstone called 'Holiday Fixtures – A Groundhoppers Delight'. 'I don't doubt that there will be someone here this morning who, at the final whistle, will be dashing off to another game somewhere, probably with a 3 p.m. kick-off, whether it be at non-League or Endsleigh League level.' There was me at least!

Appropriately, my first game was a Devon derby between Exeter and Torquay, not quite Man United against Liverpool, or Tottenham against Arsenal, but in these parts fiercely contested nonetheless. They first played each other on 24 September 1904, when United travelled to St James Fields (as it was known) for a friendly against a City team playing only their third game since the club was formed. Exeter won that match 5–0; and also the return in Torquay in February of the following year when the goals flowed again and United were beaten 6–3. The rivalry has been strong ever since.

Exeter had just been relegated to the Third Division, so the future was hardly bright on or off the pitch. Victory over their Devon arch-rivals would at least ease the pain a little for their supporters. In fact, since City were formed in 1904, by the amalgamation of St Sidwell's United and Exeter United, they'd never ventured above the Third Division. Their best-ever season in the League saw them finish eighth, in 1980.

But they had enjoyed a couple of wonderful FA Cup runs in 1931 and 1981.

During their first brush with fame they had to fight through the qualifying rounds to take their place in the first round proper, where they met First Division Derby. County's aggressive young team were tipped by many to win the Cup that year. When the sides met, Derby were third in the First Division. Their team included England international Sammy Crooks and prolific goalscorer Jack Bowers alongside George Mee, brother of Bertie, who would go on to win the double as the manager of Arsenal. Bertie was also on County's books but wasn't good enough to break into the first team.

It was to be another 50 years before Devon saw such excitement again. After beating Leatherhead, Millwall and Maidstone, they were drawn away to First Division Leicester. The first game was a 1–1 draw but the Grecians triumphed 3–1 at home to earn a tie with Newcastle at the other St James's Park. Exeter battled their way to a 1–1 draw and brought the Geordies down to Devon for a replay, which, amazingly, they won 4–0. Six of City's goals were scored by Tony Kellow, who scored 33 that season. In three spells at the club he was to score more League goals (129) than any other City player. Unfortunately, he couldn't find the net in the sixth round of the Cup at Tottenham, where City's dream died in a 2–0 defeat to the eventual Cup winners.

Exeter became known as the Grecians because of the large Greek community traditionally centred on nearby St Sidwell's. In fact, a Greek market used to take place on the land where St James Park now stands. The club even has a Grecian Gate, to the right of the Main Stand, which was paid for with funds raised by the supporters.

The club joined the Third Division in 1920 and since then have won only one major title, their Fourth Division Championship in 1990. But Exeter have had one or two star players, including Cliff Bastin, the youngest player ever to wear City's red and white stripes. He was selected for the first team at the age of 16 years and 10 days and made his début in 1928.

The following season Bastin made another 14 League appearances for the Grecians and scored three goals before he was sold to Arsenal for £2,000 – quite a large amount of money in the late 1920s. The 'Boy' Bastin, as he was called, became an England international and won FA Cup and First Division Championship medals before he was 20 as a star of what became known as the 'Lucky' Arsenal team of the 1930s.

An earlier discovery by the Grecians was goalkeeper Dick Pym. In fact, City were able to buy St James Park after their first League season in 1921 largely from the proceeds they got from selling Pym to Bolton. Wanderers got their money's worth with Pym playing in three successive FA Cup Finals at Wembley during the 1920s.

I'd arrived at St James Park by car. Once inside, the ground had a welcoming feel due partly to the warmth of the red paint used throughout St James Park. I had a seat in the Main Stand, which ran along only two-thirds of the pitch. It was built in 1926, after a delay because of the General Strike, to replace the original Main Stand (1908), which was burnt down on 17 November 1925. The fire destroyed all the players' kit except Bob Pollard's boots, which had been taken to Northampton, home of the Cobblers, to be repaired.

The wooden Main Stand was old-fashioned and quite dark partly because of the sloping roof. To the right was the Grecian Gate, which was once an entrance to the open terracing in that corner but is now used only as an exit from St James Park. To the right was the St James Road terrace, which had only 13 steps. Since there's no roof, the residents in the houses behind have a clear view of the pitch.

Opposite my seat in the Main Stand was the Cowshed, which stood in front of the Bishop Blackhall School. It was first built in 1925 to replace what had been known as the 'flowerpot terrace' – so-called because when City first moved to St James's Park, geraniums were planted along that touchline. The Cowshed, originally a short stretch of covered-over wooden terraces, was extended in 1933 and now runs from one six-yard box to the other. In 1986 the wooden terraces were replaced by concrete and it was re-roofed. You couldn't miss the Cowshed roof because it was, strangely, painted bright yellow.

To the left at the Old Tiverton Road End stood the Big Bank. It held 4,620 people and was therefore only big in relation to the rest of the ground. Older City fans will remember when this was called the Duke Bank after local Tory MP Henry E. Duke. His name was linked with the terracing because in 1911 he persuaded the owner of fields behind St James Park to sell some land so that City could extend their pitch, which was shorter than the FA minimum of 100 yards. The problem became acute when Reading, Burnley and Nelson all refused to play Cup-ties there and City had been negotiating to buy Exeter Rugby Football Club's bigger County Ground until Duke stepped in to help.

The longer pitch was first used on 14 October 1911 for a game against West Ham. Duke's daughter marked the occasion by cutting a red and white ribbon and raising a new Exeter flag. After the Taylor Report Exeter spent £750,000 on improvements to St James Park, including new barriers for the Big Bank which they'd bought from Nottingham Forest. The City faithful had congregated on the Big Bank for today's match against Torquay and were very noisy in their red and white scarves and hats.

I checked to see if there were any seagulls perched on top of the crossbars, since, according to local superstition, the result of a match at St James Park can be predicted by the number of seagulls on the goals at each end. There were none. Another boring 0–0 draw seemed to be looming. In the event, an exciting match was won by Torquay, who avenged their 2–1 defeat against Exeter in the first match of the season by winning today's game with the same score. One of their stars was a certain Dean Sturridge, on loan from Derby, who was by far the best player on the park.

LIFE'S A GAS

Bristol Rovers v Bournemouth – Twerton Park, 26 December 1994

After leaving St James Park I drove north-east through the pretty Devon countryside and into Somerset on the M5 before picking up the A39. I was headed for the spa town of Bath in the county of Avon; Bristol Rovers had played in exile for the past six years at Twerton Park, the home of Bath City.

Rovers' spiritual home remains at Eastville, where they played from 1897 until they were forced to leave in 1986. I'd passed their old ground on my way to watch Bristol City play Grimsby at Ashton Gate on 3 December.

There was something sad about the scene. The ground was now merely a shell of its former self. It was hard to imagine that a record crowd of 38,742 had once packed into the stadium to watch an FA Cup tie against Preston in 1960. All that was left of Rovers' old home was the North Stand and some barriers.

Rovers had a successful spell in the early part of the century, winning the Southern League in 1905 and being elected to the Third Division in 1920. But by 1939 they had debts of just over £15,000 and had to seek re-election. In 1932 Eastville had opened its gates to dog racing and now, in their time of need, chairman Fred Ashmead agreed to sell the ground to the greyhound company for £12,000.

The sale of Eastville was to go down as the biggest mistake in the club's history. Ashmead's fellow directors tried to stop him selling the ground and they refused to back the deal. But it was all too late. The stadium was sold and with it Rovers' security at Eastville. By 1986 Rovers were paying £50,000 a year plus expenses to the greyhound company and losing money at virtually every home game.

The last match at Eastville was the final game of the 1985–86 season, when they drew 1–1 with Chesterfield in front of a crowd of 3,576. The idiocy of Fred Ashmead's decision to sell the family silver was put into stark relief when the greyhound company added a fourth dog meeting to make Eastville Britain's busiest dog track, pulling in £250,000 a year. The company also sold 12 acres of land around the ground for £2 million and an annual rent of £150,000. How Rovers could have done with that kind of money. Instead, they had little choice but to move in with Bath City, 13 miles outside Bristol.

At least the move to Bath meant they wouldn't have to share with rivals Bristol City, known as 'The Shit' by Rovers supporters. Back in 1980 Rovers did play five home games at City's Ashton Gate after the South Stand at Eastville was burned to the ground. Fingers were pointed at City fans, though nothing was proved. But arson was definitely the cause of a fire at Twerton Park in September 1990, when City fans stopped off at Rovers' temporary home to warm things up a bit after City's away match was postponed. 'There was a wedding reception going on in the Main Stand when the fire started,' said a Rovers steward on duty for today's Boxing Day match against Bournemouth. 'Everyone had to run for their lives, including the wedding party.' Seven City fans were later convicted.

It cost £800,000 to refurbish the Main Stand and the social club. But Rovers also got lots of support. There was a security alert at Ashton Gate, but the Rovers fans didn't seek their revenge. Instead, City invited Rovers to use their ground. There was even talk of the two arch-enemies ground-sharing. Other clubs also did their bit, including Sheffield Wednesday fans, who made a collection and raised £300 in October 1990, and Bath rugby club, who had a similar fund-raising campaign.

The rivalry between the supporters of the two Bristol clubs is one of the strongest in the country. Rovers' exciting young striker Marcus Stewart (now at Huddersfield) summed up the strength of feeling when asked to name his best moments in football: 'Playing for England schoolboys, my Rovers début, and every time we beat City,' he said. And which game stood out in his memory?

'Beating City 4–0 in December 1992. The team played really well that day and we scored some excellent goals.'

Stewart was one of the best young strikers I'd see all season. He joined Rovers as a YTS trainee and signed as a professional in May 1991. He'd already been picked for the England Under-21 squad 12 times and further international honours would no doubt follow. Stewart had electric pace and a natural goalscoring ability. I wondered why no Premier League club had snapped him up yet. He was 3:1 favourite to score first against the Cherries and no wonder; he'd notched 13 goals in Rovers' last 11 games and would add to that tally against Bournemouth.

Stewart's goals had helped take Rovers up to seventh place in Division Two and they were clearly in line for a play-off spot if they could maintain their recent form. They had enjoyed very little success over the years. Rovers did finish sixth in the old Second Division twice – in 1956 and 1959, but most of their time had been spent in the old Third Division. Their 1950s Golden Era – which included appearances in the sixth round of the FA Cup in 1951 and 1958 – took place under manager Bert Tann and was inspired by striker Geoff Bradford.

Bradford still holds the club record as the highest scorer in a season (33 in 1952–53 when Rovers won the Third Division (South) Championship) and scored more goals than any other Rovers player (245 in 461 matches between 1949 and 1964). Including Cup games, he played 523 times for Rovers, scoring 260 goals. Bradford bagged nine hat-tricks and struck four times against Rotherham in March 1959. On his one England appearance versus Denmark in 1955 he trotted out alongside Billy Wright, Jackie Milburn, Tom Finney, Nat Lofthouse and Don Revie and scored in a 4–1 win. (Bradford is the only player ever to represent England while still at Rovers.)

Bradford was described by the matchday magazine as 'probably the most popular player ever to pull on a Rovers shirt'. But there have been other famous faces in Rovers' blue and white quartered shirt, including Eddie Hapgood, who began his illustrious career at Eastville in the 1920s; Tottenham captain Gary Mabbutt, whose father also played for Rovers and was a member of the team which beat Shrewsbury 7–0 in March 1964; and Leeds keeper Nigel Martyn, Britain's first £1 million goalkeeper when Rovers sold him for a then-club record fee to Crystal Palace in November 1989 after manager Gerry Francis had discovered him playing non-League football in Cornwall. (Gareth Taylor is now Rovers' most expensive sale having been transferred, also to Palace, for £1.6 million.)

It was a very wet Boxing Day afternoon when I visited Twerton Park for the match against Bournemouth. Rovers manager John Ward was not happy with the club's hectic holiday schedule. Ward followed a long line of managers at the club, including Bobby Campbell, Terry Cooper, Bobby Gould (twice), Gerry Francis, Martin Dobson and Dennis Rofe. Ward followed a long line of managers at the club, including Bobby Campbell, Terry Cooper, Bobby Gould (twice), Gerry Francis, Martin Dobson and Dennis Rofe. He had worked with Graham Taylor at Watford and Aston Villa and was known to lapse occasionally into Taylor-speak. His preferred style of play was very different to Taylor's, though. Ward favoured a passing game rather than Taylor's more direct approach. He'd taken over at Twerton Park, at the second time of asking, as a replacement for Malcolm

Allison. (Among Big Mal's more bizarre tactics was the 'whirl system', which involved all the players running round and round the ball.)

I paid at the turnstile and took my place on the top steps in the pouring rain next to a man with a colourful red, white and blue USA '94 umbrella. I was surrounded by home fans in royal-blue and white Father Christmas bobble hats with the words 'Santa's a Gashead' printed on the front. I didn't know it at the time but Rovers have been known as 'the Gas' since their move to Twerton. The nickname originates from the Stapleton Gas Works, which used to stand next to Eastville.

Rovers played their first match at Twerton in August 1986 in a League Cup tie against Reading. The match programme described Rovers as 'a club on the move'. A more fitting label would have been 'a club all over the place'. The supporters club offices were in Bristol, the club's offices in Keynsham and the ground in Twerton. All Rovers had brought from Eastville were their goalposts, ten turnstiles and the groundsman. It was hard to imagine a more disparate organisation anywhere in football.

Yet, for all that, the club had survived, and its loyal supporters continued to make the short trip to Bath, with its Georgian buildings and Roman baths, to see their team at Twerton, a few miles west of Bath city centre. But Rovers had paid a price. The ground-share was costing £65,000 a year and in their first season they attracted an average gate of only just over 3,000 – almost 25 per cent less than in their last year at Eastville.

There had been many proposals over the years for a new stadium including sites at Stoke Gifford, a mile from Hambrook; Mangotsfield; Hallen Marsh at Severnside, west of Bristol; and an area owned by ICI near Pilning, a few miles north of Hallen Marsh next to the main London to South Wales railway line. They had all fallen by the wayside as different local authorities rejected various planning applications. In fact, Rovers fans got so fed up with all the delays that they formed their own political grouping called the Bristol Party and put up candidates in ten wards at the 1994 local elections. They won 4,000 votes but still had nowhere near enough influence to find Rovers a new ground.

In the meantime, Twerton Park remained their foster home. And on a wet Boxing Day they gave their supporters something to cheer with a 2–1 win over Bournemouth, which kept their play-off hopes alive. With all those holiday games still to play manager John Ward had his team back out on the pitch long after the last fans had drifted home for left-over turkey. I watched as they warmed down by jogging in a line across the pitch in the pouring rain, before doing a series of stretches designed to relieve their muscles of the tightness which would have undoubtedly affected their performance the following day at Plymouth. Sometimes it really is a tough life being a professional footballer – though we'd all give our right arm for the opportunity to give it a try!

THE ENGLISH RIVIERA

Torquay United v Hartlepool United – Plainmoor, 27 December 1994

Dean Sturridge was the man for whom Derby wanted £7 million in the close season before the 1997–98 Premier League campaign began. On a sunny afternoon the day after Boxing Day in 1994 Sturridge turned out for Torquay United against Hartlepool at Plainmoor. I'd seen him playing for the Gulls in the Exeter match the day before and he was impressive. But £7 million? He must certainly have improved a lot in three years.

Torquay wasn't exactly a step up for the impressive Sturridge and anyone catching a glimpse of him in the multi-coloured Gulls strip could tell immediately that he was a class act. The chances of him staying in the seaside town once his loan period was over were absolutely zero. Still, you couldn't blame Torquay's chairman for hoping. A couple of weeks before I visited Plainmoor they'd lost 1–0 at home to non-League Enfield Town in a second round FA Cup replay after drawing the first match 1–1.

Their opponents today were another team from a seaside town: Hartlepool United. They too had played the day before, but unlike Torquay, who were fortunate to play a local derby, the Pool had to travel down to the south-west by coach straight after the game. Chairman Mike Bateson sympathised with Hartlepool and their supporters. 'We welcome all those who, courtesy of the League computer, have made the horrendous trip for this holiday "local" fixture. They probably think that we're neighbours because we are both near the sea!'

Torquay were certainly near the sea, although their location was more of a hindrance than a help in terms of generating support. Bateson used his programme notes to contrast the Gulls with Carlisle United, a club at the opposite end of the country in a place with a similar number of people based away from a major population centre. Carlisle were attracting average gates of 7,000 and were disappointed when only just over 5,000 turned up for their home game with Torquay. Bateson had his own theories as to why Carlisle had bigger gates and it wasn't just that they were playing better than the Gulls.

'I cannot visualise a situation where we will achieve 6,500 capacity in the foreseeable future, even if we were promoted,' he said. 'So where is the difference? I think that all will accept that the North is more of a football hotbed and that Carlisle has a more local population. By this I mean that there are fewer retired immigrants to their area in comparison with the likes of Torbay, Bournemouth and the like. The old folk who retire down here retain their loyalty to their old home-town club and never begin to show interest in this club.'

In 1921 Torquay Town joined forces with another amateur club called Babbacombe to form Torquay United. The present club turned professional in 1922 and five years later was elected to the Third Division (South). Unfortunately

Torquay's League career got off to a disastrous start and they finished bottom. In fact, in the years before and immediately after the Second World War they rarely rose above halfway in the table.

Perhaps their lack of success is responsible for the fact that Torquay had the second-highest number of managers of any League club since the war (after Stockport) – 23 in all – a distinction they shared with Walsall. Their poor track record is somewhat surprising given the star names who have been in charge at Plainmoor.

Frank O'Farrell, who later managed Manchester United and Leicester City, was the boss for two spells in 1965–68 and 1981–82. Bruce Rioch, the former Derby and Scotland midfield player, Dave Webb, the uncompromising centre-half who scored the winning goal for Chelsea in the 1970 FA Cup final replay, and the late Cyril Knowles, who played for Spurs, have all tried their luck in the hot seat.

Torquay's underachievement is also reflected in the fact that they've never had a player capped for any country, although Leeds United's Lee Sharpe began his career at Plainmoor before going on to achieve international recognition at Manchester United. The £180,000 the Gulls received for Sharpe in May 1988 is still a club record.

Torquay almost became the first Fourth Division team to be relegated to the Vauxhall Conference at the end of the 1986–87 season. The Gulls needed a draw in their last game to survive. They were losing 2–1 when a police dog ran onto the pitch and bit one of the Torquay players. The game was held up, and when it finally restarted, United equalised in the injury time added on because of the dog's antics. Torquay preserved their League status and the club chairman rewarded the dog with a steak!

The locals had long believed that Plainmoor was left to Torquay by the Cary Estate on the condition that it would always be open to the public, who could, in theory, use the pitch and watch games for nothing. But, in fact, the Cary Estate had sold the ground to the local council for £5,000 and United had paid a nominal rent ever since. After tentative plans to move to a new stadium at Newton Abbot fell through in 1991, Torquay signed a 90-year lease for Plainmoor. They were staying put.

Once new chairman Mike Bateson's plans to relocate had fallen through, he set in motion a programme to develop the ground. The first step was taken in 1992, when a single-tier stand was built at the Ellacombe Road End at a cost of almost £900,000. It came complete with a pub called Boots & Laces at the rear of the stand and six executive boxes at the front. It was now the club's social and administrative hub. And it was where I'd sit to watch today's match against Hartlepool, managed by former Man United star David McCreery.

The Popular Side on Marnham Road, opposite the Main Stand, was first covered in the early 1950s before the visit of Huddersfield in the fourth round of the FA Cup in January 1955 attracted the club's largest attendance of 21,908. A new end section made of brick and steel was added to the Main Stand at this time. Then during the '60s a concrete cantilever 'Mini-Stand' went up at the Ellacombe End in place of the 'Cowshed'. It would have covered the whole end, but the club ran out of money.

And that about summed up Torquay's fortunes over the years – lack of support, lack of resources and lack of success. It was hard to think of a club which had achieved less in its lifetime than the Gulls. Their nickname probably makes people think more of the philosophical gibberish associated with Eric Cantona than of the team that plays on the south coast along the English Riviera. Still, at least Torquay was a popular destination, not something that could be said of the home town of today's visitors, Hartlepool.

They may have driven half the night along Britain's motorways to make the journey down from the north-east, and Torquay manager Don O'Riordan may have thought they should be 'completely knackered', but, with former Coventry striker Keith Houchen playing in front of McCreery, the visitors would always be in with a shout. A hard-fought 2–2 draw gave them a point to take all that way home.

The Christmas festivities were now almost over, not that the players really knew they'd started. I left Plainmoor having watched three games in two days and having reached the magical total of 40 matches before the end of the year. And I wasn't finished yet, either, for I had three more games to see before celebrating the New Year. Compared to my itinerary the players had it easy. Thank God I didn't have to *play* 93 League games in less than 243 days. Even Manchester United didn't face that kind of punishing schedule.

IN DUBLIN'S FAIR CITY

Cambridge United v York City – The Abbey Stadium, 28 December 1994

They still talk about him in awe at the Abbey Stadium. The man has cult status. He may have flopped at Manchester United, but here, in the university town of Cambridge, the million-pound man is fondly remembered for his goal-scoring exploits in the team that John Beck built. He went on to become a hero at Coventry too, before moving to arch-rivals Aston Villa, but they'd welcome him back to the Abbey Stadium with open arms any day.

'Our lot went down when we sold Dion,' said the woman sitting behind me in the Main Stand alongside her husband and son. Dion Dublin had got his career back on track at Coventry after a somewhat surprising move from Cambridge to Old Trafford in August 1992. Many supporters around the country raised their eyebrows when Alex Ferguson loosened the purse strings to buy Deadly Dion for a cool million pounds.

Dublin wasn't the highest-ever goalscorer at the Abbey Stadium – that distinction rested with Alan Biley, who scored 74 times between 1975 and 1980. And Dion didn't score the most goals in a season – David Crown had set that record with 24 in the 1985–86 season. But the fans loved him. Company Secretary Steve Greenall summed up the feelings of Cambridge fans everywhere in his programme notes for the York match.

'At this time of year [late December], when Old Father Time gets ready to shuffle along . . . a special mention . . . to the one person without whom the pressure and heartache would have been intolerable . . . raise your glasses to the one and only Dion Dublin.' What would they give to have him back at the Abbey Stadium? Well, most things really, except the millions it would take to secure his return.

The club began life as Abbey United when they were founded in 1912, since they played in the Abbey district of Cambridge. They played first at Midsummer Common, opposite Jesus College, then Stourbridge Common. When they began to play more organised football in 1923, they moved to Station Farm, off Newmarket Road. The pitch was badly cut up and the ground was surrounded by allotments, both of which account for the nickname given to the ground by the fans: the Celery Trenches.

In 1930 Abbey United moved back to local-park football and played on a small area of a pretty recreational ground called Parker's Piece, in the centre of the city. This was where in 1848 Cambridge students publicised the first proper rules of football. The year after United moved to Parker's Piece, their president, Henry Clement Francis, offered the club land west of the Celery Trenches. While the new ground was being prepared United moved back to the Celery Trenches for the 1931–32 season. United's new ground opened in August 1932, although a wooden stand promised by Francis was not ready until 1934.

There was something of a football revival in Cambridge after the Second World War and the club turned professional in 1946. Five years later they changed their name to Cambridge United and moved up from the United Counties League to the Eastern Counties League, before joining the Southern League in 1958. The running of the club and its ground – now called the Abbey Stadium instead of the Celery Trenches, despite the fact that there was no abbey and it wasn't really even a proper stadium – was carried out for many years at the official headquarters at the Dog and Feathers pub.

After all those seasons in the minor leagues, Cambridge won the Southern League Championship in 1969. Then on 1 May 1970 a record crowd of 14,000 came to the Abbey Stadium to watch the U's play Chelsea in a friendly to inaugurate the club's new floodlights. But United had to play Margate the following day in a Southern League Championship decider. Cambridge therefore played only the first half and Chelsea's reserves filled in for them in the second half.

The next day the U's won the Southern League for the second successive year. They'd so impressed the Football League clubs that, at the League's annual meeting in June 1970, Cambridge were elected to the Fourth Division in place of Bradford Park Avenue.

Unfortunately their first season was undistinguished, although they notched up their record victory with a 6–0 win over Darlington – a feat they repeated in 1989 against Hartlepool. Cambridge finished their first campaign in 20th place, just one place clear of the re-election zone. But in 1972 they improved to tenth and a year later came third to secure promotion. The climb was maybe too quick and they were relegated the next season.

But the good times were about to roll after the appointment of Ron Atkinson as manager. They won their first major trophy, the Fourth Divison title, under Big Ron in 1977 and the following season he steered them to promotion again, before leaving to take over at West Bromwich Albion. They'd come from non-League football to Division Two in eight years, which was a remarkable achievement.

United stayed in the Second Division under manager John Docherty for five seasons during which time the Main Stand was doubled in length. Then in the October of the 1983–84 season they embarked on a disastrous run of 31 games (21 defeats and 10 draws) without a single victory – the longest-ever non-winning sequence by a League club. Gates fell to 2,000 and, not surprisingly, Cambridge were relegated to Division Three. The next year they went down again and were back in the Fourth Division.

The present-day Cambridge first made people sit up and take notice when they got promoted from the Fourth Division in 1990 – the year long-ball merchant John Beck took over the managerial reins, after hanging up his boots as a Cambridge player because of a persistent knee injury. The U's lasted only one season in the Third Division before returning to the Fourth. But there was then a remarkable rise in the club's fortunes, which saw them promoted two years running to reach the old Second Division. They had a habit of being promoted and relegated two years in a row.

Beck was unloved by football fans around the country who deplored his long-ball game. But with Dion up front Cambridge had the perfect target man and Beck's approach worked wonders. In 1992 Cambridge almost achieved promotion to the Premier League; but after that it all went wrong for the up-and-under manager and Beck left Cambridge for Preston.

I popped into the club offices next to the old Corona factory on arrival, to pick up my ticket for the match. The supporters club was ahead of me, facing the pitch next to a long covered stand, once widely known as the Corona Stand but also called the Newmarket Road End or occasionally the Abbey. I had a beer in the supporters club lounge and looked around the various glass cabinets lining the walls with displays of memorabilia from the club's past. There were newspaper cuttings of the Southern League Championship successes alongside the club's title-winning League campaigns.

To my left was the South Terrace, or Allotment End, behind which were – not surprisingly – allotments. Beyond them was Coldham's Common, an astroturf pitch and the council-owned Abbey pool. The allotments actually held the key to United's future at the Abbey Stadium. The club had failed to find an alternative site since they'd first begun looking in 1988 and now had little option but to develop their cramped ground.

United wanted to move the pitch twelve inches to the south so that they could build new stands at both ends of the ground. To do so, they needed to take over ten of the allotments, some of which weren't kept up, covering an acre of ground behind the South Terrace. United had offered to pay to move the allotment-holders to nearby scrubland and provide them with new equipment, but the council had so far blocked any development.

The match programme had asked for the views of the fans on the relocation or redevelopment of the Abbey Stadium.

'Need for a car park near the ground [for season ticket holders] – on allotments would be ideal,' wrote S. Blackwell, clearly not an allotment owner.

'If only the council could look ahead,' lamented Jean and Alan Hughes.

'Cambridge City Council do not want a football club in Cambridge,' according to a disgruntled Alan Marshall.

'Stop lining Councillor Durrant's pockets!' suggested Gary Stround.

One, Robert Wickham, had a simple solution: 'If local councillors/MP are not in favour of supporting United – then don't vote for them!'

Meanwhile, today's match against York was almost as disappointing as the council's response to United's moving plans. The second half was an improvement on the first, when windy conditions meant the ball was in the air a lot, even without the influence of John Beck. The family behind me weren't complaining, though. At least the U's were winning. They were typical of the sort of people who watch football every week all over the country. At one point their young lad returned with three Bovrils and meat pies. 'We're a real football family here,' said his dad. They were.

POSH THEY'RE NOT

Peterborough United v Cambridge United – London Road,
31 December 1994

Derby matches usually call to mind places like Merseyside, north London and Manchester, but in the Fenlands of south-east England there's another battle which is just as fiercely fought, if less well known: Peterborough versus Cambridge.

I had no idea how passionate the supporters were in this part of the country. Peterborough fans call the U's ground the Shabbey Stadium (instead of the Abbey Stadium), but to be honest London Road was little better. Still, FA Cup defeat at the hands of Cambridge had given the Posh fans extra reason for hoping their team would win. It would be a great way to welcome in the New Year.

The clubs had decided to reschedule the match to a midday kick-off so that New Year revellers would have plenty of time to prepare for the night's festivities. They'd no doubt spend much of their evening going over the incident-packed football match they were about to see. There were more twists and turns than an Agatha Christie mystery.

Peterborough had made an immediate impression when they joined the League in 1960, after gaining a reputation as cup giant-killers and dominating the Midland League in the 1950s. Before their election to the old Fourth Division, they'd put together a run of 103 matches with only one defeat between 1955 and 1960!

Their first season was spectacular. They stormed to the Fourth Division title scoring 134 goals in 46 games – a record for any division – to become the first side to win the Championship in the year of their election. Terry Bly got 52 of those goals, the most ever scored in the division; no other player has topped 50 League goals in post-war football.

In 1965 the Posh reached the FA Cup sixth round, after beating QPR and Arsenal, and the League Cup semi-final the following year. Their bubble finally burst in 1968, when they were relegated for alleged financial irregularities. Since then their only real success had been two seasons in the First Division between 1992 and 1994.

Among their former stars were Arsenal's David Seaman and Coventry's

Mickey Gynn. How they could have done with either of those two against the U's. 'Seaman was an obvious England player from the moment he came here,' according to former Posh forward Robbie Cooke. 'I phoned my dad the day he had first trained and told him exactly that. He didn't believe me but later had to admit to my being right.'

Seaman was at the other end of the spectrum from the current Posh keeper Scott Cooksey. Under the headline 'The Nightmare Continues', *The Peterborough Effect* fanzine discussed the merits of the man they called Scott Dropsey. 'Even in his better games he dropped balls for no reason whatsoever and mishandled and miskicked with monotonous regularity,' said the article.

It seemed that the only real excitement on offer at London Road these days was a derby match against Cambridge. The *Evening Telegraph*'s Alan Swann offered some idea of how much Cambridge mean to the Posh fans. In an off-beat preview of what might happen over the next 12 months he tried to warm the hearts of all Posh supporters. 'January: Cambridge are thrown out of FA Cup after refusing to switch their tie with Burnley to London Road on police advice.' Instead, they lost the tie 4–2!

The man they call 'The Posh', Peterborough's answer to the bloke in the red, white and blue top-hat and tails who follows England around the world, was also wheeled on for his moment in the sun. He was a local celebrity and always ran out on the pitch before home matches – I learned this later from a Posh fan called Julian, whom I met on a flight from Chicago to London. The appearance of 'The Posh' had been preceded by an interview with 'Barry Moore – The Number One Cambridge Fan'. Well, someone has to be!

Peterborough's ground was – well, functional would be a kind description. In *The Football Grounds of Great Britain* Simon Inglis described it as 'Born in the 1950s and barely touched since. London Road is the spirit incarnate of British ground design during that unrewarding decade . . . The basic tenet then was to copy everything that had been done in the 1930s, but replace curves with straight lines, wood with brick. Goodbye character, farewell warmth; welcome efficiency, insurability and long life.'

But at least the Posh had the first computer installed at any League ground. The large electronic counter was positioned underneath the Main Stand. The only recent development was the executive suite behind the stand, overlooking the car park, which was opened in 1985.

At the ground, the Posh supporters tucked into the London Road End gave a few clues on how they regarded their esteemed neighbours from the university town to the south: 'You're just a bunch of wankers' rang out more than once on a bright, sunny New Year's Eve. The 'wankers' chant was particularly noticeable after Cambridge striker Jason Lillis cancelled out Ken Charlery's opening strike after about 25 minutes. The abuse began after Lillis was joined in a Klinsmannesque diving celebration by Canadian-born striker Carlo Corazzin. Well, what did they expect?

Lillis was to infuriate the home fans even more after 81 minutes, when he put the U's ahead during a pulsating second half. It was end-to-end stuff in a typically frenetic derby and no surprise when Charlery equalised with six minutes left. The Posh fans went absolutely barmy.

Both sets of supporters could at least enjoy their New Year celebrations without having to drown their sorrows over defeat at the hands of the enemy. I had little time to think about celebrating anything, since I had to race across to west London for the afternoon game between Brentford and Oxford at Griffin Park. It was a hard life!

THE RETURN OF STAN THE MAN

Brentford v Oxford United – Griffin Park, 31 December 1994

Talk about ball skills. This guy was brilliant. Hoops and Hoopla. More tricks than a magician. A true maverick. Hello, Stan Bowles. The former Manchester City, Queens Park Rangers, Forest, Orient and Brentford star was propping up the bar in the executive club after the match. Fag in hand, pint on the bar and doubtless a bet on the 2.30 at Haydock Park.

Stan was larger-than-life. He still had the long locks which all true mavericks sported in the 1970s. They were grey now, but very distinguished. 'Do you miss playing?' I asked.

'No,' replied Stan. 'Not really. I loved being out there in front of the crowd and all that. But I hated the training.' And he meant it.

Stan was a conjuror on the pitch. A shimmy one way, then the other, and two opponents would be on the floor. I'd grown up watching him on *The Big Match* with Brian Moore on Sunday afternoons. I'd go straight over to the park afterwards, imagining I could dribble just like him. I couldn't. But football just wouldn't have been the same without players like Stan Bowles.

He had come back to Griffin Park for the first time since he stopped playing for the Bees in the early 1980s to see his old team-mate David Webb, now Brentford's manager. He wasn't that impressed by the football served up from the current side. 'The ball seemed to be up in the air all the time in the first half an hour,' moaned Stan. 'Why don't they keep it on the floor?' Why indeed?

Webb thought Stan and his old team-mate, winger Dave Thomas, could help his young Brentford team polish some of their rough edges and, just maybe, keep the ball on the deck. 'I wanted someone who could impress upon my players the value of their first touch,' said Webb referring to Bowles. 'I wanted to get him on the training pitch to show my players what can be achieved with one touch of the ball. Stan was a great one-touch player. He was so economic with his use of the ball.' Thomas was brought in to show the wide players how to cross the ball consistently well. 'At his peak, Dave was one of the best,' said Webb. 'He takes his own group and works on crossing and wrapping your foot around the ball.'

Webb has often used the 'greats' from the 1970s in training sessions. Players like Charlie George and Tony Currie. 'We can't live in the past, I know, but my own feeling is that the game has fewer skilful players than 20 years ago. Football has changed so much since I was playing. It's no longer the skill factor that unlocks the door. These days it's more likely to be the pace factor.'

Stan finished his career at Brentford and lives in a council flat across the road from Griffin Park. He won five caps for England and, according to Michael Hart of the London *Evening Standard*, could 'charm the birds from the trees'.

'Only two people could have got me back on the training pitch,' said Stan. 'One is Webbie and the other Gerry Francis. My touch is all right, but I'm having trouble with my breathing. But I love it. What you miss most is the banter and the atmosphere in the dressing-room. Ask any old pro. They'd all say the same.'

Stan played the day Brentford notched up their record Cup victory, a 7–0 thrashing of Windsor & Eton away in the FA Cup first round in 1982. (This was their biggest win since thrashing Wrexham 9–0 in 1963.) He really turned on the style that day, though he didn't manage to score. It was great to see him looking so well, but his addiction to gambling has clouded his career and he still dreams of getting one over the bookies with his dole money. Webb said:

> Stan is a terrific bloke. A lot of people say he's had his chance but I'd like to get him interested in football again. He'll live his life however he wants to, but it's nice to see a smile on his face again when he's playing with my lads. He's got a bit of grey hair now and when he first turned up one of my lads asked: 'Whose side is Dave Allen on?' It was the sort of crack Stan would have come up with as a player. He took it all in his stride.
>
> Most of my lads had never seen him play, but by the end of the session they knew he was no mug. At his peak I'd have put him up behind George Best. He wasn't as good as George, but he was better than Rodney Marsh. And when the going got tough, he could get stuck in a bit.

Brentford had recently matched their record Cup score against Peter Shilton's Plymouth. The last time they'd scored seven goals was against Exeter in 1983 during Stan's time at the club. They're the only League club to win all their home games (21 in 1929–30) and were, for a time, in the old First Division (1935–47) after a spectacular rise from the Third Division in only three seasons. They were relegated in 1947 and have achieved little since.

Stan's old team-mate Webbie, scorer of that memorable winning goal in the replayed 1970 Cup final against Leeds, was building a promising team at Brentford, after his earlier return to Chelsea alongside chairman Ken Bates had been predictably brief. One day the phone rang and Brentford chairman Martin Lange was on the other end asking, 'How would you like to come and work for a decent chairman?' Webb couldn't refuse. He was impressed by Lange's upbeat outlook and infectious enthusiasm for football.

The chairman's commitment stems from his genuine affection for Brentford Football Club. He first watched them from the terraces at the age of five. Lange's success as a property tycoon enabled him to take control of the club he's 'nuts' about. But that doesn't mean he lavishes millions on players. Webb had little money to spend and in recent years Brentford had sold their best players to make ends meet.

The most notable transfer was the sale of Dean Holdsworth to Wimbledon for a club record £750,000 in August 1992, but Andy Sinton, Marcus Gayle, Gary Blissett and Joe Allon, leading scorer in 1993–94, have all been sacrificed to raise funds. Surprisingly, Holdsworth was the all-time favourite player in a poll conducted by the fanzine *Beesotted,* with Stan Bowles in second place.

'Stan, who can still be found in the pubs of Brentford most days, must surely be the all-time crowd-pleaser for his antics on the playing field, and even at the end of his career his class was still there for all to see,' wrote the fanzine. Mind you, the most valuable player ever to leave Brentford must be pop star Rod Stewart, an apprentice in the early 1960s, before he switched careers.

On a very wet Saturday afternoon I was able to cast my eyes over the latest strike force of Nick Forster and Robert Taylor, plundered from Gillingham and Orient. But can the club keep hold of their promising young players?

They disposed of table-topping Oxford thanks to an impressive display by goalkeeper Kevin Dearden, who made a series of crucial saves in the second half when Oxford applied the pressure. A hamstring injury to Oxford's former Sunderland FA Cup star John Byrne had already removed the visitors' most dangerous striker. When a horrendous defensive error allowed Brentford to score a second goal late in the game, Oxford's fate was sealed.

The visitors were kept out despite a hatful of chances in the second half, and part of the ad on the roof of the New Road Stand seemed to sum up their afternoon: 'Next Time . . . ' it said, adding 'Fly KLM'. The reason for this, and the 'Forward Air Cargo' ad on the Main Stand roof, is that Griffin Park is under the flightpath to Heathrow Airport. The Air Cargo ad was thought to be the largest in the world in terms of area. There must be a bigger one in America, surely!

Unfortunately for Brentford, KLM would not be renewing their sponsorship when the deal expired later in 1995. That meant the ad would either be replaced or painted over. *Beesotted* held a competition to see who could come up with the best slogan. The suggestions were more appropriate to supporting Brentford such as, 'Next Time . . . Go Shopping with the Mrs' or 'Next Time . . . drop Westley'.

I left the ground and walked along a very wet Braemar Road past the tiny terraced houses and cottages which surround the stadium in what is a fashionable part of west London between the River Thames and the M4. Legend has it that the game of football began near Griffin Park when Julius Caesar crossed the Brent and kicked the skull of a dead Briton! I passed one of the pubs which makes the ground unique – it's the only one in the League with a watering hole on each corner. The Roman legend probably began with Brentford fans celebrating a home win in one of them on a Saturday night.

Ron Atkinson, once employed at Griffin Park painting names on the dressing-room doors, offices and boardroom, has probably tried all four pubs. So has Stan Bowles; his nights of propping up the bar are among the stories in his autobiography. 'It's all in there,' he said. 'The good, the bad and the bubbly' – as Georgie Best might say.

WEDNESDAY ON A MONDAY

Sheffield Wednesday v Southampton – Hillsborough, 2 January 1995

Hillsborough. The name conjures up one indelible image. Most football fans could tell you exactly where they were when they first heard the news. I was in the showers at a place called Leys in Dagenham, Essex, after playing football for a team called Riverside in the Romford & District League, when I first heard there had been a disaster. I can still recall my disbelief that so many people could die watching a match.

It was the worst disaster in the history of British football and had a major impact on the whole country. It was particularly devastating for the people of Liverpool, since it happened at the Liverpool end and most of the fans who died were from that city. I wondered how Sheffield Wednesday had commemorated the tragedy and paid tribute to those who'd lost their lives. I imagined there would be a sculpture of some sort or a gate. At the very least I expected a memorial stone in honour of the victims of the disaster.

There was one other thing I had to find out. Why was the club called Sheffield Wednesday? I knew it had to be something to do with the third day of the working week, but what? As it turned out, their name didn't originate from anything to do with football, but was associated with a cricket club called Sheffield Wednesday. The members played on their half-day holiday, which was a Wednesday; hence the name. It was quite common at that time for people to work a half-day on Wednesdays, since most worked a six-day week including Saturdays.

Wednesday's links to the cricket club ended in 1883 and it folded in 1924. The football team, of course, is still one of the top sides in the country. Some great players have pulled on the Wednesday shirt, including player–manager Trevor Francis. Ten goals and nine points in six days had rocketed Wednesday nine places up the Premier League and given Francis his best Christmas for 33 years. 'I can't remember a better one. It's the best I've had since I was seven and got a snooker table and a Scalextric,' said the glowing Owls boss.

Francis had experienced mixed fortunes at Wednesday. He'd taken over from Ron Atkinson just after the Owls won the League Cup by beating Manchester United 1–0 in 1991. Francis almost went one better by leading Wednesday to the final of both domestic cup competitions in 1993, only to run into a resilient Arsenal side that walked off with all the silverware. Since that Wembley double defeat, things had got tougher. Not that the Hillsborough faithful could complain – at least they'd dominated their arch-rivals from across the city. The FA Cup semi-final victory over Sheffield United at Wembley in 1993 was sweet. It was just that the Owls needed sharper competition than the Blades.

Ironically, Wednesday's original founding committee included one Charles Stokes, who went on to become a founder member of United. The Owls even used Bramall Lane for many of their key games prior to 1887. But there was little chance of the two clubs sharing the same stadium permanently. For regular games Wednesday used a variety of local pitches around Bramall Lane until 1887, when they settled at Olive Grove. They rented the ground from the Duke of Norfolk's Estate, which also, ironically, owned Bramall Lane.

By the time they moved, Wednesday were established as one of the country's leading teams. After joining the League in 1892, the same year as Sheffield United (who were founded in 1889), they caused several FA Cup upsets and finally won the trophy in 1896, after a record home crowd of 28,000 saw them beat Everton in the quarter-final. It was to be the first of the club's three FA Cup final victories, the others coming in 1907 and 1935.

Olive Grove has a place in history as the venue of the shortest-ever League game. In March 1899 the 11 minutes remaining from an abandoned game against Aston Villa were played there, and Wednesday added one goal to the three they'd scored the previous November when play was stopped at 3–1 because of bad light.

The land which was to become Hillsborough had belonged to a wealthy silversmith called James Dixon. In 1892 he gave his home, Hillsborough Hall, and its grounds to the Corporation for use as a library and public park. Wednesday formed a limited company to raise the £5,000 to buy the ten-acre ground and they spent another £5,000 or so to prepare it for League football. The club was therefore taking a big risk financially by moving outside the city boundaries to an area where there was little natural support.

The Owlerton ground (hence Wednesday's nickname) was opened on 2 September 1899, the same day as Grimsby's Blundell Park. Tottenham's White Hart Lane stadium was first used the following Monday, Portsmouth's Fratton Park opened for business two days later and the turnstiles at Coventry's Highfield Road first clicked on the Saturday. It was the busiest ground-opening period in Football League history. Almost a century would pass before the League again saw anywhere near as many new grounds open their doors for a new season.

The Lord Mayor William Clegg kicked off the first match against Chesterfield before a decent-sized crowd of 12,000. The question of where Wednesday's support would come from was answered by their new fans from remoter districts to the north of the city. In fact, gates were higher than at Olive Grove throughout the season as Wednesday marched to their first major League trophy by winning the Second Division title.

By 1901 Wednesday's fans from the north were joined by many more from the city of Sheffield as new electric trams began to pass through Owlerton. Having taken on the nickname 'the Owls', Wednesday enjoyed a period of great success at their new home, winning the League Championship in 1903 and 1904 as well as lifting the FA Cup again in 1907. The ground was also used to stage its first FA Cup semi-final in 1912.

The district of Owlerton soon became one of Sheffield's suburbs as the city grew and in 1914 became part of the new parliamentary constituency of Hillsborough. The name of Wednesday's ground was changed and in 1920 staged its first international. By the end of the decade Wednesday were the toast of Yorkshire when they won the Championship in 1929 and again in 1930.

As well as four League Championships, three FA Cups and a League Cup Wednesday have also won the Second Division Championship five times. But they've also had their share of tragedy. One of their most celebrated goalscorers was Derek Dooley, who banged in 46 goals in 30 Second Division games in the 1951–52 season. This was a club record. Sadly, his career was cut short. The following year Dooley broke his leg after an accident on the pitch and had to have it amputated.

Meanwhile, in March 1955 Wednesday installed the most advanced floodlights in the country. They were first used in a benefit match held for Dooley before a crowd of some 55,000, who had come to honour their former idol and catch a glimpse of the lights.

Just over ten year later, in 1966, Wednesday embarked on another of their famous FA Cup runs and, after beating Chelsea in the semi-final, faced Everton at Wembley. Wednesday had finished a lowly 17th in the League and won only two of their final ten League games. But they stormed into a 2–0 lead over the Toffeemen, only to squander their advantage and end up losing 3–2. Still, their young side had shown a great deal of promise.

Derek Dooley returned to manage the club in 1971, after they'd slipped into the Second Division again the year before – a season which was to mark the start of Wednesday's worst-ever period. Dooley was replaced in 1973 by Steve Burtenshaw, later the coach at Arsenal. But Burtenshaw couldn't stop the rot and in 1975 the Owls were relegated to the Third Division for the first time.

Things improved when Jack Charlton took over in 1977; he eventually moulded a team which won promotion to the Second Division in 1980. It was during that season, on Boxing Day 1979, that Wednesday chalked up a new crowd record for a Third Division match when more than 49,000 saw them win the local derby against United 4–0.

Fan power was taken to extremes in 1983, when supporter Bob Montgomery tried unsuccessfully to take the Owls to court over their performance in an FA Cup replay. He argued that Wednesday's football was so bad it couldn't be classed as such and thus was an offence under the Trades Description Act. Montgomery claimed the club had obtained his money under false pretences and should give it back.

When Charlton resigned in 1983, Howard Wilkinson was brought in from Notts County. Born in Sheffield, he'd supported Wednesday as a boy and played for them for four years. Under Wilkinson the Owls made their finest-ever start to a season by going 18 games unbeaten (14 wins and four draws). They were promoted as runners-up to Chelsea and regained their place in the First Division for the first time in 14 years.

One of the most instantly-recognisable pieces of architecture in Sheffield is Wednesday's Hillsborough ground. After sitting in traffic for ages we eventually came upon the tall floodlights towering above the stadium. Another ground, another step closer to that Guinness record. The cabbie pulled up outside one of the finest stadiums in the country. Unfortunately, if you ask anyone about Hillsborough, they'll probably still recall the disaster. It changed not just the face of British football grounds, but the image of Hillsborough itself.

Wednesday had to lead the way after the awful events at that FA Cup semi-final between Liverpool and Nottingham Forest. Hillsborough's huge capacity fell as the club made the changes necessary to bring the ground into line with the Taylor requirements for all-seater stadiums. On 17 February 1934 a record crowd of more than 72,000 packed the ground for an FA Cup fifth round match against Manchester City, and as recently as 1971 the stadium could hold 60,000. But once the redevelopment of Hillsborough was complete, only just under 40,000 would be able to fit into the all-seater stadium.

The taxi driver had dropped me outside Hillsborough's main gates and I could see the words SPION KOP painted in white on the blue entrances along the main road. The home fans were arriving for what they hoped would be their side's fourth straight win. They hadn't won all four holiday-season fixtures for 85 years. Could Wednesday break that sequence today? The fans, colourfully dressed in blue and white hats and scarves on a crisp winter day, certainly hoped so. They'd come in their thousands to see another win.

One of the main differences was the Kop, where the terracing had been extended upwards and squared off to accommodate a £1 million roof over what was a notoriously windy and exposed part of the ground. New terracing was also built on a steel frame in both rear corners, because it was cheaper than cutting back the oddly-shaped terrace in the north-west corner. The new Kop raised Hillsborough's capacity to 55,000, though it has since been greatly reduced by the installation of seats to comply with the Taylor Report. Hillsborough's standing in the game was confirmed by the fact that no less a person than the Queen opened the new Kop roof on 12 December 1986. Nowadays there's a picture of an owl and the words, THE OWLS spelt out in white seats among the blue.

But while Hillsborough was taking on a new appearance its crowning glory had not changed. The North Stand, where I'd watched that 1981 semi-final, was 'The most advanced football grandstand ever built at a British football ground,' according to Simon Inglis in *The Football Grounds of Great Britain*. It was only the second cantilever stand (that is, without supporting posts in front) in Britain, after Scunthorpe's East Stand at their former Old Show Ground. And Wednesday's cantilever stand was the first to run the full length of the pitch. The North Stand, opened by Sir Stanley Rous in August 1961, cost £150,000 and took 11 months to build. The roof, covered in ads with a clock in the middle, is 45,000 square feet and weighs 17 tons. Aluminium sheets hung under a steel frame, supported from behind by three miles of pre-stressed, pre-cast concrete. Behind the line of floodlights along the rooftop was a line of flagpoles put up for the '66 World Cup.

The approach from Leppings Lane to the back of the West Stand had been improved with the clearance of gates, railings and turnstiles which had made the build-up of fans on the day of the disaster back in 1979 far worse than it need have been. The open concourse means there's more room for supporters to congregate before a game. The West Stand still had wooden seats in the upper tier but the lower tier had been reprofiled and seated in 1991, turning the former terrace where the disaster occurred into one where such a crush could never happen again. There were four columns along the front to support the roof extension, which was put up in 1990.

Opposite my seat in the North Stand was, not surprisingly, the South Stand. Designed by Archibald Leitch, it originally cost £18,000 and was opened on 10 January 1914 for a Cup game versus Notts County, to replace the old Olive Grove Stand. Behind the stand the River Don meanders from the Pennines to the Humber. An aerial view of the ground clearly shows the tree-lined river, though it's easy to miss if you don't know it's there.

The South Stand was once from another age, but it had been upgraded with a new roof installed in 1992, a difficult task given how close the stand is to the river. It was a major engineering feat to raise the framework, with the goalpost girder constructed on a platform on top of the original main beam. The 125-metre girder is thought to be the longest clear span in Britain. The roof was angled down towards the pitch and in the centre there was a replica of the pedimented gable originally designed by Leitch as well as the copper ball.

Inside this illustrious stadium Wednesday took the lead against Southampton on 18 minutes, when Graham Hyde connected with a Grobbelaar punch and volleyed the ball spectacularly into the top corner. Trevor Francis looked like getting another Christmas present with Wednesday twice coming close to extending their lead. But Matt Le Tissier had other ideas. He'd already set up Iain Dowie with a sweet free-kick after just four minutes, but the tall blond striker headed wide. Le Tissier was to earn his side a share of the points in the 69th minute, when he fired home a penalty.

Francis's Christmas had been spoilt and he was still smarting over a failed penalty appeal late in the game, when a Mark Bright header looked as if it had been handled by Saints centre-back Richard Hall. 'I thought it was a blatant penalty. But we are not getting the rub of the green when it comes to refereeing decisions.' Still, it hadn't been a bad holiday for the Owls boss – even if his side hadn't broken an 85-year record for festive-season wins.

I left Hillsborough with the sense that I'd watched a game at one of the world's great stadiums, never mind one of the best in Britain. Unfortunately, the one disappointment was the lack of a memorial to those who died in the Hillsborough disaster. The nearby shopping centre had a small marble remembrance stone, financed by local shopkeepers and residents, and Hillsborough Park has a memorial garden with a replica of Anfield's famous Shankly gates in the middle, paid for by the Hillsborough Community Development Trust. Sheffield Wednesday owe it to the families of those who died to honour their memory.

GRAHAM'S GLOOM

Tottenham Hotspur v Arsenal – White Hart Lane, 2 January 1995

New Year's Day and one of the most fiercely-contested derbys in football, Spurs against Arsenal. Undersoil heating ensured this Monday-night fixture went ahead as planned, unlike the match at Orient earlier in the day and the west London derby between QPR and Chelsea at Loftus Road, which was to be postponed the following night, forcing Sky commentators Andy Gray and Martin Tyler to speed up to the north-east for Manchester United's match against Coventry at Old Trafford instead.

The passions aroused by a north London derby are among the fiercest in the country. I could feel the excitement building as I drove along Tottenham High Road past the Whitehall Tavern and the Hotspur restaurant with its blue and white cockerel sign hanging outside. There was no mistaking who was at home tonight as fans in navy-blue and white hats, scarves and jackets made their way to the ground.

The police were out in force to try to prevent trouble. You couldn't miss them in their bright yellow jackets with white fluorescent trim around the middle as they struggled to restrain Alsatian dogs who were trying desperately hard to break free. Police on horseback paraded along the High Street, using their higher vantage point to direct operations. They would all be needed to keep the rival fans apart tonight.

Tonight's match had been sold out for weeks, and television coverage was no deterrent for the faithful who were now arriving in their thousands. I approached the main entrance which had always been a meeting place for fans before the game. They'd congregate inside and outside the White Hart Inn. The pub was famous since Charringtons, the owners, had encouraged Tottenham to settle there in 1900 because of the profits they knew would flow from increased beer sales to fans. To my surprise the White Hart Inn had been transformed into a trendy wine bar called Rudolphs.

Rudolphs' neon sign would once have seemed out of place at the entrance to the West Stand but now it seemed to belong there. The tinted glass exterior of the £4.2 million stand, the most costly at any British ground when it was constructed in the early '80s, reflected the dawning of a new age in stadium design. Younger supporters may welcome such changes as progress, but to me something irreplaceable had been lost.

As a boy I remember one of my father's best friends, Ronnie Massey, once president of the Spurs Supporters Club, having a drink with Dave Mackay and some of the other players in the White Hart after a League match in the late '60s. The arrival of Rudolphs had dimmed the memory. It was probably the last place you'd find any of today's Spurs team after a match. Then again, times have changed since Mackay pulled on the famous white shirt, and the distance between players and supporters has grown wider outside the confines of the players' bar and the sponsors' lounge.

I turned away from Rudolphs and was walking towards Paxton Road when I suddenly heard a roar. Rival fans came running across the High Road throwing punches. The police moved in to separate them and dragged at least one supporter away with his arm up behind his back and forced him into a police van. It was the first trouble I'd witnessed on the streets outside a ground in 45 matches!

As the Arsenal followers moved towards the Park Lane End, where they'd be seated for tonight's game, there was more shouting and jockeying with the Spurs fans. The police had their work cut out to prevent uglier scenes developing. They succeeded – just. The Alsatian dogs and officers on horseback had been enough to prevent more widespread fighting breaking out. It was like a throwback to the '70s and showed that, despite innovations such as video cameras, there was an undercurrent of violence waiting to get out. After all, the pride of north London was at stake tonight!

Having seen enough of the trouble in the High Road, I popped into the Spurs kit store to see if I could get a number nine steamed onto the back of the Blackburn shirt I'd bought for my son on my earlier visit to Ewood Park (I couldn't get it done there because they only put numbers and lettering on shirts when there isn't a match on). To their credit, Spurs had the staff on hand to provide the service when you wanted it and that, not surprisingly, was when you were at the ground on match days. It doesn't take a genius to work these things out, but then not everyone involved in football is a genius.

Of course, profit is a great motivator and I know the Spurs shop isn't there out of the goodness of chairman Alan Sugar's heart. But they steamed Alan Shearer's messianic number nine onto my Blackburn shirt for nothing, which was more than I expected. The young lad who did the job, with a steam press resembling a smaller version of those used in a dry cleaners, had a concerned look on his face as he tried to assess whether his equipment would work on an alien shirt. Or perhaps he couldn't bear to work with anything other than the navy-blue and white of his beloved Tottenham.

Shirts hanging around the shop were adorned with the names of the Spurs stars: KLINSMANN, SHERINGHAM, WALKER, BARMBY. The longer the name, the higher the cost. SHERINGHAM would set you back about £10.50 – and that's just the name. Add a number, the Carling Premier League motif and the cost of the shirt and you wouldn't get much change from £50. No wonder there was a sigh of relief from dads everywhere when DUMITRESCU went on loan to Seville!

I just had time to pick up my ticket from the collection point at the main entrance and skip around the ground to the East Stand before the match began. I passed one supporter drinking a pint of beer as he walked along the High Road! I entered the ground and made my way past a door above which was a sign announcing 'The Arthur Rowe Suite' – named after the manager of the great Spurs push-and-run side which won the Championship in 1951. I climbed the stairs up to a corridor which had executive boxes leading off it on the right. My ticket took me to a box used as an overspill for guests who couldn't be accommodated anywhere else in the ground.

I found myself among a group of Jewish people who'd come to cheer on Ronnie Rosenthal – a replacement for the injured Nick Barmby. Two other guests supporting Jürgen Klinsmann were also in the box along with the Millwall boss Mick McCarthy. He was there to check out the Arsenal side which his team would play in the FA Cup third round at the New Den on the coming Saturday. I took my seat in the second row of three and sat back in a comfy chair to enjoy one of the year's football highlights.

Watching behind glass really does affect the excitement of the game. I hadn't warmed to the Premier Club at Coventry's Highfield Road because of the sterile atmosphere. It was just as bad, and perhaps worse, sitting in a box. The crowd noise could have been piped in from a speaker at the back, but it wasn't turned on. Nor was the TV mounted on the wall just above the speaker. The match therefore kicked off in virtual silence. You could have heard a pin drop.

I was desperate to join the 'real' crowd outside the glass who were in full voice all around the ground. According to Simon Inglis in *The Football Grounds of Great Britain*: 'White Hart Lane is not just a football ground, it is part of a small kingdom.' Tonight the people of the kingdom were paying homage to the family who they believed ruled north London. 'I don't think I've been at a match this season where there has been so much noise,' John Motson told *Match of the Day* viewers that night.

As usual the game itself was a close encounter of the passionate kind with little space for flair players like Anderton, Sheringham and Klinsmann of Tottenham and . . . . now if only Limpar had still been at Arsenal. The only goal of the first half was created by Howells and Anderton and clinically finished by Romanian international Gica Popescu. The Spurs fans went crazy, the Arsenal supporters sat in silence.

Popescu was called Georghe when he first arrived in England but is now known as Gica. Is that a short form of Georghe or did everyone just get it wrong? Answers on a postcard please. The confusion over Popescu's name continues a tradition at Tottenham. Former coach and then manager Peter Shreeve was called Shreeves for months after his appointment until he bravely announced at a press conference that there was no 's' at the end of his name.

It seemed even Gerry Francis had been having a little trouble with names at the club. The fanzine *Cock-a-Doodle Doo*, whilst welcoming the arrival of the former QPR supremo as the new Spurs manager, noted that: 'It would have been nice if football's most famous pigeon fancier had got our name right.' Francis called the club Tottenham Hotspurs.

The club's name comes from Shakespeare's Harry Hotspur, a character developed from the fourteenth-century ancestor of an aristocratic family of landowners called the Northumberlands, who were based in the Tottenham area in the 1880s. Hence the name given to nearby Northumberland Avenue. Harry got his name because of the spurs he wore when riding, and the club's ball and cockerel emblem is probably also linked to him, since fighting cocks used to wear tiny spurs.

The second half was also tight and the Spurs fans began to chant 'We hate Arsenal'. 'A lot of people would agree with that,' said Millwall's McCarthy. Sour grapes over the Cup defeat the year before? Ian Wright was closest to scoring when he clipped the bar with a chip over Ian Walker. The Spurs goalkeeper had made a great save by turning away a Wright effort earlier in the half, but was clearly beaten by Wright's chip and looked on helplessly as the ball bounced off the bar.

Walker, barracked by Norwich fans at Carrow Road the previous Monday for being the son of former Canaries boss Mike Walker (out of a job after being sacked by Everton), had gained some notoriety for showing off his assets in the magazine *For Women*. 'The other lads were just disappointed that they were not asked to pose naked. I suppose we're just not BIG enough stars!' said Spurs midfielder Micky Hazard.

As the electronic clock on the Umbro-sponsored scoreboard at the Park Lane End showed the minutes ticking away, the game opened up and both sides could have scored. Klinsmann fired just wide and Sheringham squandered two clear chances – one veered away past the far post and the other was driven straight into the arms of Seaman. Arsenal also applied pressure, but failed to find the net.

Late in the game Stefan Schwarz was sent off for a late tackle on Klinsmann, who almost waited for the Swedish international to throw himself at the ball before falling to the ground. It was almost the famous dying swan act, but not quite. The Arsenal fans jeered, the referee held up the red card and Schwarz departed.

The referee blew the final whistle and the Tottenham fans went delirious. The Spurs players hugged each other as if it was a cup final and then applauded the fans. The Arsenal players shook hands with their assailants and left the field dejected. The pressure on George Graham was growing as his side's poor form added to the controversy surrounding his role in the transfer of Danish midfield star John Jensen from Brondby and revelations that Paul Merson was a cocaine addict.

For Spurs fans Arsenal's troubles were like manna from heaven. After all the problems surrounding the Scholar years, the bust-up between Sugar and Venables and financial irregularities which led to an FA Cup ban and six-point penalty (eventually overturned), the inquisitor's spotlight had at last moved to the arch-enemy.

Under a headline 'The Arsenal World of Sleaze', the Tottenham fanzine detailed an 'Early History of Arsenal Misdemeanours' and a 'Rogues Gallery' of the '70s and early '80s, before moving on to 'The Recent Past'.

It's not hard to understand why Spurs fans hate Arsenal when you look at the historical background. A scandalous series of events in 1919 saw the Gooners unjustly take Tottenham's place in the First Division. That year the Football League decided to expand the First Division to 22 teams. However, instead of retaining Chelsea and Spurs, the two clubs who were at the bottom of the First Division before the war in 1915, only Chelsea kept their place as the top two teams in the Second Division were promoted and Arsenal were voted into the First Division instead of Spurs, despite finishing fifth in the Second Division. Perhaps that partly explained the animosity.

Tottenham's fate was also sealed by a fixed match in which Manchester United beat Liverpool in 1915 – a result which kept United above Tottenham at the bottom of the table. Some players were suspended but United were not penalised! And everyone complains about corruption in the game today. As always it just seems like things used to be better. Older people tell you how much better things were. Usually, they weren't.

After the game I returned to the bar with my acquaintance from the executive box. We just caught a glimpse of World Cup winner Martin Peters, now on the Spurs payroll as a PR man, leaving the ground. In the bar, supporters were listening to interviews with a satisfied Gerry Francis and an under-fire George Graham.

I didn't catch the interviews on Sky but later that night the views of the two managers were aired on *Match of the Day*. There are times when football is like a war and the comparison wasn't lost on Francis as he told John Motson: 'Obviously, John, it was a hell of a battle. We had to dig in there at times. Arsenal came at us with a lot of pride and didn't want to lose the local derby and neither did we. It was obviously going to be very tight. Even before the game started we thought it was going to be like that – maybe one goal was going to win it and, fortunately, we got the goal.'

Surprisingly, George Graham was upbeat. The master of disguise. 'I was very pleased with our attitude and our overall performance. Really pleased. And we had some chances in the second half. I thought the commitment and effort was there. I think if we'd have got the equaliser, things would have been different. They were full of it tonight. As long as we can repeat that a bit more often we won't have any problems.'

Motson then asked the question on everyone's lips. 'That's only two wins in 12 games in the League now, George. Do you think that any of the off-the-field publicity which has been directed towards Arsenal has affected your form or the confidence of the team?'

Graham's answer was short and to the point. 'No.'

I wandered over to the trophy cabinet past a couple of old Spurs favourites. Martin Chivers had retained the stature he had as a player, while Cliff Jones, a member of the 1961 double-winning team, looked very smart in a jacket and tie. It was nice to see old stars returning to the scene of their greatest triumphs. It drove home to me how short a footballer's career really is. And I bet they expect it to last for ever when they're at the top and making the headlines. It doesn't.

The first trophy I laid eyes on was a silver presentation plate. The inscription said: 'Presented by the directors of Watford Football Club to Tottenham Hotspur Football Club on the occasion of the Semi-Final of the Football Association Challenge Cup Competition. Saturday, 11th April, 1987. Villa Park, Birmingham.'

There was a display of colourful pennants from AS Monaco, FC Metz, Aberdeen, Sparta Rotterdam, Atletico de Madrid and Ajax of Amsterdam – all old-time foes from European competitions over the years. There was also a pennant from a team called Wydad Athletic Club, Casablanca. I wondered if Humphrey Bogart had played centre-forward.

The cabinet also contained the answer to a question I'd pondered since visiting Brighton's Goldstone Ground. At Brighton the only sign of their Wembley appearance in the 1984 final was a dog-eared programme on the bottom shelf of the trophy cabinet in the directors' lounge. What does a club receive when it loses an FA Cup final?

A gold-trimmed white pennant with the Football Association's crest gave me the answer and somewhere at the Goldstone Ground there must be a similar memento. It said: 'Runners-up, Challenge Cup. Tottenham Hotspur FC. Season 1986-87.' Not much for all that effort! Spurs had only ever lost one FA Cup final and at the time held the joint record for the number of wins with eight – the same as Manchester United. The one blemish was in 1987, when they lost 3–2 to Coventry.

As I was leaving White Hart Lane I noticed a tall copper ball with a cockerel perched proudly on the top displayed outside the Arthur Rowe Suite. 'Was that the cockerel which used to sit on top of the East Stand?' I asked the girl on the front desk.

'That's right,' she said.

'How old is it?'

'There's an inscription on the wall. That'll tell you.'

I wandered over to the tall weather-beaten sculpture to take a look. 'The Tottenham cockerel, manufactured in 1909 by Mr W.J. Scott of F. Brady and Co., London at a cost of £35. Scott had also been an amateur player with the club in 1896. The cockerel was originally positioned in the gable end of the old West Stand and was moved to the East Stand in 1958.' Some fans believe the ball contains Tottenham's League registration papers from 1908 as well as coins and old newspapers.

As I walked back along the High Road I could have been in Milan or Madrid instead of north London. Car horns were tooting and flags were waving as the Tottenham fans savoured the victory. Icicles hanging from the roof of an underground parking garage near my car reminded me of the coldness of winter. But for Spurs fans the night was a warm one. They'd witnessed a famous victory – all victories over Arsenal are famous – and were in the mood to celebrate.

PSYCHO

Wrexham v Leyton Orient – The Racecourse Ground, 14 January 1995

I thought I'd take the train to Wrexham, and then on to Port Vale on the Sunday, since it would be such a tiring drive from London to north Wales and back via

Stoke. After half an hour on the phone with British Rail's information service I changed my mind. A run through the itinerary shows just how complicated the journey is by train. Who draws up these train schedules anyway?

The 9.05 from London Euston would get to Birmingham by 10.39; from there I'd have to get on the 10.47 train to Glasgow which would reach Wolverhampton at 11.21; from there I could jump on the 11.38 to Wrexham General Station, arriving at 12.56.

That would be the easy part. Getting from Wrexham to Port Vale on a Sunday morning would be nearly impossible. The first train was due to leave at 2.40 in the afternoon, obviously far too late for a 3.00 kick-off at Vale Park. If I could get a local bus to Chester, I would be able to link up with the 10.19, which would reach Crewe by 10.42. Just under an hour later, the 11.32 would leave Crewe for Stafford, where it would arrive at 11.59. Over an hour after that, the 1.03 would depart from Stafford to reach Stoke-on-Trent by 1.25! Then on to Vale Park.

The cost of this little excursion would be £33 for the return fare to Wrexham plus £3.50 for the return from Stafford to Stoke, plus the bus fare from Wrexham to Chester. Apparently, I would have to buy a return from Stafford to Stoke to be able to use the remainder of my return ticket from Wrexham to London Euston, even though I would be going directly south from Stoke and would not be returning to Stafford! The British Rail information desk could not explain why. But to use my return ticket from London to Wrexham that's what I would have to do. There was also a suggestion that I should get off at a little hamlet called Norton Bridge, the first stop after Stafford, to be able to use the return from Wrexham, though I never managed to figure out how that related to my return from Stafford.

Meanwhile, the town of Wrexham was buzzing after the club had performed another giant-killing in the FA Cup the previous Saturday with a 2–1 win over Ipswich Town, secured four minutes from the end of regular time by a Gary Bennett penalty (more about him later). Today, according to the *Wrexham Leader*, it was back to the bread and butter of League soccer. Is that what they call football in this part of the country?

I thought it must be the influence of all the American tourists who flock to nearby Chester in the summer. But then again former Wrexham player Eddie McIlvenny was captain of the United States team which beat England 1–0 in the 1950 World Cup at Belo Horizonte. Perhaps they do call it soccer around here!

Wrexham's priority today was to get back among the play-off challengers with a win over Orient. But the programme was nonetheless full of coverage of that famous victory over Ipswich, including a centrefold picture of the players in the bath. The caption read: ' . . . this is the least revealing! However, we still have the negatives and are prepared to listen to cash offers from certain players!' Surely, you can afford it lads?

This item was balanced morally by the God Spot. 'A question often asked is "What makes a person a Christian?",' noted club chaplain Paul Brown. 'It is a question which can be easily answered. For example, we know that a football kit does not make a man a footballer. It is the skill he or she has that makes them a special player. If you were to see me in a football strip you would know exactly what I mean.' Words of wisdom indeed. By the way, in case you're wondering, the ability to love and be loved is what makes you a Christian.

Back to the football. Or, at least, the journey to the football. Now, I'd read about all the sheep in north Wales and the valleys and the coal mines – all of which is true. I passed countless sheep on my journey north, a couple of gorgeous valleys and one coal mine. But nobody had told me about one hell of a striker called Gary Bennett, who had joined Wrexham on a free transfer from neighbouring rivals Chester City three years before.

On the sheep front, even the Wrexham fanzine is called *The Sheeping Giant* and has a mascot sheep called Arfon – no doubt named after Wrexham's most famous son Arfon Griffiths, who made a record 592 appearances for the club between 1959 and 1979. He was also the manager from 1977 to 1981, taking the Robins into the Second Division in 1978 – their highest-ever League position. But his finest moment was probably the goal he scored against Austria at the Racecourse Ground in November 1975, which took Wales, in their centenary season, into the quarter-finals of the European Championships for the first time. No wonder he's a local hero.

Bennett had to be good, since all the young fans standing by the players' tunnel an hour before the match were calling his name, albeit interspersed with boos as each Orient player emerged from the tunnel for a pre-match warm-up. But I didn't know he was that good. Joey Jones, the former Liverpool and Wrexham defender, now the coach, didn't mention him when we chatted outside the dressing-room before the match.

Jones had more to say about his former colleague Mickey Thomas, who was sold to Manchester United for £300,000 in November 1978, Wrexham's joint record transfer, before returning to the club and scoring a memorable winning goal from a free-kick in the 1991 FA Cup third round giant-killing win over Arsenal. Now 40, Thomas had just become caretaker manager at Porthmadog in the Konica League of Wales.

'Are you still playing?' I asked Jones, Wrexham's record signing at £210,000 from Liverpool the month before Thomas left for United.

'Only in the reserves,' he replied, 'but Mickey's still playing at Porthmadog. He's in the side today.' Indeed he was, for the away trip to Newtown. He was in charge as caretaker-manager-player. He would always be welcome as a legend at the Racecourse Ground.

The drive to north Wales had been less traumatic than I'd expected. It was a cloudy day, with the sun trying to break through (sunny intervals, the weatherman would say) and I had a clear run from London without any hold-ups. Cars passing me in both directions bore the insignias of their teams as scarves trailed out of their windows. Green and white, blue and white and red and white were all represented, though I couldn't work out exactly which teams their occupants were following today.

One colourful van really caught my eye. Painted in red, white and blue it had 'Jesus Christ's Army' and 'We fight for you' emblazoned on the side. I assumed the latter was a metaphorical, rather than literal, statement. It could have contained a mob of supporters whose chanting of 'Jesus Christ and his red, white and blue army' might have been heard in some northern church later that afternoon, though I had my doubts. I knew Jesus had followers, disciples even, but an army?

When the signposts showed Wrexham in both English and Welsh (Wrecsam) I knew there wasn't far to go. When I finally reached the ground, which lies north-west of the town centre, there was a big board strapped to one of the floodlight pylons. It read: 'Wrexham v. Orient. Saturday, 14 January.' At last I'd arrived.

After popping into the programme shop to pick up a copy of *The Sheeping Giant* (the Christmas Special, no less), I wandered into the club shop, where fans were booking coach trips for the fourth round FA Cup tie against Manchester United at Old Trafford. According to the programme, the coaches would 'leave the Racecourse at 12.30 p.m., arriving in Manchester with plenty of time to cope with the capacity of 43,000 that we always attract to Old Trafford!' Now there's confidence for you.

Wrexham's average home gate was about 5,000, but the prospect of a voucher for the Man United game would swell today's attendance to more than 6,500. 'Who are all these people?' moaned one fan.

'Why aren't they here every week?' said another who was scrambling around to get vouchers for his mates.

In case you're wondering about the name of the ground, by the way, it was a racecourse in Victorian times and had been used for various sporting events since 1850. At that time it was described as 'a place where drunkardness and vice were encouraged to a terrible extent' – sounds more like the football stadiums of the '70s!

The Mold Road side of the ground had been closed since 1985 and, for an international venue, the facilities were quite basic. As the birthplace of the Welsh FA the locals believe they have a historic right to have internationals played at the Racecourse. But the stadium holds the unenviable record of having attracted the lowest gate (2,315) for any international in Britain since 1892. Part of the reason was live television coverage of the replayed 1982 Cup final between Spurs and QPR on the same night. But still!

The Racecourse once had one of the oddest stands ever seen at a ground in Britain. I've described Coventry's Premier Club as being like a cinema, but in the early 1960s Wrexham actually erected a stand whose steel frame and seats came from a real cinema – the Majestic. The stand was called the 'Pigeon Loft' and stood on top of the Kop. It had a curved balcony wall, just like at the pictures, and held 1,000 fans. Unfortunately, by 1978 it was considered unsafe and sold to the local rugby club.

I walked around to the so-called popular side of the ground and into the club shop. On the wall hung the number seven shirt with PSYCHO on the back. I knew all about Stuart Pearce, but he doesn't play for Wrexham. I wondered who this psycho was. I would find out soon enough. The trophy cabinet inside the entrance for players and officials contained a pewter tankard marking Wrexham's victory in the 1978 Welsh Cup final. They had won the Welsh Cup no less than 22 times, a record number of victories, and had been runners-up 22 times, another record.

Welsh Cup victories had provided a lucrative avenue into the European Cup-Winners' Cup on seven occasions since 1972, the last time in 1991, raising much-needed revenue and an exciting series of foreign trips to places like Anderlecht in Belgium and Werder Bremen in Germany. The trophy cabinet bore testimony to the club's overseas adventures, with pennants from many European clubs. I wondered what the top continental players made of a ground which contained a hotel on one side!

I had a seat in the popular, or main, stand, opposite the more interesting Mold Road, or Plas Coch, side of the ground, which includes the Turf Hotel. This was originally used as a dressing-room from which the players walked down a wooden staircase and across the terracing, or paddock, onto the pitch. It belongs to Border Breweries, who also own the ground itself, and serves a fine pint of Marston's bitter, as I later found out.

I glanced at the teams in the programme and noticed only one Hughes (Bryan) – a very skilful young player – and one Jones (Barry). In 1967 one Graham Jones became the 100th player with that surname to represent the club since they joined the Football League in 1921 as founder members of the Third Division (North).

I looked over to my right where the travelling Orient fans, numbering less than a hundred, were watching a drummer for inspiration. He sat in the middle of them with a red drum, trimmed with silver, and drove the Wrexham fans mad orchestrating an endless series of chants. 'Orient' bang, bang, bang. 'Orient' bang, bang, bang. I was already getting a headache. The meagre away support certainly needed help to be heard, but I'm sure that if one of the home supporters had a gun he'd have shot him.

The Orient fans continued to make the most noise but it didn't last long. Only six minutes had gone when that man in the number seven shirt headed the first of three superb goals which would take him to 32 for the season and keep him well ahead as the Second Division's leading scorer. His name: Gary Bennett, FA Cup hero of the week before. 'Psycho, psycho, psycho,' chanted the crowd. So that's who Psycho was.

Bennett was already known as Psycho when he caused an injury to Sheffield Wednesday centre-half Ian Knight during an FA Cup replay with Chester that enhanced his reputation. Lee Chapman, in his book *More than a Match: A Player's Story* described it as 'the worst injury I have ever witnessed on a football field'. Chapman recalled how Knight went for a ball that was 60:40 in his favour:

> From where I was standing Bennett's subsequent attempt to win the ball from Ian seemed to me to be the most diabolically reckless tackle. It was so high and late it left Ian with a double compound fracture of his leg. Such was the severity of the injury that his fibula had been forced through his calf muscle and out of his sock. The sight of his bone protruding out of his leg turned even the strongest stomach.

Back at the Racecourse Ground I half-expected the Yale Stand to ring out with a chorus of 'You're not drumming anymore' directed towards the silenced Orient fans at the Plas Coch End, but it didn't. The home fans were more interested in seeing Wrexham add to their lead. Despite further pressure they'd have to wait until the second half for more goals.

Bennett's second goal, just after half-time, was superb. An intelligently taken quick free-kick released him down the left wing. He took the ball on, cut inside and unleashed an unstoppable shot with his right foot from about 20 yards; the ball flew into the top corner past the bewildered Orient keeper Paul Heald. By the time Bennett side-footed home his third, and Wrexham's fourth, the celebrations were already in full swing.

The Wrexham number seven ran towards the Kop, ripped off his shirt, as he'd done after scoring the winner against Ipswich in the Cup the week before, and pretended to throw it to his adoring fans. They lapped it up. He pulled his shirt on again and made his way triumphantly back to the centre circle punching the air. The supporters in the Popular Side began an ironic chant of 'Chester reject, Chester reject, allo' and 'What a waste of money'. Bennett looked up at them with a half-bewildered smile on his face. He knew it sounded strange, but the joke was on rivals Chester – and Orient.

Bennett had scored in each of Wrexham's first seven home League games in 1993 and failed to score at the Racecourse Ground on only seven other occasions all season. He was a much-travelled 31-year-old who began his career at Wigan before spells at Chester, Southend, Chester again and Wrexham. The Robins fans couldn't believe their rivals had actually given him away. How bottom club Chester could have done with him now.

The Orient supporters did have one moment to cheer. Their number six, Ian Bogie, tucked away a 67th minute penalty, which sent the visitors into raptures. They jumped up and down, ran around, sang, danced, you name it, they did it. Anyone would have thought they'd just scored the winning goal in the Cup final. Even the Wrexham fans had to laugh when the Orient faithful started singing 'We're gonna win the League.'

The triumphant Bennett posed for photographs with the matchball after the final whistle, and I made my way to the Turf Hotel for a drink. The bartender told me they used to serve beer to the fans standing on the terraces through a window at the back of the pub until the Mold Road side of the ground was closed in 1985. Nowadays, a select few could watch the game and enjoy a pint from the hotel balcony overlooking the pitch. It was more like a cricket pavilion than part of a football ground. I'd noticed about 15 lucky supporters up there during the match. What a way to go.

WEMBLEY OF THE NORTH

Port Vale v Tranmere Rovers – Vale Park, 15 January 1995

My journey to Port Vale took me north along the A51 towards Nantwich and Crewe, past a pub called the Headless Woman and a place called Barbridge on the Shropshire Union Canal. There were lots of coloured boats painted red, white and other bright colours. Most had been hauled up onto the banks of the canal for repairs, leaving only a few anchored in the water. It was the wrong time of year to be floating up and down canals.

I knew I was getting closer to the ground when I passed a company called Price and Kensington Potteries, complete with factory shop where you could purchase some of their wares. The area around Stoke has been the centre of Britain's pottery and ceramics industry for 400 years.

The factories have distinctive chimneys: tall and thin at the top and wide at the bottom. They were the kilns where the pots were fired. Men wrapped in cloth would walk inside the kilns to take out the pots. It was very hot and could be dangerous. They were paid well but it must have been an awful job.

These were the sort of men who relished Saturday afternoons and the chance to go along to Vale Park or the Victoria Ground to see their heroes. And they've had some heroes to cheer down the years, including Stanley Matthews who, of course, began and ended his playing career at Stoke before going on to manage Port Vale in the mid-'60s.

As I approached Vale Park I stopped to take a picture of the stadium. A neanderthal Tranmere fan with a skinhead haircut and leather jacket walking on the other side of the road suddenly stopped. He looked across at me and began shouting, 'We hate Vale. We hate Vale.'

'Don't look at me, mate,' I thought. 'I'm not a Vale supporter.' I hadn't come across too many unsavoury characters on my travels, but this bloke fitted the bill. He was one fat meathead. It was as if he'd missed his era and should have gone back to the '70s.

Vale Park stands in one of the many marl-pits which are common in the area. They have been created as the result of excavations for lime clay deposits. The pitch sits on what might best be described as a levelled crater. The Valiants have been based at Vale Park since 1950, when they were in the middle of implementing grand plans to build a 'Wembley of the North'. The directors, led by chairman Alderman Holdcroft, wanted to build the finest stadium in the north, with a capacity of 70,000.

Port Vale had actually bought the ground next to Burslem Park in 1944. But there was a lot of work to be done before they could move in – not least the need to move 30,000 cubic yards of earth to create a level playing surface. The club was in the Third Division (South) after the war and basically broke. First Division Stoke City dominated football in the Potteries, overshadowing their neighbours from Burslem. But none of this deterred the Vale directors and their ambitions for the club.

Vale had been a founder member of the Second Division in 1892, the year in which they suffered a record 10-0 defeat against Sheffield United, after their goalkeeper lost his glasses in the snow! They failed to win re-election in 1896, but returned in 1898 before resigning in 1907 over financial difficulties. They regained their League status in 1919, when they replaced Leeds City, the forerunners to Leeds United who were expelled from the League for illegal payments to players during the war.

Vale's best performance in the FA Cup came in 1954, when, as a Third Division side, they reached the semi-final. No Third Division club has reached the FA Cup final but Vale came close. Swept along on a tide of support across the country they beat Queens Park Rangers, Cardiff, Blackpool and Leyton Orient on their way to the semi. A crowd of just over 68,000 came to Villa Park for the match against Staffordshire neighbours West Brom. Vale led until the second half but lost 2–1, the winning goal coming from their former player Ronnie Allen.

Vale played a record 30 League games in a row without conceding a goal that season as they ran away with their second Third Division Championship by a record margin of 11 points. Their previous Third Division title was in 1930. Their other main achievements are the Fourth Division Championship in 1959 and the Autoglass Trophy in 1993.

I had to pick up my ticket from the back of the Main Stand on Lorne Street.

The temporary offices, built when the stadium first opened, were still in use. My seat was on the opposite side of the stadium in the Railway Stand, where Vale supporters had draped a huge black, yellow and white flag over the empty seats in the far left corner.

The atmosphere was buzzing despite a crowd of only 8,000. The presence of the Granada Television cameras covering the game live hadn't helped the attendance. It was Vale's second Sunday afternoon appearance in front of the cameras since the start of the season. The first occasion was the opening weekend of the campaign in the sunshine at Swindon when Midlands Central cameras covered the game.

Vale's location has been a source of confusion for years, since the club is in a sort of no-man's-land between north and south – hence the different television companies covering the two games. Vale have played in both the Third Division (South) and the Third Division (North). In the Autoglass Trophy they were in the southern section, whereas they've played in both regions of the Freight Rover trophy.

The television cameras at least captured the enthusiasm of the Vale supporters who had showed up. The Railway Stand's low roof made the stadium feel closed in and the noise seemed to reverberate around the ground. I'd been to stadiums with much bigger crowds where the decibel level was nowhere near as loud as that generated by the fans at Vale Park on this sunny Sunday afternoon.

The Bycars Lane End to my left is now called the Sentinel Stand after the local evening newspaper which sponsors the club. The cover was bought from Chester when they left their Sealand Road ground for the new purpose-built Deva Stadium. The travelling Tranmere fans were tucked away in the corner between the Railway and Bycars Lane stands.

Vale Park is still very spacious both inside and out with lots of room for further development.

The club had unveiled plans to install 4,500 seats at the Hamil End over the summer and to put a new roof on the Railway Stand. There was also talk of a restaurant in the Main Stand on Lorne Street and rumours that the club had bought one of Blackburn's old stands so that they could use the roof as a cover.

But the council had thrown a spanner in the works with its own plans to provide a new stadium for arch-rivals Stoke City. The diary in the fanzine *The Memoirs of Seth Bottomley* takes up the story. 'Councillor Ted Smith, he of red and white stripy tunnel vision, announces a wonderful new local initiative with benefits to us all – an £18 million super stadium for Stoke City.'

There were rumours that Vale would share the new ground or even merge with their arch-rivals. *The Memoirs of Seth Bottomley* suggested this could involve a combined team with a new name consisting of a couple of the letters from Stoke – like the S and the K – and three letters from Port Vale – such as the O, T and E. These could be rearranged to give the new side a catchy five-letter name. Similarly, as Vale play in black and white, and Stoke in red and white, the council might propose taking the white of Vale and the red of Stoke and putting them together in an eye-catching striped shirt design.

The council had responded to the criticism with plans to develop sporting facilities behind the Bycars Lane End of Vale Park, 'although quite how far behind is not clarified, and rumours that it's somewhere near Tunstall Park are neither confirmed nor denied,' said the fanzine. I thought I could detect a touch of irony in there somewhere.

Vale Park had seen a number of quality players in the Valiants team over the years, including Robbie Earle, now at Wimbledon, Sheffield Wednesday striker Mark Bright and midfield dynamo Ian Taylor, and Keith Houchen, Coventry's FA Cup winner before becoming player–manager at his first club, Hartlepool.

Scottish Under-21 international Lee Glover was bought for £200,000 from Nottingham Forest over the summer to bolster the midfield. Kevin Scott, a solid central defender who helped Newcastle win the First Division Championship in 1993, was making his début. He had been signed on loan from Tottenham to steady the back four.

The Valiants took the lead against Tranmere in an entertaining first 45 minutes when left-back Allen Tankard drove the ball with the outside of his left foot into the top corner past a stranded Eric Nixon. It was his first goal for the club. The half-time break was livened up by the appearance of two larger-than-life-sized Mr Blobbys. The bright pink characters had white neck ties and big red lips. They walked around the pitch throwing sweets to the crowd and were loudly booed in mock fashion. Kids from all over the ground began running down to the front of the stands to claim their packages.

Vale's second goal came 15 minutes into the second half when Guppy chipped the ball over the Tranmere defence to Martin Foyle – Vale's £375,000 record signing from Oxford. The balding number nine dropped his left shoulder and clinically hit a low right-foot volley into the far corner of the net. The *Daily Mail* called it 'one of the goals of the season'. The home fans at the Hamil Road End began taunting any of their local rivals who might have been watching on TV with chants of 'We hate Stoke. We hate Stoke. We hate Stoke.'

Near the end of the match a fierce 25-yard drive by Vale's Dutch midfielder Robin Van der Laan whistled over Nixon's bar. The reaction of Vale fans imitated the response usually reserved for a certain Frenchman at Old Trafford: 'Ooh, aah Van der Laan, sing, ooh aah Van der Laan'. I was hoping to hear a rendition of 'The Wonder of You', the Vale terrace anthem sung as a tribute to Elvis Presley, but I didn't. After the match Tranmere manager John King, a former Vale player who captained the side to promotion in 1970, said: 'They trampled all over us.'

Vale's John Rudge, the longest-serving manager in the League after Crewe's Dario Gradi, was understandably upbeat about his struggling side's performance. 'They were magnificent, they showed their fighting spirit today. I couldn't be more pleased. We've had no luck whatsoever in recent weeks and this could hopefully be the spark that helps us turn the corner.'

Today's victory over Tranmere was Vale's first win in an eight-match run that included an unexpected defeat by the League's bottom club, Scarborough. The fanzine wasn't that shocked by the Cup defeat: 'hardly surprising . . . if you take into consideration that half the squad were plastered the night before, with Van der Laan and [Joe] Allon the chief culprits. Rumours circulate that VdL needed to be helped to his hotel room, and some suggest even worse from Allon. Who knows?' Allon was swiftly put on the transfer list.

Apart from the players' drinking habits, another explanation for Vale's poor form could have been their taste for pizza. According to a letter in the local paper from one S. Smith of Shelton, the players were often at his local Pizza Hut. In fact, they were usually there twice a week on the days of the 'eat as much as you can' offer!

I left the ground and made my way past the Elms Television Centre, not the local equivalent of the BBC Television Centre in London but a local shop selling TVs for £45. A pub called the Vine was conveniently located opposite the police station.

As I was driving home listening to BBC radio coverage of Newcastle versus Manchester United from St James's Park, the commentator interrupted the match to say he'd just received important traffic information for drivers on the M1. 'That's it,' I thought. 'A massive hold-up. Just what I need.'

I didn't find out what the problem was, or indeed where it was, until some minutes later, because the action at St James's Park was just too exciting for the commentator to break away – even to give out the important traffic information. So much for priorities. Eventually, he said there were long delays on the M1 northbound because of a five-car pile-up. Fortunately, I was going south.

ECHOES OF FINNEY

Preston North End v Mansfield Town – Deepdale, 21 January 1995

I arrived at Preston's ground 120 years to the day after the club, then called Preston Nelson, moved to the Deepdale Farm in 1875. It would be four years before the first football match kicked off at the new ground, because cricket, rugby and athletics were the games usually played by the members. But Deepdale would soon be famous as the club expanded and the football team took the domestic game by storm.

In their first game at Deepdale Preston were thrashed 16–0 by Blackburn Rovers, the start of a rivalry which is just as fierce today. The former Premier League champions are not known as Bastard Rovers for nothing in this part of the North-West. The Lilywhites, for their part, are usually called Preston Nob End by rival fans, including those at Blackburn and Blackpool.

The feud with Blackpool is the most intense. Preston had been drawn out of the hat to play the Tangerines in an FA Cup first round match shown live on Sky – the first time the Lilywhites had been on television since the 1964 Cup final. Preston won 1–0 and their fans went barmy. 'This was MEGA. Like birthday, Christmas, first shag, a gallon of Diamond White and winning the lottery rolled into one,' wrote one fanatic in the *Preston Pie Muncher* fanzine. Can anything be that good?

In the early years Preston played some of the great old teams like Old Carthusians and Queens Park and the crowds began to grow. Sheep were still allowed to graze on the pitch, but fences were put up around the ground and Preston's policy of allowing ladies to watch for free was abandoned because so many came along to see the new craze of the day.

Preston made their mark in the record books when they beat Hyde 26–0 in the first round of the FA Cup in 1887 – the heaviest defeat suffered by any club in the competition's history. They were helped by the referee, though. He apparently lost his watch and didn't blow the final whistle until 120 minutes had been played!

Preston never looked back and in 1889 became the first double-winners in the League's first season. Nicknamed the 'Invincibles', they won the Championship without losing a match and the FA Cup without conceding a goal.

Preston pioneered the use of paid players and continued to dominate English football through the early 1890s. The club retained the title in 1890 and were runners-up in the following three seasons. They have not been champions since then (though they were second in 1953, by the narrowest of margins, and again in 1958). Preston last won the FA Cup in 1938. George Mutch hit the winner from the penalty spot against Huddersfield with the last kick of Wembley's first extra-time final – the first to be shown in full on television.

There's no doubt that Tom Finney was the greatest player ever to pull on a Preston shirt. One of his descendants ran out onto the pitch at Deepdale before the Third Division game against Mansfield. His Preston shirt carried the name of sponsors Coloroll, the Preston badge with the famous PP, which stands for Proud Preston, and another badge with the word footy. But this young Finney was not in today's line-up. Tom's great-great-nephew, four-year-old Matthew, was the mascot.

Tom Finney is the president of Preston. His company, Tom Finney Ltd, were today's match sponsors and had taken out a half-page ad in the match programme. It said: 'Tom Finney Ltd. A long standing local firm just a phone call away for all your electrical, plumbing and heating problems, however large or small.' The firm was certainly long-standing. Finney wasn't known as the Preston Plumber for nothing. The man who ranks alongside Sir Stanley Matthews as the greatest English footballer of all time began his business during his playing career.

Finney joined Preston from school and really began to shine after the Second World War, when English football entered something of a golden era. He was famous for his dribbling and burst of speed. Finney played for England 76 times between 1946 and 1958, scoring 30 goals and appearing in every position in the forward line.

He was the first player to be named Footballer of the Year twice, in 1954 and 1957, and a host of clubs were after his signature. But Finney remained loyal to Preston despite lucrative offers from clubs like Palermo in Italy, which offered him £10,000 plus a car, a villa and a huge salary.

He retired after 569 first-class matches at the end of the 1959–60 season. Despite his legendary status, he never won a Championship or Cup winners' medal, ending his career with two League runners-up medals and a Cup runners-up medal. His last game at Deepdale attracted a huge crowd who sang 'Auld Lang Syne' as Finney bade farewell.

After Finney retired in 1960 Preston's form slumped. The following year they were relegated. The club suffered a slow decline throughout the '60s, though they reached the '64 Cup final when, as a Second Division team, they lost to West Ham. Preston then moved between the top two divisions until they dropped into the Third for the first time in 1970.

They have since mostly divided their time between the Second and Third Divisions, apart from a brief spell in the Fourth between 1985 and 1987 and relegation to the new Third Division in 1993.

John Beck, former Cambridge manager and arch-exponent of the long-ball game, orchestrated the drop to the Third Division. But he took them to Wembley in the play-offs the following season. A dramatic 4–1 semi-final second leg victory over Torquay at Deepdale overturned a 2–0 deficit from the first game at Plainmoor. The fans dubbed that Wednesday night, 18 May 1994, one of the all-time great nights at Deepdale.

Promotion fever gripped the town and 20,000 tickets for the play-off final were sold in one day. Wembley was a sea of blue, white and yellow. Preston lost 4–2 to Wycombe and remained in the bottom division, but the fans were philosophical.

Beck followed some great players into the manager's seat. Unfortunately most of them failed to bring success. Bobby Charlton took over in 1973, but was gone by 1975. Harry Catterick, fresh from a largely successful 13-year spell at Everton, lasted three years. Nobby Stiles was in charge until 1981, when Tommy Docherty took over. The Doc's reign was brief. After losing the Preston job he said, 'They offered me a handshake of £10,000 to settle amicably. I told them they would have to be a lot more amicable than that.' Gordon Lee, former Manchester City centre-half Tommy Booth and Manchester United's current assistant manager Brian Kidd have also had spells in charge.

Beck was appointed in December 1992. He put the players on a weightlifting programme. They wore tights on Deepdale's plastic pitch. They were faster, fitter. 'We played a system whereby the goalie booted the ball out to the winger, he crosses and the big striker shoots. This is repeated until PNE score enough goals to win the match,' said the fanzine. By May they were relegated.

So what did the players think of him? New signing Graham Lancashire was asked whether Beck's departure had made any difference to his decision to join the club. 'No. The other players haven't really told me about John Beck, but they do say there's a much better team spirit now, and they all enjoy their football more.' Precisely.

And what about the fans? 'Until December 1992 Preston North End was stagnant. Now there is passion and commitment behind the scenes and on the terraces . . . he made every player proud to pull on a white shirt. He also divided the supporters, something no other manager has ever done, but at least the feeling was there. John Beck did PNE more good than any manager since the war, and fair play to him. The foundations for success are now in place, and for that we should all be eternally grateful to one person . . . John Beck.' At least some supporters liked him.

Beck's assistant Gary Peters took over and had an immediate impact. The fanzine described the 4–2 win over Hereford as 'another step along the road from Stone Age football to New Age football'.

This New Age football was being played in a stadium which looked as if it had come out of the Victorian era. It almost had. The only English League club to have been at their present ground longer are Stoke. Football was first seen at the Victoria Ground in 1878, three years before it was played at Deepdale. But Preston had been based at their ground since 1875, even though it wasn't used for football at first.

It was dark and wet when I arrived at Deepdale but I didn't care. I was just relieved to get to another match after a wash-out at Wigan (see Wigan v. Hereford). I stood on the terraces in the Pavilion Stand. The ground was somehow magical in the fading light of the winter afternoon. It's hard to explain why it felt that way, but it was certainly different to any other ground I'd been to. Perhaps it was echoes of the 'Old Invincibles' reaching me from down the years. The fans of both teams were brilliant, probably the best I was amongst all season.

Opposite me was the elegant West Stand, built in 1906 – a unique feature. The old wooden stand was probably the best preserved of its age in the country. It looked majestic in the winter gloom. More a pavilion than a stand, it would have been at home on a cricket ground. Thin white posts, roughly ten feet apart, supported the roof, giving it an almost delicate look.

Sadly, its days were numbered. By the summer it would be gone. The club was replacing it as part of a £10 million scheme to redevelop the ground along the lines of the Luigi Ferrari's stadium in Italy, home to Sampdoria and Genoa. Plans for a public share offer to raise £4 million to strengthen the first team and speed up the development of Deepdale would also be announced before the start of the 1995–96 season.

The stadium redevelopment was made possible by the local council, which had given Preston security by offering the club a new 125-year lease, costing over £300,000. The rebuilding plans included a new 6,000 all-seater West Stand, due to be finished by March 1996. The only chance of preserving the famous old stand was to take up a suggestion from one Dutch football enthusiast who believed it should be carefully dismantled, reassembled and preserved as a reminder of football's glorious past.

There was little chance of that happening. But there were plans for a National Football Museum inside the new West Stand. Preston hoped the museum would be open by the time the European Championships began in May 1996. The club would also begin negotiations during the summer with FIFA to persuade football's governing body to place its museum collection at Deepdale. I couldn't think of a better place for a shrine to the world's football legends given Proud Preston's place in the history of the beautiful game.

Opposite the West Stand was the Pavilion Stand, where I stood to watch the match. Built in 1934, it was originally 50 yards long and straddled the halfway line. There were new offices, guest rooms on three floors, dressing-rooms and a lift. The South Pavilion, effectively an extension of the original Pavilion, was built in 1936 – the same year that local firm Abbotts of Lancaster made specially designed stained-glass windows for the boardroom. The name of the South Pavilion often confuses away supporters who aren't familiar with the ground. It's actually on the east side but lies to the south of the original Pavilion. Behind me, between the two, was the club crest proudly displayed on the front of the stand roof.

The pitch was treacherous after all the rain but Preston played neat, attacking football in a lively match and beat Mansfield 2–1. I was just glad the game was played and owed a debt of gratitude to the referee, ironically a Mr Flood, for passing it fit on a day when half the League programme was wiped out by rain. The home fans were certainly happy. The win kept Preston on the heels of the Division's leading pack. What better time for the musicians amongst them to finish with a flourish as they treated everyone to some of the Glenn Miller big-band sound and a medley of Brazilian samba songs. Great stuff.

Tranmere Rovers v Oldham Athletic – Prenton Park, 22 January
1995

The Beatles. That's what most people think of when they're asked about
Liverpool. Just around the corner from my hotel was the world-famous Cavern
Club in Matthew Street, where the Fab Four played over 200 gigs. Tragically,
Liverpool Council knocked down the warehouse above the club and filled in
some of the underground arches in the mid-'70s. It's almost unbelievable that
they could destroy a piece of history. After all, it was the birthplace of popular
music.

Tranmere Rovers have retained a separate identity, but the club is definitely a
third-class citizen in this part of the world. The local supporters, known as
Wirralites because they come from the Wirral peninsula (which lies between the
Dee and Mersey estuaries), would like nothing better than to join Liverpool and
Everton in the Premier League. They've been close – in 1993 Tranmere came
fourth before losing in the play-offs – but they've yet to take that final step into
the top flight.

I'd arrived in Liverpool from Preston the night before in the pouring rain,
desperate for a hot meal and a bed for the night. Burger King supplied the meal
and I was hoping the Feathers Hotel would provide the bed. I left the main station
and went into a posh hotel to ask if they'd heard of the Feathers. 'It's just around
the corner,' said the bellhop. The Feathers was listed in the *Rough Guide* as a
frequent winner of the Merseyside Tourist Board's Hotel of the Year Award, so it
had to be good. It was the largest commercial hotel in Liverpool and mainly
catered for students. Flags from different countries hung on large poles outside
the hotel, which was part of a converted terrace of Georgian houses.

I noticed that everything in the rooms at the Feathers Hotel, from the TV to the
electric kettle, was screwed down. They'd obviously had a lot stolen in the past.
Before showering I decided to ring a girl I'd taken out the week before. Her
answerphone was on, so I left a message and got in the shower.

Suddenly my phone rang. I put a towel around me and walked across the room,
dripping everywhere. 'Hello,' I said, as you do when you pick up the phone.

'Hi there. It's Nicky,' she replied – the girl I'd called a few minutes earlier. But
how did she know I was at the Feathers Hotel in Liverpool? I didn't tell her before
I left London and I didn't leave any details on her answerphone.

The mystery was soon solved. 'I phoned a special BT service which tells you
the telephone number of your last caller,' she explained. This is one smart girl, I
thought, and she must be keen to have taken the trouble to track me down in
Liverpool. She was to play a big part in my record attempt.

The next morning a taxi dropped me off in the car park at the main entrance
to the ground on Prenton Park West. I'd come to watch Rovers play Oldham as

they struggled to move into a Second Division promotion spot. But Oldham had lost only one of their previous ten matches and would be a stern test for the home side.

The cameras from Granada's *Sunday Match* were covering the game. That probably explained the crowd of only 5,581, Tranmere's second-lowest in the League all season. Rovers used to play on Friday nights, but the Football League had banned the practice. The *Daily Post*'s chief soccer writer, Vic Gibson, one of those unfortunate souls who had to work on Saturday afternoons and couldn't watch his team Tranmere much anymore, had the task of reporting on Everton and Liverpool 'whenever and wherever across the country'. The previous day's match at Goodison was the 52nd of the season he'd covered so far.

At least Rovers would receive £60,000 in compensation from the Football League for staging today's match on a Sunday afternoon. But what about the crowd? Alyson Rudd in *The Times* said that even the Granada television officials must have begun to wonder why they bothered with Tranmere, who always promised to deliver a quality game but never quite did so.

Former Ipswich star Bryan Hamilton, Tranmere's manager in the dark days of the '80s, was at today's game against Oldham as a radio colour commentator. He received a friendly welcome from those who remembered him. When Hamilton was in charge, the team was bottom of the old Fourth Division, and the whole community became involved in round-the-clock survival efforts.

A 'Save the Rovers' appeal was launched after the club announced it would be closing down in two weeks. Liquidation day was delayed many times with the help of a friendly against Manchester United, which raised £8,000, and a match versus Liverpool, which attracted 8,000 to Prenton Park. Tranmere were finally saved when they sold off part of the car park for £100,000 and took a £200,000 loan from Wirral Council.

The ground has been developed into a fine stadium. The Kop End has been transformed into a modern all-seater stand, with TRANMERE ROVERS picked out in white from the shiny new blue seats. The new Kop was finished in February 1995. The Borough Road side is also now a smart new stand, albeit still very low. The Prenton Road End is a modern all-seater stand, completed in October 1994.

The fanzine *GUAR*, an acronym for Give Us An R, is rightly proud of the transformation. 'It just seems like half a season ago that our ground was the laughing stock of the division. Now it would serve us well in the Premier League, and we've probably got the team to match as well if they'd believe it more often.'

It was one of the best fanzines I'd read. The match reports had me in stitches. For example, Burnley 1, Tranmere 1:

> The press had highlighted the game as the clash of the Everton old boys, with Adrian Heath and Alan Harper playing for Burnley and Gary Stevens and Pat Nevin playing for us. We'd certainly got the better end of the deal. Inchy Heath, like Pat Nevin, wears a kit you could hang up in the back of your car . . . Burnley, as their team colours would suggest were marooned near the bottom of the division . . . A quarter of an hour into the second half they were having most of the possession and their crowd had woken up. Flat caps were removed and whippets placed to one side as the Burnley fans broke into song . . .

Perhaps the humour helped cover up the disappointment associated with watching Rovers play. They had reached the Coca-Cola Cup semi-finals in 1994, but their only major honours are the Welsh Cup, which they won in 1935 (though they're not even Welsh), the Third Division (North) title in 1938 and the Leyland Daf Cup in 1990. Hardly ranks up there with the Liverpools and Evertons of this world, does it?

Still, Tranmere have had their moments – and some great players. Centre-forward Bunny Bell holds the club record for the most League goals in a season with 35 in the Third Division (North) in 1934, while centre-half Harold Bell holds the club's appearance record with 595 games to his credit between 1946 and 1964, including a League record 401 consecutive appearances. The Everton legend Dixie Dean also played for Tranmere, as did Roy McFarland, later to star with Derby and England, and Steve Coppell, who moved on to Manchester United and also became an England star.

I was escorted on a tour of the ground, with a mum and dad and their son, by a delightful lady who worked for Tranmere. She took us first into the main entrance, where a picture of Dean takes pride of place. He started his career at Tranmere before moving on to Everton to score a record 60 goals in just one season. Will it ever be beaten?

The Tranmere trophy room was next. It was very impressive, extending along one wall and crammed full of silverware. Out on the pitch there was time for a photograph in the home team dugout. I sat there wondering what the place must have been like during the Second World War when the club car park was used as a site for anti-aircraft guns and for producing black smoke clouds as a screen defence against the Luftwaffe. There were tank traps in Borough Road, where the roof of the stand was destroyed by German bombs. Like Manchester and Liverpool, Birkenhead suffered repeated bombing because of the importance of the docks and shipbuilding in the area.

The war years also threw up a few oddities in the Rovers' fixture list. The programme for today's Oldham game recalled a match in September 1940 when Tranmere beat a Czech Army X1 5–2, while the 'B' team slaughtered a side called Heyworth 25–0 to set a new record. The great Harold Bell bagged ten of those goals. On Christmas Day 1940 Tommy Lawton guested for Crewe against Rovers after playing for Everton in the morning! Three days later Tranmere beat Liverpool 3–2 at Anfield with the help of five Everton players guesting for the day.

Probably the fastest hat-trick on record was scored by Blackpool's Jock Dodds in 1942, when Rovers were thrashed 15–3 at Bloomfield Road. Dodds scored seven goals that day including a hat-trick in two and a half minutes. In another wartime match Rovers fielded their youngest-ever player, 15-year-old Stanley Wright.

After the war the club did a deal with the local council in which the authorities were given six feet of land behind the Borough Road side so that they could widen the pavement and build bus loading bays. In return, the council helped to lift the ten hundredweight tank traps over to the Kop End so that Rovers could use them as the foundations for some new raised banking.

Today's Tranmere side included John McGreal, who was interviewed in the match programme feature 'The Flip Side of . . .' Asked which luxury item he'd take with him if he was marooned on a desert island, he said Linda Evangelista. Wouldn't we all, John.

Rovers manager John King had more realistic ambitions. 'I can only hope we put on a performance to wipe away the memory of the horror show at Port Vale last Sunday. We were awful. There's no other way to describe such a lacklustre performance.'

King was amazingly apologetic in his programme notes. 'Obviously, I'm sorry that we were again unable to put on a decent performance for the TV viewers, however I was desperately sorry for those fans who took the trouble to follow us down to the Potteries. They deserve better and I can only apologise on behalf of the players who knew they had let themselves, and the fans, down. Get behind the lads today. If you've made the effort to come today despite the live TV coverage make yourselves heard and help us to victory.'

Oldham, in their bright tangerine away strip, obviously hadn't read the script. They took the lead after 15 minutes when Norwegian international Gunnar Halle feigned a right-foot cross, fooling Rovers defender Ged Brannan, and laid the ball back for full-back Chris Makin to score. Tranmere equalised just seven minutes later when their centre-forward looped a header into the top corner over Paul Gerrard in the Oldham goal from a hopeful cross to the back post by Brannan. The PA system boomed out James Brown's immortal lines 'I Feel Good, I Feel Good, I've Got You.'

In the second half Brannan took it upon himself to more than make up for his earlier errors. First, he crossed from the right in the 74th minute for Ian Muir, Tranmere's all-time top scorer, to head their second goal. Muir was only in the side because John Aldridge was injured, but he was making the most of his chance. Then Brannan hit a screamer on the stroke of full-time from the edge of the box. 'Sharpie, Sharpie, what's the score? Sharpie, what's the score?' sang the Prenton Park faithful in the direction of Oldham player–manager Graeme Sharpe, the former Everton striker.

The scoreline reflected harshly on Oldham, who had dominated much of the game but only had themselves to blame for missing several clear-cut chances. Still, their luck was out. At Millwall recently they were pulled up for offside, only to find that the linesman had mistakenly flagged a safety stewards jacket.

After the match I waited for a bus back to Hamilton Square metro. As I stood at the bus stop, Rovers' young forward Chris Malkin walked past with his arm around his girlfriend. 'Well played, Chris,' said one fan.

'Nice game, son,' said another.

'Thanks,' said Malkin, raising his hand in acknowledgement.

I caught a bus back to the metro station but I wasn't sure where to get off. 'I'll show you,' said a guy on the bus who'd overheard me ask the driver. We talked about the Oldham game and football in general, as you do, to pass the time. He had one of those player-by-player books on Everton which includes pictures of all the great stars. 'I'm collecting autographs,' he said. He was in his thirties but as enthusiastic about his collection as a young kid with Panini soccer cards. 'I got Duncan McKenzie and Martin Dobson today as well as Pat Nevin,' he told me. I looked at him as if to say 'That's nice'.

'It's something to do,' he said.

GRAHAM ON THE RACK

Arsenal v Southampton – Highbury, 24 January 1995

Highbury in crisis? The Queen will be filing for divorce next! George Graham could handle it – he'd been there before as a player. Not as a manager, though. And certainly not with allegations of taking a £285,000 'bung' hanging over his head. The players? Paul Merson certainly couldn't handle it. He was just back in training after rehabilitation for cocaine addiction. Merson had a strong incentive to return to work, though – the need to pay off thousands of pounds in gambling debts. But what about the rest of the team? Arsenal hadn't won at Fortress Highbury in 13 weeks and were slipping down the table.

I made my way along Avenell Road towards the East Stand. Above the main doors was Arsenal's AFC insignia and over that the club's red cannon emblem picked out in relief between the tall windows. I entered the ground through the main entrance to the East Stand, famous for its marble halls. A black marble bust of the legendary Herbert Chapman stands in the hall from which a sweeping staircase leads to the boardroom and guest rooms on the first floor. (The club's late secretary, Bob Wall, claimed Chapman's ghost walked the corridors of Highbury.)

New striker John Hartson passed me in the main hall, where former Arsenal keeper and ITV presenter Bob Wilson was talking to BBC commentator John Motson. Lee Dixon emerged from the dressing-rooms to the right and shuffled past in his Arsenal kit in stockinged feet. He expertly spun a letter under the teller's window in the main office. At the top of the stairs I was greeted by the famous Arsenal commissioners, smartly dressed in their black military-style uniforms with peaked caps. They were there to usher guests to the various rooms and to keep an eye on the trophies displayed on a table to the right. The European Cup-Winners' Cup, decorated with red and white silk ribbons, was flanked by the FA Youth Cup and another trophy.

Then it was up another flight of stairs to the trophy cabinets housing the silverware collected by some of the great Arsenal teams of the past, including the one shaped by Chapman which won the League Championship five times and the FA Cup twice in the 1930s. There was a striking figure of a Russian bear presented to Arsenal by a club from the former Soviet Union, a pennant from the Racing Club of Argentina dated 1950 and a silver presentation plate from arch-rivals Tottenham commemorating the first FA Cup semi-final between the two teams and the first played at Wembley in 1991 when Spurs won 3–1.

I wandered out into the directors' box in the middle of the East Stand where each red seat is personally labelled with the name of an Arsenal director. The Southampton players were already outside inspecting the pitch. Ironically, shortly after they emerged from the tunnel in their smart suits, Highbury's state-of-the-art Jumbotron screens, one in each corner of the ground, began showing highlights of previous Arsenal matches against the Saints. The Southampton players smiled as they pointed towards the big screen where Ian Wright, Paul Merson and Alan Smith were finding the back of the net with the Saints defence in disarray.

I left the East Stand's marble halls and walked around the perimeter of the pitch, marvelling at the modern Highbury. The famous West Stand, complete with electric lift, stood opposite. It was opened in 1932 by the Prince of Wales (later Edward VIII). At one end the new North Bank rose steeply into the sky, while at the other the distinguished Clock End with its shimmering executive boxes also towered over the pitch. The Arsenal Stadium wasn't always like this.

A feature in the match programme marvelled at the changes. 'They'd be amazed now, those Church Commissioners – the men who sold a 21-year lease on the playing fields of St John's College, Highbury to a struggling south-east London football club in 1913. So would those 20,000 fans who filled the stadium on opening day – September 6, 1913: Arsenal 2 Leicester Fosse 1.'

By the time of Chapman's arrival in 1925, Arsenal had bought the stadium outright for £64,000. Chapman transformed the team; and manager and board developed the ground to keep pace with the Gunners' success. In the summer of 1931 work began on the most ambitious project yet – the £50,000 West Stand, which opened in December 1932. The Stand remains, with only minor alterations, as it was built 60 years ago. In 1935, the year after Chapman died, his famous clock was moved to the South End, known ever since as the 'Clock End'.

The 1988–89 season saw the start of the first major redevelopment at the ground since 1937. Gleaming executive boxes were built above the Clock End along with offices, banqueting facilities and a new Arsenal Sports Centre. Following the Hillsborough disaster of 1989 and the Taylor Report, Arsenal laid down plans for the North Bank to be turned into a state-of-the-art superstand. On 2 May 1992 Arsenal played in front of the old North Bank for the last time, firing five goals past tonight's visitors Southampton.

The new £16.5 million North Bank stand opened in August 1993. It includes facilities rarely seen before in this country. If you get tickets for the North Bank today, you'll be entertained by a live pop group in the main concourse, you can visit the club shop under the stand, or perhaps walk around the museum containing memorabilia (including Don Howe's tracksuit, replicas of major trophies, England caps won by Arsenal stars of the past, pennants, medals and even a waxwork dummy of George Graham if it's still there!), watch a 20-minute film, *The Story So Far*, recounting great moments in the club's history (it was narrated by Graham when I was there), or see the man whose goal against Liverpool in the 1971 FA Cup final won the 'double'.

Charlie George, famous for his flowing locks, flamboyant lifestyle and spectacular goals, works for Arsenal in the museum and is on hand to talk to supporters, autograph photos of himself at his peak in action against Manchester City's Francis Lee and Mike Doyle and pose for pictures. The long hair has thinned and he wears glasses now but there's no mistaking him.

'Hello, Charlie. How are you doing?' said two fair-haired young lads entering the museum.

'I'm fine, boys. How are you?' Charlie replied politely. They were far too young to have seen him play but they had seen his goal, and his celebratory slide to the ground, arms outstretched behind him as he waited to be mobbed by his elated Arsenal team-mates. North London (well one side of it anyway) was in raptures for weeks. Champagne Charlie had brought home the 'double'.

I would have loved to have talked to him about the old days, how it felt scoring the winner against Liverpool and whether he missed playing, but the game was about to start, so I was moved on by my guide. He later told me that Charlie didn't miss playing football any more. I suppose there's a time and a place for everything. In 1971 Charlie George was in the right place at the right time and his goal will live on in the memories of Arsenal fans for ever.

I took up my place in the press-box – front row, over the halfway line. On my left was a journalist from a Dutch football magazine called *Football International*. 'There is a lot of interest in English football again,' he told me. 'When English teams were banned from Europe, there wasn't so much interest in the game here. But now people back home want to know about the stars they see on television. The Premier League is very fast, very direct and exciting. In Holland there are only a couple of big teams but here there are at least half a dozen Championship contenders. Also the crowds are much bigger and more passionate. It all makes the game more exciting.'

Behind me sat the radio commentator for Radio Solent, who would be keeping the people of Hampshire up-to-date with all the action from tonight's match. In fact, the first-ever radio commentary on a football match took place at Highbury on 22 January 1927, when a certain H.B.T. Wakelam covered Arsenal v. Sheffield United. The first televised match was also at Highbury when Arsenal played Arsenal reserves on 16 September 1937. Was it a defensive encounter I wondered? The location of the BBC's broadcasting unit at nearby Alexandra Palace, from where the first-ever television pictures were broadcast, was the main reason for Highbury being chosen.

According to an article I'd read in *The Independent* the week before, the first radio broadcast also involved a blind man and another commentator. The blind man's job was to nudge the main match commentator if he wasn't getting enough information about what was going on in the game. Meanwhile, the other commentator kept track of where the play was on the pitch according to a grid of squares over the pitch published in that week's *Radio Times,* to help listeners follow the play. This is where the saying 'Back to square one' comes from, since square one was positioned over the goal areas.

Back to tonight's match. Matt Le Tissier, worshipped by the Southampton fans, was strangely off-form and missed three good chances in the first half. The Saints would pay for his profligacy. Wright got the better of full-back Francis Benali and drove in a shot which Grobbelaar could only parry onto the head of Hartson. The former Luton striker gratefully nodded the ball into the empty net. It was his home League début and he had crowned it with his second goal for the club after a winning strike at Coventry the previous Saturday.

At half-time the journalists returned to the warmth of the press lounge, where tea and sandwiches were waiting for them. Outside in the cold the Arsenal fans were watching highlights of the first half on the Jumbotron screens. It didn't last long.

The second half was better and belonged to Southampton. They should have equalised from one of a hatful of chances but eventually settled for Jim

Magilton's close-range drive over the stranded Seaman inside the 18-yard-box, after Le Tissier had threaded his way past three or four bemused Arsenal defenders. The Saints manager Alan Ball leapt from the dugout, took off his checked flat cap and punched the air in triumph as his players surrounded the delighted Magilton. The Southampton fans rang out with a chorus of 'When the Saints go marching in'. The Arsenal fans rumbled in discontent.

The tabloid journalist behind me rang his office. 'Are we too late to change the intro?' he asked urgently. The answer must have been no, since he quickly dictated a new story incorporating the latest twist in the match for consumption at the morning breakfast-table. The Arsenal fans, meanwhile, had decided to try to lift their team and sang 'We're by far the greatest team . . .' George Graham stood beside the pitch with his hands in the pockets of his manager's touchline coat.

'A tense finish here,' said the Radio Solent commentator. Then, it was all over. The final whistle was greeted with boos from the Arsenal fans. It wasn't a great game, but better than the recent match against Villa – rated by some of the reporters as the worst League game they had ever seen.

After filing their match reports the journalists gradually began to file into Arsenal's impressive press-room. Built like a small theatre, there was a smart varnished pine top-table decorated with the Gunners' imposing cannon crest. The managers would sit behind the table in turn to answer questions from the assembled hacks comfortably positioned in soft, cinema-style seats. Among them was Brian Glanville of *The Sunday Times* – one of only two journalists spoken to on first name terms by either Ball or Graham.

Ball was the first to come into the press-room. He seemed reasonably pleased with the draw.

'Was that a fair result?' asked one reporter. Ball replied:

> Yes, it was two halves, wasn't it? In all fairness to Arsenal they came out and worked very hard at closing us down first half; beat us up in many ways. That's what I said to my players at half-time, 'You're being intimidated here, you're being outfought, you're second on all sorts of stuff.'
>
> I said, 'I don't want you to be intimidated. I want to see if you're coming on as the good players I'm hoping you to be; the good little team that I'm trying to fashion you into. You must go out and compete. You must pass the ball. You must try and play through them through the middle of the pitch. Third man runs and get after them. Play your football. Bounce it off Shipperley. Runners getting after them.' And I thought we were terrific second-half. Playing football all over the pitch. And we got our just rewards in the end. And it's important we did because young lads, if they don't get what they deserve, you know, they can go under very quickly. And, thank God, they got what they deserved trying to do what their manager wanted them to do.

'Seaman made a great save,' noted another hack.

'Both keepers made good stops today,' said Ball, who then remarked on Grobbelaar's outfield play. 'Bruce was a bit better than Seaman out on the flanks,' he said to ripples of laughter around the press-room. 'He drops the old left shoulder.'

Graham came into the press-room as Ball was leaving. They shook hands and greeted each other like old friends. Their mutual admiration was obvious and Graham would refer to Ball with the utmost respect in his press briefing. Graham began by asking the reporters to tell him what 'Ballie' said first. The journalist with the droopy moustache gave him a quick summary.

'He said that you stopped them playing in the first half. You dominated them and stopped them passing the ball.'

'I agree with him,' replied a dapper-looking Graham.

The journalist returned to his summary. 'Second half they outpassed you and they were well worth a point.'

'I agree with him,' repeated Graham, 'a good summing up.

'There's a lack of confidence,' said the Arsenal manager. 'I mean a lot of the players just now are going through a period they've never known before. In the last eight years we've either been winning things or up there and nearly winning them. They know how to handle success, now they've got to handle the other situation. And this is a new experience for some of them. And I hope they don't like it.'

'A new experience for you as well,' pointed out one hack.

'Yes, but I've handled it as a player. You know I know what it's like. As a manager it's probably the worst period I've had. But I know what it's like because I've been in the situation where you do go through a bad spell.'

'George, did you ever envisage a situation where you could go 13 weeks without a win at home?'

Graham had a sharp answer. 'No, I'll have to phone up Tottenham and ask them what it's like,' he said, sparking a round of laughter from the assembled hacks. He went on:

> No, that wasn't actually meant in cheek. You know sometimes it goes like that, doesn't it? No, football's a great game for turning itself on its head. You know what I mean. You know this. Something just may happen that just sort of sparks it off again. As long as you keep doing the right things – we're not doing anything basically different.
>
> Never mind all the headlines about the long ball. We've never played intentionally long balls. I like the players to get out there and play and pass the ball as they see fit whether they play a short ball or whether they play a long ball. I've never instructed anybody. We do press in. We've never changed the football philosophy since I've come here. We've played the same way for eight years. Some people say that's wrong.

'How much does the criticism hurt you, George or do you try to deflect it off your players?' was the next insightful question. Graham replied:

> I've never been under any illusions in football. I've been in football too long, since I was 15. And if you're winning, you're good, you get the points, enjoy the success. And if you're not winning you'd better take the flak that's flying. It's not becoming the best of pieces, is it?

I had plenty of problems as a player. I was an average player. I had good success as a player. But I had plenty of problems in my playing career as well, you know. But I played for a lot of good clubs, I picked up some trophies. I did okay as a player. But it wasn't all plain sailing in the way that some of the so-called experts on television now go straight from top-class player into expert analysis, you know, because this life's too tough for them.

Graham had obviously been upset by former England captain Gary Lineker who had appeared on the BBC's *Football Focus* programme the previous Saturday lunchtime, joking about allegations that Graham had received a £285,000 bung as part of the transfer deal that took John Jensen to Arsenal from Danish club Brondby.

Asked about the crisis at Highbury, Lineker said: 'There's a lot of pressure on George Graham at the moment. But I think the real issue is not lack of form, more what's going on off the field. Whether or not he has taken a bung, or what the inquiry is going to come up with, I don't know what George Graham's defence is. But for his sake, I hope it's better than Arsenal's against Millwall.' The Gunners had just been beaten 2–0 by the south London side in the third round of the FA Cup in a replay at Highbury.

The impact of Lineker's remarks were shown clearly when the under-fire Arsenal manager refused to appear on *Match of the Day* that night following Arsenal's 1–0 win at Coventry. The former Leicester, Everton, Barcelona, Tottenham and Grampus 8 striker had clearly touched a raw nerve and it hurt. Graham chose instead to use the post-match press conference after the 1–1 draw with Southampton to air his views on the criticism handed out by television 'experts'. He didn't name names, but it was clear who he was pointing the finger at and Lineker was the target:

There are a lot of ex-players who have taken the easy route by going into TV instead of management. They have earned a lot of money, these boys, without ever having to put their head in the noose as managers do. They have never coached, never managed. But they think they can tell me how to do my job. They are entitled to their opinions on what happens on the pitch. But don't tell me how to run Arsenal when you have never been there. Who wants to go into management these days? It is far too hard for these people. They have no pedigree, yet they tell people like me what should be going on in the game.

A man like Alan Ball I can respect. He has managed down at Exeter, he has been at the sharp end. But not these guys. Arsenal are well respected within the game and as long as I have the respect of my peers I will be satisfied. Their views are what I take on board, not those of people whose only qualification to talk is that they were once top-class players.

I have regrets. I wish I'd been able to make the signings I wanted. I came very close with Chris Sutton. I tried for Marc Overmars and David Ginola, but those deals didn't come off because their teams were playing in the Champions League. With hindsight, maybe I should have switched my attention and made other signings.

Graham then addressed the issue on everyone's lips. Would he be staying at Arsenal? 'Some papers have called on me to resign. It's not my nature to walk away from problems. I think back to last season. We were written off after we'd lost to Bolton in the FA Cup. A few months later we were parading with the Cup-Winners' Cup. Let's go for a repeat performance.' On their current form Arsenal would struggle to do so.

HOLTE – WHO GOES THERE?

Aston Villa v Tottenham Hotspur – Villa Park, 25 January 1995

This match was a mouth-watering prospect. A revitalised Villa under new manager Brian Little against a rejuvenated Tottenham, unbeaten in 11 matches, under Gerry Francis. 'It's one of those fixtures, I suspect, which neutrals would like to see because it has such promise as a spectacle,' said the Villa boss. They did, it had and, most important of all, it was. This was one of the best games I'd see all season.

Unfortunately, the match at Villa Park was overshadowed by a little incident at Selhurst Park involving a certain Eric Cantona. There wasn't any kung-fu fighting here, but Villa keeper Mark Bosnich did his own version of the can-can, which ended with his knee in Jürgen Klinsmann's head.

Only 20 minutes had gone when the ball was knocked over the top of the Villa defence by Spurs defender Colin Calderwood. Klinsmann ran onto it pursued by two defenders, Bosnich rushed out of his goal, the German striker knocked the ball forward with his head and felt the full force of the Villa keeper's challenge.

Klinsmann was carried off unconscious on a stretcher and took no further part in the game to the disappointment of the supporters of both teams. A black, red and yellow German flag draped over one of the exits among the Tottenham fans proclaimed: *Klinsmann der Meister*. Tonight he had little chance to live up to the slogan.

Herr Francis was not amused. 'I'm sure Jürgen got to the ball first and their keeper smacked into him after that. I'm surprised the ref didn't see that. In the end, it cost us dearly. He had a bad knock full in the face, which has left him with a terrible headache. I thought he was very brave going for the ball.'

Bosnich said the collision was 'unfortunate'. He'd hoped to head the ball away as it swirled in the wind. 'I was sorry for what happened, but I saw Jürgen at half-time and he seemed fine. In fact, he wanted to come out and play.' The pictures in the following morning's papers showed the true nature of the challenge. Bosnich had his boot in Klinsmann's face with his feet almost as high as the heads of the defenders around him. The headline in *The Sun* was 'Jürgen Horror. Klinsmann KO'd by Bosnich'.

Klinsmann was carried to the Villa first-aid room where he was seen by the club doctor. The diagnosis was an injured nose, a bump on the back of his head and concussion. He would later have X-rays and a scan on his face and nose as a precautionary measure.

Meanwhile, out on the pitch Bosnich was booed by the Spurs fans every time he touched the ball. But they couldn't stop Villa snatching a 1–0 win. After 18 minutes full-back Steve Staunton hit a ball down the line on the left. Dean Saunders picked the ball up with his back to goal. The Holte End rose to their feet together as he turned and cut inside Calderwood. Saunders then sprinted across the edge of the box and drove a low shot beyond Spurs keeper Ian Walker into the bottom corner of the net.

Tottenham stepped up the pressure in the second half of an evenly balanced match. A good old-fashioned, blood-and-thunder contest between two committed teams. Spurs' Romanian international Gica Popescu was put clear by Teddy Sheringham early in the second half but was caught and tackled by Villa's other full-back Earl Barrett.

'Typical bloody Romanian,' said the Villa fan next to me.

I thought hard. 'What's a typical bloody Romanian?'

I'd arrived at Villa Park early on a wet Wednesday night for a tour of the ground. I threaded my way around the infamous Spaghetti Junction and under the Aston Expressway towards the stadium. The name Holte is famous in these parts as the largest Kop in the country – the Holte End. It's named after Sir Thomas Holte, who built Aston Hall, a red-brick Jacobean mansion, in 1618. I could see the mansion at the top of a hill in nearby Aston Park. The Holte pub was also named after him.

I parked in the club car park and walked around the stadium past a few early arrivals from North London. I checked out the new Holte End, home of Villa's die-hard supporters, which replaced the famous huge standing terrace at the end of the 1993–94 season. The last match with the Holte End terracing was against Liverpool in front of 45,000 – the largest League crowd of the season.

Around the back, on Trinity Road, stands probably the most distinguished facade at any football ground in the country. The Italian-style architecture seems out of place at a stadium, though Soldier Field, home of the Chicago Bears American football team, looks like a Roman coliseum and is more imposing than Villa Park.

Nevertheless, with its sweeping steps leading up to the top tier of seats, the Trinity Road entrance oozes class. The red-brick walls have the authority of a local council building from the 1930s. There was a circular window on each of the twin towers either side of the stairs and the word Aston and then Villa painted on each of the towers in the team's colours. Above the stairs, between the towers, was the club crest topped with a flagpole. Only the facade of the Main Stand at Craven Cottage came close to reminding me of Villa Park, but Fulham's ground on the banks of the Thames doesn't boast such a majestic staircase.

The Trinity Road Stand was completed in 1922 and first used for a match against Blackburn. The official opening came two years later, when the Duke of York, the future King George VI, made an appearance – though not in a claret and blue shirt. The stand was used as an air-raid shelter during the Second World War and was also home to a rifle company which lived in the Villa dressing-room, giving a whole new meaning to shouts of 'shoot'!

I walked back towards the car park and wandered into Villa's plush reception area. The VIPs were already mingling, some drinking tea and coffee as they waited to be escorted to the various executive suites. Regular fans were also arriving for the match, many picking up their tickets at the front desk, where the receptionists told telephone callers the match was a sell-out. Klinsmann was the big attraction. 'Hello, Aston Villa Football Club. No, I'm sorry all tickets for tonight's match have been sold,' said the blonde. It was an apology she'd give repeatedly.

I wondered if Villa's most famous fan, the violinist Nigel Kennedy, was at the match. If he was, at least he'd be sure of a ticket. Fans queuing for tickets outside the main entrance were as disappointed as those jamming the switchboard.

A group of Spurs fans kitted out in Holsten-sponsored replica shirts came to pick up their tickets. 'You're in amongst the Villa supporters,' said the blonde. 'We can't put you there. Not wearing Spurs shirts.' A quick phone call sorted out the problem. They could sing their hearts out for the lads in the corner of the new £5 million two-tier Doug Ellis Stand, formerly the Witton Lane Stand, with the rest of the colourful entourage of away fans.

I joined a group of Villa supporters for the ground tour and discovered some Spurs fans sprinkled among them. We were taken past the entrance to the tunnel and through to the home dressing-room. The tour in front of us was just emerging from the sanctity of the Villa changing-room as we arrived. It was like visiting a cathedral or stately home on a busy Sunday afternoon. Some of the Villa players had already arrived, including a smiling Andy Townsend. The players' shirts were hung around the walls ready for battle. Their shorts and socks were neatly folded underneath each peg.

Then it was down the tunnel, underneath the club's gold Lion crest with the motto 'Prepared', and out into the damp night air to see the pitch – or rather the plastic covers protecting the playing surface from the torrential rain which had engulfed the stadium. The covers are mechanically rolled out from behind the advertising boards in front of the Witton Lane Stand whenever the stadium is hit by heavy rain.

Next stop was the trophy room – a cornucopia of silverware. It contained a mini replica of the European Cup, won by Villa in 1982 under Tony Barton when they beat Bayern Munich 1–0 in Rotterdam thanks to a Peter Withe goal. Villa went on to win the Super Cup the following year, beating Barcelona. There were also replicas of the FA Cup they've lifted seven times – though not since 1957.

Villa have also won the Championship seven times, six of those successes coming between 1894 and 1910, the last occasion being 1981. They also won the elusive 'double' in 1897 – only the second team to do so after the achievement of Preston's 'Invincibles' in the first season of League football in 1889. One week later they played their first match at what is now Villa Park, though it was then called Aston Lower Grounds, in a friendly against Blackburn.

After Villa clinched the double, one journalist went along to their headquarters at the Tavistock Hotel to congratulate them. But while talking to the players, including Athersmith – a winger who once played on a rainy day with an umbrella held over his head – the reporter rashly said he was sorry they'd deprived Preston, the greatest team of all time, of their unique record. The Villa players threatened to drop him out of the window into the courtyard below! John Campbell, Villa's Scottish centre-forward, shouted: 'Preston? Ha! Football was in its infancy then. They had no one to beat.'

The Villa guide continued his tour by taking us through the restaurant, where supporters were tucking into a three-course meal before the match. A portrait of the club's first chairman, William McGregor, was on the wall. His place in the history of the game was secured when he founded the Football League. It's not surprising, therefore, that Villa were one of the 12 founder members.

We were then taken back outside the ground to be given a fascinating account of the history of Villa Park. Apparently, the stadium was built on what was the Aston Lower Grounds amusement park during Victorian times. The range of activities almost rivalled those at London's Crystal Palace – the building, not the south London football club! Villa were formed in 1874 and first played in Aston Park, across the road from the amusement park. But the Lower Grounds were a logical place for a stadium and part of the park was taken over in 1895 so that Villa could start to build.

Over time the amusement park was changed so that, by the time Villa Park was used as a World Cup venue in 1966, nearly all trace of the Aston Lower Grounds had disappeared. Simon Inglis outlines the changes: 'The old aquarium, skating rink and restaurant became Villa's new offices and gymnasium. The ground's maintenance man took charge of the rifle range. At the rear, a practice pitch and car park was laid on the site of a theatre and concert hall, and on the far side of Witton Lane housing was built where once had been a boating lake with ornamental island. The Witton Lane Stand covered what had been a sub-tropical garden. Another lake became, as at Crystal Palace, the site of the new pitch.'

The Lower Grounds' bowling green was covered by a new social club as part of the preparations for the '66 World Cup. All links with the amusement park were lost in the mid-'80s when the Victorian buildings housing Villa's offices were pulled down as part of a new development underneath the imposing North Stand, which replaced the Witton Lane Stand in the late '70s.

After the tour I was taken to an executive suite from where I could walk to my seat in the North Stand, which was as tall as the Holte End. There were hardly any supporters there yet, but a steward was in position, ready to help the thousands who would pack the stadium. He was less than happy about the recent sacking of manager Ron Atkinson. 'We couldn't believe it here,' he said, shaking his head. 'Big Ron shouldn't have been treated like that. He just needed more time.' I asked about the new boss, Brian Little. 'It's too early to say how well he'll do. We'll just have to wait and see, I suppose,' said the steward.

One of Little's early signings was Tommy Johnson from Derby. At least he was guaranteed a run in the first team, unlike Prime Minister John Major's son, a trialist who didn't make the grade. Johnson had joined Villa because of his respect for Little and the chance to join one of the biggest clubs in the country. But asked in the match programme whom he respected most, he answered Mother Theresa. Johnson must have been praying for a goal against Tottenham tonight.

As the ground began to fill up the covers were removed and the players emerged from the tunnel a good half an hour before the kick-off to warm up. Just before the game a fleet of cars were driven around the perimeter of the pitch as part of an advertising campaign for a local showroom. It was a world apart from the concrete cycle track used for major events until 1914. But then many things had changed at Villa Park since then. Not that Jürgen Klinsmann would remember much about it in the morning!

DID THEY NOT LIKE THAT?

Lincoln City v Hereford United – Sincil Bank, 28 January 1995

Lincoln is one of the few places in England, along with Watford, where Graham Taylor is welcomed with open arms. He took City to the Fourth Division Championship in the mid-'70s with a club record number of points.

'He was a good manager and player as well in his day,' said the local hospital radio commentator sitting behind me in the Main Stand. 'We had a good team then.' Not now, though. At half-time in this appalling match the players were jeered off the pitch. It didn't happen in Taylor's day.

Lincoln have had some famous players in the past, though they've never achieved much. Their best-ever League position was fifth in the Second Division in the 1901–02 season. They won the Third Division (North) three times in the 20 years from 1932 and the Fourth Division Championship in 1976. But their main claim to fame is probably as the first team ever to be automatically relegated to the Vauxhall Conference, in 1987. They bounced straight back to the old Fourth Division the following season.

The nature of their relegation was bizarre and owed much to a police dog called Bryn. On the final day of the season Burnley, Torquay and Lincoln were battling relegation. Torquay went 2–0 down against Crewe knowing that if they lost they'd go down. They clawed one goal back and then, with 10 minutes left, Bryn ran onto the pitch and bit Torquay's Jim McNichol, the scorer of their goal. The referee stopped the match and in the time added on Paul Dobson hit the equaliser sending Lincoln into the Conference. Torquay chairman Lew Pope gave the dog a choice steak for his efforts!

The legendary Raich Carter, a superstar at Sunderland in the 1930s, was once coach at Lincoln. 'I played with him during a practice match, but I never made it as a player,' said the local hospital commentator, who saw his first Lincoln game in 1940. Jock Dodds, once the scorer of a shock winner against Arsenal in the FA Cup, was also at Sincil Bank. 'He was a drunk by the time he came here near the end of his career' said the commentator. 'He didn't run around but made the ball do all the work. He was brilliant.'

More recently, the peripatetic Mick Harford and Luton's former Coventry defender Andy Peake also wore the Imps colours. How Lincoln could have done with some up-and-coming stars now. The club was going through a hard time both on the pitch and financially, with debts estimated at about £300,000.

Their most controversial boss was Willie Bell, who resigned in 1978 to become manager of a team belonging to the religious sect called the US Campus Crusade for Christ, which tried to convert sportsmen to Christianity. (I was to meet the national co-ordinator of a similar organisation called Christians in Football at a Watford Crystal Palace match the following September.)

Of the ten managers who have followed Taylor, only Colin Murphy, in two spells, has had even modest success. The club spent money in the transfer market during the 1993–94 season but still slumped to 18th place in the Third Division, their worst performance since they regained their League status in 1988. Then-manager, Sam Ellis, had the distinction of leading Taylor's side to that Fourth Division title as club captain and centre-half.

I'd arrived at Lincoln station via Peterborough after a journey which began opposite two young lads who were intrigued at my football-ground hopping. One supported Stoke whereas his mate followed Liverpool. He was at Hillsborough the day 89 Liverpool supporters were killed before the FA Cup semi-final against Nottingham Forest. 'We didn't really know what was going on at the time,' he told me. 'I'd gone with my uncle but someone else had offered me a ticket at the Leppings Lane End, so I could just as easily have ended up there. Thank God I didn't.'

The young Stoke fan then told me everything I never wanted to know about Stoke City and wasn't afraid to ask. We covered the 1972 League Cup final when the Potters beat Chelsea 2–1 at Wembley; Stanley Matthews; Alan Hudson; Peter Shilton; their chances of promotion; and anything else he could think of to do with the men in red and white stripes. His pal was less voluble about Liverpool. I suppose most people know what there is to know about the Merseyside club. It was almost a relief when they got off.

When I arrived, I went to get a local paper but there wasn't a preview of today's game. I could have bought a copy of *Farming News* but decided against it. I looked around for someone to help me with directions to Sincil Bank and asked a short man with a bushy moustache.

'You want the football stadium?' he replied in a surprised tone which indicated that watching Lincoln wasn't everyone's favourite way of spending a Saturday afternoon. He told me the way, I thanked him and set off.

The commentator on Radio Lincolnshire was waxing lyrical about the new Sincil Bank stand. He described how it was almost finished except for some scaffolding on the right side and the need to put the letter 'N' on the end of LINCOL, which was picked out in red from the other seats. He said the bright new stand, with its 14 skylights, was something the club could be proud of, although he criticised the lack of foresight in not building a stand on the opposite side of the ground that ran the full length of the pitch.

One of the saddest aspects of a visit to Sincil Bank is incorporated in the Stacey West Stand, which was to my right in front of the cathedral and the castle. Stacey and West are the surnames of two Lincoln fans killed in the Bradford fire in 1985. The club named the stand after them so that they'd always be remembered at Sincil Bank.

The first half was goalless and awful. Probably among the worst football I'd seen all season. The second half improved slightly, and at least there were some goals. Lincoln took the lead about eight minutes into the second half, when a cross from the right was turned in by David Hill after Hereford's central defender misheaded the ball. Four minutes later another cross from the right to the far post was met by the promising Matt Carbon. He rose above the Hereford defence to power a header past goalkeeper Tony Pennock. And that was that.

At half-time the announcer behind me in his red bobble hat, with the word Imps embroidered across the front in white, gave the half-time scores from other matches. The club's nickname has some historical significance and a link to the Usher Gallery in Lindum Road, which contains a collection of watches and clocks from the seventeenth century. These were given to the gallery by its benefactor, James Ward Usher, a local jeweller and watchmaker. But what's the connection with Lincoln City Football Club? Well, Usher made a fortune by making up the legend of the Lincoln Imp, which he turned into the city's emblem in the 1880s. According to his story, there were a couple of imps hopping around the cathedral until one was turned into stone because he tried to talk to the angels carved into the roof of the choir. The other imp fled on the back of a witch. And that's why Lincoln City are known as the Imps.

GOING DOWN

Chester City v Wycombe Wanderers – The Deva Stadium, 31 January 1995

Archie Gemmill, Stuart Pearson, Arthur Albiston, Mike Smith, Alan Parry, Simon Garner, Cyrille Regis and Nicky Reid. It was like a who's who of football personalities past and present at Chester's Deva Stadium on a windswept night when rain had caused floods and chaos on the roads and railways. High in the Pennines one person had died and dozens were injured after two trains collided.

The first train was believed to have been derailed by a landslide. The Chester players knew how it felt to slide. Promotion from the Third Division one year, bottom of the Second the next. Two managers had already departed and the present incumbent, caretaker boss Derek Mann, was spending as much time trying to defend his team as they were trying to defend their goal. High-flying Wycombe were not the kind of opponents to let you off the hook.

I was originally going to Hereford on this wet Tuesday night, but that match was called off in the morning because of a waterlogged pitch. Chester's playing surface was in better condition, so I travelled north in the hope of watching a match that had originally been postponed the day after New Year's Day because of – you guessed – a waterlogged pitch. The London Weather Centre had already reported twice the average rainfall in parts of the south in January – the highest for some seven years.

'You'll be alright in the autumn and the spring but the winter will be your problem,' I was told by a number of people before my record attempt. In fact, postponements were a big help because they meant I could fit more midweek games into my already tight schedule. I had to get to places like Chester on a Tuesday night, but I'd passed my 50th match of the season and it was worth it.

The home defence lasted just 26 minutes against Wycombe before new boy Miguel Desouza, a £100,000 buy from Birmingham, put the away side ahead. 'Going down, going down, going down,' sang the Wycombe fans.

'We're already down,' said a Chester fan behind me.

The Wycombe manager, former Northern Ireland international Martin O'Neill was steering his side towards a second successive promotion drive. He was without the services of former Manchester City defender Nicky Reid, who was recovering from a cartilage operation. 'Apart from that the manager hates my guts,' Reid told a former QPR scout, who had inquired about his position at the club in the bar before the match.

Reid played in the classic 100th FA Cup final between Manchester City and Spurs in 1981, memorable for a five-goal replay which Spurs won 3–2 thanks to a mazy dribble from Argentine international Ricardo Villa which ended with the ball being slotted through Joe Corrigan's legs. That was the peak of Reid's career. This was the nadir. Out of the Wycombe side through injury and unpopular with the manager.

The scout, who said he'd discovered Les Ferdinand and Andrew Impey, was working for Charlton's managerial duo of Alan Curbishley and Steve Gritt. He'd left QPR after ten years following a series of disputes surrounding everything from the cut he thought he deserved from the sale of the players he'd discovered to the fact that they wouldn't give him a car and hadn't compensated him for a theft from his own.

The scout said former QPR manager Jim Smith had promised him a 1 per cent cut of the fee if Ferdinand was sold but, when Newcastle came in with a £3.8 million offer, he was told by then-Rangers boss Gerry Francis that his deal had been negotiated under a different manager and he wasn't entitled to anything from the sale of players he'd brought to the attention of the club before Francis took charge.

The scout would get a cut from the sale of players he'd discovered under Francis but nothing more. The scout claimed it was all so unfair because he reckoned Francis was allegedly on a share of the transfer fee from the sale of Ferdinand. (An insider at Spurs later told me Francis was entitled to a percentage of any increase in a player's value at QPR between the time he'd taken over as manager and the time they were sold, but not a cut of the whole amount.)

The question of managers receiving money from selling players seemed to me to be a conflict of interest. It meant that a manager would profit from selling the club's best players. His personal gain would therefore come at the expense of the team and the fans unless he was selling to buy other players who would improve the side – usually not the case.

Since Ferdinand wasn't sold while Francis was QPR manager, I suppose all this is academic. But the scout was incensed at how unfair the system was. 'I'd been there ten years as well,' said the scout. 'There's no loyalty in the game today,' said Reid.

As he was leaving, the scout gave Reid his card. 'If there's anything I can do for you, let me know. I'm always getting calls from people who want players.' Then he left to take up his seat in the Main Stand, while I was busily totting up what a 1 per cent cut of £3.8 million would be – £38,000, not bad if you can get it. And if you can't, there are always other players to discover.

Outside, the fans were settling into their seats in the Deva Stadium, named after the Roman word for Dee, the river which winds its way around this county town. The club had sold their Sealand Road Ground for about £3 million in 1990 and built a new 6,000-capacity stadium on a greenfield site a mile and a half south-west of the town centre.

After ground-sharing with Macclesfield for two years, Chester moved into their new stadium in 1992 and played their first match there on 5 September, beating Burnley 3–0 in front of almost 5,000 fans. It was a very smart ground, similar to Wycombe's Adams Park, but it had no soul and was a bit like a new shopping complex: very smart, very comfortable, but ultimately sterile.

The 150 or so Wycombe fans who'd made the trip from west of London did their best to enliven the atmosphere among a crowd of only 1,500. Decked out in yellow, one of them banged a drum throughout the match, much to the annoyance of the middle-aged lady behind me who at one point pleaded for him to stop. Without the drummer, however, the ground would have resembled a wake. 'Come on Wycombe, Come on Wycombe,' sang their fans. The Chester followers had little to cheer.

It was all so different from the glory of promotion the season before, but perfectly understandable given two changes of manager and a clear-out of players. 'There was an Arsenal scout at the last home game watching our keeper David Felgate and defender Chris Lightfoot. At half-time he said he'd wasted his time,' said the young supporter. 'Tranmere made a £750,000 bid for Lightfoot last season. We should have taken it when we had the chance.' They'd since come back with a lower offer, but Chester had again turned it down. I told him about the former QPR scout who'd discovered Les Ferdinand. 'Well, he won't discover anyone here,' said the young season ticket holder.

Former Wales and Everton defender Kevin Ratcliffe was assistant manager at Chester and in the side, according to my programme – the one printed for the postponed 2 January match because it was too expensive to print another.

'Why isn't Ratcliffe playing?' I asked the noisy fan next to me.

'Well, he's paid so much a game, I've heard, and it's cheaper not to play him. These are minimum cost matches.' Things sounded tight.

Chester's team was once graced by players of the calibre of Liverpool's Ian Rush, Arsenal's Lee Dixon and Wimbledon's Aidan Newhouse. Dixon was allowed to leave on a free, as was Gary Bennett whose transfer was particularly galling. He was the top scorer in the League with 32 goals already this season and had scored them all for Chester's arch-rivals Wrexham.

'We don't like any of the Welsh teams,' a taxi driver told me on the way to the match, 'but I suppose Wrexham are our main rivals.' I mentioned Bennett. 'Don't talk to me about it,' said the cabbie, obviously still smarting from the embarrassment. I assumed he was proud of Chester winning the Welsh Cup three times – in 1908, 1933 and 1947. Not until 1975 did they achieve any success in English competition when they were promoted from the old Fourth Division and reached the League Cup semi-final.

The conditions in the second half were atrocious with rain driving across the pitch. It was a miracle the players could see, let alone play football. The weather didn't stop the home fans from complaining, though.

'It's like bloody ping-pong out there,' yelled one supporter.

'Oh dear,' mumbled his wife as she pondered the downside of playing in the Endsleigh League Second Division on a night like this. Fifteen minutes before the end the Chester fans began to leave.

'I've got to go. They're giving me a migraine,' said one, joining the early exodus back to town.

A photographer trying to get some close-up shots at the end of the match looked as if he was starring with Gregory Peck in *Moby Dick*. His fisherman's mac definitely had the wet look as he struggled to focus his camera on the celebrating Wycombe players. They stood there in triumph applauding their travelling fans, before heading off for a shower and a quick pint in the warmth of the vice-president's lounge.

A Chester official stood on the door to the lounge barring anyone without a pass.

'But we're Wycombe players,' said one handsome young lad as he led the injured and discarded to the bar.

'That's all right then,' said the official, smartly dressed in a royal-blue jacket. He'd supported Chester for 40 years and said this was the worst side he'd ever seen. He enjoyed meeting all the football celebrities who visited the club, though.

'Ronnie Moran showed up the other week unannounced. He didn't have a ticket and I didn't have one for him, but you've got to find somewhere for people like that, haven't you? A scout showed up the other week in a tracksuit, but I couldn't let him in because we have a dress code. He said no problem I've got a suit in the car. Well, then Dario Gradi (Crewe's manager) came along in a shell suit. What could I do? I had to let him into the lounge. There are certain personalities in football and you have to look after them. Suppose we want one of their players on loan?' He had a point.

The official recalled the days when Chester played at Sealand Road, especially the night they knocked the mighty Leeds United out of the League Cup 3–0. 'It was the only time I could remember Billy Bremner being substituted.' The famous victory over the reigning League champions took place on 13 November 1974 in front of 19,000.

The fanzine *Hello Albert* published a map of the old ground showing where the celebrations had taken place. Little reminders like, 'Centre circle Leeds kicked off from four times' and 'Where we sang our hearts out' were dotted around the map. 'Pandemonium on the kop when Chester score second and third goals,' was followed by, 'One man loses wedding ring . . . another his false teeth!'

If you're wondering why the fanzine is called *Hello Albert*, here goes. Chester's Sealand Road ground was one of the first in the League to have a PA system. From as early as 1931, when Chester entered the League, the announcer would greet supporters with, 'Hello, Spion Kop! Hello, Albert.' He was apparently welcoming a long-standing supporter. Obvious, really.

As my thoughts turned to getting a taxi back to town the official told me about the time Jack Charlton was asked to compare the current Leeds team with the one he played in.

'They're pretty close in terms of ability, so what would the score be if you played them?' Big Jack was asked.

'Probably 1–0.'

'Only one?' said the official, surprised.

Jack looked at him with a sparkle in his eye, 'Well, we are all over 50 now!'

PELÉ PLAYED HERE

Plymouth Argyle v York City – Home Park, 4 February 1995

The Brazilian team Santos came to England at the start of the 1987–88 season to play a series of exhibition matches against much less glamorous teams, including Barnsley, Bradford and Wolves. But it wasn't the first time the club had visited these shores to play more humble opposition. During the heyday of the World's Greatest Footballer, Edson Arantes do Nascimento, the Black Pearl, better known as Pelé, Plymouth hosted the Brazilians in an exhibition match before a crowd of 36,000.

The match was not without controversy – at one stage it was nearly called off – and eventually world football's governing body, FIFA, had to sort out the mess. The reason was money. Plymouth had agreed to pay Santos a total of £11,000 in appearance money – a large sum in the 1970s. Twenty minutes before kick-off, with the Argyle fans packed into the ground, bubbling with anticipation, a club official popped his head around the door of the away dressing-room to make sure the Santos players were okay. He was shocked to find that they hadn't yet got changed for the match.

'I asked what was going on and was stunned when they told me they'd seen the size of the crowd and wanted another £3,000 in cash or else they wouldn't play,' said the official. 'There was a quick meeting and we decided we'd have to pay them. I scurried around the turnstiles to get some of the gate money. I remember sitting there with all this cash on my lap. We paid them, and they played.'

Plymouth reported the Brazilians to FIFA and eventually they returned the extra money after being threatened with a ban from international competition. I just couldn't resist sitting in the corner where Pelé had – eventually – changed for the match. 'We've never cleaned it since,' joked the official. It was hard to imagine the World's Greatest Footballer sitting in the humble surroundings of the away dressing-room.

A visit to Home Park was like going back in time. The ground, the atmosphere, even the fans and officials – everything was 1950s. The music they played as the home team came out of the tunnel, remarkably topped with flowers in little window boxes, sounded like it was salvaged from the Second World War. A picture of the black and white puppy from His Master's Voice had to be on the record label. I half-expected the supporters to be wearing flat caps, holding rattles and drinking Bovril and it wouldn't have surprised me to see the Argyle players in baggy shorts.

I'd left London bright and early to travel down to Plymouth by car with my girlfriend Nicky (a recent addition to my travelling entourage – basically just me up to now). We'd arrived in plenty of time for the tour of the ground and the match. Home Park is next to a large open area called Central Park with its Mayflower sports centre and swimming pool, a sports club which has a cricket pitch, squash and tennis courts and an Astroturf pitch, a golf course, bowling greens, training pitches and lots of fields. There was clearly plenty of room for expansion if Plymouth ever decided to join the growing band of clubs building new stadiums. (They have since unveiled plans for a 25,000 all-seater stadium which, it's hoped, will be built on the lines of Huddersfield's Alfred McAlpine Stadium in partnership with Plymouth County Council.)

I pulled into the vast car park and asked the man in the ticket office if he could find out who would be giving me a tour of Home Park. A few minutes later our guide appeared. After being shown around we were taken to an executive box which was actually more like my nan's front room than one of those sleek, glass affairs with tinted windows you see at most Premier League grounds. We shared it with two middle-aged ladies, a younger woman and a boy of about ten. They were keen Plymouth fans but all of them, with the exception of the youngster, had seen better days at Home Park.

The ground was first used in the 1890s not for football but for rugby by Plymouth Albion and then the Devonport rugby club. The Argyle Athletic Club, formed in 1886 for amateur rugby, football and cricket as well as athletics, took it over in 1901. At the time there was only a roped-off pitch and a cinder track.

The Argyle Football Club, which came under the Athletic Club umbrella, was formed in September 1886 by former schoolboys who wanted to continue playing football. They first met in a room above the Borough Arms Coffee House in Bedford Street and also got together in Argyle Terrace, Mutley. The name Argyle, or Argyll, was fashionable throughout the country because of Queen Victoria's interest in Scotland. It was also the custom in those days to choose the name of a local street or terrace as a club name and so the new football team was called Plymouth Argyle.

The ground hosted pony-trotting, whippet-racing and motorcycling, but the owner, one Clarence Spooner, was more keen on Devon's main city matching Bristol, Portsmouth and Southampton by having a professional football club. He arranged a series of exhibition matches to try to promote the game. Aston Villa were the first big-name team to come to Home Park and exhibited their skills before a crowd of 16,000 by beating Argyle 7–0. The Wednesday and Notts County were the next First Division teams to arrive in the city, though they played each other just to show that evenly balanced matches were possible and could be just as exciting.

Rugby was still the most popular sport in the area, but interest in football, particularly among the Armed Forces stationed in Plymouth, was growing. In 1903 the Argyle Athletic Club dropped cricket and rugby to concentrate on football and the whole club was renamed Plymouth Argyle after the football team. They signed a new lease and in September 1903 the club played its first senior competitive match in the Southern League against Northampton before a crowd of almost 4,500. Home Park was circled by farms and allotments with most people walking to the ground between hedges and over a stile on a country path called Pennycomequick. As you can imagine, it was a bit crowded on match days.

In 1920 Argyle followed many of their Southern League opponents when they became founder members of the Third Division (South). They drew their first League match 1–1 at home to Norwich. For six consecutive years between 1921 and 1927 they finished runners-up, twice missing out on promotion by a point and once on goal average. One of the most amazing matches ever staged at Home Park was in 1926, when a team of strikers played the police during the General Strike. The controversial game was preceded by clashes between the strikers and mounted police as the crowds tried to block local transport taking fans to the ground. But the game was played and the strikers won 2–1. In a calmer, though no less excitable atmosphere, Argyle were finally rewarded for their consistency when they won the title by seven points in 1930.

After the war Plymouth had to be reconstructed, a process made easier by its growth into by far the largest city in Devon. A new board at Plymouth Argyle also had to set about rebuilding the football ground. Simon Inglis described the process in *The Football Grounds of Britain*: 'Tons of rubble from the ruins of the town centre were dumped in the craters or used to raise the banking around the pitch. Old tramcars were used as offices, army huts became dressing rooms, railway sleepers were laid on the terraces. In the south-east corner a pavilion was built for the directors, while the stand wreckage was cleared and seating placed on the bank. Thus Home Park re-opened, battered but unbowed for season 1946–47, and was greeted by an all-time record average gate of 23,375.' The two tramcars, which replaced the bomb-damaged terraces, provided temporary accommodation for supporters and remained in use, as the headquarters for the supporters club and a base for groundstaff, until the 1950s.

Plymouth began the new decade by being relegated to the Third Division in 1950 but bounced back quickly with the current double-decker Main Stand built in time for their return to the Second Division as champions in 1952. It was the best stand they'd had, but was the last of its type ever built and would have been more at home in the '30s than the '50s. Still, it served its purpose and the club continued to make small improvements to the stadium.

In 1953 the floodlights were officially unveiled in front of a disappointing crowd of only 2,000 for a friendly against local rivals Exeter. City have always been utterly despised by Argyle fans and any player with connections to the Grecians is guaranteed a hostile reception at Home Park. Unfortunately, Exeter had recently fallen on very hard times. 'I bet most fans had at least a quiet chuckle to themselves when they heard the news that City were in receivership,' said the Plymouth fanzine *Rub of the Green*. But were Argyle fans really rubbing their hands with glee at the thought of Exeter going bust?

'One of the pleasures of football is laughing at the misfortunes of others, especially your closest rivals, but this time it is a bit too close to home,' wrote the fanzine. 'Firstly, if [Plymouth chairman] Dan McCauley were to walk out it is not hard to see that Argyle could end up in the same state. Secondly, if the worst did come to the worst and City did go to the wall who would we take the piss out of? You can't beat a team that doesn't exist. So I for one hope that City survive, but only just. And, while I'm feeling benevolent, I hope City get a new ground, at least that might have a roof on the away end and a decent stand.'

McCauley, owner of the Exeter-based engineering firm Rotolok which sponsored Argyle, took over Plymouth in 1991 when the club was deep in debt after years of neglect. He'd provided money for players and nobody doubted the good he'd done for the club. But his efforts were yet to be rewarded by success on the pitch. McCauley was treading a well-worn path of underperformance, which had littered Argyle's history.

I watched their latest attempt to garner some League points from an executive box as green as the rest of the stadium. Green comfy chairs, a green door, green walls, green crush barriers on the terraces, green signs, officials in green uniforms and, of course, the team in a mainly green home strip – the only one in the English League. Peter Pan would have fitted in well.

'Dwight Marshall was a good player, Gran,' said the young lad in his green and white scarf.

'I know dear, but he won't be coming back,' she said apologetically. 'He's at Luton now.' I felt really sorry for the boy. Marshall was obviously his idol and now he was deprived of watching him because Plymouth needed the money.

The multi-million pound transfers and five-figure weekly wages being thrown about in the Premier League and the First Division were light-years away. But the youngster's disappointment was close enough. He could only relate to the fact that the player he looked forward to seeing every other week wasn't wearing Plymouth's green and black shirt anymore.

His gran had supported the Pilgrims since she was a child and listed Paul Mariner and Dwight Marshall as among the best players she'd seen at Home Park. Perhaps even she was too old to remember three of the club's record-holders from the 1920s – Sammy Black, Moses Russell and Jack Cock. Black is the club's highest scorer with 180 goals between 1924 and 1938, Russell has the most caps of any Plymouth player (20 for Wales whilst at the club and 23 in total) and Cock rammed in 32 goals in the Third Division (South) in 1925–26 – the most League goals any Argyle player had scored in a season.

Paul Mariner, of course, went on to fame and fortune in the great Ipswich team which lit up the First Division under Bobby Robson. But before he left Home Park, Mariner had been the club's top scorer and was voted Player of the Year for two consecutive seasons. The second of those feats had been matched only by Shilton's successor at the Home Park helm, newly installed player–manager Steve McCall.

McCall had also made his name under Bobby Robson at Ipswich as a member of the team that created two club records – 23 undefeated League matches and 33 games unbeaten at Portman Road. He was also a key player in Town's UEFA Cup-winning side of 1981 when they beat AZ67 Alkmaar to lift a European trophy for the first time in the club's history. McCall moved to Sheffield Wednesday for £300,000 in 1987, before becoming Shilton's second signing for Plymouth in March 1992 at a cost of £25,000.

After taking over from Shilton, McCall appointed former Nottingham Forest midfielder Ian Bowyer as his assistant, with ex-Sheffield Wednesday keeper Martin Hodge put in charge of the youth team. Together they hoped to steer Plymouth clear of the relegation zone. McCall was still able to have the most influence on the team, not just because he was the manager but by virtue of being out there on the park, where he could urge on his players and use his own skills to change the pattern of play.

Plymouth dominated the first half and should have scored at least four times against York instead of the one goal which divided the teams at half-time. Nevertheless, the Plymouth fans in the executive box seemed reasonably happy with the way the game was going. The most opinionated was the grandmother. She had firm views on football, life and everything. She certainly had the experience to back her.

At half-time she switched on the TV to find out how England were doing against France in the day's rugby international. They were winning.

'What's the score?' said the middle-aged lady in the corner.

'We're beating the frogs, of course,' said gran. She then turned swiftly and said to me, 'You're not French, are you?'.

'*Oui*,' I replied in my best accent, but there was no fooling gran.

'Sure,' she said, a glint in her eye.

Plymouth began the second half on top but gradually lost their grip. All those missed chances from the first-half were preying on the minds of the players and York, so far anonymous, began to look dangerous on the break. Eventually, the inevitable happened and they broke away to equalise after a dazzling mazy run from their winger. The more the game went on, the more you felt York might even snatch a winner. They did.

The Plymouth fans were very tolerant. They wanted McCall to succeed. He was a firm favourite on the pitch and that support had carried over into his job as player–manager. Relegation might change their views, but for now they were right behind their new boss. I told the fans I was going to Shrewsbury on the following Tuesday night where I'd see Plymouth again. 'Cheer them on,' said the ladies. 'They need all the help they can get.

THE CORACLE MAN

Shrewsbury Town v Plymouth Argyle – Gay Meadow, 7 February 1995

Fred Davies. Not the former world snooker champion, nor the manager of Shrewsbury Town, but *the* Fred Davies. Any self-respecting football fanatic has heard of him, probably seen him on *Football Focus* or *On the Ball* and, if really privileged, may have watched him rowing along the River Severn on match days to retrieve a ball.

Fred was a legend. For years he spent Saturday afternoons, and some evenings, in his round, wooden boat, called a coracle, waiting for a Tony Adams-style hoof to take the ball out of the Gay Meadow stadium into the river. He would then row his boat to wherever the ball had landed and retrieve it for the princely sum of 25 pence.

'Fred Davies, isn't that the name of your manager? He's not the same guy who used to collect footballs in his boat, is he?' I asked the middle-aged man standing next to me at the Abbey Foregate End of Gay Meadow.

'Well, some of the supporters might wish the manager was otherwise employed, but he isn't the same guy,' he said. 'Poor old Fred isn't with us anymore.' I wondered if perhaps he'd been transferred for several million pounds to another riverside team like Nottingham Forest.

In fact, Fred retired aged 86 and handed over the oars to his son. But the young Mr Davies had trouble controlling the coracle, so Fred came out of retirement to resume his role as the oldest retriever at the Town. Sadly, Fred has since passed away; but his legend lingers on. He is more famous than any Shrewsbury player or manager (not difficult, perhaps, but how many coracle owners do you know?).

I was told by a supporter that Fred was buried 'at river', so to speak, in a ceremony befitting a Viking leader. All and sundry supposedly gathered along the banks of the Severn to watch Fred's body being pushed out into the river in his beloved coracle. The boat was set on fire and Fred was given the send off he would have wanted. There was hardly a dry eye in the town. I'm not certain the story is true, but it would be nice to think so.

Fred Davies, more than anyone or anything else, sums up the spirit of Shrewsbury Town. The ground is tucked away across a bridge leading from the delightful town centre with its olde-worlde shops, hotels and restaurants. Even the local McDonald's and Burger King restaurants exude class (at least in the buildings and decor, if not the standardised food). The back of the Riverside Enclosure is lined with tall trees which offer the ball some protection from the River Severn.

The pitch has suffered from being so close to water. Tonight's match against Plymouth was originally scheduled for New Year's Eve but a waterlogged pitch saved the south-coast team a long journey. The original programme for that match, on sale tonight with a one-page update to save reprinting costs, hoped the Plymouth players would be home in time to celebrate the New Year. In the event, they never left!

One feature at Gay Meadow is the ornate iron Victorian turnstile at the Station End. There were so few Plymouth fans at the match that Shrewsbury had moved them into the Main Stand seats and the Station End was closed tonight.

'Mind if I take a look at your famous turnstile?' I asked a steward.

'I didn't know it was that famous,' he replied, but kindly took me through to see it anyway.

It really is special, unlike any other turnstile I'd ever seen. Its origins are cloudy but it may have come from the Crystal Palace ground (not Selhurst Park) which staged the FA Cup final between 1895 and 1914.

'How old is it?' I asked another steward.

'I don't know exactly but it's Victorian. Queen Victoria herself has been through there.'

'Sure,' I thought. Did the old dowager ever visit a football ground?

Gay Meadow had seen some great players and memorable games over the years. The bearded middle-aged man in the check flat-cap standing next to me recalled seeing the great Johnny Haynes in his prime. 'He was knocking the ball across the pitch straight under someone's toe. I'd never seen anyone pass the ball so accurately. Then there was the match when Ivor Allchurch was playing for Swansea and Peter Broadbent for Shrewsbury. They were in a completely different class from the others.'

He also told me about the time Shrewsbury played Scunthorpe in the early '70s. They were awarded a free-kick near the left touchline, level with the 18-yard box. Three Scunthorpe players lined up to take the kick. The first ran over the ball; then the second; and finally the third. They all looked at each other in bewilderment and the Shrewsbury crowd fell about laughing. The programme for that match included an article on a promising youngster called Kevin Keegan. He wasn't even in the Scunthorpe first team then!

Plymouth made all the running in the first half and could have scored four. But they only managed the one goal. It would prove to be fatal for the second time in a week. If only they had a young Paul Mariner or could bring back Dwight Marshall from Luton. They created goalscoring opportunities at will in the first half, but there was just nobody to put the ball in the net.

SIMPLY THE BEST

Stockport County v Chester City – Edgeley Park, 11 February 1995

Georgie Best once played for Stockport. Not a lot of people know that, as Michael Caine might say. (Best had a punch-up with the film star in a London nightclub once, but that's another story). When County were struggling to survive in the mid-'70s they signed a 29-year-old Best for a month – his third comeback attempt after two years out of the game. On his Fourth Division début against Swansea he more than trebled the gate at 9,240, made two goals and scored the winner in a 3–2 victory.

Best's comeback was ironic in a way. At the height of his fame at Manchester United a much younger Georgie Boy often joined his friend and rival from Manchester City, Mike Summerbee, at Edgeley Park on Friday nights to watch the Third Division football on offer in the 1960s. 'I usually start by watching one particular player and end up watching the referee,' said Best at the time. The referee was a very important character for me today, since he'd decide if my trip to Stockport was worth while.

Water, water, everywhere – but which game would be on? The rain hadn't stopped falling for days. All over England the heavens had opened and the match I'd planned to watch, York against Hull, was in doubt. York told me on Friday night they were 99 per cent certain it would be off, so I checked the fixtures on teletext. There were pitch inspections at Derby and Mansfield, as well as York. I decided to try either Bury or Stockport, but I'd have to wait until the morning, possibly even Saturday lunchtime, before I was sure either game would go ahead. It would be a close call.

On the tube platform at London's King's Cross I just had time to call Gigg Lane to see if I could arrange a ticket for Bury's match. A recorded message said there would be a pitch inspection at one o'clock. That did it. I decided to take my chances by travelling to Stockport for the game against bottom club Chester. I'd have no trouble getting a ticket and at least there was a chance it would be on. It was a wise choice.

I reached London's Euston Station ten minutes before the next train to Manchester. The train stopped at Stockport, one station and eight minutes before its arrival at Manchester Piccadilly. There were plenty of Manchester City fans on board travelling to Maine Road for the derby match against United. Strangely, I didn't spot any Reds supporters. Euston was always full of fans in their colours on Saturday mornings. Today I saw Liverpool and QPR supporters going to Anfield for the match between their teams. They'd share the spoils in a 1–1 draw.

245

The journey to Stockport highlighted the weather problem for the groundstaff in both the Endsleigh League and, to a lesser extent, the Carling Premiership. The countryside was under water. Rivers were filled to the brim and some had broken their banks; fishermen were trying their luck in what were usually green fields.

I arrived at Edgeley Park in the rain to find just one fan outside the players' entrance. I passed him as I made my way to the ticket office.

'Is the game on?' I enquired.

'Pitch inspection at one o'clock,' said the office manager. Great.

I asked the lone fan where else I could go if the game was called off. He suggested Wigan, Sheffield United, Rochdale or Liverpool. Bury had already been called off, justifying my decision not to travel to Gigg Lane. Now all I could do was wait.

I talked to a couple of Stockport fans outside the Main Stand to find out more about the club. They'd reached the final of the Autoglass Trophy a couple of years earlier, but their success in recent seasons was limited. They were currently just out of the running for a play-off spot but would be right back among the contenders if they could string a few wins together. The big story was the recent loss of the tallest player in the League to Birmingham – six feet seven inch Kevin Francis.

Francis had Stockport's Uruguayan-born manager Danny Bergara to thank for his success. The charismatic Bergara had a reputation as a bit of a miracle-worker – and he needed to be. As he said:

> Basically, you've got to get people for £10,000 and sell them on for £100,000. You've got to work really hard with people like Kevin Francis. When he first came to the club – I love the kid and he's done brilliant for us – but I put my hands on my head and said, 'I've got it wrong this time.' But we worked on this, we worked on that, and you've got an all-round deal of £800,000.
>
> What you've got to do is go to games and watch players and you see something in these players and the others don't. The biggest example is Kev. When I went to watch him two or three times, people were laughing. I left before the end and I'm out on the car park rubbing my hands and I'm thinking, 'This is my chance, son.' Nobody wanted big Paul Williams – bad boy this, that and the other. Get him for free from Hartlepool, he scored 14 goals in 27 games to take us to second from top in the Fourth Division and we sell him to West Brom for £250,000. You're talking about Tony Barrass – a free from Hartlepool – and Andy Preece for £15,000 from Wrexham and the rest.
>
> These guys don't grow on trees. You've got to take them out on the training ground and show 'em what to do – you don't tell them, you show them – and, if they're really interested in improving themselves, they'll do it. It's all a matter of getting players that desperately want to do it and, if you've got somebody who desperately wants to do it, I know that I'm one of the best at instructing them how to do it.

The Edgeley Park faithful adored Francis. Ironically, he had to play against Stockport in his second match for Birmingham. Faced with an open goal, he hit the post. 'I didn't enjoy it!' he said afterwards. But he did enjoy the reception given to him by the County fans at St Andrews. He was so overcome that he contacted the local *Stockport Express* newspaper to say how he felt. 'I would like to thank all the County fans who gave me such a marvellous reception,' he told the paper.

The *Express* itself highlighted how laudable it was to witness supporters cheering rather than jeering their erstwhile hero. 'In an era when chants of Judas are commonly hurled by fans at former favourites who have moved on, it was refreshing to hear Francis, a hero for four years at Edgeley Park, being cheered before, during and after the game.' The fanzine *IO County* put a picture of Francis on the front cover with the tribute 'Thanks for Everything Big Man. Good Luck'.

The £800,000 Birmingham had paid for him would help Stockport cover some of the costs of developing their ground, including the new Cheadle End which was going up fast. The skeleton iron structure behind the goal to my right looked like something out of H.G. Wells's *War of the Worlds*. Mind you, not everyone was happy. The two doddery old geezers behind me, wearing check flat-caps and smoking pipes, were less than pleased.

'A waste of bloody money,' said one.

'We need new players not a new stand,' said the other.

The club were more enthusiastic about the stand. Commercial manager John Rutter was certainly keen. 'Whilst it may be true that the stand will not be full every week [a criticism echoed by the fans in the Main Stand around me], I am convinced that the facilities within the stand will reach capacity. The 250-seater restaurant will be an obvious attraction. The social club too will provide a facility that we have sadly lacked in recent years.' He may be right, if the team is winning. If they're not, it won't be just the stand that isn't filled every week.

As I waited outside the ground before the match the time was getting on and I was getting wet. Finally, an official emerged from the players' entrance with the news that it was on. I'd come to the right place. Stockport had spent a lot of money re-laying their pitch and improving the drainage. The expense was paying dividends. However, I was a bit concerned that a former Wigan groundsman was on the staff at Edgeley Park. Was this the same man who had put sand on the pitch at Springfield Park and ruined the playing surface?

Stockport's game was completely overshadowed on the day by the Manchester derby. Piccadilly Gold, the Manchester radio station, was previewing the Mancunian clash with former City and Scotland defender Willie Donachie. He was asked if the weather conditions would affect the game. 'If the ball skids on the pitch, then it will suit Manchester United; if it doesn't skid, it will suit Manchester City.' I tried to work out the logic but failed.

The Stockport announcer was also aware of the big match up the road. 'I hope you're all wrapped up and ready for today's action at the Theatre of Dreams,' he said ironically, referring to Edgeley Park not Old Trafford. I didn't know if he'd said it with a straight face, but the Stockport defence gave a good impression of a comedy act in the first half. Defender Tony Dinning was particularly entertaining, scoring his second own goal in succession following an astute lob over his own keeper at Birmingham.

Perhaps the Stockport defenders thought bottom club Chester would be easy pickings. They certainly looked relaxed in the first half-hour. After sustained pressure the visitors went ahead in the 22nd minute through Roger Preece. Stuart Rimmer, formerly of Everton, Watford and Barnsley, broke down the left wing before laying the ball back to the edge of the area. The cross was slightly deflected but fell perfectly for Preece, who volleyed sweetly into the top left-hand corner.

Worse was to follow for the home side. Two minutes later a cross from the right was headed down into the six-yard box where first Stockport's Michael Wallace and then the hapless Tony Dinning between them steered the ball over the line as they made a desperate attempt to clear. The Stockport fans behind me were livid. 'You're a load of dummies,' said the flat capped, pipe-smoking pensioner.

County's new signing Ian Helliwell, £20,000 from Rotherham, was anonymous and certainly not a replacement for Francis. 'I don't know why we bothered to buy him,' said the man whose son played for Stockport's youth team. It all looked pretty hopeless, but things would brighten up for the home fans in the second half with a goal just after half-time and an equaliser three minutes from the end. Anyway, Valentine's Day was approaching and at least the announcer didn't disappoint the home supporters. 'I have a Valentine's message for you: Hilda loves Squidgy Bunny.' Right!

I asked the father of the youth-team member to name the best player he'd seen at County. Kevin Francis was the only one he could come up with. He'd obviously missed the silky skills of Georgie Best. Then again, don't we all.

HODDLE FAILS TO SHINE

Chesterfield v Barnet – The Recreation Ground, 14 February 1995

If you've ever wondered why Chesterfield's nickname is the Spireites (and you probably haven't), it's because of the crooked spire of the Church of St Mary and All Saints which dominates the town. The Church was finished in about 1360 and is the largest in Derbyshire.

So how did the spire become as crooked as a football manager taking a bung? Legend tells of a powerful magician who persuaded a Bolsover blacksmith to shoe the Devil. Unfortunately he drove a nail into the Devil's foot. Howling with rage and pain, the sort of noise you make after being tackled by Vinny Jones, the Devil fled to Chesterfield. Skimming over the church, he lashed out in agony, caught the spire and twisted it out of shape. Another theory is that Lucifer sat on the church and spitefully let his massive weight crush its elegant spire. The truth, as usual, is probably less fanciful and linked to the ravages of the Black Death, which spread across Britain in the fourteenth century when the church was being built. Many people died in the Plague, among them skilled craftsmen. The survivors built the spire out of timber which, over the years, has become twisted beneath the heavy lead covering.

Chesterfield's Recreation Ground – also known as Saltergate after the main thoroughfare at the Kop End – stands on a hill above the town centre. The stadium is surrounded by suburban houses. From the open Cross Street End the famous spire is to the left, hidden by the Main Stand on St Margaret's Drive. After catching a mid-afternoon train from London's St Pancras station and a taxi from Chesterfield to a small hotel around the corner from the ground, that's where I found myself. I was sitting between a Blackburn scout and an elderly man who'd been evacuated as a child to a town called New Whittington, north of Chesterfield, from his home in Barnet during the Second World War.

Evacuation was to cause unforseen problems later in his life – the main one being who he should support when Chesterfield played Barnet as they would tonight.

'The Chesterfield chairman kindly gave me a ticket for tonight's match as his guest but he asked me who I would be supporting first,' said the elderly man.

'Is that because you wouldn't have got a ticket if you said you'd be cheering on Barnet?' I asked.

'No, but if I said I'd support Barnet he'd have put me over there,' he said, pointing towards the hundred or so Barnet fans sitting on our right.

After Chesterfield had taken a two-goal lead through David Moss and teenage prodigy Kevin Davies, the reason for the presence of the Blackburn scout, Barnet made a substitution. Carl Hoddle, brother of the more famous Glenn, was replaced by former Spurs and Wimbledon forward Terry Gibson. 'Gibson is playing out of position,' said the elderly man. 'He's a forward.' I looked for Gibson. He was playing as a forward. In fact, he was closer to the Chesterfield goal than any other Barnet player!

The Blackburn scout had, like me, been to the West Ham–Everton match at Upton Park the night before. He worked every day, including weekends, and saw five games a week. I never did find out what he did on the other two days. 'He's a hard task master Mr Dalglish,' he said in a serious tone. The scout was watching Chesterfield's exciting young teenage forward Kevin Davies. 'I've seen him 104 times, Kenny's watched him twice. I get a look at him every three weeks.' 'Is he a good prospect?' I asked.

'No,' said the scout.

The 17-year-old Youth international was tall, strong and keen. In October 1993 he became the youngest player to make his début in the Coca-Cola Cup when he played against West Ham at the age of 16 years, 104 days. He put a lot of effort in against Barnet and scored the second goal, his eleventh of the season, with a chip over the advancing keeper from just outside the 18-yard box after a long ball out of defence. But he also missed chances. He fluffed the best opportunity of the first half with 17 minutes gone when, finding himself with the ball at his feet six yards out, he shot poorly and Barnet keeper Paul Newell parried the ball. Davies still had much to learn, but Derby seemed to think he was on a fast learning curve all the way to the top.

The fans also loved the lad they associated with that boyhood hero Superman. The *Crooked Spireite* fanzine had nothing but praise for him. 'Wonderboy, with his Pocket Full of Kryptonite, has been nothing less than transformational. He and Robbo [Phil Robinson], I guess, have been the difference between a side with a magnificent defence and one which actually wins a lot of games. It's Pocket Full of Kryptonite who holds the ball up royally, who beats players at will, who can move the side forwards, sometimes as much as 50, 60 yards . . . with a surging, helter-skelter run . . . Make the most of him everyone, while he lasts.'

The other player who captured the imagination was Carl Hoddle. He was built like his brother, Glenn – tall and well balanced on the ball – but that's where the similarities ended. Hoddle was his name, but he wouldn't grace Wembley like his brother. He missed a glorious chance to put Barnet ahead seven minutes after the break, when he slid across a muddy penalty area to get on the end of a flick. The ball spun wide from ten yards out. Carl's brother Glenn would probably have stopped it on a sixpence, waited for the keeper to commit himself, then tapped the ball into an empty net. Chesterfield stretched their unbeaten run to nine games with this 2–0 win at Saltergate and remained on course for automatic promotion.

The next morning I checked out of the Tullamore Hotel. The owner wanted me to present the town and its team in a good light. 'I hope you've written a good report,' he told me, 'or else we'll have to charge you double.'

'Well, they won, didn't they?' I replied. 'How could I write a bad report?' With that I made my way back to the station to catch the train to London, where I'd connect with another to Swindon for the next leg of my marathon. I passed the church with the crooked spire, which I couldn't see the night before in the dark, thinking: 'How the Devil did it get twisted?'

MAD MAC

Swindon Town v Bristol City – The County Ground, 15 February 1995

Steve McMahon has always been hot-tempered, even when he played for Aston Villa, Liverpool and Manchester City. But in those days there was someone higher up to answer to, namely the manager. Now he was his own boss. So who would keep him under control, calm him down, focus his aggression positively? The answer was nobody. And that was dangerous, both for his opponents, his team-mates and, ultimately, Swindon Town Football Club. Mad Mac was on the loose.

Tonight, with his team 2–0 down against West Country rivals Bristol City, ahead with goals from midfielder Junior Bent and on-loan striker Robert Fleck, McMahon decided it was time to return to action. He hadn't played since breaking his arm on New Year's Eve – an injury sustained playing rather than celebrating, I assumed. Mac had already burnt the ear of a linesman, nicknamed 'Chicken George' by the home fans, earlier in the second half. The Roots lookalike had kept his flag down on a number of occasions as Swindon fans and the bench repeatedly screamed for offside.

In his first column for the *Evening Advertiser* McMahon spelled out the importance of a local derby to the players and the fans:

> Local derbies mean local pride is at stake and I can assure you we will be trying every bit as hard to win tonight as last Sunday [the first leg of the Coca-Cola Cup semi-final against Bolton, which Swindon won 2–1]. These are the games that matter to the people who are most important in football – the fans.

I've played in Merseyside derbies and Manchester derbies, with all the emotion and excitement those games can generate. But it really doesn't matter whether it's Swindon Town against Bristol City or Liverpool against Everton. The fans hate to lose these games and so do the players. Of course, there are also three very important League points at stake tonight and we shall be doubly determined to get a win. But it's not just about players. Supporters can play a big part on nights like this. There are times when the crowd can act like an extra man.

Given McMahon's track record for being sent-off, the team would need that extra man on quite a few occasions, just to even out the numbers on both sides!

McMahon had used his newspaper column to give supporters an insight into what it's like for a player–manager to be on the sidelines rather than on the pitch. 'I've included myself in the squad tonight and I'm looking forward to playing again as soon as possible. People ask why I get so animated during a game, well it's because I'm still a player at heart. Even when I'm on the bench like Sunday [in the Coca-Cola semi-final], I'm kicking every ball. I've been on the bench since breaking my arm on New Year's Eve, but I'm just about ready to return. And being honest, I can hardly wait.'

It wasn't hard to notice. McMahon's reaction to Bristol City's second goal was to start warming up. A few sprints along the touchline in front of the main North Stand; a few minutes chatting to the linesman; then a return to the dugout to await his opportunity to stamp his mark on the game. Midway through the second half, when frustration got the better of him, he came on to replace Andrew Thomson, Swindon's number six.

McMahon's impact was immediate. Within a few minutes he had given away a free-kick near the left touchline after chasing around the pitch like a headless chicken. The ball was swung onto the head of City's number five Matthew Bryant and in a flash it was 3–0. Mac turned towards the centre circle, head down, determination oozing out of his tensed body. Shortly afterwards he lunged into another tackle and was promptly booked.

Joe Jordan, the former Leeds, Manchester United, AC Milan and Southampton forward, renowned for his toothless grin and now in his second spell as manager of Bristol City, was off the bench in a flash. He stood on the edge of the touchline sneering at McMahon. A few years ago he'd have been squaring up to him. Now all he could do was point an accusing finger before being ushered back to the dugout by his assistant John Gorman, the former Swindon manager who was succeeded by McMahon. 'Super, Super John, Super, Super John, Super, Super John, Super Johnny Gorman,' sang the Bristol City fans away to my left.

Midway through the second half the rain which had been threatening all night finally arrived. It came driving across the stadium, swirling as it went and showering the supporters under cover in the North Stand as well as in the rest of the ground. The Bristol City fans at the Stratton Bank End were wet but happy. The home fans began to sing, 'Come on, you rain,' clearly hoping that divine intervention might see the match abandoned and salvage what had become a hopeless cause. 'Maybe it will be called off,' said one optimistically. It was their only hope, but a forlorn one.

For all McMahon's kamikaze tackles, the match against Bristol City was overshadowed by events at Lansdowne Road, not Swindon's former ground but the stadium across the Irish Sea in Dublin. It was the night so-called England fans ripped out seats in the upper tier and used them as missiles to attack Irish fans in the paddock below, after David Kelly had given the Republic the lead in a friendly international. I watched the pathetic events unfold on Sky at half-time in the Swindon match alongside the home fans – tucking into their meat pie, chips and peas, washed down with beer – in the executive suite.

A debate was raging about whether England's hooligans should have been kept inside the stadium so that the police could identify the troublemakers on video and arrest them immediately. 'You can't do that,' said one Swindon fan. 'They'll cause a riot.' I disagreed and said it was the perfect opportunity to arrest them because they were trapped. Sky presenter Richard Keys looked pretty cheesed off as he sought reactions from former England stars Gerry Francis and Alan Ball. 'I've seen trouble at the Swindon–Bristol City match before,' said the Swindon fan. 'But it doesn't happen these days.'

It must have been hard for the Swindon fans who thought their team would be playing in the top flight for longer than the one season they managed in 1993–94, especially after their 1990 play-off win failed to lead to promotion because of a financial scandal involving former manager Lou Macari (now in charge at Stoke). Their first taste of life in the top division was short, but definitely not sweet.

Those supporters with long memories might have recalled how unfair the world was as far back as the '60s. Undoubtedly Swindon's greatest triumph was their shock 3–1 win over Arsenal in the 1969 League Cup final. Who could forget Don Rogers skipping around the Gunners' defence and sliding the ball past Bob Wilson after running through from the halfway line? It's a moment etched on the collective football memory.

Unfortunately Third Division teams weren't allowed to compete in the European Fairs Cup. So, although Swindon had secured promotion to the Second Division as runners-up, that wasn't good enough to qualify. But they did win the specially created Anglo-Italian Cup by beating AS Roma 5–2 on aggregate in the competition's inaugural year. They won it again in 1970, overcoming Napoli 3–0.

DULL CITY

Hull City v Stockport County – Boothferry Park, 18 February 1995

If you imagine a game between Hull and Stockport to be about as interesting as watching paint dry, you'd be right. I got out of bed at 8 o'clock in the morning, raced to the local tube station, discovered I couldn't get a connection to King's Cross because of work on the line, jumped in a taxi, ran to the train, changed at Doncaster and arrived in Hull . . . on time. And for what? No goals, no excitement, not one move throughout the whole 90 minutes worth writing home about.

Earlier, as the train passed the Humber Bridge, I had high hopes that the afternoon would bring good things. The North Sea water glistened in the bright sunshine and seagulls poked around in the sand looking for food. It was a glorious sunny day. So different from the weather at most of the matches I'd been to over the past few weeks in pouring rain and high winds. Factories were dotted along the coast on one side of the railway tracks, whereas suburban houses stretched out for miles along the inland side.

Boothferry Park used to have its own railway station, Boothferry Park Halt, behind the East Side. Supporters entered the ground directly through the turnstiles on the station platform which backed onto the terraces. 'It was a great way to handle away fans,' said a steward with short-cropped hair and a Roy Keane-style goatee beard. 'They'd come in on special trains and go straight into the ground without going near the town centre. That's what happened when we played Manchester United in the Cup.'

Unfortunately, the club's railway station, opened in January 1951, was now closed. 'British Rail wanted too much money to keep it open. It just wasn't viable,' said a club official. The railway wasn't the only part of Boothferry Park no longer open to the public. Most of the East Side, apart from a section for away fans to the left and a members-only area in the middle, was closed. The crumbling terraces on the East Side were unsafe and the club didn't have the money to redevelop the stand.

The rest of the stadium was in better condition, particularly the South Stand which towered over the ground. The Boothferry Road End was dominated by a Kwik Save store, which replaced the old North Stand when the club sold out to the supermarket chain. There was little alternative but to sell the huge car park for redevelopment after the club dropped from the Second to the Fourth Division between 1978 and 1981, and in February 1982 the receivers were called in and the club was put up for sale.

Hull leased the land back on a long-term contract and kept 15 steps of open terrace in front of the supermarket for away fans. The land sale, and a wage cut for the players, enabled Hull to wipe out debts of £1.2 million. 'We're going to develop that end with executive boxes built on top of the supermarket and make it all seater,' said an enthusiastic Hull fan dressed in a blue blazer and official club tie. But how could they? Where would the money come from? 'We need £125,000 and the rest will be a grant from the Football Trust,' said the Hull fan.

'Has the club got £125,000?' I asked.

'No,' came the reply.

The enthusiastic fan went on, 'This is a very friendly club'. And indeed it was. But the local *Hull Daily Mail* carried a front-page story headlined 'Irish were warned of Hull soccer hooligans'.

The story said City fans were pinpointed in a police intelligence report on yobs travelling to the recent England–Ireland match at Lansdowne Road. The game was abandoned in the first-half after rioting English fans in the upper tier at one end of the ground ripped out seats and threw them onto the Irish fans below. 'Known thugs who follow the Tigers were among 15 English gangs identified in a report by football intelligence officers for their Irish counterparts,' reported the *Hull Daily Mail*. I wondered if any of them were at Boothferry Park for the Stockport match today.

The story said Humberside police had expected up to a dozen Hull City troublemakers to go to the England game. Inspector Bryan Calam, match commander at Boothferry Park, was aware of the hooligans because they'd caused trouble in the past. 'They learn their trade at Hull City and graduate to internationals. They often meet up with hooligans from other clubs who may be enemies in local games but unite at international level.' Unless I was mistaken, incidents of seats being ripped out and thrown at visiting fans were unknown at Hull. What exactly were these thugs learning at Boothferry Park?

At the time, a debate about whether England should host the 1996 European Championships was raging around the country in the wake of the horrific scenes at Lansdowne Road. Former Hull City favourite Ken Wagstaff, a member of the side which won the Third Division Championship in 1966, thought the country couldn't afford to stage the finals. 'Euro '96 will take place in the summer when it's warm and there will be lots of families and children about. Their lives are at risk. We know these thugs go to football just to cause trouble. They loot stores, terrify shoppers and attack police and other fans. What will they do if thousands of fans from the likes of Germany, Italy and France come over here? It will be all-out war,' said Ken, clearly trying hard not to overreact.

Hull are under-achievers par excellence and that lack of success is reflected in modest attendances. 'Don't follow crowds of people to help find the stadium, as they're probably going to watch the ice hockey or do some shopping,' warned Hull fan Andy Metcalf in *Total Football*. Not that there are a lot of other things to do in a town which many people think of a plain dull. Hull's most famous adopted son, the poet Philip Larkin, who worked as librarian at the university, once wrote, 'I wish I could think of just one nice thing to tell you about Hull, oh yes . . . it's very nice and flat for cycling.'

Most people would imagine Hull's main rivals to be nearby Grimsby, but in fact the Uniteds of Sheffield and Leeds (The Team Whose Name Dare Not Be Spoken For They Are So Evil, according to Metcalf) are the most hated by Tigers fans. Grimsby fans hate Hull, but apparently the feeling isn't mutual, even though each club is known by the others fans as Codheads. Perhaps it's because Hull supporters want to identify with the bigger clubs in the area rather than a team which at the time of my visit was just one division above them and would never be considered a 'big' club.

Hull have had their share of star players in the past and a couple of promising players in today's side as well. Dean Windass had made 163 appearances for Hull and clearly had great potential. Linton Brown, the great-nephew of the elderly man next to me was also one of Hull's better players on this dull afternoon. But the man's best memories of Hull were a long time ago. He told me Raich Carter was the best player he'd ever seen pull on a Hull shirt. Carter joined Hull as player–manager towards the end of his career in 1948. He was described as the finest inside-forward of the '30s and '40s.

Carter inspired the Tigers to the Third Division title in 1949, and attendances rose to a peak of more than 37,000, against a pre-war high of just over 11,000 when the club played at Anlaby Road. The reason Carter left the town in 1952 had nothing to do with his performances. 'He left Hull because of his divorce,' said the elderly man next to me in the Main Stand. 'He had to leave town. You see it just wasn't accepted back then. Nowadays it happens just like that and nobody bats an eyelid. Times have changed.'

They certainly had and not only in terms of social behaviour. I was sure the football served up by the Tigers in Carter's era was better than that on offer today.

At least Hull had more of an excuse for a rusty performance than Stockport. They had only played one League match in a month because of postponements through bad weather. They were so desperate for a game that Dolan had fielded his first team in a reserve fixture against local rivals Grimsby the previous Tuesday. 'Unfortunately, after two days of dry weather the game was played in gale force winds and driving rain, which didn't help.' But Dolan had a solution for the atrocious weather – a switch to summertime soccer!

The trouble was I didn't want to watch football like that dished up at Boothferry in the Stockport match – whether it was played in summer, winter, spring or autumn.

NO PRICE INCREASE

Darlington v Gillingham – Feethams Ground, 21 February 1995

Darlington is one of those towns whose names you hear on the football results every week without knowing anything about the place. Each Saturday during the season James Alexander Gordon's resonant voice can be heard announcing the Darlington score on BBC radio and every self-respecting fan is aware that the town exists. But apart from the hardy souls who've followed their teams away in the GM Vauxhall Conference or Third and Fourth Divisions in recent years, few fans have been there.

Darlington's single claim to fame is that in 1825 George Stephenson's No.1 Locomotion left the town on a journey to Stockton-on-Tees; the inventor was at the controls and horsemen with flags rode ahead to warn that the train, travelling at a speed of between 10 and 13 miles per hour, would soon be coming. Edward Pease, the line's instigator, had wanted a fast and cost-effective way of transporting coal from the Durham pits to the docks at Stockton. But the Stockton to Darlington Railway soon became the world's first passenger line, which was a bonus for Pease.

Darlington's Feethams Ground was one of the most delightful I'd see on my travels. There were alms-houses by the main gate; and the River Skerne, its banks lined with trees, ran along the east side, faced by a line of neat, well-kept Victorian villas. The narrow, cobbled Polam Lane was along the west side of the ground leading to a footbridge which you could use to cross the river to a lodge and a park.

The main entrance had an ornate gateway and twin towers. Above the gates was a plug for the local *Northern Echo* newspaper welcoming visitors to the Darlington Cricket & Football Club. After entering the gates the first thing I saw was the cricket pitch with its pavilion and groundsman's house. I walked along the driveway past the cricket scoreboard to another set of gates, which marked the entrance to the football ground.

The Darlington Cricket Club first rented the ground in 1866 from a Quaker called John Beaumont who'd campaigned for the abolition of slavery and also owned Feethams House. That historic connection explained the football club's nickname of the Quakers and also the connection with the cricket club from whom Darlington rent Feethams. In fact, their ground is the last in the League still connected to a cricket club. The Quakers are also one of the few clubs to have used only one ground.

When Feethams was first used for cricket, the pitch was laid out with turf from the town's older cricket ground in Old Park Street; but football was also played on the field next to the cricket pitch for many years. Indeed, a football club existed in the town as early as 1861, before Darlington were formed in 1883. They reached the final of the Durham Senior Cup in their first season, losing to Sunderland in a replay after complaints they'd been intimidated in the first game! The Quakers won the trophy the following season and for many years were one of the leading amateur clubs in the area.

The cricket pavilion was built in 1906 at a time when the football club was playing in the Northern League. They turned professional in 1908 and joined the North-Eastern League. But it was in 1911 that they made the country sit up and take notice. According to the fanzine *Mission Impossible,* it was 'one of the very few occasions in Darlo's meagre history that the nation's eyes have focused on the happenings at Feethams'. The reason for all the attention was their great FA Cup run.

They had started in the first qualifying round of the competition and by the time they faced First Division Sheffield United at Bramall Lane they were playing their ninth Cup Tie. An astonishing 1–0 victory made the Quakers the first non-League team to win at a First Division ground. Their reward was a home draw against Second Division Bradford Park Avenue, who were mid-table and had yet to win away from home.

The Darlington players prepared for the next big Cup game with six-mile walks, Indian club training and rowing on South Park Lake. Footballs seemed to figure little in their routine. As a special treat they spent Thursday in the Saltburn Brine Baths and turned down the offer of a game of football on the beach against Newcastle, who were getting ready for their own Cup match against Northampton.

Bradford won the toss and elected to play into a breezy north wind. A few minutes into the game a fence collapsed and the crowd spilled onto the pitch. There were no casualties and play quickly restarted. The first half was niggly with many fouls. In the second half Darlington roared forward. With 15 minutes to go a neatly judged pass by Denham dissected the full-backs and Cornock, a Scot from Airdrie, ran onto the ball, rounded the keeper and scored the winner. There was one gut-twisting moment three minutes from time when Turnbull broke free, but he stubbed his shot and the ball span away to safety. Darlington had made it to the last 16 of the FA Cup and become the first non-League club to beat First and Second Division opposition in consecutive games.

The Quakers were thrashed 3–0 at home to Swindon in the quarter-finals by which time they'd played 11 matches in eight rounds of the competition – a record which is unlikely to be beaten.

But the Quakers have had very few star players over the years. Indeed, *The Football Almanack* lists David Brown, Alan Walsh, Ron Greener and David Currie – none of whom are household names. You could add Ken Furphy, though he was better known as a manager with Workington, Watford, Blackburn and Sheffield United. Another famous name associated with the club was an outside-right called Baden-Powell from the 1950s, though he wasn't the same man who founded the Boy Scouts.

One of the most highly thought-of managers at the club was the former Tottenham left-back Cyril Knowles, who was in charge from 1983 to 1987. The *Mission Impossible* questionnaire in the fanzine had probably the highest tribute that could be paid to anyone when, asked to name the manager she most admired, Darlo fan Lynda Smith had no hesitation in voting for Cyril, adding that 'he was a great man'. Nice one.

Under Knowles, Darlington won promotion in 1985, this time managing two seasons in the Third before being relegated once again. Two years later, in 1989, they left the division again, though this time losing their League status altogether as they went into the GM Vauxhall Conference under (current Villa boss) Brian Little, who's obviously come a long way since then! After just one season among the non-League clubs Darlington finished top of the Conference and the following year the Quakers won their only major trophy by collecting the Fourth Division Championship. Once again they had no staying-power and were instantly relegated to the bottom division again.

And that's where they were when I turned up for a midweek game against Gillingham. The match was originally scheduled for Saturday, 28 January but a waterlogged pitch had put paid to that fixture; now, almost a month later, the match would finally go ahead. As I peered out across the pitch from the dark recesses of the East Stand I could make out a steel structure (at the end of the West Stand) which looked as if the club had begun to build a new stand and had then run out of money.

'What's that rusting steel at the end there?' I said to one of the Darlo faithful who'd come along with his dad for tonight's match.

'That's the stand we were going to build until we ran out of money,' he said.

In fact, the Quakers had taken delivery of a 1970s stand from Teeside Park racecourse in 1992 and they planned to re-erect the roof over the south terrace. Unfortunately this would have cost £80,000 on top of the £30,000 they'd already spent to dismantle and store the steel frames. In the end, the only use they made of the steel was to erect a TV camera platform, which is what I could see in the murky darkness of a cold February night. I doubted it got much use, since Darlington were hardly *Match of the Day* material.

Still, I was looking forward to watching former Middlesbrough star Bernie Slaven, described in *Mission Impossible* as a 'goal machine' and 'ace marksman'. While at Darlington Slaven had reached the milestone of scoring 200 goals in his career and was something of a hero to the success-starved Quakers fans. Not that even Slaven could meet the wishes of Darlo fanatic Lynda Smith. Asked which players she'd like to see wearing the black and white stripes at Feethams, she replied, 'The Brazilian forward line!' Still, the Darlo die-hards would be warmed tonight by two goals from 'goal machine' Bernie Slaven, who proved there was still some life in the old dog yet.

After the game I had a swift half with the chairman in the club bar. We talked about Slaven and his impressive performance. 'The trouble is he's getting older now and suffers more than his share of injuries,' said Weeks. Nevertheless, Slaven had proved that, when fit, he still knew where to find the goal – which is more than most people can say about Darlington.

NICE ONE CYRIL

Hartlepool United v Exeter City – The Victoria Ground,
25 February 1995

Hartlepool United are famous – if that's the right word – for two things. Their
Victoria Ground was the only stadium in Britain bombed by Zeppelins in the First
World War. And on 15 March 1971 they drew 0–0 with Brentford in the one-
millionth game to have been played since the Football League was formed in
1888. The Pool are certainly not renowned for their achievements on the pitch,
since there are so few.

Even Brian Clough, who launched his managerial career at Hartlepool in 1965
with right-hand man Peter Taylor, couldn't lead them to success. In fact, during
Cloughie's reign they were so hard up that he had to repair the Main Stand, carry
150 sheets of corrugated iron across the pitch to re-roof one of the end terraces,
drive the team bus and even work without pay for a while.

The Hartlepools club had been formed in 1908 as a professional team to
emulate the success of West Hartlepool, winners of the FA Amateur Cup in 1905.
They became founder members of the Third Division (North) in 1921 and stayed
there until 1958, when they moved to the newly formed Fourth Division. And
they've stayed in the League's basement division ever since with the exception of
the 1968–69 season.

In 1956–57 they did score 90 goals and came runners-up in the Third Division
(North), but they weren't promoted, since only the League Champions went up in
those days. When they were finally promoted in 1968, it was in third place,
behind Luton and Barnsley. They lasted just the one season in the Second
Division, finishing in 22nd place. They've had to apply for re-election to the
League more than any other club.

Hartlepool had never got past the fourth round of either the FA or League Cup
and between 1927 and 1930 they were knocked out of the former every year by
a non-League club. The closest they've come to an FA Cup giant-killing was in
1957, when the club almost beat the great Busby Babes Manchester United team
before ultimately losing 4–3 to the eventual League champions. Two years later
they beat Barrow 10–1 to chalk up their record win and, five years after that, lost
by the same amount to Wrexham.

As I took my seat in the Mill House Stand I could see that the Main Stand
opposite had been flattened and there was a clear view out to the dockyards, with
their cranes and the North Sea beyond. United had plans for a new stand and had
even chosen a name but had no money. It was to be called the Cyril Knowles
Stand in memory of the former Spurs and England full-back who once managed
the Pool and got them promoted to the Third Division in 1991. They came straight
back down again under Alan Murray, who'd taken over from Knowles who died
at a very young age. The stand was to be a fitting tribute and I could personally

vouch for the fact that the club badly needed to cover the open side.

Although it was a clear, sunny day, the wind came whistling in off the North Sea without the protection of the Main Stand; and my girlfriend Nicky and I were freezing as we sat in the Mill House Stand, named after a local pub. It was an impressive cantilever stand, which had been built for 40,000 after the club's first taste of Third Division football in 1968. There were plans to move the club's offices and the players' facilities, including the dressing-rooms, underneath the stand but the money ran out.

In fact, the financial situation was so tight that United had to sell the ground to the council for £10,000. They failed in a bid to buy it back in 1980, leading the chairman to threaten to move the club to Scarborough. But the financial problems remained and the year after the Main Stand was taken down the two end covers were removed for safety reasons. Things were so bad that the bailiffs took away the goalposts in 1986.

That was the low point. In 1990 a cover was put over what's known as the Rink End of the ground after the Queens skating rink, which stood behind that end of the ground until it was demolished in the 1970s. (The rink and the Victoria Ground itself were named after Queen Victoria because the ground was first laid out by the West Hartlepool rugby club in 1886 in honour of the Queen's forthcoming Golden Jubilee.)

A new chairman called Harold Hornsey, who'd made his fortune from DIY, gave the club even more hope when, in 1994, he pulled together money from a City Challenge grant, the Football Trust and the local council. The £650,000 Cyril Knowles Stand would be built after all – not that the club's finances had improved that much.

Besides, the fans were more concerned with events on the pitch than the prospect of a new stand. 'The news that work on the now infamous Clarence Road Stand seems to have started at last seems to have caused little reaction amongst Pool fans,' according to the Hartlepool United Supporters Club. The worries were reflected in the fact that I'd be watching their first match since the sale of captain Phil Gilchrist to Oxford.

Manager David McCreery used his programme notes in the *Pool Review* to explain why Gilchrist had to be allowed to leave for £100,000. 'I know that many of you will be no strangers to this situation at the club. We were forced to sell Phil simply because we had to have the money. Our chairman Mr Hornsey and his colleagues on the board are under severe pressure to clear the club's debts, and it would not have been fair on those who are owed money if we continued to turn down Oxford's offers.'

The club had debts of around half a million pounds and not a penny of the Gilchrist money would be spent on the team. Nicky Loughlin was realistic in his 'Off The Post' column. 'It's a harsh fact of footballing life that when there's a player worth his salt on the books at Hartlepool United he will be snapped up by bigger clubs before too long. Over the years there's been a long list including a young Keith Houchen, the Linighan brothers, David and Andy, and the big money break up of the 1990 promotion team.'

Chairman Harold Hornsey was also frank in his 'From The Boardroom' column. 'I would personally like to thank the supporters, around 1,500 who turn up week after week to support their team. I am sure that with a successful team we could double this figure – and here lies the problem. Will the support come back if the club is successful, or do we need the support to ensure success? I know what my answer is.'

Hartlepool survived reasonably well without their old captain and fought out a 2–2 draw with Exeter thanks to solid performances from former Coventry hero Keith Houchen up front and new captain Ian McGuckin at the back. The next result a Pool fan looks for after his or her own team is that of arch-rivals Darlington.

The talking-point in the Corner Flag, the pub built by the Supporters Club in 1993, was today's hard-fought draw and the Gilchrist transfer. I had a swift half with my girlfriend before leaving to take a quick look around the recently refurbished quayside. The £20 million Historic Quay, built by the Teeside Development Corporation, was a re-creation of life in the eighteenth century. It included theme pubs and a marina as well as what the publicity material called a 'unique shopping experience'. We would love to have taken a leisurely look around, but we had to get to Derby for the next match.

THE BIGGEST CRIME IN FOOTBALL

Derby County v Bolton Wanderers – The Baseball Ground, 26 February 1995

'The biggest crime in football is to give the ball to the opposition,' said the sign on the wall above the exit from Derby's home dressing-room. Brian Clough put that sign up there, according to the official showing us around the ground. It must have done the trick. Within two years of Cloughie's arrival in May 1967 the club roared into the First Division led by captain Dave Mackay, a double-winner at Tottenham in 1961.

Derby won the League Championship in 1972 for the first time in the closest race ever seen. With Clough at the helm and Peter Taylor by his side, they clinched the title by one point from Leeds, Liverpool and Manchester City. The players, including Colin Todd, Roy McFarland, Archie Gemmill, John McGovern, Bruce Rioch and Frannie Lee, found out they'd won the League in Spain, where they were relaxing on holiday!

The history of the club was laid out in a long cabinet which ran the length of the directors' lounge back wall. 'We won the Championship twice in the early '70s and the FA Cup in 1946, but we can't show you those because we had to hand them back,' said the tour guide. Victory in the first post-war FA Cup was largely due to the skills of Raich Carter, Peter Doherty and Jack Stamps.

Derby Chairman Lionel Pickering was hoping to repeat that Cup success. 'I look back to the glory days of the 1940s when we won the FA Cup. If you speak to some of the great players of the past, they say that team was even better than our side from the 1970s,' said Pickering.

Mind you, they may have had some gypsy fortune on their side. When Derby first moved to the Baseball Ground in 1895, gypsies camping on the site had to leave and as they did so one of them put a curse on the ground. A local journalist was so worried about the curse that he found a gypsy camp and had the curse lifted before the '46 Cup final at Wembley. It must have worked, since the Rams beat Charlton 4–1.

'This trophy means a lot,' said the official, pointing to a silver galleon given to the club by Real Madrid. There was also a bronze ball, another gift from Madrid, and a bronze eagle from Benfica. 'We have a lot of Spanish trophies for the simple reason that for over 20 years Derby used to go to Spain, mainly Majorca.' Next came the Player of the Year trophy given to the club by the family of Jack Stamps, hero of that '46 Cup victory, when he died. It was now presented every year in his memory.

Derby were one of the 12 founder members of the League in 1888, though they were formed four years earlier by members of the Derbyshire County Cricket Club; they attracted attention for their amber, pale blue and chocolate-coloured strip based on the colours worn by the cricket club. The football team quickly established itself as one of the top sides in the country and reached 13 FA Cup semi-finals between 1895 and 1909. Unfortunately they lost all three of the finals they contested during that time.

The Baseball Ground itself was developed in the 1880s as a sports ground for foundry workers. In 1889 the foundry owner, Francis Ley, went to America and was so taken with baseball that he decided to develop the game among his workers and spent £7,000 adapting the ground for what we'd probably call rounders.

Baseball was played at the stadium for years after Derby County arrived and many football clubs, including Orient and Aston Villa, sent teams to play at the ground in a national competition. Derby won the baseball title in 1897 with the legendary Steve Bloomer on second base! Nevertheless, football was still the ground's main sport.

The 'Stan the Fan' feature in one of the tabloid newspapers had its own verdict on the current Baseball Ground. 'Some great ideas but little chance of putting them into practice. Living on its past with little hope of a future. I'd rather take the mother-in-law out than come here. Team's lacking sparkle and so is the entire club. Shame that a once grand club now looks so tatty.'

The engine of the current team was Craig Short, Derby's record signing at two and a half million pounds. He was outstanding, at the heart of the home side's defence, in this match against promotion-chasing Bolton. But he could not prevent Derby going behind after less than a minute when the ball broke for Jason McAteer in the box. He turned and slotted it into the corner. The away fans in the corner of the Toyota Stand went barmy. Two Trotters supporters behind me, placed incongruously among the Derby faithful, also jumped up to celebrate, much to the annoyance of a sandy-haired Rams supporter of about twenty sitting in front. 'They can't stand a bit of banter,' said the older Bolton fan. 'He thinks we shouldn't be in this stand. It's pretty pathetic, isn't it?'

The match itself was notable not for the skills of any one player but for an incident after ten minutes which left Bolton defender Simon Coleman with a broken leg. Derby striker Marco Gabbiadini was elbowed in the face by Coleman, a former Rams player. Gabbiadini, anger etched across his face, reacted with a crunching tackle, though he did seem to go for the ball. Coleman fell to the ground writhing in agony under the weight of the challenge. The St John's Ambulancemen rushed on with a stretcher and taped Coleman's legs together. It didn't look good.

The whole episode overshadowed a game which Bolton desperately needed to win to keep up with Middlesbrough at the top of the First Division table. After about 25 minutes of non-stop talking and shouting by the Bolton fans behind me the Derby supporter in front of me got up out of his seat, turned around and put his fist in the air. He wanted a fight. I stood up to calm him down as his dad held onto his arm. An elderly man with thinning grey hair, plain round glasses and a grey raincoat turned around and told the Bolton fans to shut up. The atmosphere was definitely hotting up around me. I turned to my girlfriend Nicky and shrugged. Typical behaviour for agitated football fans.

'Where was the lob over the top then?' said the Bolton supporter, undaunted by the turmoil his earlier comments had caused. 'That was bloody awful finishing. We should have been four up by now. That was crap. It sat up for him perfectly.' He was complaining about the Trotters' Dutch star Richard Sneekes, who was clean through with only the keeper to beat but shot tamely into his arms. 'This lot will get half a chance and score. You watch, the first chance they get they'll score.'

In the second half Derby tried to claw back an equaliser, but missed another chance when a header flew over the bar. 'Score in a brothel, you couldn't score in a brothel,' sang the Bolton fans. Very original. But also untrue. Bolton had led from that early strike by McAteer until the 82nd minute, but Derby were to snatch victory from the jaws of defeat. Eight minutes from time there was a scramble in the box and their latest arrival Dean Yates, signed from Notts County, stubbed the ball over the line. Derby had equalised totally against the run of play.

With only three minutes left Lee Mills picked up the ball midway into the Bolton half, ran unchallenged to the edge of the box and drove a flyer into the top left-hand corner, giving the keeper no chance. The Bolton fan had been right all along.

THE TOTTENHAM CONNECTION

Barnet v Exeter City – Underhill, 28 February 1995

When Jimmy Greaves was still trying to fight the booze, one of his distractions was playing for Barnet at their sloping Underhill ground. Since Jimbo saw life through an alcoholic haze at the time, it wasn't surprising that his goalscoring feats didn't match up to his previous track record. Another famous Spurs striker, Martin Chivers, also pulled on the gold shirt of Barnet when his days at the top were over. Employing former White Hart Lane stars had become something of a tradition at Underhill.

It was hardly surprising then when former Liverpool, Spurs and England keeper Ray Clemence took over as manager. Clemence, of course, had been in the business of stopping goals rather than scoring them, but the Bees needed all the help they could get after a stormy period under the volatile combination of manager Barry Fry and eccentric owner Stan Flashman.

There was an international flavour to the proceedings the afternoon I arrived for the game against Exeter. Tor Mollatt Eriksen and some of his friends from the Norwegian branch of the Barnet Supporters Club were at the match. Three of them had arrived in England at Christmas hoping to take in a couple of Bees fixtures. Why they followed Barnet was anybody's guess. But their fanaticism even stretched to producing their own fanzine, which was available at the ground!

Tonight's match against Terry Cooper's Exeter City had originally been scheduled for Monday, 2 January but a frozen pitch had put paid to that and the match had been re-arranged. Barnet were still selling the programme for the original game, though it did include an extra sheet updating the League table and the teams. When you're a struggling Third Division side reprinting programmes is a costly option.

At the start of the year Barnet were in fourth place, behind leaders Carlisle. Not any more. They'd just lost 4–0 to Fulham at Craven Cottage, leaving them with just one win in ten games and none from the last seven. Barnet had slipped down the table to 12th place. Their hopes of promotion were fading fast and the 'Bees' had simply stopped buzzing.

The club's nickname comes from the colour of their kit – amber shirts with black shorts and socks. It's almost impossible to escape the references to bees throughout Underhill. The club shop was called the Buzz Stop. The programme had a section covering future games called Buzzing Around. Barnet needed to after their recent run of poor form. It wasn't in their nature to give up without a fight. Former chairman Stan Flashman and ex-manager Barry Fry could vouch for that.

The appointment of Barry Fry as manager in 1978 was to mark the beginning of an eventful period in the Bees' history. Fry was unorthodox, determined and very loyal. He was caught mowing the pitch by moonlight before one game and in 1984 took out a second mortgage on his home to try to rescue the club.

But Fry's efforts, though welcome, were not on a grand enough scale to provide a solution. In fact, Barnet would have gone to the wall had Fry not enlisted the help of renowned ticket-tout Stan Flashman. When Fat Stan arrived like a white knight, he put champagne in the boardroom and bought Yves St Laurent jackets for the players.

The Bees eventually won promotion to the Fourth Division in 1991 after winning the Vauxhall Conference. The crowds flocked to Underhill and the attendances doubled within three years. Meanwhile, Fry's astute activity in the transfer market yielded a profit of some £2 million. But the honeymoon didn't last. Fry and Flashman were at each other's throats, with the former resigning repeatedly only to be lured back by Stan.

It was almost a miracle that the club not only survived the traumatic 1992–93 season but actually won promotion to the Second Division. When Flashman resigned and Fry left to join Southend, the club was in disarray. Mounting debts, partly due to fines imposed by the Football League because of financial irregularities, were a real burden.

Barnet were chased by the Inland Revenue and a host of debtors as well as the League. Many of the players were eventually allowed to leave on free transfers, since they hadn't been paid. The future looked grim. Under the circumstances, the turnaround achieved under new chairman David Buchler was nothing short of miraculous.

The biggest problem, however, remained the ground. Capacity had shrunk to less than 4,000 and there was little hope of being able to expand it to the 6,000-level required by 1998 for Third Division clubs, including 2,000 seats by 1998. It wasn't even clear if Underhill could meet the requirements of the GM Vauxhall Conference.

On arriving at the ground I could see the problems immediately. The view from the main stand was great but I was astonished by the price of the tickets, which was close to what a member would pay to sit at White Hart Lane. It was certainly a bit strong for Third Division football. Down to my left Ray Clemence stood talking to supporters. This was a tightly knit club and the former England keeper was quite happy to discuss the match with the fans. They chatted to him as if they were friends.

At half-time we popped into the social club for a drink. Barnet had spent £2 million on the ground since 1991 to bring it up to League standards. The social club, built to replace its predecessor which burned down in January 1991, was part of that expenditure. It was very basic but quite homely. More of a youth club than a wine bar.

Back on the pitch the game was less than enthralling and finished 1–1. Clemence was clearly not satisfied, though given his team's recent run he must have been relieved to pick up one point. Nevertheless, Barnet's promotion push looked dead and buried – not unlike Underhill itself, whose days seemed to be increasingly numbered.

SCOTLAND IN ENGLAND

Berwick Rangers v Meadowbank – Shielfield Park, 4 March 1995

It was on the train to Berwick that I suddenly decided my record-breaking attempt was sheer madness. The miles were being eaten up by the British Rail express and, to be honest, it wasn't exactly a hardship sitting there sipping a cup of tea and turning my thoughts to the next match. But it was then that it dawned on me just how far I had to travel to set a new world record as the most peripatetic football supporter.

Of course, there wasn't a Premier or Football League team to watch in Berwick, but there was a Scottish League team playing at home in England. Confused? So was I when I realised that to break the Guinness record and secure my place in history I would have to visit Shielfield Park, the home of Scottish Second Division club Berwick Rangers.

This was the farthest I had to travel from my home in London on my football odyssey. I felt I had to go now for a variety of reasons: first, it was spring and the weather wasn't too cold; second, I could see the match at Berwick on Saturday and then move south to watch Sunderland play Tranmere the following day.

When the woman who helps 'authenticate' records for inclusion in *The Guinness Book of Records* confirmed I had to visit Berwick, I thought she was joking. 'But Berwick play in the Scottish Second Division,' I said, with a sense of injustice at the thought of having to travel so far to see a match.

'Ah, yes,' she replied, 'but their ground is in England isn't it?' She wasn't looking for an answer.

Berwick began as members of the Northumberland Football Association and for years competed against Northumberland and Border teams. But by 1919 the club's allegiance was definitely to Scotland. This was partly explained by the fact that if they'd joined the Football League, Berwick's longest journey would have been 470 miles to Plymouth, whereas their farthest trip in Scotland was 170 miles to Aberdeen. Berwick thus became the only team in the Scottish League with a ground in England – the reason I had to go there to become a record-breaker.

On 28 January 1967, the part-timers of Berwick pulled off one of the biggest shocks in Scottish football history when they beat Glasgow Rangers 1–0 in the first round of the Scottish Cup before a record crowd of 13,365. Sammy Reid, a former Liverpool player, scored the historic 32nd minute goal. For the rest of the match Berwick's 35-year-old goalkeeper–manager Jock Wallace (who, ironically, later managed Rangers as well as Leicester, Motherwell and Rangers again) held out.

It was one of Scotland's great giant-killing acts. Glasgow Rangers had been beaten by a Scottish Second Division side based in England! Until then they'd never been beaten by a team from the Second Division and many of the 7,000 supporters who travelled from Glasgow to Tweedmouth that day still can't believe their beloved team lost. They still talk about that result in the bar at Berwick to this day. It's the club's only real claim to fame and they'll probably never see such glory again.

I walked down to the main entrance and was told I would find my guide for the day, the club's public relations manager Conrad Turner, in the social club. There was a jovial atmosphere and it was more like a local pub than just a place for a beer before the match. Early arrivals were playing cards and darts and I imagined they'd have been there whether Berwick had a game or not. Unlike the sterile executive lounges springing up at Premier and First Division clubs this place was clearly part of the community. Many of the men drinking there were at Shielfield the day Berwick beat the other Rangers from Glasgow. The memories still brought a smile to their faces.

Outside I noticed that the pitch was some distance from the stand and was told that this was because of the cinder track used by the Berwick Bandits speedway team from the late 1960s until they left in 1981. It made the ground seem very open and with crowds of only a few hundred turning up to watch the first team it didn't help the atmosphere. This was one place where an enclosed ground would have really helped.

The crowd of 455 watched the game in bitterly cold conditions and the players were able to produce little in the way of exciting action to warm them up. I later learned that there were all of 18 Meadowbank fans present – not exactly a big enough contingent to generate much support for the visitors. An advert in the eight-page match programme for Bell's Scotch whisky said: 'You can't call yourself a supporter if you don't go to the match.' It could have been written for the absent Thistle fans.

The programme included a column by manager Tom Hendrie headlined 'Give Us a Quick Flash Lads!' The flash referred to the inspiration he was looking for to swing the result Berwick's way after a recent epic Scottish Cup encounter with the Wee Jags, as Meadowbank are known. The match went to a replay which Berwick lost at home. Still, at least they were pushing for promotion, while Thistle were struggling against relegation.

'I've said it many times before, and I'll say it again, that there is very little difference between those at the top and those at the bottom of the Second Division in terms of ability,' wrote Hendrie. 'The gap between ourselves and Meadowbank Thistle is obvious in our respective League positions, but it will not be so obvious when the teams take to the pitch this afternoon.' He could say that again. Both sides were poor and a single goal was enough to secure the points for Berwick in a nondescript match.

After the game I wandered back to the station to catch a train to Newcastle. On the platform I met a neutral fan who'd travelled up from Newcastle to watch the game for no better reason than having something to do on a Saturday afternoon. Get a life, I thought. Watching paint dry would have been only marginally less interesting. Still, he was friendly enough and we chatted about the state of Scottish and English football.

His wife and kids met him at the station and he kindly offered me a lift to the B&B where my friends were staying. Map in hand, his wife drove around the back streets apologising for the roadworks which meant the journey was taking longer than normal. The hospitality in the north was really something special.

WEAR AND TEAR

Sunderland v Tranmere Rovers – Roker Park, 5 March 1995

Sunderland definitely have an inferiority complex. The success of their rivals on Tyneside and Teeside had left the Wearsiders casting envious glances over their shoulders. The rebuilt St James's Park and the shiny new Cellnet Riverside Stadium had left the once-impressive Roker Park lagging behind. I'd heard for years about the famous 'Roker Roar', but the fans had recently had little to roar about.

The fanzine *A Love Supreme* assessed the merits of Roker Park and St James's: 'Well, it's like a Mercedes and a Robin Reliant really. Even the turnstile doors [at St James's] look impressive and stylish. A small flight of stairs takes you to . . . a communal drinking, eating and socialising area. No, we're not talking the pie counter at Roker, but a long promenade of fast-food counters . . . I eagerly checked out the toilets – a long way from the draughty brick-walled holes in the floor I'm used to.'

(The Stadium of Light would put paid to all that.)

Sunderland were known as 'the Team of all the Talents' after they joined the League in 1890, clinching four First Division Championships by 1902 and another in 1913. Centre-forward Raich Carter inspired them to a sixth in 1936, when they were known as the Bank of England team, and they won the FA Cup for the first time the following year. Great players like Len Shackleton and Billy Bingham failed to build on that success and in 1958 their record 68 years in the First Division ended. Brian Clough's goals got them back into the First Division in 1964, but they went down again in 1970.

Then came that famous 1973 FA Cup final win over the mighty Leeds thanks to a brilliant performance by keeper Jim Montgomery and a goal from Ian Porterfield. It was the first time the Cup had gone to a team outside the First Division since West Brom's success in 1931. Porterfield's golden boot sits proudly in the Roker Park trophy room as a reminder of that glorious day.

Despite the doom and gloom at the time of my visit, things were about to start looking up for the Wearsiders. For a start, Buxton would soon be leaving to be replaced by former Everton and England midfielder Peter Reid. There were also plans to build a new stadium. The club had talked about moving to a new ground many times before but such notions were played down by the fans, who called them 'grandiose statements'.

I'd taken the metro from Newcastle to South Shields, where I met up with a Rokerite called Jimmy. He'd been coming to watch Sunderland for years and remembered the good times. He worked with local kids and said he'd noticed more of them wearing the black and white Geordie stripes over the past couple of seasons – a worrying trend. Unemployment and Sunderland's poor performances on the pitch had already eaten into the team's support. Defections to their arch-rivals were hard to swallow.

Jimmy and I were driven up to the suburb of Roker, once an Edwardian seaside retreat, in the driving rain. Roker Park is very close to the North Sea and that partly explained why it was so cold. We walked in through the main entrance, where I expected to see a famous picture of Sunderland's former ground at Newcastle Road painted by one Thomas M. Henry. It shows a goalmouth scramble from a fictional match against Aston Villa in the late 1800s. Unfortunately the oil painting was on loan to the Sunderland museum.

Despite their recent lack of success, and a deteriorating stadium, there was still something magical about coming to Roker Park. There are some grounds so steeped in tradition that they have a presence all of their own. This ranked up there with Old Trafford, St James's Park, Molineux, White Hart Lane, Highbury and the rest. Its proudest moments probably came in the 1966 World Cup when the ground was chosen to stage Group Four matches and the quarter-final between the USSR and Hungary

Sunderland had recently played Tottenham in the fourth round of the FA Cup – the first time Spurs had been to Roker Park in the Cup since a quarter-final tie in 1961, when they were on their way to the first 'double' of the century. The match drew a crowd of over 61,000 and record gate receipts of £14,000. Tottenham's captain, Danny Blanchflower, said it was the greatest crowd he'd ever played before and that the semi-final and even the final were an anti-climax after the game at Roker Park. The tour guide told me that the Roker Roar was so loud it could be heard seven or eight miles away in South Shields, on the banks of the Tyne. But the Spurs players kept their heads and held on for the draw. Sunderland were beaten 5–1 at White Hart Lane.

Jimmy and I were taken down into the home dressing-room just before the match. The players, including defender Gary Bennett and striker Phil Gray, were already in their Sunderland colours. In the corner was a blackboard with comments on each player's performance in the previous game – a reminder of how well, or badly, they'd played.

You could keep a check on the players' appearances in the club programme, *Roker Review*. Now most clubs provide the basic information on matches played, the score, team line-ups, scorers, penalties, substitutions, goalscorers, players booked or sent-off – the regular information needed by any self-respecting football fanatic.

Sunderland went one better. The key was so complex even regulars must have been baffled. For example, the small circle next to Lee Howey's name for the Cup match against Spurs meant he 'Operated as 3rd central defender in 5-3-2 formation'. So, if a player operated as the third central defender in a 5-3-2 formation and scored two penalties on his début before being sent off (unlikely I know) you'd have seen: oDPx2x&. Even Einstein would have had trouble working it out!

As I took my seat in the Grand Stand I noticed that the flag on the Clock Stand opposite was at half-mast.

'Don't tell us it's Maggie Thatcher who has died,' said one supporter.

'No, if it was Maggie we'd have the flags out,' said his mate.

It was clear that the locals were still bitter about the rise in unemployment during the last recession. I looked out across the Roker End towards the docks and beyond to the sea. Cranes towered over the River Wear like giraffes, but they were now sadly idle. Unlike local industry Sunderland fans were hoping that the club's recent decline could be reversed. Time would tell.

EMLYN HUGHES WOZ 'ERE

Rotherham United v Cambridge United – The Millmoor Ground, 7 March 1995

They still talk about him in glowing terms at Millmoor. Player–manager Emlyn Hughes. The defender with the squeaky voice who also captained England and Liverpool. He was the nearly man at Rotherham. After winning the old Third Division championship in 1981 they missed out on promotion to the top flight by just one point in the next campaign. The chance of glory was gone and the following season so was Emlyn.

The Merry Millers, named after the local steel mills (and not a windmill as is often incorrectly assumed), had been through it all before. In 1955 they won eight of their last nine Second Division games, including a final 6–1 win over Liverpool, to finish level on points with Birmingham and Luton. They'd scored more goals than the Blues but missed promotion on goal average, the measure used by the League to divide teams back then.

Arguably their greatest triumph was in 1961 when, under manager Tom Johnston, they reached the League Cup final at Wembley against Aston Villa. The competition had only just started and didn't include all the First Division teams, but it was a great achievement for Second Division Rotherham to reach the final. They didn't win, of course, but at least they'd been to a Wembley final.

The Millers have had their fair share of famous managers, including a young Tommy Docherty in the late 1960s and former Leeds hard man Norman Hunter in the mid-1980s. Docherty tells the story of how he was in Greece with his wife, having been offered the job as manager of Panathinaikos. 'It could be worse,' he told her. 'I could be manager at Rotherham.' Shortly afterwards he was! Some great players have also pulled on the red shirt over the years, such as former Manchester City and England centre-half Dave Watson, sold to Sunderland for a then club record £100,000.

Today's crop of managers and players was no less distinguished. At the helm were joint managers Archie Gemmill and John McGovern – seasoned pros who played together at Derby and Nottingham Forest and had surely learned a lot about the art of management from Brian Clough. Rotherham were struggling near the foot of the Second Division but at least they could share the burden together, like that other management double Alan Curbishley and Steve Gritt at Charlton.

Gemmill and McGovern used their jointly signed programme notes to ask the fans to 'Stick with us'. But their main message was about character:

> Part and parcel of a manager's job is improving his playing staff by recruiting new players. This usually entails endless telephone conversations regarding a player's ability, temperament and skill level. There is, however, one overriding factor that is less and less prevalent in the overall make up of a player and that is the ingredient of character.
>
> People of character will roll up their sleeves when the going gets tough and will be absolutely ruthless when they are on top. Players are always going to make mistakes but if you happen to possess this rare attribute of character you always want the ball, even if you are making mistakes, to come through a lean spell and show what you are capable of.

The Gemmill–McGovern axis had passed on that character to their players judging by a narrow 1–0 win over Cambridge in a relegation dogfight at Millmoor on a cold Tuesday night. I sat in the main stand, opposite the Millmoor Lane Stand. (The ground is also named after Millmoor Lane, the thoroughfare that runs behind the stand.) Former Derby striker Bobby Davison led the line with as much determination, if a little less speed, than in his younger days. And, when Davison began to tire, the much-travelled Imre Varadi took up the mantle.

Tommy Docherty's joke about having more clubs than Jack Nicklaus is overused but certainly applies to Varadi. The 35-year-old striker began his career with Sheffield United before joining Everton, Newcastle, Sheffield Wednesday, West Brom, Manchester City, Sheffield Wednesday again, Leeds, Luton, Oxford, on loan, and finally Rotherham. He applied himself with enthusiasm to the task of replacing the impressive Davison and clearly still had a zest for the game. I wondered if even he could remember all the teams he'd played for.

The local Sheffield paper, *The Star*, was full of praise for Rotherham's solid performance. 'In pulling off a vital win last night, Rotherham United fell back on three of the major qualities which have edged them steadily through the depths of winter to where they can see light at the edge of the wood [poetic or what?]. Their five-month long Millmoor invincibility, a growing reputation for being difficult to beat, and another Shaun Goater goal all combined to nudge aside visitors Cambridge United.'

The win pulled Rotherham further away from the relegation zone and plunged Cambridge into deeper trouble. The away fans, less than a hundred of them, were huddled together in what used to be called the cow shed (I could see why) but was now known as the Railway End. Opposite was the Tivoli End, named after the cinema that used to occupy the magnificent building on Masborough Street. It was a fine example of cinema architecture, built before the First World War, but was now a furniture store.

I was worn out. I'd been up since 3.30 a.m. and after a very stressful day at the office caught an afternoon train to Doncaster to link up with the local service to Rotherham. I understood why Edward Wood, the previous holder of the Guinness record for visiting all the League grounds, had taken a year off to go on his travels. I was completely knackered and needed a break. I wasn't sure I could manage one more game, let alone another 27.

It's strange how anything taken to excess ceases to be much fun. I'd always thought complete freedom to travel to every football ground in the country would be brilliant. In reality, long train journeys to rundown industrial towns to watch mediocre football is not the best way to use your time. It was certainly a challenge – and, after visiting 66 grounds, not a challenge I was about to give up – but freedom for me now was not having to go visiting 93 football grounds in one season. Funny how your outlook on life changes with experience. Next stop Wolverhampton.

THE CRY OF DE WOLF

Wolverhampton Wanderers v Sunderland – Molineux, 8 March 1995

John de Wolf. Hero. Villain. Aptly named pillar of the Wolverhampton Wanderers defence. A larger-than-life character who had captured the hearts of the fans. They loved him, opposing fans hated him. De Wolf, known locally as the Wolfman, generated strong reactions among all football supporters. He's that kind of guy.

The strength of feeling towards the guy was amazing. One Dutch football fan, Damien Degreef, a 19-year-old supporter of de Wolf's former club, Feyenoord of Rotterdam, had an 8 by 10 inch colour portrait of the great man tattooed on his right shoulder. De Wolf signed the tattoo in recognition of the fanatical fan's devotion.

Now Degreef may strike you as someone a few cards short of a full deck, but what about the businessman who offered him £10,000 for the post-mortem rights to the tattoo which he wanted surgically removed after Degreef's death! 'It was gruesome,' said Degreef. 'At first I thought it was a joke, but he was deadly serious.'

The businessman had a contract drawn up offering a large downpayment if

Degreef insured the tattoo and got it touched up every five years. After consulting Rotterdam police, Degreef decided to turn down the businessman's offer. 'I was tempted, but the police said someone else might buy the contract and want to collect on it early!'

I had first seen de Wolf play for Feyenoord at White Hart Lane, when he marked Gary Lineker out of the game in a European Cup-Winners' Cup tie. He looked clinically efficient on the night. Strong in the tackle; good in the air; sure with his passes. Nothing had changed judging by his performance tonight.

Molineux was almost full for the Sunderland match. The crowd of almost 26,000 was the biggest that night. It was larger than at either of the fizzy drink cup semi-finals at Selhurst Park and Burnden Park between Crystal Palace and Liverpool and Bolton and Swindon. It was also above the gates at Blackburn versus Arsenal, Tottenham against Ipswich and Newcastle West Ham. Molineux's superb facilities deserved Premier League football.

After a series of injuries as long as your arm Wolves, under former England manager Graham Taylor, were still in the hunt for a play-off place and would face Crystal Palace in the quarter-finals of the FA Cup the following Saturday. They badly needed the contributions of de Wolf and Bull after losing Tony Daley and Steve Froggatt to long-term injuries. Sunderland were battling against relegation and had come to Molineux in an uncompromising mood following the 1–0 defeat at home to Tranmere.

Molineux had been transformed from the ramshackle stadium I had first seen on television in the UEFA Cup final of 1972, when Wolves lost 4–3 on aggregate to Tottenham after a 2-1 defeat at home and a 2–2 draw at White Hart Lane. The club, under the stewardish of President Sir Jack Hayward, had already spent more than £14 million to redevelop the ground. 'I hate recessions, but they are certainly the time to build,' said Sir Jack, obviously believing that it was money well spent. 'Terrific value,' was how he described the stadium Wolves had built to provide first-class facilities for up to 28,500.

The main entrance to Molineux in the Billy Wright Stand takes you into a foyer notable for a bronze bust of Sir Jack Hayward. A plaque on the wall to the right of Sir Jack explains that a time capsule has been buried in the wall and will be unearthed in the year 2,015. It contains a pair of Steve Bull's boots and an international cap and player's contract both belonging to the late Billy Wright.

When Sir Jack Hayward took the reins and started the ball rolling to redevelop the ground, the architect was told to 'assist the Football Club in achieving a multi-purpose functional venue for business pleasure and sporting activities capable of operating six or seven days a week and achieving income generation to assist in maintaining the financial longevity of the Club.' In other words, a stadium that could be used by the locals and pay its way!

The first phase of the building of the new Molineux began in October 1991 with the demolition of the North Bank, the traditional home end, which had been declared unfit for use since the Bradford fire in 1985. The Stan Cullis Stand was opened on 7 August 1992 in a friendly against Aston Villa. It has a propped cantilever support (in other words, no pillars to block your view) which weighs 60 tons and measures 76 metres. The stand contains a ticket office and travel bureau as well as the commercial department, club shop, social club, community development facilities and function rooms. Fancy getting married at your favourite football club? You can do at Wolves.

In 1992 a new pitch was laid and realigned with the new stand along with a fully computerised pop-up sprinkler system. The new pitch was first used in a pre-season friendly against Arsenal on a Friday night. The former Arsenal manager George Graham came out with the well-worn comment, 'If you can't play on that, then you can't play on anything.'

SINGING THE BLUES

Birmingham City v Swansea City – St Andrews, 11 March 1995

As I walked towards the Main Stand at Saint Andrews one of the first things I saw was a sign for the Trevor Francis Suite. Francis, later to return to the club as manager, was, 'A Hero, a Star, a Legend . . . darling of the Kop, an idol for Brummie schoolboys everywhere. He was quick, skilful and intelligent – some would say the complete striker.'

The description comes from a booklet called 'A Historical Look at the Fortunes of Birmingham City Football Club during the Years of the Spion Kop', but it could just as easily have been said by any Blues fan who had the privilege of watching the young Francis in action. He was deadly in the penalty area with a lightning turn of speed.

Francis had come up through City's youth scheme, although he didn't follow the Blues. 'I actually supported Plymouth Argyle as a lad, but I was tempted to sign for Birmingham City through the kindness and persistence of the then-Chief Scout Don Dorman,' he says.

It wasn't long before the precocious youngster broke into the first team. In the February of his first season in the City side he bagged all four goals in a First Division match against Bolton – the first 16-year-old to achieve such a feat. Francis netted 15 goals in his first 15 games for City and ended the season with 16, earning himself the nickname 'Superboy'. His exciting brand of attacking football attracted the fans to St Andrews and the average home gate rose from 18,000 to 25,000 in his first season as a teenage scoring sensation.

The following season he teamed up with the two Bobs: Latchford and Hatton. The triumvirate reined supreme and the crowds at St Andrews soared from 25,000 to an average of 36,000 and often swelled to more then 40,000. 'These were special days and times I will never forget,' says Francis. 'To hear the Kop singing "Keep Right On" was always a great spur for the team and often intimidated the opposition. To play with Bob and Latch was great, we seemed to hit it off from day one. There was a great understanding between us.'

In 1979 he became the first £1 million footballer when he joined Nottingham Forest. 'On leaving Birmingham I was disappointed that my efforts over the nine years had not brought success to St Andrews,' says Francis. 'We had a good side and I think we deserved to win something. It was a great honour to have such a big move and I was lucky enough to have the chance of playing with a successful side at Notts Forest.'

Under Brian Clough, Francis won the European Cup for Forest when he scored the only goal right on the stroke of half-time in the final against Malmo before 57,000 fans in Munich on 30 May 1979. He also won a League Cup winners' medal in that first season. Francis added a second European Cup winners' medal the following season when, as holders, Forest retained the trophy with a 2–0 win over Hamburg in Madrid.

Birmingham began life as Small Heath and became founder members of Division Two in 1892. In 1905 they changed their name to Birmingham and the following year moved to St Andrews. The site was a wasteland of stagnant pools and muddy slopes, but director Harry Morris believed the former brickworks had the potential to rival the new Midlands grounds of Villa Park and the Hawthorns.

Everyone was happy with the new ground except a group of local gypsies who used the area as a winter stopover. Their angry leader put a curse on the site to ensure City would always just fail to achieve success while they stayed at St Andrews.

The club changed its name from Birmingham FC to Birmingham City in 1945 and soon began rebuilding the ground. The new two-tier Main Stand had a propped cantilever roof and the damaged Kop also got a new cover. The next major development was the two-tier Railway, or City, Stand built during the 1963–64 season. It was virtually the same design as the Main Stand, which had been erected more than ten years earlier.

The Blues enjoyed something of a golden age in the '60s and '70s and even managed to bounce back at the first attempt after being relegated in 1979. Wise spending by manager Jim Smith of the £1.2 million received from the sale of Trevor Francis to Notts Forest was mainly responsible for the revival. But it was short-lived. When Ron Saunders moved across from Villa Park in February 1982 to become the first manager to have been in charge of both clubs, the Blues were heading for trouble.

Saunders believed Birmingham's dismal run in his first full season was due to the 'Curse of the Kop'. So convinced was he that the gypsies had taken revenge on him that Smith had a holy cross put on each of the four floodlight pylons as well as having the soles of the players' boots painted red to ward off the evil spirits. The fans responded by sending the club scores of lucky charms, heather and crosses.

In 1992 things took another turn for the worse. The club's owners from Manchester, the Kumar Brothers, who'd been struggling to get the club back onto a sound financial footing, found their own business heading for liquidation after the BCCI banking scandal rocked the City of London. The Blues were put into receivership and after rumours of bids from across the world, David Sullivan, best known for his ownership of the *Sunday Sport*, took over.

The new chairman had big plans for his new plaything, including the redevelopment of the ground and money for players. But still City couldn't shake off the gypsy curse. During the 1993–94 season they suffered another dismal run of 14 matches without a win after a string of unbelievable injuries and bad luck. With the team sliding towards the bottom of the First Division manager Barry Fry requested the help of the club chaplain. The Reverend Ken Hawkings, an ardent Blues fan, was sure the curse was still active. He performed a series of exorcism readings and sprinkled holy water around the ground. 'As far as I am aware what

I have done today has never before been tried at St Andrews,' said Hawkings. The remedy didn't save the Blues from relegation to the Second Division, but the following season promised better luck.

Meanwhile, Sullivan was true to his word on plans to spend £4.5 million on the ground's redevelopment. Sullivan and the Gold brothers insisted that the new stadium should reflect the club's personality. St Andrews was to be a venue for top class football whilst showing the drive and forward thinking approach so successfully applied to the development of the city centre.

The new Kop and Tilton Road stands were officially opened on 15 November 1994, when a crowd of almost 20,000 saw a 1–1 draw in a friendly with Aston Villa. The Kop was sponsored by local brewers Bass Mitchells & Butlers and was named 'The Brew XI Kop'. Ironically, almost 90 years earlier Sir John Holder had opened St Andrews after his brewery had just merged with M & B. Back then the gypsies had only just cursed the ground; now it was hoped that by clearing the terraces the club had removed the curse. One Blues fan working on the rebuilding of Aston Villa's Holte End actually put a piece of rubble from St Andrews into the cement at Villa Park to transfer the curse!

Having provided all this, David Sullivan wanted the fans to spend their money at the club. A note in the programme for the Swansea match headlined 'The Scum of YOUR CLUB' set out to put the record straight. 'Do you realise that there are people stealing from YOUR CLUB? Yes, thiefs [sic] and YOU may be helping them.' So what heinous crime had these thiefs [sic] committed? Had they robbed the programme seller? Blasted their way into the club safe? Had their fingers in the refreshment bar tills? No, they'd been selling Birmingham City souvenirs outside the ground – the cheek of it!

'Have YOU bought from a street trader, today or at any other game?' asked Sullivan:

> The SCUM that steal from your club sell SCARVES, BADGES, HATS, T-SHIRTS that the CLUB does not benefit from. EVERY PENNY YOU GIVE THEM IS STEALING FROM YOUR CLUB. We want to be able to buy more new players, even spend £1,000,000 on one player in the summer, we will NOT do this if SO-CALLED supporters buy merchandise from these thiefs [sic].
>
> WE BEG YOU, AS GENUINE BLUES SUPPORTERS PLEASE DO NOT BUY FROM STREET TRADERS, BUY ONLY FROM THE CLUB SHOPS.

Sullivan didn't stop there. In his 'Sullivan Speaks' column he brought up the issue of support. He doesn't mince his words:

> Our gates are still very disappointing. Our last two games in the league (and one of these included 4,000 children at just £1 admission) have averaged only 16,500. Huddersfield, only a small town, got 17,500 last Saturday – we are the second biggest city in Britain so we hope for and deserve bigger gates. PLEASE DRAG ALL YOUR FRIENDS AND RELATIONS along to our remaining home games. Get all those people who claim to be Blues supporters and who have not been to the ground in years to TURN UP AND SHOUT THE TEAM ON.

And the team had at last started doing the business where it mattered: on the pitch. The efforts of the Reverend Ken Hawkings, who'd kept secret his formula for ridding the club of the gypsy curse, finally seemed to be having an effect. At the time of my visit for the Swansea match the Blues had lost only one of their 26 home games – the longest unbeaten run of any team in any division that season. 'I have never believed in things like this [the gypsy curse],' said Fry, 'but the fans who witnessed that [previous] bad run will surely agree that no team can be that unlucky. After the vicar blessed the changing rooms and physio room our injuries cleared up and the team started to get results. Surely that must be more than just coincidence!' So had the curse finally been lifted? Would success return to St Andrews? In a word, no.

The players emerged from the dressing-rooms behind the disabled area between the Railway Stand and the Main Stand. Among their stars were midfielders Liam Daish and Mark Ward, Louie Donowa and Steve Claridge (later a hero at Leicester after scoring the winning goal in the replayed 1996 Coca-Cola Cup final).

Before the match the club mascot, a furry round royal-blue ball known as Bluenose, ambled around the pitch waving to the fans. It was the oddest mascot I'd seen all season. The guy inside wore black leggings and royal blue gloves and the word BLUENOSE was picked out in white letters on his blue furry outfit. I wasn't sure why City fans had the nickname Bluenoses, apart from the obvious fact that the team play in blue. Where the noses came into it was a mystery to me.

The fans did their best to meet David Sullivan's appeal for vocal support. They shouted. They sang. They screamed. But their support was conditional. After City went behind, they resorted to abuse. They shouted angrily at the players, their own and Swansea's. The mood change was swift and affected those in the directors' box as well as the regular fans. The atmosphere was the most intimidating I'd come across so far on my travels but it didn't help Birmingham who were as much in the firing line as Swansea. Clearly the Blues fans wanted success, and if they didn't get it, they'd be the first to let everyone know what they thought of the team and the manager.

Curse or no curse Sullivan remains determined to bring the good times back to St Andrews. 'Now I've got a message for every Bluenose, and it's simple – I am grateful for your support and for making me feel that I am one of you. Together we can and will make Birmingham City Football Club realise its potential to become one of the greatest clubs in the land. Tell your sons, your fathers and your friends and hold your head up high for we will be great. The slumbering giant has awoke.'

Watch this space.

BORING, BORING, YORK

York City v Wycombe Wanderers – Bootham Crescent, 14 March 1995

This was the most boring game I'd seen all season. Incredibly, York had gone 20 League games without a draw – until the visit of Wycombe Wanderers. The chance of an entertaining match was therefore remote. The *Yorkshire Evening Post* was full of letters criticising York for being boring. After watching this performance I thoroughly agreed. 'Utter rubbish' was one fan's reaction.

It was the sort of game in which ultimately you didn't want either side to score. Having watched crap football in the freezing cold, eaten a cold chicken and mushroom pie, drunk two cups of weak tea and sat on a hard wooden seat for 90 minutes, I was beginning to enjoy being a martyr. A goal would have somehow compromised my suffering.

A sprinkling of post-match reaction provides a good idea of just how bad the Wycombe game was. Malcolm Huntington, chief sportswriter at the *Evening Post*, wrote under the headline 'Mix and match City struck by flair play loss. Snore point reward for Minstermen'. His report described the evening's entertainment as 'very much a match of the bread and water variety and it set up an unwanted record as far as this scribe is concerned in that it was the first time since I first watched City back in 1941 that a team has gone through a game without managing a single direct shot on target . . . neither side deserved to win a forgettable match in which there was little goalmouth action or excitement to keep spectators warm on a cold night.'

York manager Alan Little, formerly a player at Aston Villa, gave his patched-up team a sterling tribute and was satisfied with their overall performance. 'We're at the stage of the season when you get games like this, when it's dour and scrappy and teams don't want to give anything away. At times the quality was not there, the passing was not there, nor sometimes the final ball. But I cannot fault the effort put in by the team. I have to be pleased with that.' No quality, no passing, no final ball equalled no goals.

But what about the supporters? After all, they were the ones who'd paid to watch the fare dished up by two promotion-chasing teams. Martin Fowler, 51, a technical sales rep from Dringhouses (wherever that is) was hooked by the attractions of watching York after a 3–3 draw against Southampton in the FA Cup in January 1971. But what about tonight's match? 'This was a game when not a single player seemed able to play a simple pass to feet . . . this has to be the poorest playing surface at Bootham Crescent in living memory.'

There have been few momentous moments at Bootham Crescent, the ground bought by York City from York Cricket Club in 1932. But it was actually one of the quaintest grounds I'd visited. Bootham Crescent, which leads to the stadium, was full of the sort of guest houses you expect to see along the seafront at a coastal resort. Handy for away fans who feel like spending some time in the historic city.

I'd arrived on an afternoon train from London for this Tuesday-night match. York Station, just outside the city walls on the south side of the River Ouse, was a short walk from the historic centre of the city and a bit further from Bootham Crescent. The city walls enclosed narrow streets, lined with overhanging rows of old buildings, that wound their way along an irregular medieval course. The city is dominated by York Minster, which is the largest medieval English cathedral (and second in importance only to Canterbury) and gives rise to York's nickname, the Minstermen.

The most interesting bit of history is that the highwayman Dick Turpin was tried and hanged at York in 1739, though his famous ride to the city was in fact made by Swift Nick (William Nevinson) in the seventeenth century and added to the Turpin legend by William Harrison Ainsworth in his novel *Rookwood* (1834). The only robbery I saw was the money taken from supporters by the gatemen at Bootham Crescent!

However, one tragic event that shocked everyone at the club, and led to the stand at the Shipton Street End being called The David Longhurst Stand, was the death of a player affectionately known as Longy. His dad takes up the story. 'My wife and I were returning from holiday in Scotland . . . when we heard the shattering news on the car radio that our son David had died on the pitch at Bootham Crescent.'

It was a tragedy. 'Like everyone else at Bootham Crescent I will never forget the horror of seeing David suddenly collapse on the pitch, soon followed by the devastating realisation that he had died. It was a crushing blow to our club and to the city of York,' said the York President at the time, John Greenway.

'Longy' began his career at Nottingham Forest under the watchful eye of Brian Clough before moving to Halifax, Northampton, Peterborough and then York. 'Throughout the whole of his 25 years David loved football,' said his dad. 'It was his whole life and he was looking forward to the new season at York. But what happened could not have been prevented.'

The highlight of Longhurst's career came when he played for Peterborough in an FA Cup first-round clash at Gillingham. He scored all three Posh goals in a 3–3 thriller – including the dramatic equaliser three minutes from time. He clutched the matchball with pride that day and ended the season as the supporters' Player of the Year.

A special memorial match between his home-town team Corby and neighbours Kettering was full of glowing tributes to the young man. 'David was a great favourite with our supporters,' said Greenway. 'There could be no more fitting tribute to his memory than a stand at the home supporters' end of the ground.' David Longhurst's name still lives on at York on top of that stand.

THE THEATRE OF DREAMS

Manchester United v Tottenham Hotspur – Old Trafford, 15 March 1995

Home to legends like the Busby Babes, so tragically killed in the Munich air disaster of 1958; and home to one of the greatest forward lines the world has ever seen, the trio of Best, Law and Charlton – Old Trafford is unique. For a start, no other ground in England, with the exception of Wembley, has been so perfectly designed. Most stadiums have been developed piecemeal over a number of years with no clear long-term plan. Not so United's ground, with its unbroken elliptical shape encircling the pitch. An early drawing of the ground shows that it was the same shape as it is today.

Old Trafford lies to the south-west of the city centre, on the border between Manchester and Salford, the biggest town in England without a League club. England's largest canal, built by the Duke of Bridgewater in the middle of the eighteenth century to transport cotton and coal, runs behind Old Trafford. It was the first of a system of waterways which, by the early 1800s, linked Manchester with Ashton and Oldham, Bolton and Bury, and Rochdale.

When the ground was opened in 1910, after United won the League in 1908 and the Cup in 1909, Old Trafford was one of the most advanced stadiums of its time and the envy of all the other League clubs. I couldn't work out why it was called Old Trafford, even when it was new. I mean, it can legitimately be called Old Trafford now, since it's 85 years old, but surely it should have started out as New Trafford or just plain Trafford back in 1910!

It was designed by Archibald Leitch and could hold 80,000, though it never did. The luxurious cushioned tip-up seats were more comfortable than those used at League grounds today and attendants were even on hand to take United fans from the tea-rooms to the seats. The ground also boasted magnificent changing-rooms with lavish bathing facilities, including a plunge-bath. The players were pampered in the club's own massage parlour, or they could relax in the billiards room. More serious work-outs took place in the gymnasium.

Old Trafford's location near the Manchester ship canal (built in 1894 to attract ships away from the burgeoning city of arch-rivals Liverpool) and its closeness to the key Trafford Park industrial estate was to be a problem for the club during the Second World War. German planes repeatedly carpet-bombed the area in a bid to destroy Manchester's industrial capacity. In March 1941 the inevitable happened; the ground suffered serious damage from two bombs after a Luftwaffe raid on Trafford Park and Salford Docks.

The Main Stand was a burnt-out shell, the covered terrace on United Road was damaged and the pitch was scorched from the explosions. The War Damage Commission gave United money to clear the rubble and rebuild the stands, but, in the meantime, the Reds had to share Maine Road with Manchester City. That's where the largest crowd ever to watch an English League game showed up: 82,950 for United's game against Arsenal in January 1948.

Ironic, then, that City striker Uwe Rosler should pose before press photographers during the 1994–95 season wearing a T-shirt saying: 'Rosler's Grandad Bombed Old Trafford. February 21st 1941'. United fans were understandably upset. The first-ever United fanzine, *Red News*, summed up the feelings among the Old Trafford faithful. 'We think that "prat" is too soft a word for Uwe Rosler – someone who obviously thinks it's great fun to wear a T-shirt celebrating German bombing raids on Manchester. That City supporters could be so sick to produce the shirt is not surprising, but the fact that the Bitter Blue player in question actually wore one for the media cameras leaves a stink as fermenting as any polluted river.' The fact that City allowed the Press to take the pictures inside Maine Road had added insult to injury.

This time I'd come up by train from London for a midweek game which had been rearranged because of both sides' FA Cup commitments on the Saturday when it was originally supposed to be played. United were battling with Blackburn to secure their third title in a row – a feat that had only been achieved three times in the history of the game by Huddersfield, Arsenal and Liverpool. Tottenham were having a good run and had become a hard team to beat since Gerry Francis arrived from QPR.

As I walked up the steps of the Main Stand to my seat I could see a blanket of snowflakes falling in the crisp, cold Manchester night sky. The two teams walked out onto the pitch together, like they do in the Wembley Cup final, just as my guide said they would. A red balloon floated across the seats in front of me as I squeezed my way along a row near the front of the stand to my seat amongst the United faithful.

United dominated the opening exchanges. I grimaced every time the Reds attacked the Spurs goal, hoping Tottenham could keep them at bay. United have been known as the Reds, obviously because of the colour of their shirts, since the club was reformed in 1902, after Newton Heath, their predecessors, were put into liquidation. The black third strip used by United in the 1994–95 season was based on the kit originally worn by Newton Heath, after the club was founded by railway workers in 1878 as the Newton Heath (Lancashire and Yorkshire Railway) Cricket and Football Club.

Since the 1950s United have also been known as 'the Red Devils'. The name was originally given to the Salford Rugby League Club who made an unbeaten tour of France in 1934. The French papers were so impressed by their performances that they nicknamed the team *Les Diables Rouges*, or Red Devils. Like Salford, United also played in red and thus became known as 'the Red Devils'.

A red devil was added to the club badge in the early 1970s when United, following FA advice to stamp out pirate sellers of goods bearing the club crest, decided to copyright the existing club badge. However, they found they couldn't do that because it was based on the City of Manchester Coat of Arms and so they replaced the part of the crest showing three diagonal stripes on a red shield with a devil. The two roses on either side were replaced with footballs, but the ship symbolising the Manchester ship canal was kept.

Meanwhile, all around me the home fans were becoming more and more frustrated as United failed to penetrate the Spurs defence. Tottenham were still clinging to hopes of a UEFA Cup place, but for United the prize was ever so slightly bigger – another Championship and a path back into the European Cup. For all their possession, the Reds could not break Spurs down. The match ended goalless.

The loss of two points against Tottenham was one of those games that would ultimately cost United a third title in a row and the chance to emulate Huddersfield, Arsenal and Liverpool. The possibility of a second successive double, and the immortality that would go with being the only side ever to achieve the feat, was slipping away. It's hard to imagine any other team coming close to dominating the domestic game in such a fashion. Doing the 'double' once is a great achievement, doing it twice would be something else.

LET'S GET BEHIND THEM

Swansea City v Shrewsbury Town – The Vetch Field, 17 March 1995

One of the fascinating aspects of my travels was finding out the reasons for the various names attached to grounds, stands and teams. At Swansea I discovered that the stadium's strange name, the Vetch Field, relates to the use of the site for growing vetch, a type of bean used to feed cattle. By the time the farmer's field was converted to a football pitch it was covered in cinders and the players had to wear knee-pads to avoid injury.

Swansea were just off the play-off spots and desperately needed to beat their local rivals to climb up the table. At Birmingham they were brilliant. At home to Shrewsbury they were mediocre. 'They can't play at home. They're frightened,' said the supporter in front of me. He was wearing a thorn jacket and black jeans. He was the noisiest one there. 'Let's get behind them,' he shouted repeatedly. 'Come on, City,' he sang, almost alone. His friends joined in half-heartedly, but without any passion.

As the game drifted towards an inevitable goalless draw this particular fan became increasingly frustrated. 'We've got to get behind them,' he kept saying. 'What's wrong with this lot?' he added motioning towards the other supporters in the Centre Stand, which was built in 1913 just after Swansea won their first Welsh Cup final – they'd since lifted the trophy another eight times.

'You could hear a pin drop here,' agreed the bulky Welsh lad next to him. Most of the hard-core home fans were in the North Stand opposite. But even their sporadic chants of encouragement began to wane in the second half.

How distant seemed the days when former Liverpool striker John Toshack took over as player–manager and led the Swans from the Fourth Division to the First in just three seasons in the late '70s and early '80s. The late Bill Shankly said Toshack should be given a 'manager of the century' award for what he'd achieved in such a short time.

For a brief spell in March 1982 Swansea topped the First Division. I remember listening to a classic match at Anfield during which the Swans took a 2–0 lead but were eventually pegged back to 2–2 in a thriller. They'd only rub shoulders with the élite for two seasons. In an effort to keep pace with their First Division rivals the club overspent in the transfer market, culminating in their record signing of Colin Irwin for £340,000 from Liverpool, but with little reward. By October 1983 they were bottom of the Second Division and, more seriously, threatened with closure.

In less than five months Toshack left the club, came back and departed again. Two years after briefly being the best team in the League, Swansea were back in the Third Division. They'd slipped down as quickly as they'd climbed up and by 1986 were in the Fourth Division. Football can be cruel sometimes, ask any Swans fan.

Tonight's match against Shrewsbury was played in a gale-force wind, which didn't help the players to put on a classic. The conditions were partly to blame for the dour performance that prevented the Swans moving within a point of a play-off spot. The home side didn't force Shrewsbury keeper Tim Clarke to make a save until the 53rd minute. That sparked Swansea's best spell. Club captain John Cornforth, hoping to win his first cap for Wales against Bulgaria in Sofia a couple of weeks later, almost broke the deadlock with a fierce angled drive that Clarke tipped over.

Shrewsbury, managed by former Cardiff keeper Fred Davies – assistant to John Bond at Swansea a decade ago – were equally lacking in invention. Swansea keeper Roger Freestone, once of Chelsea, only had one save to make in each half. That was hardly the form to enable them to record a fifth successive League win at the Vetch. And they didn't. This was my third match in a row without a goal and meant that I'd seen 270 minutes of League football without the ball hitting the back of the net. To be honest, I'd have cheered if the ball had even trickled over the line. I was cold and tired.

It was hard to imagine the local football team once hosting the likes of Manchester United and Liverpool. Tonight most of the excitement surrounded the next day's rugby international at the National Stadium between Wales and Ireland. The hordes of Irish fans who'd come over early to celebrate St Patrick's Day had filled all the hotels and B&Bs along the seafront. Almost every establishment had a NO VACANCY sign. One hotel covered in neon lights said they might be able to fit me in later if the booking for their double room didn't show up. Meanwhile, my search continued.

Eventually I found a place, the Hotel Glengarrick, which had a VACANCIES sign in the window.

'Do you have a single?' I asked, slightly desperately.

'Yes,' replied the matronly lady behind the reception desk.

'How come it's so hard to get a room?'

'It's the rugby.'

'Yes, but that's in Cardiff, isn't it?'

'Ay, but Cardiff is packed tonight, so a lot of supporters are staying in Swansea and will travel up to the game tomorrow.'

It's amazing how many obstacles a record attempt has to overcome! But at least I had a bed to sleep in – and boyo did I need one.

A LOAD OF BULLS

Hereford United v Scarborough – Edgar Street , 18 March 1995

I left Swansea's Glengarrick Hotel by taxi, stopping off to take some pictures of the players' entrance and the strange crane-like floodlight at the Vetch Field. I had to get to the station for the 8.32 train to Newport and my connection to Hereford.

Hereford stands in a loop of the River Wye near the Welsh marches. Its strategic position gave it a long and bloody military history and it was once a Saxon border garrison town against the Welsh. A cathedral city since it was founded in AD 700 , the modern city of Hereford only really began to develop in the nineteenth century with the arrival of the railway. The city is still firmly connected to its agricultural base. Indeed, the cattle market with its pedigree bulls is next to United's Edgar Street ground.

But while Hereford is widely known for its cathedral, medieval treasures and cider, the place was only really put on the map in the minds of football fans after a famous FA Cup third-round replay on 5 February 1972. Hereford had been drawn against First Division Newcastle and after a thoroughly deserved 2–2 draw at St James's Park, which United were unlucky not to win, the two teams spent the next 12 days waiting around for the rain to stop and the waterlogged Edgar Street pitch to dry out.

Hereford were more than ready to do battle. Newcastle's centre-forward Malcolm Macdonald had inadvertently helped to motivate the Hereford players with his comments in the papers after the first game. Super Mac said they'd had their moment of glory and he'd score ten goals in the replay. Hereford player–manager Colin Addison simply pinned the article on the dressing-room wall.

The game finally went ahead on a grey February afternoon on the day of the fourth round. The excitement in the city had been building for almost two weeks and a crowd of 15,000 was packed into United's Edgar Street ground. Local cider makers had brought in hundreds of wooden crates for schoolboys to sit on in the grassed terraces behind the goals.

Newcastle had the better start, hitting the bar twice in the first half as they forced the first six corners of the match. But Hereford had the slope in their favour in the second half and began to get on top. Addison was bossing the midfield and McLaughlin was doing a good job on Macdonald. Then, against the run of play, Viv Busby crossed from the right and Super Mac headed Newcastle in front with just eight minutes left.

Macdonald may not have scored ten but it looked as if he'd grabbed the winner. Four minutes later Ronnie Radford won the ball in midfield from John Tudor and played a one-two with Brian Owen which came off his shin. Rocket Ronnie then hit a screamer from fully 40 yards into the top right-hand corner of Ian McFaul's goal.

'It sat there, just waiting to be hit,' said Radford. 'Colin Addison shouted, "My ball, Raddy", but then he slipped so I went for it. I just hit it and it flew in. I'd done it before and since, but the difference was that it was on TV. Once we'd equalised, Newcastle had gone.'

The Southern League side were dominating extra-time when full-back Roger Griffiths, who later discovered he'd played almost 80 minutes with a fractured left fibula, was replaced by Ricky George. After 102 minutes of this epic Cup-tie George met a short pass from Radford and slid a shot across McFaul and inside the far post. It proved to be the winner and made George the most famous FA Cup substitute of all time. It was the first time a First Division team had been knocked out of the Cup by a non-League club since Yeovil's win over Sunderland in 1949.

Today I had a seat in the cold, windswept Main Stand, which was sparsely populated with die-hard Hereford fans. The few Scarborough supporters who'd made the long journey down from the North-East were in the upper tier of the Len Weston Stand opposite. They could see the cattle market, the cathedral and the southern hills from up there – a much prettier sight than the football.

The match itself was a pretty dour Third Division affair with the ball in the air a lot. The very windy conditions didn't help, but the poor quality of play was the main reason. Hereford managed to secure the points with a 2–1 win despite losing their star player, Ashley Ward, to Norwich the week before the game. I was just pleased the match was a midday kick-off because it gave me the time to reach Stoke's Victoria Ground for an afternoon game against Reading. Every match helped my quest.

WIZARD OF DRIBBLE

Stoke City v Reading – The Victoria Ground, 18 March 1995

There's nothing in the trophy cabinet at Stoke's Victoria Ground to indicate that one of the best dribblers in the game once played for the Potters. But he did, and he was there on a bright Saturday afternoon for the visit of play-off contenders Reading.

In 1933 Sir Stanley Matthews was just a promising young winger playing alongside Freddie Steele in a team that brought First Division football back to the Potteries after a 10-year absence and took the club to a runners-up spot in 1946. Stan left Stoke for Blackpool and the road to the highlight of his career: the Matthews Final at Wembley in which his wizardry helped Blackpool to a famous 4–3 win over Bolton. But he returned in 1961, aged 46. Manager Tony Waddington paid a bargain £35,000 to bring the 'Wizard of Dribble' back to the Potteries to play alongside Jimmy McIlroy and Dennis Viollet.

Matthews put 30,000 people on the gate at the Victoria Ground and helped his old club back to the First Division in 1963, playing in 36 of their 42 League games! The star-studded team of has-beens and cast-offs had the highest average age in the Football League. But their experience was invaluable. Stan was 50 when he played his last game for the club.

Some people claim that Stoke were formed in 1863, but a more plausible date is 1868 when workers at the local railway formed Stoke Ramblers. But there's no doubt that they were one of the original 12 Football League clubs in 1888 and the second-oldest League club after Notts County. Stoke had also been based at the same ground longer than any other British club – since 1878.

Until Stoke's League Cup win over Chelsea in 1972 (2–1: Eastham and Conroy) Matthews was their only claim to fame. Sure, they won the Second Division (North) title in 1927, and the Second Division Championship in 1933 and 1963. And they'd had some great players. Gordon Banks, a key part of that League Cup winning team, had been a legend between the posts for six seasons from 1967 until a car crash resulted in eye injuries that ended his career. He was succeeded by another England great, Peter Shilton, while other stars to have worn the red and white stripes include Geoff Hurst, Adrian Heath, Garth Crooks and Mark Stein.

But the club had failed to add any silverware since the League Cup apart from the Second Division title in 1993. They'd enjoyed some success under Lou Macari in his first spell at the Victoria Ground. He led Stoke to the Third Division Championship and victory in the Autoglass Trophy after a miserable spell under Mick Mills and Alan Ball which resulted in relegation to the Third Division for the first time since 1927.

The jewel in the Stoke trophy cabinet thus remained the tankard inscribed with 'League Cup Winners 1972'. I remembered how, when I was 12 years old, I'd tossed a coin with another lad in our school team to see who'd get the ticket one of our mates had for the final at Wembley. I lost and he went. I got to Wembley the following year to see Tottenham play Norwich, when Ralph Coates scored the only goal for Spurs in one of the most boring League Cup finals in history.

I remained bemused by the fact that there was nothing in the Stoke boardroom to celebrate Sir Stan's achievements. I'd seen one of his England shirts and a few caps and medals on display at a shopping centre in Stoke the year before.

'Hasn't he donated one of his caps or a medal or something?' I asked a club official.

'No, I don't think so. But as president he comes to most games. He was here today.' Still, I thought, there should have been something from the great man apart from the bronze bust which stands proudly inside the club's main entrance.

I'd driven to Stoke from a morning game at Hereford and arrived just in time for the kick-off. The Potteries are widely known as 'the Five Towns', but the city of Stoke-on-Trent is actually made up of six large towns which stretch for about eight miles along the A50. The joining together of the towns of the Potteries in 1925 to form the new corporation of Stoke-on-Trent persuaded Stoke to add City to their name.

The district around Stoke-on-Trent has been Britain's main pottery centre for 400 years. A Toby Jug of Matthews, part of a series commemorating Britain's great footballers and which I was to come across in the Blackpool club shop later in the season, was made in Stoke by Wedgwood – just one of the companies, along with Royal Doulton and Spode, which gave the area its worldwide reputation.

The process of modernising the Main Stand on Boothen Road, a narrow street overshadowed by the Boothen Stand, began in 1960 with the first part of a three-stage rebuilding plan. The final stage coincided with the club's promotion to the First Division in 1963, when the players were offered a shilling an hour over the summer to help lay the concrete for the terraces!

The River Trent passed by the ground a few yards behind the corner joining the Boothen End and the Butler Street Stand. The foundations of the old roof in the south-west corner of the Butler Street Stand were actually sunk deep into the river bed. The Trent is narrower here than when it passes Nottingham Forest's City Ground and Notts County's Meadow Lane stadium because Stoke is closer to the river's source a few miles north of the Victoria Ground, east of Vale Park in Burslem.

How Stoke needed Stanley Matthews' wily skills on the wing today! Another defeat – this time by a single goal – had left City struggling near the relegation zone. Indeed, Macari would have been grateful to have any of Stoke's galaxy of stars at their peak. Freddie Steele, George Eastham, Jimmy Greenhoff, Sammy McIlroy, Lee Dixon, Steve Bould – the list is almost endless.

The latest 'star' to appear in the famous red and white stripes was Paul Allen. I'd seen the former Spurs and Hammers midfielder sitting in the stands at Southampton when he was recovering from injury. Allen then popped up at Luton where he was making his début on-loan. Now he was just finishing a two-month loan spell at Stoke. Lou Macari hadn't made him an offer, so the second-youngest player ever to appear in an FA Cup final was hoping another club would buy him before the transfer deadline.

'Coming to Stoke was the first time I had played my football in the North and it opened my eyes, If the right club came in for me now, the geography would not matter.' And I thought the North was places like Sunderland and Blackpool! Isn't Stoke somewhere in the Midlands? Let's hope Allen's knowledge of geography is better on the pitch. At least he should have had no trouble finding the Victoria Ground, since you can't miss it from the motorway link road!

SING WHEN WE'RE FISHING

Grimsby Town v Sunderland – Blundell Park, 19 March 1995

'If you want to win this division, you've got to come to places like Grimsby and win,' according to Middlesbrough manager Bryan Robson. 'I'd rather play for Grimsby,' screamed the headline on the back of the *News of the World,* quoting, Paul Gascoigne, who'd just fallen out with Spurs in a dispute over a tax bill. A young couple on *The Big Breakfast*, who couldn't answer five simple questions to win a holiday in Guadeloupe, were offered a luxury weekend in Grimsby as a consolation prize. They turned it down.

Not that the club is short of ideas. On the day of the Sunderland match there was a special initiative to get more local children into the ground. Any Grimsby or Sunderland fan could take in two kids under 16 for free. The offer was also to compensate the supporters for what happened the previous year. 'The corresponding fixture last season was postponed owing to torrential rain after just six minutes and therefore as a gesture of goodwill to both sets of fans we wanted to introduce a special scheme for all supporters,' said Grimsby spokesman Steve Wraith.

Fifteen minutes into the second half the rain came pouring down. The wind also swept across Blundell Park, making it difficult for the players and miserable for the Sunderland fans in the partly covered Osmond Stand to my left, most of whom were getting soaked. But worse was to follow. The rain gave way to snow, then sleet. Suddenly it stopped, and late in the match the sun came out again. I'd experienced the sort of weather the fishermen have to put up with in Grimsby.

The Grimsby fans behind the goal at the Pontoon End, named after the docks, cheered the loudest. They're renowned for a dance resembling the canoeists in the title sequence of the television series *Hawaii Five-O* and for waving inflatable haddocks on the terraces. Rival fans call them 'Codheads'. But these supporters don't resent their fishy connections, they revel in them – and they have a sense of humour to boot. Not for them an attempt to play down their seafaring roots.

Take Harry the Haddock for instance. He swam into the nation's consciousness during Grimsby's 1989 FA Cup run when, as a struggling Fourth Division side, they knocked out First Division Middlesbrough and Reading, before going down 3–1 in the fifth round to Wimbledon, where Harry made one of his first appearances. The Grimsby fanzine *Sing When We're Fishing* says Harry is a forename of 'deep, mystic significance' at the club. If you want to sound authentically local, by the way, you should drop the 'H'.

Grimsby had only recently lost their successful manager Alan Buckley to West Brom. Despite taking the Mariners from the obscurity of the Fourth Division to mid-table respectability in the First, Buckley had not got the crowds flocking back to Blundell Park. The average home gate was still less than 6,000. Fanzine contributor Phil Ball believes this was partly because Buckley didn't really understand the town. So what is it that makes Grimsby different to similar coastal towns around Britain?

'If you want to get the crowds back, you have to understand the Grimsby area,' says Ball. 'You have to understand that the place has a special psyche, a weird cut-off sort of identity that you only find in places like Barrow-in-Furness or Penzance. We only want characters to represent us, not pretty football. If you come from Grimsby, or Cleethorpes, you spend the best part of your life as a figure of fun. What is most important about being from this area is that we hate the rest of the world because it's always taking the piss out of us. We need to feel that the personnel of Grimsby Town Football Club understands this and goes out onto the field of play with the appropriate attitude. We are the most proudly parochial people on the planet. We still swoon if we get a mention on the telly, or if one of the quality papers deigns to mention us. The football at Town has to reflect how we are here, how we regard the rest of the world from out of our special shell.'

The fans wanted local heroes John Cockerill and Paul Futcher, the former Luton and Manchester City defender, to be given the job. They were put in charge temporarily, but Grimsby opted for youth and eventually chose former Nottingham Forest defender Brian Laws.

Fanzine editor Steve Plowes explained the local reaction. 'We loved Futch and Cockers; fans would applaud when Futcher bent down to lace his boots. Then Laws appeared in a suit, and in Grimsby we don't trust people in suits.' If Buckley didn't understand the area, is there any hope of Laws becoming more integrated into the Grimsby 'psyche'? The initial signs weren't good. One of the main changes he made in his first few weeks in charge was to take fish and chips out of the players' diet!

The fans' natural pessimism goes back a long way. Blundell Park started out on three miles of boggy turf on the coastal approach to Grimsby. Like the City Ground in Nottingham, Blundell Park is not based in the town that bears the team's name but is actually in nearby Cleethorpes. The ground takes its name from a Peter Blundell who, in 1616, left money to Sidney Sussex College, Cambridge. The college used the funds to buy the manor of Itterby, including land which would be named Blundell Park in honour of Pete, whoever he was. As to why Sidney Sussex College, Cambridge, was buying land in Cleethorpes, that's anyone's guess.

I was sure the fans behind the goal in the Pontoon Stand didn't know, or care for that matter. Their main concern was a win for Grimsby and a place in the play-offs. Five minutes into the second half Sunderland's Craig Russell had run through the middle of the Grimsby defence, twisting and turning past two, then three, defenders before laying the ball to Steve Agnew on the edge of the six-yard box. Agnew took the ball in his stride before planting it into the corner of the net. The Sunderland fans ran onto the pitch to celebrate and two of them were caught by stewards and led away by the police. 'We are Sunderland, say, we are Sunderland,' they sang.

After 27 minutes Grimsby took the lead again when Livingstone scored his second with a header. With the home team back in control a group of about 50 youngsters ran along the terraces in front of the Findus Stand towards the Osmond Stand containing the away supporters. They took up a position on the open terracing beside the Findus Stand and began chanting at the much bigger contingent of Rokerites to their right. The Sunderland fans looked at the rabble, most wearing their designer Grimsby shirts, and sang, 'What the fucking hell is that? What the fucking hell is that?'

But they'd all go home happy today. Late in the match on-loan signing Jamie Forrester from Leeds capped a fine performance with his first goal for the club to make it 3–1. Here was one young man who was definitely happy to be in Grimsby. What's so great about Guadeloupe anyway?

PRIDE OF EAST ANGLIA

Norwich City v Ipswich Town – Carrow Road, 20 March 1995

It had been 43 years since Norwich last did the 'double' over Ipswich in the East Anglian derby. Having won 2–1 at Portman Road in September they now had the perfect opportunity to take maximum points by winning this Monday-night game at Carrow Road. Ipswich were almost certainly relegated, standing second from bottom of the Premier League with only Leicester below them. But pride was at stake tonight.

City's under-pressure manager John Deehan was particularly keen to win the match. 'It would mean a lot for me if I could become the first manager in recent history to achieve the double over Ipswich.' The importance of the match for Deehan was clear from the moment I walked across the River Wensum towards the ground. 'Bring Back Mike Walker' said a home-made placard surrounded by City fans organising a petition for his reinstatement. They'd already gathered 3,000 signatures.

The fans desperately wanted former manager Mike Walker reinstated. But Walker hadn't left on the best of terms, and with a proud and stubborn chairman like Robert Chase at the club, it was fanciful to think the Canaries' former manager would be invited back. Even if Walker's return wasn't on the agenda at the time, Deehan's days still looked numbered. There were rumours some of the players weren't happy playing under him. And a lot of the fans weren't happy watching the players playing under him. Not that a win over rivals Ipswich would do Deehan, or indeed Chase, any harm.

Carrow Road is a sea of green and yellow except for the South Stand, which has an odd combination of red and blue seats. Both end stands have yellow seats on the upper tiers with the word CANARIES spelt out in green, whereas each of the lower tiers has green seats with two canaries picked out in yellow at either end. The link with canaries comes from Huguenot refugees who arrived in the city in the sixteenth century. They kept pet birds, including imported canaries, which they bred.

The club was founded in 1902 by two schoolteachers, who arranged the inaugural meeting in the Criterion Café. Norwich joined the Norfolk and Suffolk League and their first competitive match was against Ipswich. Fred Witham, who'd attended that first meeting, scored the only goal. They joined the Third Division as founder members in 1920 and were promoted to the Second Division in 1934 as Third Division (South) champions. Norwich first met Ipswich in the Football League at Portman Road on 2 September 1939, but their 1–1 draw never made the record books because war was declared the next day and League football was abandoned.

When the League programme resumed in 1945, City weren't ready and were immediately relegated to the Third Division (South). By the time floodlights were installed at Carrow Road in 1956 Norwich were really struggling. They only just managed to make the repayments on an £8,000 loan they'd received from the FA to build their ground in 1935. In 1957 the Canaries reached rock-bottom and had to apply for re-election.

It was in the 1970s that Norwich really came into their own. In 1971 the club bought the Carrow Road freehold from Boulton Paul with its seven acres of land. The following year, under manager Ron Saunders, they reached the old First Division for the first time, after winning the Second Division title. In their first season back their average crowd was more than 28,000 – a record for the club – but they only lasted two years. Norwich would spend the next 20-odd years moving between the top two divisions without ever being able to consolidate their position in the First Division.

Norwich weren't alone in finding life tough at the top. Ipswich were also struggling in the competitive world of the Premier League. Their supporters had little to cheer but they were nothing if not loyal and for tonight's game were packed into the old South Stand. They were in full voice and much noisier than the home fans before the match. And, despite a tenuous hold on their Premiership position, they displayed a sense of humour. 'Down with the Ipswich, You're going down with the Ipswich,' they sang.

Finally, the players walked out onto the pitch together, generating a sharp increase in the number of decibels from both sets of fans. The Norwich keeper, Andy Marshall, ran towards the Barclay End and jumped into the net as the faithful roared his name. A most unusual manoeuvre. The early pace of the game was hectic, as you'd expect from a derby match. Norwich forced a corner early on and the scoreboards at both ends flashed up IN THE NET . . . as if the players needed a reminder of where to put the ball!

With half an hour gone and the match evenly balanced, the Town contingent decided to have some fun. 'One Robert Chase, There's only one Robert Chase,' they chanted, obviously deliriously happy that their team no longer had to face players like Sutton, Fox and Robins – at least not at the same time and in yellow and green shirts. Their joy was short-lived, however, since the long-serving John Wark was sent off shortly afterwards for a late lunging tackle.

Without the inspirational Wark Ipswich caved in and Norwich won the game comfortably 3–0. Cue a quick rendition of the club's anthem 'On the Ball, City' – a music hall song written by one Albert T. Smith in about 1890 and adopted by Canaries fans shortly after the club was founded in 1902. It's supposed to be the oldest football song still regularly heard at any football ground in the country.

The win over Ipswich meant John Deehan would go down in history as the first Canaries manager in more than 40 years to steer the club to the 'double' over their arch-rivals. It meant a lot to him and just as much to the fans. But Deehan's achievement wasn't the only thing to go down, since Norwich would join their rivals on the slippery slope to the First Division. It was to be Deehan's last moment of glory.

RISING FROM THE ASHES

Bradford City v Swansea City – Valley Parade, 21 March 1995

They still hold an annual service for the dead outside Bradford City Hall. Ten years on there were three commemorations for those who died in the fire which swept through City's Valley Parade ground in May 1985. At the club there were many reminders of that fateful day, if anyone needed reminding. The people of the city will never forget the afternoon on the very last day of the season when 56 people lost their lives and more than 200 suffered serious injuries watching a football match.

The irony of the Bradford fire is that the 77-year-old Main Stand was being used for the last time that day. Builders were due to demolish the timber-framed construction the Monday after Bradford's last game of the season. Indeed, the *Bradford Telegraph & Argus* published a souvenir edition including an article headlined 'Spit and Polish for the Parade Ground'. The paper, which outlined the work to be done on the ground, noted that it was 'inadequate in so many ways'.

It was a tragedy the city would never forget and, along with the Hillsborough disaster, triggered major changes in Britain's football stadiums.

As you approach the main entrance to the ground on South Parade it's impossible to miss the sculpted memorial to the fire victims. Designed by Patricia McAllister, it shows a mother grieving with players leaping around her. Inside the main entrance the trophy cabinet is full of tributes from other clubs, like Oldham, and from as far away as Canada. The local miners, themselves no strangers to disaster, had presented Bradford with a miner's lamp. A silver presentation plate marked the opening of the new Valley Parade. On the wall is a case containing the ribbon cut by Lord Justice Popplewell when he opened the rebuilt ground in 1986. Alongside was a commemorative stone.

'The sad thing was that they were going to start work on redeveloping the main stand the Monday after the match,' confirmed Catherine, the pretty Bradford fanatic I'd met at York with her friend Caroline the previous Tuesday night. They'd travelled to arch-rivals Huddersfield to watch Bradford reserves' 2–2 draw at the new McAlpine Stadium while I was at Old Trafford for the Spurs game.

It was strange to see them again. They were the only two fans I'd meet up with at two different grounds all season, with the exception of the footballing entourage of commentators, ex-players, scouts and managers which follows the game all across the country. Another day, another town, another game. When asked what he would have liked most during his days as a manager the peripatetic Malcolm Allison said a chauffeur to drive him to games and save him from the exhaustion. I knew how he felt.

I'd actually reached the stage where exhaustion was beginning to take over. If I could have stopped right then and not seen another game for the rest of the season I'd have been deliriously happy. But I knew that with a few days' rest I'd recapture my enthusiasm.

The club was quite successful in its early years, winning the Second Division title in 1908, and Valley Parade was turned into one of the best grounds in England with a capacity of 40,000. By 1911 City had reached their highest-ever League position of fifth and also won the FA Cup. Bradford were in fact the first winners of the present FA Challenge Cup when they beat Newcastle 1–0 at Old Trafford after a goalless draw at the old Crystal Palace. On their way to the final City attracted their biggest-ever crowd when more than 39,000 saw them play Burnley. It's the oldest attendance record of any Football League club. Ironically, the trophy they lifted – the third FA Cup – was designed by a Bradford company called Fattorini's and cost 50 guineas.

Bradford held the record for the most consecutive Cup games without conceding a goal. They went 12 games from the third round in 1911 to the third round replay the following year without letting a single goal past them. But they had to enjoy their moment of glory because that was to be the best season they'd ever have. They were relegated in 1922 and by the early 1960s had slipped into the bottom division. Bradford moved between the Third and Fourth Divisions until that fateful day in 1985 when they were promoted to the Second Division under manager George Mulhall.

The Pulse Stadium had not exactly set pulses racing with the standard of football on show at Valley Parade in recent seasons. There were few top-class players turning out in City's colours. The exception was central defender Dean Richards, or 'Deano' to his adoring fans, whose name was splashed across the back page of the local *Telegraph & Argus* after his call-up as a reserve for the England Under-21 squad. He looked an accomplished player, very dangerous when making forward runs from the back, as he did frequently. With Bradford 3–0 down, Deano was pushed up front and made an immediate impact with a late consolation goal.

Catherine told me scouts from all the big clubs came to watch him regularly. The fans behind me said they'd heard Manchester United, Forest, Liverpool, West Ham and Blackburn were at the game to check on their idol. Coventry had already had a £1.5 million bid rejected. But it seemed almost inevitable that he would be sold. 'Deano scores his last goal for Bradford,' said one fan anticipating what he considered to be just a matter of time. (He joined Wolves during the close season.)

The Bradford supporters' biggest idol of all time, though, was Stuart McCall, the Rangers midfield dynamo who was sold in June 1988 to Everton for £850,000 – the highest fee City had ever received for a player. They thought so much of McCall at Valley Parade they'd even named an executive suite after him. He'd donated a signed Rangers shirt for an auction City were holding as part of a testimonial for Gavin Oliver.

'I'm going to offer my week's wages for that,' Catherine told a fellow supporter as we queued for a hamburger at half-time.

'It's too late,' said the tall City fan with short-cropped dark hair. 'I've heard some businessman has offered £500 for it.'

'That's not fair,' she said.

'Life isn't about being fair, it's about this . . .' said her friend, rubbing his fingers together . . . 'Spondoolies'. He looked at her with a glint in his eye: 'I've heard it hasn't been washed either.'

'Well, I'll just have to ask him to sign another one,' said Catherine, rather dejectedly.

Does everything come down to money?, I thought. The answer, of course, is *almost* everything – especially in football.

PROMOTION BATTLE

Bury v Mansfield Town – Gigg Lane, 25 March 1995

Bury and Mansfield. Fourth and fifth in the Endsleigh League Division Three. Both desperate to snatch the second automatic promotion spot behind Michael Knighton's runaway leaders, Carlisle. Mansfield had already scored a massive 71 goals – by far the highest total in the Third Division and a bigger haul than any other club in the League, including Premiership leaders Blackburn, who'd scored a mere 70!

Bury is a small town known for its open-air market and black pudding – inflatable versions of which have found their way onto the Gigg Lane terraces!

Its most famous sons are: politician Sir Robert Peel, whose grandad introduced calico-printing to Lancashire – he was born near Bury and there's a statue of him in the market place; John Kay, inventor of the fly-shuttle – he was mobbed by the people of Bury and died a pauper in France; and Mark Carter, hot-shot striker – he hits the back of the net with a frequency that's destined to deliver him into Lancastrian folklore.

Unfortunately the crowds do not flock to see the club's star striker, since the attractions of Old Trafford and Maine Road lie less than five miles along the motorway. But the sense of occasion at today's game was heightened by the carnival atmosphere of a Family Spectacular organised as part of the Football League's Season of the Family campaign, a national event involving every club.

Unlikely as it seems, Bury once graced the old First Division. They've even won the FA Cup twice – in 1900, and then 1903 with a record 6–0 win over Derby. A replica of the Cup was proudly displayed in the trophy cabinet which Bury had thoughtfully put in the social club. There was also a programme from a match against Arsenal in the 1928–29 season and a celebration of Bury's 1985 centenary year. A portrait of Colin Bell, the midfielder who later found fame at Manchester City and was in England's 1970 World Cup squad, hung on the social club wall. At least the regular fans who go there for a drink can see the mementos, unlike at most clubs where they're hidden away in the boardroom or put on display in the executive suites.

The ground, once part of the Earl of Derby's estate, remains much as it was before the Second World War. Indeed, the South Stand opposite my Main Stand seat, has been around for some 90 years and was one of the oldest in the League along with Preston's since-demolished West Stand.

After the game Mansfield boss Andy King was less than pleased with his players or the referee. He also thought the scoreline should have been slightly different. 'We went 2–0 down to a bad mistake and a bad refereeing decision. We should have been 4–1 up at half-time, there was only one team in it. We made Bury panic. The better team drew and that was us!'

The next day the local paper used Mansfield's nickname as the metaphor to pep up their reports. 'Wounded Stags prove a dangerous species' was one eye-catching headline. 'On a day when there were no Premiership games to tickle the palate, these two hopefuls proved there is life beyond millionaires' row,' wrote Chris Bailey. 'Even the most jaded of appetites couldn't have failed to have been revived by this rich feast of entertainment. Bury and Mansfield traded blow for blow in a pulsating contest.' And it was.

Bury's nickname originates from the Lancashire Cup final of 1892, when the Shakers were clear underdogs against Blackburn. The Bury chairman, rumoured to have been eating black puddings at half-time, shouted, 'We'll give them a shaking, for we are the Shakers!' The name has stuck ever since.

Burnley v Port Vale – Turf Moor, 28 March 1995

Burnley always seem to produce great players but somehow they never hang on to them. The club's youth policy was designed to nurture local talent and then sell it to keep Burnley solvent. Tommy Lawton (Everton), Willie Morgan (Manchester United), Martin Dobson (Everton), Ralph Coates (Spurs), Steve Kindon (Wolves), Dave Thomas (QPR), Leighton James (Derby), Brian Flynn (Leeds) and Tony Morley (Aston Villa) to name but a few of the players who went on to star for other teams.

The sales policy has damaged the team in the past, and no doubt will do so in the future. But Burnley had turned things around quite dramatically since 1987, when they almost lost their League status. Everything hinged on the last match of the season in what became known as 'the Orient Game'. Burnley had to beat the O's and hope that other results went their way, otherwise the unthinkable would have happened.

A crowd of 17,600 were packed into Turf Moor (the average gate that season was a mere 3,360) to see if Burnley could complete the great escape. On 9 May 1987 they won the crucial final match of their Fourth Division campaign by 2–1 while the other candidates for the drop, Lincoln City, lost to Swansea. The Clarets had survived and Lincoln joined the GM Vauxhall Conference. If Burnley had lost and been relegated, they'd have begun the 1987–88 season outside the Football League for the first time since starting out as founder members in 1888, almost exactly 100 years before.

That last match has left an indelible mark on the club, the town and the people of Burnley. A local artist painted a picture called 'Never Again' showing the scorer of one of Burnley's goals being embraced by a team-mate inside the six-yard box. Manager Brian Miller called it 'the worst and the best day of my life'. Thankfully he managed to avoid being remembered as the man who'd lost Burnley their League status.

Burnley have occupied Turf Moor continuously since 1883 – longer than any other League club except Preston, who've been at Deepdale since 1875. (Stoke had been at the Victoria Ground since 1878 but would move to the Britannia Stadium at Trentham Fields in 1997).

Their first League Championship came in 1921, when they played 30 consecutive matches without defeat. That stood as a League record until Leeds went 34 matches before losing in the 1969–70 season. Burnley keeper Jerry Dawson played in both the FA Cup-winning side and the Championship team, chalking up 522 League games from 1907 to 1928. He played in goal so long that he had 47 understudies during his time at Turf Moor!

Burnley were relegated to the Second Division in 1930 and lost their way until after the Second World War. They returned to the First Division in 1947, conceding only 32 goals in 51 games. But most of their post-war success was down to a blunt local butcher called Bob Lord, who took over the club and began one of football's great adventures.

Lord looked like a throwback to a footballer from the 1930s, but his ideas were anything but old-fashioned. Lord's mission was to drag this sleepy Lancashire club into the twentieth century. Burnley's larger-than-life chairman presided over a team which won the First Division title in 1960 with stars like Jimmy Adamson and Jimmy McIlroy. 'The winning of the League Championship by a small-town team, as Burnley did for the second time in 1960, stands as a remarkable achievement in a competition almost totally dominated in its history by big-city clubs,' wrote Albert Sewell in *Soccer*.

As champions, Burnley were eligible for the European Cup. After receiving a bye in the first round they were drawn against Rheims of France. A crowd of 37,742, including hundreds of French supporters, turned out for the first leg at Turf Moor. The Clarets won 2–0 with goals from the two Jimmys: Robson and McIlroy.

Hundreds of Burnley fans travelled to France for the second leg. Burnley lost 3–2 but went through 4–3 on aggregate. The programme for that match, a single A4 sheet, was given away free to each supporter entering the ground. It's now one of the rarest post-war Burnley programmes, worth more than £80.

They came up against West German champions Hamburg and their legendary forward Uwe Seeler in the quarter-finals. They won the first leg 3–1 at home, but the away goal was to prove decisive. In the return leg in front of a 71,000 crowd Hamburg were unstoppable and powered their way to a 4–1 win. If McIlroy had scored instead of hitting the post in the last minute, the Clarets would have been through to the semis.

Bob Lord died in 1981 on the eve of Burnley's centenary celebrations. His legacy was the training ground, the youth scheme and the modernised Turf Moor. But there were those who felt that if the money had been spent on players, or on keeping the home-grown stars Lord was so proud of, then Burnley might have held on to their place in the First Division. Many other clubs were to follow the same path with the same result.

Being among the élite is one thing; losing your League status is quite another. And if the Clarets had dropped down into the GM Vauxhall Conference, Dave Burnley for one might never have recovered. One of the club's most famous fans, Dave had changed his name from Beeston to show his loyalty to the cause after the Clarets were relegated in 1976. His daughter was christened Clarette because 'her mam refused to let me call her Burnley Burnley'. If they have a boy, he'll be either Ralphie Coates or Turfmoor!

Dave Burnley is the man who took a girlfriend out for a curry and made her answer 150 questions about whether a relationship would affect his love for the club. 'She passed with 97 per cent' . . . but things still didn't work out. How he managed to get a date in the first place under such conditions is beyond me! Dave had missed only one game in 20 years – a 12-times postponed match at Newcastle during a rail strike!

The fanzine *Who ate all the pies?* included a problem page for fans like Dave. 'GOT A PROBLEM? WRITE TO UNCLE JIMMY FOR SOME HEALTHY ADVICE.' It said the Uncle Jimmy in question was a spoof of then-manager Jimmy Mullen. The 'letters' included the following gem:

Dear Jimmy,

I have 2 girlfriends who have found out about each other and both have given me an ultimatum to ditch the competition. Flo is a grand lass but is a bit lacking in the beauty department, though she is mad keen on the Clarets and goes to all the matches with me. (Sounds like just the girl for Dave – ed!) Desirée on the other hand hates football but is a real party animal and looks just like Pamela Anderson in all departments. Who should I choose?

Desperate Dave.

Dear Desperate,

What do you expect me to say, 'Go with the Flo'? Get real, stick with Pamela Anderson and go to matches on your own!

Having climbed back to the First Division the Clarets were now desperately trying to avoid going straight back down. 'In the four years I have been here we have known only about success,' said Mullen, 'we all have to dig very deep now and show what we are made of.'

According to the fanzine: 'To complete the great escape all we have to do is win all eight remaining home games and grab a couple of draws on our travels.' Sounded easy.

'Port Vale will be keen to re-establish the lead they had when the Boxing Day clash was washed out,' said Mullen. 'It is essential for us to get the right result to put us on the right track for the final push.' Burnley did just that, winning 4–3 in a pulsating end-to-end match. But the Clarets were relegated anyway. And Mullen eventually quit the club after so-called supporters set fire to his wife's dress at a local Chinese restaurant!

MIKHAIL GORBACHEV'S TEAM

Wigan Athletic v Hereford United – Springfield Park, 29 March 1995

Wigan Athletic. Former Soviet President Mikhail Gorbachev's team. You think I'm kidding? Gorbachev came to Springfield Park with a Russian team in his younger days when he was an official at the club. He took a liking to Wigan and has followed them ever since.

Wigan found out about Gorbachev's interest when someone connected with the Latics saw an article in the *Straits Times* newspaper at a hotel in Singapore. He was so intrigued that he brought a copy of the paper back to the club's directors. They contacted the Russian Embassy in London, who knew nothing about it. Well, what did you expect? But Wigan decided to invite the then Soviet President to Springfield Park. He never came, but the Latics have since hosted a number of Russian teams and have also played in Russia. The last Russian team to visit was Moscow Torpedo.

Tonight's match against Hereford was my second attempt to see Wigan play at home. It was also my 35th birthday, which meant that I'd never forget this particular game for the rest of my life. If anyone ever asks me 'Where were you on the night of your 35th birthday?' I'll remember instantly. Springfield Park: Wigan 1, Hereford 1.

Back in January I'd travelled to the ground for a game against Hartlepool, but it was postponed because of a waterlogged pitch. I was given a quick look around the ground anyway, since I'd travelled all the way from London. Springfield Park was very spacious with plenty of room for development if the club decided to invest in the stadium. There was talk of a move to the outskirts of town and a new leisure complex with cinemas, sports facilities and two pitches – one for rugby and one for football. So far that's all it was – talk.

There's only one major sport in Wigan, as I learned from the taxi driver who picked me up from the station, and that's rugby league. The rugby club regularly attracted 20,000 or more fans to their ground, while the football team struggled along on gates of about 2,000. With the Hartlepool game postponed Wigan had only played one game at Springfield Park in over a month. Since the home team now takes all the revenue from League games (but not the FA Cup where non-League clubs get a 50 per cent cut of the gate receipts and League sides take 40 per cent), Wigan's income had been badly hit.

'We've still got to pay the players' wages and other expenses,' said one director, 'but nothing has been coming in through the turnstiles in gate receipts. It's a problem for a small club like ours.'

My problem was where to go from Wigan to see a game of football on a very wet and windy day which had wiped out half the league fixtures, mostly in the south.

'Why don't you go up to Preston, they're at home today?' said one of the directors. Another director gave me a lift back to the station in his Range Rover and I was soon on my way to Prenton Park, the home of Tom Finney.

As I waited on the station platform I was asked by a Manchester University student if the Wigan game was off.

'Yes,' I replied. 'Waterlogged pitch. Do you follow Wigan then?' I asked him.

'Yes, I'm from Wigan. I get back here most Saturdays to see them play.' The conversation turned to Andy Lyons, their Blackpool-based winger signed from Crewe. If the game had been played that day, Lyons would have made his 50th appearance.

Lyons was born the year England won the World Cup, had missed only eight games since his £15,000 transfer 15 months before and was a favourite with the fans. They named him as their Player of the Year in 1993–94 after a season in which he was the club's top scorer with 11 league goals. Lyons had already notched six more in 1994–95, including his first-ever hat-trick in the 4–1 win over Darlington at Springfield Park in November.

The student boarded his train back to Manchester and I got back to reading the Wigan match programme. Imagine my surprise when I looked up to find a freshly showered Lyons waiting on the station platform, with his kit-bag, for a train.

He was disappointed the Hartlepool match had been called off. 'I hate it when this happens. You know, you don't go out on Friday night and you psyche yourself up to play and then it's called off.' Wigan were struggling near the foot of the Third Division and needed all the points they could get, but a last-minute goal at Mansfield the week before had cost them the match.

'Are you still in the FA Cup?' I asked.

'No, Altrincham beat us,' said Lyons. 'I suppose it was a giant-killing,' he added with a wry smile. The difference between the top non-League teams and those at the bottom of the Third Division was not that great.

The biggest matches Lyons had played in all season were the two-legs of the Coca-Cola Cup second-round match against Aston Villa. Wigan lost the first leg 5–0 at Villa Park and the second leg 3–0 at Springfield Park. 'Any time we looked like we might get back in it they just stepped up a gear. They were able to raise their game to a whole new level. It was frightening. Still, just to be out there with all those great players was an experience. It's a different world in the Premier League. The stadium, the facilities, everything. Their players were in the bar after the match and they all had mobile phones,' said Lyons, hinting that you couldn't really afford one on Third Division wages.

Wigan had enjoyed better times in the FA Cup in January 1980, when they beat Chelsea at Stamford Bridge in the third round with a goal from Tommy Gore, one of the Liverpool-born members of the team. They wore a Liverpool-style all-red strip on the night described by their Scottish manager Ian McNeill as the 'greatest win in Wigan's history'. They went on to play Everton at Goodison in front of the biggest crowd of the fourth round (51,863) and lost 3–0. It was the first time they'd got that far.

Wigan Athletic were known as 'the finest non-League club in the north' when they were in the Northern Premier League. A non-League match against Southern League Hereford drew their largest-ever crowd of 27,500 in 1953. But they became the League's newest members in 1978 when, after a recount, they were elected in place of Southport with their 35th application for membership!

For years the town was best known for its rugby league club, but now they faced competition from the Latics. They were promoted to the Third Division in 1982 and won their only cup, the Freight Rover Trophy, in 1985. But they were relegated in 1993 to the new Third Division.

Andy Lyons knew all about playing in the Third Division, though not today. I said goodbye to Lyons, a really nice bloke, and we went our separate ways. He switched platforms to get a Blackpool train; I made my way out of the station to catch a taxi to Prenton Park – one of only 17 League grounds staging any football at all on a very wet Saturday. Most of the countryside on the train ride north, that January afternoon, was waterlogged; it was hardly surprising so many games were off.

APRIL FOOLS

Rochdale v Barnet – Spotland, I April 1995

The first day of April, the one day in the month when you could suffer fools gladly. The Football League had put together an interesting batch of linesmen for various League games. There were G. Monk and A. Monk at Vicarage Road, C. Francis and G. Lee at St Andrews, S. French and R. Saunders at the Abbey Stadium (surely the Monks should have been sent there), M. Arch and B. Bishop at Ninian Park, R. Smith and J. Wesson at Field Mill and M. Ryan and P. Giggs at the Bescot Stadium. The list was endless. It seemed the League was entering into the spirit of the day.

There had been times on my travels when I'd felt rather foolish getting out of bed at four o'clock in the morning to rush to work, complete my shift and then run off to a British Rail station to board a train for some godforsaken part of Britain I'd never been to before and was unlikely to go back to again. Not today, though, and I was full of the joys of spring as I journeyed with my son Lyle to Spotland, the home of Rochdale. The ground is named after the local area and the team are known locally as the Dale.

We found the town easily enough nestling in a valley with its tourist office, museum and post office. It had been a wool town and a cotton town in its heyday but those industries had declined leaving Rochdale to survive as just another small English town of just over 90,000 people. Sadly, it wasn't football that attracted visitors to this part of Lancashire, but a woman whose songs had made her famous as Our Gracie.

'Rochdale is still more famous as the birthplace of Gracie Fields than for the deeds of its football team,' wrote Albert Sewell in *Soccer*. Our Gracie was born in Rochdale in 1898 and the Rochdale Museum pays tribute to the singer who died in 1979. The town's only other real claim to fame is that the Co-op was started there when the Society of Equitable Pioneers opened a grocery shop in the town in 1844.

The football team has always struggled to make an impact in a region of the country better known for rugby than for soccer. The difficulties faced by those trying to establish an Association football club were not surprising given the locals' love of the oval-ball game.

The football club's consistent under-achievement was summed up by a club history titled *The Survivors*. Resolution and perseverance were the words used to describe the dogged determination of Dale and their supporters. A leading member of the National Football Supporters Association once said that 'to be a lifelong Rochdale fan shows a passion for the game above and beyond the normal realms'.

As I pulled my car into the entrance I could see the words SPOTLAND STADIUM boldly announcing that we'd arrived at our destination. The

298

Lancashire dales were clearly visible over the top of the terraced houses behind the Wilbutts Lane Terrace with its low blue roof covering the centre section. To the left was Knowl Hill and in front stood Rooley Moor. They were both more than 130 feet high and gave the ground a very rural feel. They were certainly prettier than the football on display in the Endsleigh League Division Three game against Barnet.

Barnet striker Freedman had already bagged four goals for his new club against Rochdale back in September when Barnet had thrashed the Dale 6–2 at Underhill.

Since then Freedman had become one of the most consistent goalscorers in the Third Division. He'd hit a hat-trick against Hartlepool a fortnight ago and his strike in a 1–1 draw with Wigan the previous weekend had made him the division's leading scorer with 23 goals in all matches. His 18 League goals were just two short of the club record set by Gary Bull in the 1991–92 season. And he needed only another three goals to match Bull's 26 goals in all games during that campaign.

His pedigree was already drawing attention from other managers and his international career was also about to take off. He'd scored the winning goal for the Scotland Under-21 side against Russia in a European Championships qualifying match the Tuesday before the Rochdale game.

Freedman didn't disappoint against Rochdale and was always dangerous whenever Barnet attacked. The game was an end-to-end affair, though it didn't impress my son Lyle, who was more interested in his hamburger than the match. Having just seen Liverpool play Southampton, the delights of watching Rochdale were lost on him.

ONE STANLEY MATTHEWS

Blackpool v Birmingham City – Bloomfield Road, 4 April 1995

'There have been many, probably too many, who have been tagged great in my time, but there is only one Stanley Matthews.' These are the words of Jimmy Armfield, himself one of the greats and a club colleague of Matthews during his Blackpool days. Armfield made 568 League appearances for the Seasiders and was capped 43 times at full-back for England, both club records. He knows all about Stan.

Matthews is now the President of Stoke City and the undisputed 'King of the Potteries' but his fame comes from Blackpool. His finest moment in a tangerine shirt was against Bolton in the 1953 FA Cup final, a match named after him long before a ball had been kicked at Wembley.

I travelled to Blackpool, 'famous for fresh air and fun', looking forward to seeing the Tower and the Illuminations, with its half a million lightbulbs, that decorate the promenade. But I was more excited about delving into the legend that was Matthews.

Blackpool were a top-class team when Matthews wore the tangerine shirt which was famous all over the world. Football supporters everywhere know the names of Mortensen, Johnstone and, of course, Matthews. Everyone in Blackpool who was old enough had seen him play; to them he was simply the best.

'He had this knack of pushing the ball forward to invite the full-back to make a tackle and then, as soon as the defender had committed himself, Stan was gone,' said the balding middle-aged man with the beer belly sitting next to me with his son in the original Main Stand at Bloomfield Road. It was the night of Blackpool's promotion battle against Birmingham. 'Stan was very quick over short distances and that's what made him great. You'd often see him on the beach running or doing exercises.'

But was Stan really that good? 'Other football legends such as Pelé, Finney, Di Stefano and Charlton really bring magical memories back as well, but with Matthews there was a sort of mystique that made him different,' said Armfield, now a BBC radio commentator:

> He had a ruthless streak. Once he got on top of an opponent, he showed no mercy. He could taunt defenders almost like a matador with a bull. He was totally confident. It was all down to his fanatical drive for physical fitness that was superior to other footballers.
>
> In Blackpool he went down to the beach at eight o'clock every morning where he did light jogging, exercises and, just as important to him, deep breathing. He came to the ground and trained with the rest of us as well. His fitness level was never in doubt, even when he was past 40. He didn't smoke or drink and he experimented with health foods long before any other athlete had even considered them. Carrot juice was on the Matthews menu, although I can also recall when he would purposely go on a fast and start to build up for his next game with salads and light meals.

Matthews has never lost the will to train alone and still works out today. Armfield believes that's probably what made him better than all the rest. 'Stan took great pains so as not to disappoint his public. Whenever we played we knew that Stan would be the focus of attention. We knew, as well, that there were critical eyes on him – many waiting and eager to write him off. He disappointed the cynics, as he wasn't like other footballers who start to worry about the future when they pass 30. Incredibly, even after retiring, he told me he thought he had gone out too soon.'

Stan was the first winner of the Player of the Year award in 1948, helping the Seasiders reach their first FA Cup final. They lost 4–2 to Manchester United. In 1951 Blackpool got back to Wembley where they played a Newcastle team spearheaded by Jackie Milburn. They lost 2–0. Matthews was 38 years old. Today his chances of having another crack at winning the Cup would have been almost non-existent. How many Premiership players are older than that?

But Stan was far from finished. He believed he'd get another chance. Everybody wanted him to get another chance. And in classic fairytale tradition he did. It was Coronation year and a time to celebrate. When Blackpool reached the final again, everybody in the country, except the Bolton fans, wanted Matthews to pick-up a winners' medal. The Post Office had to make special deliveries to Bloomfield Road to carry the huge volume of letters wishing Matthews success at last.

In a Wembley classic the Seasiders came back from 3–1 down to win 4–3. Mortensen was one hero, scoring the only ever hat-trick in an FA Cup final. But it was Matthews who stole the headlines. Stan caused havoc down the Bolton left in the last half-hour and laid on the winner for Bill Perry. That was to be his finest performance in a tangerine shirt. He came closest to a League Championship medal in 1956, when Blackpool were runners-up to Manchester United. In 1961 Stan left Bloomfield Road and returned to his roots, rejoining Stoke for £35,000.

Blackpool's flame flickered briefly after Matthews' departure when they reached the League Cup semi-final in 1962. But they were relegated from the old First Division in 1967. The Seasiders bounced back in 1970 but their comeback only lasted one season as they finished bottom – a sad ending to the career of Jimmy Armfield. The club has remained outside the top flight ever since and, after relegation again in 1978, has spent its time in the bottom two divisions. The glory years of the late 1950s are nowadays just a fading memory.

You can't miss Bloomfield Road, and there's certainly no doubt that it's the home of Blackpool FC. The club's name is spelt out in huge tangerine letters across the front of the Main Stand. I'd written to the club the previous May and received a reply from Managing Director Gill Bridge – one of only two women in such a lofty position in the Premier or Football League. The other, of course, is Karren Brady, Managing Director of tonight's visitors Birmingham.

I looked up at the empty Kop, which was closed tonight, and imagined being there in the '50s when Matthews and Mortensen ran out in their baggy shorts to the cheers from supporters in flat caps and woolly scarves waving their wooden rattles. I was brought back to the '90s when the two teams came out onto the pitch.

At half-time a gorilla wearing a Blackpool kit came onto the pitch and started trying to kick plastic footballs into the crowd. He failed the first few times, much to the amusement of the crowd, but eventually got the hang of it. The Birmingham fans applauded when he managed to kick a ball in their direction. Meanwhile, the cheerleaders had returned for another show in the centre circle. Suddenly, the music died on them and the away fans started booing. I felt sorry for the girls, none of whom was older than about 17. They were trying their best and deserved encouragement.

The second half began and Birmingham were soon on the attack again. Their six feet eight inch striker, Kevin Francis, recently signed from Stockport, tried a shot but miscued completely. 'His legs look like they're too long for him,' said one Blackpool supporter. The Seasiders equalised in the second half to the relief of their fans. But the Birmingham players weren't happy. They needed the points for their promotion drive.

As they left the pitch the Birmingham number six squared up to the Blackpool fans in the Family Stand. I thought he was about to launch himself into the supporters Cantona-like, but his team-mates quickly came over to drag him away. I couldn't believe it as he stood there in front of the home fans shouting, 'Come on then, come on then'. He was spoiling for a fight and was clearly frustrated that the Blues hadn't secured all three points. Not the sort of end to a fine evening's football that you want to see.

Fortunately, for millions of football fans, thoughts of Blackpool turn to Stanley Matthews. What did it mean to Jimmy Armfield, who'd been reporting on tonight's match, to play with the maestro? 'The name still conjures up something magical to me and I suppose that when I look back on my career with Blackpool and England I still feel that one of my greatest honours was to play behind the great Stan for six seasons. He was to football what Fred Perry was to tennis, Len Hutton to cricket and Henry Cotton to golf. Self-taught, they were the people's champions – there was an aura about them that presented professionalism and clean living, and Englishmen everywhere loved them.' A shame you can't say that about too many of today's footballers!

LIFE AND DEATH

Liverpool v Southampton – Anfield, 5 April 1995

'I know that I had the best dad in the whole world and I'm proud of that. Thanks, Dad. Love and miss you very much. Pat.'

'A true Koppite joining those so tragically killed at Hillsborough. Rest in peace, Bob. Your loving wife and children.'

'Terry, you are so very precious to me. I will always love you. Sandra.'

'Happy Birthday, Grandad. All our love. Gareth and Ben.'

These were just some of the dedications among the flowers laid beneath the Anfield Memorial to those who lost their lives so tragically at Hillsborough on 15 April 1989. The dead were aged between 14 and 67 years old. Tommy Anthony Howard, Eric Hankin, Paul Brown, Lee Nichol and Adam Edward Spearritt were the youngest; Gerard Baron (Snr) was the oldest. The names are listed in alphabetical order from Jack Anderson, who was 62, to Graham John Wright, 17.

The everlasting flame in the middle of the marble stone was burning brightly on a damp night in Liverpool before a home League match against Southampton. Bill Shankly used to say, 'Football's not a matter of life and death. It's much more important than that.' Here was clear evidence, if any were needed, that his maxim was patently untrue. Nothing is more important than life itself.

It was heartwarming to see the mementoes from rival fans lying among the wreaths. A mini 'We Follow Bolton Wanderers' scarf; a copy of *The Gooner* fanzine signed 'From all at the Arsenal'. They bore testimony to the links between supporters around the country. At the end of the day it's just a game. It's as well to remember that amid the clamour for success in modern football.

Next to the memorial stood the famous Shankly Gate, topped with the words to the title of the famous song 'You'll Never Walk Alone', dedicated to the former Liverpool manager. It was here that supporters tied scarves and laid flowers in the wake of Hillsborough. 'The saddest and most beautiful sight I have ever seen,' said Liverpool manager Kenny Dalglish. Supporters have to pass through the gates to reach the main stand.

Anfield may now be a Red Fortress standing proudly on top of the hill overlooking Stanley Park and the home of arch-rivals Everton across the park at Goodison, but it was once the Toffeemen who played at Anfield. Everton even won their first Championship there. But an argument with their landlord, John Houlding, saw them move to Mere Green, later Goodison, in 1892.

Houlding set up his own club and wanted to keep the Everton name, but the Football League ruled against it so, he chose Liverpool FC. That name was then challenged by the local rugby union club, so he settled on Liverpool AFC. Today few people even know that it was once the home of the team in blue across the park.

The area around Anfield remained relatively run-down. Portsmouth fans claim that they penned the words to the version of 'My Liverpool Home' first heard in the early '80s which begins: 'In your Liverpool slums'. Not that Liverpool Football Club can be accused of lagging behind in redeveloping their Anfield stadium in line with the Taylor Report. Sums of £8 million to redevelop the Centenary Stand, £9 million to rebuild the Kop and another couple of million for a second tier on the Anfield Road Stand showed the club's commitment to providing their fans with a first-class ground.

Indeed, Anfield was chosen as one of the eight venues for the European Championships, to the chagrin of the Blues across Stanley Park. The club conducts tours of the stadium and the museum: 'An Absolute Must for Every Football Fan or Visitor to Merseyside' says the club. 'At Anfield, the image of success is a shining one, as befits one of the most famous and successful football clubs in the world . . . follow in the footsteps of Bill Shankly and the hundreds of legendary players over the years.'

I was aiming to do just that before the match against the Saints. I began in the historic Anfield Museum and Trophy Room. The place is a cornucopia of footballing memorabilia from one of Bill Shankly's Scotland caps (he won five) to the boots worn by Billy Liddell, the Scottish-born winger known for his sportsmanship and his role in the Liverpool team of the '40s and '50s who were nicknamed Liddellpool.

There was also a telegram from Dixie Dean, the famous Everton centre-forward, the shirt worn by Ian St John in the 1965 FA Cup final and a shield presented by the Football League to commemorate Liverpool's achievement in winning three successive League titles between 1981–82 and 1983–84 (matching Huddersfield, Shankly's former team, in the '20s and the Arsenal side of the '30s).

Liverpool have never been outside the top two divisions. They had won a record 18 First Division Championships, four European Cups, four FA Cups, four League Cups, the UEFA Cup and the Super Cup. They are the only team to win three major trophies in one season (the League title, Milk Cup and European Cup in 1983–84). No other British club has appeared in more European competitions.

I took my seat in the Centenary Stand, opened by Lennart Johanssen, the President of UEFA, in the summer of 1992, the club's centenary year. It used to be the Kemlyn Road Stand, but was renamed after a second tier was added. The car park behind the stand had replaced the row of houses which was demolished to make way for the new development.

It had turned into a beautiful spring night and the drizzle which had dampened the city earlier in the evening had disappeared. Out in the middle of the pitch on the centre spot stood a small table. The Coca-Cola Cup sat on top. It was the perfect stage for the Liverpool team to parade the trophy they'd won the previous Saturday at Wembley by beating Bolton 2–1.

As I'd discovered on my travels, several stands around the country had taken on the name of Spion Kop. They were mostly mounds where the most fanatical fans stood to watch their team. But this was the most famous of them all – even if Arsenal claim to have had the first Kop. The name comes from Spion Kop, the hill in South Africa that was fought for by British troops, mainly from regiments in Lancashire, many of whom came from Liverpool, against Boer forces in January 1900.

More than 300 soldiers died in the attack on the hill including many of those from Liverpool. The Liverpool Kop got its name at the suggestion of journalist Ernest Edwards, sports editor of the local *Post and Echo*, as a tribute to those who died. Spion Kop actually means 'look-out' in Afrikaans and is therefore an appropriate name for a stand behind the goal.

The Southampton fans sat away to my right in the Anfield Road Stand with its seats of orange, ochre, violet red, green and cream – so different from the red seats around the rest of the stadium. The multi-colours were chosen deliberately when former Liverpool boss Bob Paisley complained, after watching a reserve match, that his players were almost invisible in their red shirts against the red seats originally installed at that end of the ground.

Bruce Grobbelaar was returning to Anfield for the first time since his free transfer the previous summer with match-fixing allegations hanging over his head. That didn't stop the Anfield faithful chanting his name as the 37-year-old keeper came out to warm up. He'd been a hero at Liverpool for 13 years, helping them win 13 major trophies.

The Saints took the lead after 14 minutes through Richard Hall after Grobbelaar's successor in the Liverpool goal, David James, could only palm out a Matt Le Tissier corner. The away fans went barmy at the Anfield Road End, singing their theme tune 'When the Saints Go Marching In'.

Liverpool were obviously still celebrating their Cup win and suffering a hangover and Southampton's goal had quietened down the celebrating home fans. Ian Rush soon revived their spirits, though, with a free header just before the half-hour for his 16th goal of the season. It seemed that the players had after all heeded demands from Evans to keep their feet on the accelerator after their Wembley win.

The Kop gave Grobbelaar a rapturous reception as he took up his position between the posts for the second half. The larger-than-life keeper responded by blowing kisses and bowing to his once-adoring fans. 'It was a great welcome and just what I expected,' he said after the match.

'It was lovely,' chipped in the Saints manager Alan Ball.

In the second half the referee gave a decision against Southampton which the Saints fans clearly disagreed with. 'Who's the Scouser in the black?' they sang accusingly. Shortly afterwards, Rush put Liverpool ahead with a 25-yard left-foot shot that beat Grobbelaar after a deflection off Hall. The Zimbabwean international keeper should have saved it and the Kop saw their chance for some fun. 'Who's the Scouser in the yellow?' they sang at Grobbelaar. Even he could see the funny side of it.

In the 70th minute Jason Dodd brought down Liverpool substitute Mark Walters, a replacement for defender Stig Inge Bjornebye, who'd been carried off on a stretcher after breaking his left leg. Robbie Fowler put away his 29th goal of the campaign from the spot. 'Evans, Evans, Evans,' sang the home fans. They were clearly delighted to see the Reds canter to another win.

After the match I took the lift down to the hospitality suites beneath the Centenary Stand. The walls of the Bill Shankly Suite were lined with pictures of the great man and photos of the teams he'd steered to success. Shankly had a successful playing career with Carlisle and then Preston, with whom he picked up an FA Cup winners' medal in 1938. His first managerial job was at Carlisle but he was also in charge at Grimsby, Workington and Huddersfield before joining Liverpool.

One of the local newspaper reports on his arrival at Anfield recounted his approach to the game. 'Shankly came because he thinks he can make Liverpool one of the greatest teams in the country. He will make a player kill a ball and move it all at the same time . . . ' Shankly wanted no hard drinking and no smoking amongst his players, though they were allowed to drink herbal tea!

The Bob Paisley Suite was similarly full of photographs of his Championship-winning teams and Paisley himself with Joe Fagan in the Anfield boot room. Paisley won a Championship medal with Liverpool in 1947 and first joined the coaching staff in 1954, eventually becoming Shankly's right-hand man. He inherited the manager's job in 1974 and became the most successful manager in the history of the English game before stepping down in 1983.

HEADING FOR THE DROP

Cardiff City v Rotherham United – Ninian Park, 8 April 1995

Cardiff City won the FA Cup in 1927 – the one and only time the trophy has been held aloft by a club outside England. Their team included an Englishman, three Scots, four Irishmen and just three Welshmen, but there can be no dispute that Cardiff are definitely a Welsh team. After all, they've won the Welsh Cup 21 times. They also reached the semi-final of the Cup-Winners' Cup in 1968 – a good year for British clubs in Europe with Manchester United winning the European Cup at Wembley.

The Bluebirds' League form has been less inspiring, although in the 1923–24 season they were runners-up in the First Division. Cardiff needed two points from a win in their final match against Birmingham to win the League title, but missed a penalty late in the game and only managed a draw. Since 1962 they've played their football outside the top flight and in more recent years have spent most of their time between the bottom two divisions.

On a bright sunny Saturday afternoon in April they faced the dreaded drop back to Division Three, the lowest rung on the League ladder after the formation of the Premier League and the changing of the divisional labels which abolished the Fourth Division. Their visitors were Rotherham, a few places higher and almost out of trouble, but still mathematically within reach of the relegation net.

Ninian Park, a former rubbish tip on the edge of Leckwith Common, between Sloper Road in Grangetown and the Taff Vale railway line, has changed little over the years as I would discover when taking my seat in the original part of the Main Stand. The ground is named after Lord Ninian Crichton Stuart, second son of the third Marquis of Bute. It was to have been called Sloper Park, after the nearby street, but Lord Ninian's name was used instead to acknowledge his help in securing the lease.

The first international at Ninian Park was in March 1911 when Wales played Scotland, but it was the visit of England in October 1961 that attracted the record crowd of more than 61,000. It was the biggest gate for a Welsh international match played in Wales. Traditionally, Ninian Park staged about two-thirds of the national team's home matches, but in recent years the venue had been on a more equal footing with other grounds like Swansea's Vetch Field and Wrexham's Racecourse Ground.

I knocked on the door of the club secretary's office at Ninian Park. 'Come in,' he said. 'Take a seat. I won't keep you long.' His desk was piled high with letters and papers. One of them was a long list of questions from the *Rothmans Football Yearbook* – an annual task for all the clubs. 'What can I do for you?' he asked. I explained that I'd come along as part of my record attempt and would like to see the ground. Could he show me round? Well, actually, no; he was quite busy today. But I could take a look around myself.

I walked into the main foyer to see what the club called 'a pictorial display of practically every player to have appeared for the Bluebirds in our history' – the nickname coming from Cardiff's blue kit.

The display began at the foot of the main staircase and continued up into the John Charles Suite on the first floor. There was also a trophy cabinet in the foyer containing a couple of international caps, pennants from some of the great European teams who have played at Ninian Park in the Cup-Winners' Cup, including Real Madrid, Dynamo Berlin and Real Zaragosa, and an old photo of the 1927 FA Cup-winning team with the Cup they proudly brought back to Wales.

The defeat of Arsenal at Wembley is the most memorable event in Cardiff's history. Ironically, it was an error by a Welshman, the Gunners keeper Dan Lewis, which allowed Hughie Ferguson (a good Welsh name if ever I heard one) to score the goal that secured a famous victory. There's a painting of that precious moment on the wall in the main entrance. Underneath, it said: 'The most famous goal in Cardiff's illustrious history. Len Davies follows up as Arsenal's goalkeeper Dan Lewis allows Hughie Ferguson's shot to drift into the net for the only goal of the game.'

Meanwhile, Mystic Meg was trying to forecast the winner of the day's big race on the TV at the far end of the John Charles Suite as I wandered in. The suite was dominated by a black and white photograph of the famous Welshman in action during his playing days. Charles was nicknamed *Il Buon Gigante* (the Gentle Giant) by his adoring Italian fans, since he weighed almost 14 stone and was more than six feet tall.

Charles ended his career at Cardiff, retiring in 1966 after returning to Wales from Roma in 1963. Born in Swansea, he joined Leeds in 1947 and in 1950 became the youngest player ever to win a Welsh cap. He helped Leeds win promotion from the Second Division in 1956 and was the top scorer in the First

Division the following season with 38 goals. He left Leeds for Juventus, and won three League titles and two Italian Cups before briefly rejoining Leeds in 1962 and then Roma.

'Who's the best player you've seen at Ninian Park over the years?' I later asked the elderly man next to me in the Main Stand.

'I've seen great players here. Stanley Matthews, Tom Finney, the Busby Babes, George Best. I suppose Best was the most exciting. But we had some good players ourselves you know. Ivor Allchurch, John Charles and his brother, Trevor Ford. They were the best.' He didn't mention John Toshack but he must surely rank alongside the greats Cardiff have produced.

'Eddie Mays, Eddie Mays, Eddie Mays,' sang the crowd as the manager took his seat in the dugout for an hour and a half of nailbiting relegation football which would go a long way to determining his side's fate. Cardiff started well and created most of the chances in a scrappy first half. The breakthrough came in the 35th minute after a spell of pressure. Cardiff's skilful winger Cohen Griffith scored from inside the six-yard box after a shot was blocked by Rotherham keeper Matt Clark.

The Rotherham players had names on their shirts in contrast to the Cardiff team which just had white numbers on the back of their royal-blue tops. Late in the first half I noticed two Millers playing for Rotherham and, after a bad foul, the fan behind me said jokingly to his mate, 'The ref should book that Millers.' I suddenly realised that every Rotherham player had the word Millers on his back and the penny dropped. It's the club's nickname! I know it seems impossible not to have noticed but there you go.

Each bad Rotherham foul, and there weren't that many, was greeted with 'You dirty English bastards,' by the Cardiff faithful seated in the Canton Stand to my left. I figured the chant simplified things, since the fans didn't have to differentiate between the north and south of England. One chant would cover almost every team they played with the exception of arch-rivals Swansea and almost arch-rivals Wrexham.

The hostility between Cardiff and Swansea was intense. The League encounters had resulted in trouble, with the Swansea fans pelting the home supporters with coins, cans and anything else they could lay their hands on during the match in September when they drew 1–1. The Cardiff fans were banned for the return game at the Vetch Field in early March, which Swansea won 4–1, and that ban would again be in force for the first leg of the Welsh Cup semi-final.

Against Rotherham, Cardiff seemed to take control after their goal and should have added to their tally, but they missed a couple of excellent chances in the second half. They'd live to regret their largesse. In the 87th minute Rotherham equalised. All Cardiff's good work had been undone in an instant and their chances of avoiding relegation hung by a thread. Most of their rivals near the bottom of the Second Division had won and the Bluebirds faced tough away games at table-topping Brentford and Birmingham.

The fans took the blow well. I suppose they must have known their hold on the Second Division place, which they'd earned by winning the old Fourth Division Championship in 1992, was slipping. They trooped to Ninian Park station behind the Popular Stand after the match. Their average age couldn't have been more than 15, but they made a lot of noise and, as they banged the roof from inside the train, sounded intimidating. But they were basically a bunch of school kids. I couldn't believe they'd brought Cardiff such a notorious reputation for hooliganism over the years.

THE MYSTERY OF THE ORIENT

Leyton Orient v Bristol Rovers – Brisbane Road, 11 April 1995

I took my dad along to Brisbane Road to watch the Orient play against Bristol Rovers. It was the least I could do, since he'd encouraged me every step of the way with my record attempt. But there was another reason why it was appropriate for him to accompany me to what's more formally known as the Leyton Stadium. He'd actually played for the O's in the late '40s and early '50s when Alec Stock was the manager.

He wasn't a first-team regular, mind you, since in those days it was very hard for a youngster to break into the side and the old pro's tended to extend their careers by slipping down the leagues and ending up at places like Orient. Today the speed of the game and the lack of resources in the lower divisions means young players tend to get more opportunities to show what they can do. So my dad never really got his chance.

But he played against Tottenham's international full-back ('I ran rings around him,' he claims) and the O's have always been his team. It was inevitable really, since his dad was an Orient fan and I guess his mum was too. Not that I would be subjected to following a team of no-hopers whose highest League placing was bottom of the First Division in 1963. I was spared years in the supporting wilderness and followed Spurs.

Although the O's have never been very successful there's something attractive about the club. They are almost always the underdogs and most neutrals support them. There's also something magical about their name. Its origins can be traced back to the Orient Steam Navigation Company. A number of the company's employees became involved with the club and, at the suggestion of a player, it adopted the name Orient.

In 1898, while playing at the Whittle Athletic Ground, they changed their name to Clapton Orient, because they thought it made the club sound more respectable. Then in 1946 they changed their name to Leyton Orient and in 1966 simply to Orient when the local council became part of the borough of Waltham Forest. Since 1987 they've gone back to Leyton Orient. But whatever they decide to call themselves doesn't really matter. Everyone knows them as Orient, or the O's. And most people known their ground as Brisbane Road rather than the official title of the Leyton Stadium.

In March 1937 a record crowd of almost 20,500 crammed into Orient's ground at Lea Bridge for a Third Division game against Millwall and the club realised that the stadium wouldn't be suitable for big games unless a lot of money was spent on refurbishment. Instead, they moved to Brisbane Road in 1937, replacing

Leyton Amateurs. At that time there was one stand on the west side and no concrete terracing.

By the time England were lifting the World Cup in 1966 Orient had slipped into the Third Division and were so broke that buckets had to be passed around the crowd to prevent the club going bankrupt. In 1970 Orient had at least got it right on the pitch when they won the Third Division Championship. But in October that year their existence was threatened again by debts of £100,000 – an alarming figure at the time. A public meeting was called and only a generous response from the fan and the sale of Tommy Taylor to West Ham for £100,000 saved the club.

The O's held their own in the Second Division for 12 years during which little changed, except for seats being installed on the West Terrace in 1977 to meet the requirements of the Safety of Sports Grounds Act. By 1982 they'd slipped back to the Third Division and in 1985 the O's dropped into the Fourth Division for the first time in their history. They regained their Third Division place in 1989 which is where they were when I saw them, except that the Third Division had become the Second Division by then after the Premier League was started in 1992.

My dad's connection with the Orient (he eventually left for Crystal Palace after playing for his battalion in the Army) ensured that I'd always have a soft spot for them. In fact, most Londoners look up the Orient result whichever team they follow and most people want the O's to do well – unless they're playing their own team. But situated between West Ham and Spurs hasn't helped attendances. I'd been to Brisbane Road, which surprisingly has the widest pitch in the League, on many occasions. If one game stands out, then it has to be a famous Cup match against a flamboyant Chelsea side.

It was 1971 and the Blues arrived with a team of stars including Peter Osgood and David Webb. They were the Cup-holders having beaten Leeds 2–1 in a replay at Old Trafford during which Webb scored the winner with a header. The First Division side stormed into a 2–0 lead, but Orient fought back to 2–2. When they equalised, the wooden box I'd been standing on was destroyed as the crush barrier behind us collapsed and the crowd surged forward As a small boy I was frightened and wanted to leave, but my dad insisted on staying to see Orient snatch the winner through the bearded Barrie Fairbrother. It was a famous victory and the O's went on to the quarter-finals.

Towards the end of the decade, in 1978, the O's went on another Cup run under manager Jimmy Bloomfield, who was in his second spell at the club. They beat three First Division teams before losing to Arsenal in the semi-final at Stamford Bridge. Although they just missed out on a Wembley appearance, the O's had played there in the League in November 1930. The Football League had ruled that the speedway track at the Lea Bridge Speedway Stadium, which Orient used as a home ground, was too close to the touchlines. Since the pitch was already the minimum width, they were told to lay extra turf, but the speedway company refused and the O's had to find another ground.

Wembley agreed to Orient playing their next League match against Brentford at the national stadium. A crowd of just over 10,000 turned up to see the O's win 3–0. Their next home game was at Highbury where they entertained Luton in an FA Cup tie. Two days later they were back at the twin towers against Southend, but only 2,500 came along which didn't cover Wembley's cut. Fortunately, by then the speedway company had agreed to widen the pitch and Orient returned to Lea Bridge. Wembley has never staged a regular season League match since.

The chances of Orient getting back to Wembley are pretty remote, though it's possible they could make the play-offs some day. Their chances had improved since snooker impresario Barry Hearn had taken over the club in March 1995. The Matchroom boss had arranged for an open meeting with the fans to outline his plans for the future of the club and to answer their questions. Hearn's plans included stepping up Orient's community work, staging boxing bouts at the ground and giving local kids season tickets for £10. Not surprisingly, season ticket sales went up four-fold.

At the time of my visit for the game against Bristol Rovers the club had other, more immediate concerns – like trying to improve their performances to avoid the drop to Division Three. The O's were second from bottom of the table with only Chester below and an 11-point gap to Cardiff above. The game against the Gasheads had been rearranged because the original fixture had been postponed because of a frozen pitch. But it was Rovers' fourth visit to east London.

Before the match my dad and I were given a quick tour, which didn't amount to much apart from a brief walk on the pitch and enough time to pop our heads around the dressing-room door to wish the lads good luck. Our seats were in the wooden East Stand which, though dated, was at least brightly painted in red and white. Apparently, the gable on the roof of the stand, which isn't quite centered because it was put in the middle when the first phase was built, may have once been used as the steward's box at the Mitcham greyhound track.

To our left was the uncovered South Terrace, which was to be replaced with a new 3,000-seater stand containing an indoor sports hall for the club's Football in the Community scheme as well as the obligatory bars and executive suites. On our right was the North Terrace, which, it was hoped, would be replaced by a new stand that included club offices and a conference centre. To the west of the West Stand were the famous Hackney Marshes, which had spawned many a talented footballer over the years and was once said to have more football pitches in one place than anywhere else in the world. The plans for a new West Stand included workshops, a performing arts centre and a studio. It would, indeed, be a brave new world.

Whether or not Orient could produce a team to match their grandiose plans for a new stadium remained to be seen. Today's match was being billed as 'the decider', since Rovers had knocked Orient out of the FA Cup, though the O's had gained revenge in the Auto Windscreens Shield. The return League match at Twerton Park wouldn't take place until 22 April. Meanwhile, the Gasheads were pushing for a return to the First Division and stood in fourth position. The respective League positions meant that a 2–1 home defeat came as no surprise to the Orient faithful. Unlike their predecessors in the 1950s the fans took it all in their stride. In a way their passive acceptance of defeat showed just what a big job Barry 'I won't tolerate failure' Hearn had on his hands.

A MATTER OF LIFE AND DEATH

Crystal Palace v Tottenham Hotspur – Selhurst Park, 14 April 1995

Palace season ticket holder Paul Nixon had been killed in Walsall the previous Sunday before the Eagles' FA Cup semi-final against Manchester United at Villa Park. Today there would be a minute's silence in front of the Selhurst Park faithful – and at grounds across the country – in memory of the unfortunate Paul Nixon. This event overshadowed the match against Spurs and, indeed, all the other games played on this Good Friday. It seemed that some things are more important than football after all.

Cantona's kung-fu attack on Palace fan Matthew Simmonds the night I was at Villa Park, and the Frenchman's subsequent ban, had fanned the ill-will between United and Palace supporters. It had become clear very early on the day of the FA Cup semi-final in Birmingham that most United fans held a grudge against their Palace counterparts. But few could have expected those bad feelings to result in the death of a supporter.

The match programme for the Spurs' game included a regular column called 'Selhurst Standpoint' by Paul Romain. His message was clear. 'Whilst the Frenchman can obviously not be held responsible for what happened last week, this latest tragedy should bring it home to all players that their actions on the pitch can have far reaching consequences. It is a huge responsibility they bear, however unreasonable they think it to be, to act with restraint and with due regard to the potential for supporters of any club to adopt them as some sort of martyr for a dubious cause.'

Palace manager Alan Smith had started his programme notes 'From the Boss' expressing his sympathy for Nixon's family. 'Both myself and all of the players were shocked to hear the sad news on returning to our hotel after the game. Let me make it clear that violence in sport, both on and off the field, is completely unacceptable. The game of football is to be enjoyed by everybody participating, whether as a spectator or as a player. The sooner that any form of violence within our game is eliminated the better, and when it so tragically ends in someone's death it really does put the whole sport into perspective.'

Palace haven't always played at Selhurst Park. The club was formed in 1861 by workers of the company that owned Joseph Paxton's famous iron and glass Crystal Palace Exhibition building in Hyde Park. The team played in the park grounds before moving to Upper Sydenham heights in south London, where Paxton's Crystal Palace building was rehoused after the Great Exhibition. Selhurst and the surrounding area lie at the foot of the hill on which the palace stood until it was ruined by a fire in 1936.

Palace entered the very first FA Cup competition in 1871, when they got to the semi-final, but their association with the competition would soon become much closer than that. By the turn of the century their ground was the country's main sporting venue and from 1895 until 1914 it staged the FA Cup final. The pitch was beside Paxton's glass palace in what was once the bed of an artificial lake. The supporters could stroll around the grounds and enjoy picnics before and after matches. Those were the days!

It has changed a lot since then. The Whitehorse Lane Stand, with two tiers of executive boxes, was built in the summer of 1993, whereas the massive Holmesdale Road, or Kop, terracing was demolished in May 1994 to make way for a two-tier all-seater stand. The roof of the new stand had just begun to take shape: when the first section was hoisted into place the week before my visit. The roof sections were built in Fleetwood, Lancashire, and transported to Selhurst Park on huge low loader vehicles. It was sad that the old Kop had gone, but the new stand was impressive.

I'd been to Palace twice before, once for a League Cup tie against Spurs back in the early 1980s, when Steve Perryman inspired the away side to victory; and again at the end of last season, when a poor Tottenham team was well beaten by Palace's tenants Wimbledon. I stood up in the corner of the Holmesdale Road End for the game against the Dons and was amazed at how ramshackle it was for a Premier League side.

Before this match, I was given a tour of the ground which took in the various hospitality suites and restaurants. Palace seemed to have more of them than most other clubs I'd visited. The directors' room included a large trophy cabinet. One side was filled with Palace's silverware and the other with Wimbledon's. Now that's what I call sharing! The large Zenith Data Systems Cup, won by the Eagles in 1991, was displayed on a small table opposite the trophy cabinet, near the bar.

There was, however, a space on the Palace side of the cabinet. 'That's where we usually put the First Division Championship trophy,' said my guide. 'I think they've taken it away to be cleaned today.'

Palace's only other major success was as Second Division champions in 1979 and Third Division champions in 1921. Their most successful manager was Steve Coppell who has since returned to the hot seat after Alan Smith's departure. Coppell took the Eagles into the old First Division in 1989 and to a best-ever League finish of third in 1991, the 1990 FA Cup final and the 1993 League Cup semi-final.

I took my seat in the Main Stand on the Clifton Road side of the ground, in the corner near the Sainsbury's End. Palace had leased that part of the ground and the large car park behind for £2 million in 1983, bringing much needed funds into the club. The supermarket was built on the car park with the terraces refitted along the back wall. Sainsbury's now dominates the entrance to the club from Whitehorse Lane.

Opposite was the Arthur Wait Stand, completed in 1969 when Palace reached the First Division for the first time after a remarkable rise from the Fourth Division in 1961. It was named after the club's long-serving chairman who, being a builder, helped in the construction of his stand. Imagine Sir John Hall or Jack Walker doing that!

After the match I went for a drink in the social club underneath the Main Stand. The TVs hanging from the ceiling were showing an interview with Jürgen Klinsmann. The main question on everybody's lips was 'Would he stay or would he go?' He said at the time that he hadn't made his decision yet, but would consider his options after the season was over. He did, and he went. Alan Sugar was impressed, wasn't he?

ONE GILBERT ALSOP

Walsall v Rochdale – The Bescot Stadium, 15 April 1995

I couldn't miss Walsall's Bescot Stadium. The home of the Saddlers, just off the M6 motorway, was marked by a large illuminated sign on the William Sharp Stand in Bescot Crescent. When I drove past, it was advertising the Korean electronics firm Daewoo. The pulling power of a sign standing next to what's thought to be the busiest section of motorway in Europe was reflected in the rush of advertisers queuing up to replace Daewoo when their contract came up. Walsall appreciated the advertising income, but would have been even more ecstatic if they had a team good enough to fill the ground.

The club moved to their new home in 1990, when Sir Stanley Matthews opened the £4.5 million stadium for a friendly against Aston Villa. The H.L. Fellows Stand, where I sat to watch them take on Rochdale in a Third Division match, was named after a former popular club chairman who was on the board from 1921 to 1938. Like all the other stands at the Bescot, the Main Stand was an anonymous grey colour with touches of red. It contained the club offices and some executive lounges plus 13 boxes.

Len Fellows' star was falling, since he'd had the name of Walsall's previous ground, Fellows Park, all to himself. There was now a supermarket where the stadium used to be. You could see the site on the left just before turning off the M6 into Bescot Crescent. It was one of only four League grounds named after individuals (the others are Bournemouth's Dean Court, Wycombe's Adams Park and Cardiff's Ninian Park). Nevertheless, I was sure Fellows wouldn't begrudge sharing the new ground.

The William Sharp Stand, to the right, got its name from the engineering firm based in nearby Bescot Crescent. Opposite, between the Highgate Mild Stand, named after a local brew, and the H.L. Fellows Stand, was the Gilbert Alsop Stand where the die-hard home supporters congregated. Gilbert was a legend in his own lifetime among Walsall fans. Holder of the club scoring record for his 40 goals in the Third Division (North) in both the 1933–34 and 1934–35 seasons, Gilbert scored one of the most famous goals in the Saddlers' history in a shock FA Cup win over mighty Arsenal. He went on to join the groundstaff and worked at the club for 20 years in that capacity before passing away in 1992. There really was only one Gilbert Alsop.

Walsall haven't achieved much since they were formed as a result of the 1888 amalgamation of Walsall Town and Walsall Town Swifts (hence the club's red swift crest). They had to apply for League re-election a record seven times. The club's highest League position was sixth place in the old Second Division in 1899 and their only major honour was the 1960 Fourth Division title.

But in January 1933 Walsall's name was on everyone's lips. They'd drawn

Arsenal in the third round of the FA Cup at Fellows Park. The mighty Gunners team, fashioned by the legendary Herbert Chapman, was full of internationals and rated as the best in the country. Arsenal were known as the '£30,000 aristocrats'. They sat proudly on top of the First Division. Walsall were tenth in the Third Division (North), ten points behind leaders Chester. Their entire team cost £69 – less than the Arsenal team's boots. Walsall were truly unexceptional and hadn't won a game for a month. They'd only been beyond the third round of the Cup once. Nobody gave them a chance.

For various reasons Chapman left out four regular first-team players, including Hapgood, from the Gunners' line-up. But the side still included David Jack, Alex James and Cliff Bastin. *The Times* said they should beat Walsall easily, but added that 'when there are so many strange faces, one can never tell.' How prophetic. The narrow, muddy, sloping Fellows Park pitch foxed the Gunners. Alsop headed the first goal and was brought down in the penalty area to set up the second. The noise from the home fans could be heard two miles away.

Walsall not only won, they deserved to win. The *Times* report reflected the balance of the game. 'Walsall's football was better, much more virile, and so roused to the occasion that from the start they had Arsenal in difficulties.' It was one of the most sensational giant-killings of all-time. Newspapers double-checked with their correspondents for confirmation they'd reported the score the right way round. Arsenal fans at Highbury watching a reserve match laughed when they were told the result. They thought it was a joke. But, unfortunately for them, it wasn't.

Cliff Bastin recalled the match in his book *Cliff Bastin Remembers*: 'On my way home to my lodgings that night in the Underground Railway I felt positively suicidal. Visions of the Arsenal goals that might have been rose up before my eyes; hopes that the events of the afternoon had been nothing but an evil nightmare would delude me for a brief moment, only to be banished away by the cold, grim reality. Walsall 2, Arsenal 0. Nothing could change those figures.'

Even Arsenal fans with shorter memories were unlikely to have a soft spot for Walsall. In 1984, the Saddlers reached the first Cup semi-final in their 96-year history after beating the Gunners again along the way – this time by 2–1 in the fourth round of the Milk Cup. They went on to reach the semi-final and took 9,000 fans to Anfield – double their average home gate – where they fought a magnificent 2–2 draw with holders Liverpool. The West Midlands club were just one game from Wembley. Fellows Park was packed with 20,000 fans for the second leg against the Reds, but the fairy-tale ended when Walsall were beaten by 2–0.

They'd achieved little in recent years beyond their move to a new stadium. The fact that David Kelly, the Saddlers' record transfer at £600,000 to West Ham in 1988, was rated as one of their famous players in *The Football Almanack* spoke volumes about the quality of their team in the '80s and '90s. But they'd had a good season and needed just one point from the match against Rochdale to secure a play-off spot.

Player–coach Kevin Wilson, former Chelsea forward and a Northern Ireland international, looked sharp up front alongside Bermudan striker Kyle Lightbourne. Keeper Trevor Wood, also in the Northern Ireland set-up, looked secure. Former Spurs midfielder Scott Houghton hustled and bustled. But for all their effort, Walsall could not break down the Rochdale defence. It finished 0–0 at the Bescot – a ground more than capable of hosting a higher class of football.

The Black Country town is best known for its leather industry, hence Walsall's nickname, the Saddlers, and to some it is known as the birthplace of Jerome K. Jerome, author of *Three Men in a Boat*. As long as Walsall's football team remains overshadowed by nearby Birmingham City and Aston Villa, the football club is unlikely to steal the limelight.

STARSHIP ENTERPRISE

Huddersfield Town v Hull City – The Alfred McAlpine Stadium, 17 April 1995

'We call that the Starship Enterprise,' said the steward walking along the touchline in the shadow of the Main Stand. Light rain was drizzling across the stadium on a damp spring Saturday afternoon. The steward, a short woman in her thirties, looked up at the control box supported by two of the huge concrete struts which form the base of a floodlight pylon at Huddersfield's futuristic McAlpine Kirklees stadium. Science fiction meets the Endsleigh League.

I'd heard a lot about Huddersfield's super new stadium from other supporters on my travels and I was looking forward to seeing it first-hand. The ground was hard to miss. As I turned off the High Road the banana-shaped roof of the Main Stand appeared like a huge alien spacecraft out of the film *Close Encounters of the Third Kind*. I wondered if Spielberg had been called in to help design the state-of-the-art arena. I thought I might see aliens, but the only ones I came across were the away fans.

The new 51-acre site was close to the banks of the River Colne, near the club's former ground at Leeds Road. It was an emotional afternoon on 30 April 1994 when Huddersfield said goodbye to the ground that had been their home for the past 83 years with a League match against Blackpool. The game was billed as the 'End of an Era' and many of Town's former stars turned up, including Ray Wilson, England's full-back in the '66 World Cup final.

Huddersfield were founded in 1908 after a meeting in the Imperial Hotel two years earlier at which it was decided that a football club could be formed in what was a strong rugby area. The competition from the oval ball is still there today and Town actually share their new ground with the local Rugby League club. The football club ticket office was to the right of the main entrance, while the rugby club offices were to the left, decked out in claret and gold. I walked around the stadium to the open end where the North Stand would be built when the club could afford it. From the car park behind the goal I could see the whole town down below me.

In the mid-'20s Huddersfield dominated League football. They won the FA Cup in 1922 and were runners-up in the First Division in 1923 before becoming the first club ever to win the Championship three seasons in a row, between 1924 and 1926. Town were presented with a large shield by the Football League to commemorate their achievement and visitors to the ground can see the trophy at the top of the stairs on the first floor of the executive suites. They were also runners-up in 1927 and 1928 before the glory days ended. If they'd won all six titles, the record would have stood for ever!

Only Arsenal (1933–35) and Liverpool (1982–84) have emulated that triple title feat. Ironically, it was the great Herbert Chapman, who later took Arsenal to three successive League Championships, who steered Town to their first two League titles. Chapman's Arsenal also ended Town's record-breaking unbeaten home run in the FA Cup which lasted from 1913 until 1932!

Town stayed in the First Division until 1952, got promoted at the first attempt, were relegated again in 1956 and then spent 14 years in the Second Division. Bill Shankly was in charge for the first three of those campaigns, before joining Liverpool in 1959, and thus managed Denis Law who played for the Terriers in the late '50s. Other great players to grace Huddersfield's old Leeds Road ground were Ray Wilson, who went on to become a member of England's World Cup winning team in '66 when he was playing for Everton, and Steve Kindon who also played for Burnley and Wolves.

Huddersfield regained their place in the top flight in 1970, when players like Trevor Cherry and Frank Worthington wore their colours, but lasted just two seasons in the First Division. By 1973 the Terriers had dropped into the Third Division for the first time and two years later they were in the Fourth.

The McAlpine Stadium was certainly built for a higher level of football. When the club assessed its options for a new ground, it followed a number of clubs who'd already moved into new stadiums. Paul Fletcher, chief executive of Kirklees Stadium Development and Huddersfield Town, and a director of Huddersfield Rugby League Club, explains:

> The answer could have been very simple. We only needed to visit other stadiums recently built. Walsall's Bescot Stadium, Scunthorpe's Glanfield Park, even St Johnstone's McDiarmid Park Stadium seemed to answer the problem. But if we had followed any of these straightforward examples we would have ensured Huddersfield Town would never be a big club ever again. A basic eight, ten or twelve thousand seater stadium would relegate the club to the lower divisions for ever. We chose not to visit any of these stadiums. We had bigger plans for Huddersfield Town. We all had a dream, a vision, a mission.

On Valentine's Day 1992 the project team left Manchester airport for Toronto. They decided to start by visiting probably the best stadium in the world: the Skydome. Canada's premier arena, and home of the Toronto Blue Jays baseball team, was finished in 1991 at a cost of $300 million. It's used for about 200 events a year, more than any other stadium in the world. Its features include a sliding roof, which closes in 20 minutes, and a hydraulic seating system used to create purpose-built pitches for a variety of sports and other activities including baseball, American football and soccer.

The term 'spectator friendly' became the theme for every decision from the quality seats to the 'knee room', toilets, concourse flooring, concessions and everything else. The project team constantly sought quality rather than quantity.

The Kirklees Stadium design is based on computerised calculations of the ideal viewing distances and sightlines, resulting in an oval plan with four shell-like stands all close to the pitch.

The early plans also showed a completed 25,000 all-seater stadium with a 5,000-seater North Stand including a gymnasium and a health club. However, the Football Trust insisted that the club didn't overstretch its resources, pointing out that success on the pitch would attract enough money to build the fourth stand. The club hopes to start building within the next couple of years, keeping in mind that the foundations will have to be able to take 5,000–10,000 seats if Huddersfield reach the Premier League. There were also plans to include a cinema and a ski slope in the design for the new stand.

According to Town's chief executive Paul Fletcher it will become 'a venue for legends. It will see tears of joy and tears of sadness'. And it will witness 'great victories by Huddersfield Town and Huddersfield Rugby League Club and also, without doubt, disastrous defeats. Fabulous memories of goals, tries, tackles, sending-offs. Memories that will be traded in bars, often distorted with age. Grandchildren will visit the stadium with their grandads . . . and one day bring grandchildren of their own.'

And talking of disastrous defeats . . . Hull almost caused one when they took the lead through their big centre-back Rob Dewhurst seconds after the break. Most of the 12,000 crowd fell silent whereas the Hull supporters went barmy in the South Stand. 'I thought we did well in the first half against the wind and I told my players at half-time, if it takes until into injury time to make it 1–0 that will be enough – but Hull scored before I sat down in the dugout,' said Town manager Neil Warnock. After that it was one-way traffic as Huddersfield sought the equaliser.

Huddersfield had 17 goal attempts in the last 34 minutes during which they won eight of their 11 corners. There were shots, headers, penalty claims, goalmouth scrambles. You name it, the Terriers threw it at Hull. But the Tigers held out gallantly to survive the second-half onslaught until centre-back Lee Sinnott grabbed his first goal for Town 17 minutes from time with a header at the far post from a fine angled cross by Mike Duxbury. With a minute to go Huddersfield drove in a corner which came back off the far post and was followed by a goalmouth scramble. But still the Terriers couldn't score the winner. Then it was all over.

I'd enjoyed the electronic scoreboard almost as much as the football. In the first half Huddersfield had a shot which sailed over the bar. DEAD BALL flashed up on the screen with a picture of a gun alongside. Each time there was a corner a big white hand appeared pointing to a corner spot. The scoreboard also gave weather flashes. IT'S GETTING WINDY, it announced towards the end of the first half, just in case I hadn't noticed as the rain swirled down across the front row of seats in the Riverside Stand – the only complaint I had about the design of the stadium.

And that wasn't all. At half-time there was an announcement over the PA system as details flashed up on the scoreboard asking for volunteers to attend an identity parade. 'Six foot tall, of slim build, mousey hair, clean shaven. £5 per hour plus travelling expenses. To be held at Dews Police Station.' (I wondered what would happen if one of the volunteers was picked out as the villain.) And if you were hungry at half-time the scoreboard had some suggestions. GET 'EM

317

WHILE THEY'RE HOT flashed up after a picture of a hotdog being garnished with relish had appeared in full, delicious colour.

ARE YOU WATCHING, EXETER?

Scarborough v Darlington – The McCain Stadium, 18 April 1995

Some teams have a chip on their shoulder. They should be in Scarborough's position. The team based just outside the North-East coastal town know all about chips. Their sponsors are McCain – famous for the frozen variety you shove in the oven to go with your eggs, beans and sausages. You can't fail to establish the connection. The ground is called the McCain Stadium. Then there's the McCain Stand, the McCain Lounge and the McCain tracksuits worn by the players. The main match sponsors for tonight's match against Darlington? McCain of course.

What's it like to be propping up the Endsleigh League? Well, it changes your perspective on life and scales down your ambitions. Manchester United may have been chasing another Premiership and FA Cup double; Scarborough's sights were set just slightly lower. 'We desperately want to finish off the foot of the table – the goal I set the team when I took over,' said manager Ray McHale. The injured Stuart Hicks was also getting excited. 'The lads have got us on a bit of a roll at the moment and to get off the bottom would be brilliant for all of us and you the supporters as well.'

The *Scarborough Evening News* was also pinning its hopes on the team climbing off the bottom of the league. Under the headline 'Win or bust for Boro' local reporter Pete Oliver outlined the importance of this Tuesday-night match against Darlington. 'It's D-day for Boro who must send Darlington packing at the McCain Stadium tonight to keep their season alive.' Keep it alive? Most fans believe a season is dead once their team have been knocked out of both domestic cups and is out of contention for a championship, play-off or relegation place. But not at Scarborough.

Here was an ambitious club. There wasn't much money about, but what they had they used well. On the wall in the boardroom was a plan for the new stadium they hoped to build. Part of it already existed. The new Seamer Road Stand had just been officially opened by the legendary Tom Finney before the previous home match against Preston.

Some supporters were overwhelmed by the new developments. During the match I overheard two supporters talking about the impact the new stand had made on the team. 'Isn't it strange how we always seem to be attacking the new East Stand in the second half, the way Liverpool usually attack the Kop?' I didn't like to tell them that was where the similarity ended. In fact, they spent most of the match talking about who would win the Premiership and the FA Cup. Scarborough was way down their list of conversation topics.

I had earlier been taken into the boardroom, where this evening's invited guests were indulging in a pre-match drink at the bar. On the wall hung a certificate from the Football Association presented to Scarborough to commemorate their participation in the 100th FA Cup competition in 1981. A shelf around the wall held some of the trophies won by the club since they were founded in 1880. Pride of place went to the GM Vauxhall Conference trophy from the 1986–87 season – their passport to League football. On the far wall was a painting of the match against Arsenal in the Coca-Cola Cup in 1992 which Scarborough lost 1–0. They'd hoped for a draw and a lucrative replay at Highbury.

Scarborough had hit a rich vein of form of late and had narrowed the gap at the bottom from eight points to two. The crowd of just over 2,000 were in good voice: 'Come on, Boro, Come on, Boro,' they sang as thoughts of moving off the bottom of the League inspired them to get behind their team. They wouldn't get a better chance of winning than the match against Darlington. The Quakers were in 18th position and hadn't won in a ten-game stretch, nine of those under new manager Paul Futcher, during which they'd scored only two goals. Former Grimsby star Futcher, a surprise replacement for sacked Darlington boss Alan Murray, was already feeling the heat.

Scarborough's task seemed more daunting on the night as lanky centre-forward Jason White was shown the red card after an elbowing incident on the halfway line. But two goals from Boro number seven Robert Scott, on loan from Sheffield United, helped them to a 3–1 win. His second goal was superb. Scott side-stepped one tackle, just inside the 18-yard box, before driving the ball into the top left-hand corner of the net. He stood in front of the home fans in the East Stand, his arms raised in triumph. 'Ray McHale's barmy army,' sang the delirious Boro supporters.

After the second goal the fans in the new East Stand began singing, '2–0 to the Scarborough, 2–0 to the Scarborough' followed by 'Are you watching, Exeter? Are you watching, Exeter?' I was baffled. I conjured up a map of Britain in my mind and located Exeter down on the south-west coast. 'That's miles from here,' I thought, recalling the usual circumstances in which such singing occurs when the fans of one team taunt their local rivals, usually when the game is televised live. Exeter were not local rivals and this match was definitely not on the telly. Then it hit me. Of course. Exeter were second from bottom of the Endsleigh Third Division.

Towards the end of the match the Darlington fans decided it was time for another appointment in the managerial merry-go-round at Feethams. 'We want Futcher out, say we want Futcher out,' they sang. They would soon get their way. Just in case the message hadn't got through they decided to reinforce it with an assessment of their team's qualities. 'We're shit, and we know we are, we're shit and we know we are,' rang around the ground to the familiar tune of the Pet Shop Boys 'Go West'.

At least the Football League's rules on ground safety had erased the possibility of the bottom club being relegated to the GM Vauxhall Conference because Macclesfield, runaway leaders of the Conference, had failed to meet the League's requirements by the December deadline. The decision was controversial, since Chester had ground-shared with Macclesfield, whose stadium had therefore already been used to stage League football. As it turned out, Scarborough managed to achieve a Houdini-style escape from the bottom rung of the League ladder, finishing above Exeter and achieving their goal in life. I wondered if they'd had the champagne corks popping to celebrate.

IN SEARCH OF KEVIN KEEGAN

Scunthorpe United v Scarborough – Glanford Park, 22 April 1995

'Did you see Keegan play here?' I asked the St John's Ambulance man standing in the corner of the ground near the refreshment stall which served the best chips I'd had all season.

'No. I'm not even interested in football. Bloody cold today, isn't it?'

'What was Keegan like when he was here?' I asked the tall distinguished supporter with the Clark Gable moustache at half-time.

'I never saw him play. I've lived in the area all my life, but I've only been coming to the football since my lad was about ten years old. He's in his twenties now.' Hadn't anyone seen King Kev play before he became rich and famous?

Scunthorpe was an old iron and steel town of just over 65,000 people and home to one of the largest steelworks in Europe. 'There's 12 miles of road in there,' said the taxi driver who took me to the match at the club's new purpose-built Glanford Park stadium on the outskirts of town. The history explained the club's nickname: the Iron. 'The mill is about one and a half to two miles square, I'd guess. I worked there once. Hard work it was. People don't like hard work these days. I always remember when they tipped the slag. There was a red glow like a sunset. It was beautiful.'

So this was the club where Kevin Keegan began his career as one of the best footballers of his generation. After establishing himself as Scunthorpe's top scorer in the 1970–71 season with 11 goals, Keegan was sold to Liverpool where he joined up with former Iron goalkeeper Ray Clemence at Anfield. In those days Scunthorpe played at the Old Showground, so called because it was once the venue for all sorts of events including horse jumping and the Scunthorpe Show. The stadium was the first in the history of football grounds to have a cantilever stand, three years before Sheffield Wednesday had one built at Hillsborough.

Since Scunthorpe was an iron and steel town, it should come as no surprise that the local football club should have the first stand that wasn't supported by posts to obscure the view for their fans. The United Steel Structural Company Limited, based in the town, built the stand in 1958 on favourable terms, no doubt hoping that orders for cantilever stands would come flooding in. They didn't, but at least Scunthorpe was on the map as the first club to have one.

The new cantilevered East Stand was opened for the start of Scunthorpe's first season in the Second Division after their promotion as champions of the Third Division (North). To mark the opening of the new stand, the second half of the Iron's opening game against Ipswich was covered live on BBC radio. Now that may not sound like much of an accolade, but Scunthorpe don't get live coverage on national radio every week. Twenty years later they played their last game at the

Old Showground in the Fourth Division promotion play-offs in May 1988. Sadly, they lost to Torquay.

By the start of the following season they'd become the first League side of modern times to move to a new purpose-built ground when they opened their new £2.5 million Glanford Park stadium one and a half miles outside the town centre on a greenfield site just a mile away from the Old Showground. The stadium, which took 11 months to build, was paid for by the sale of the home they used for 90 years to a supermarket chain. There was enough money left over to clear the club's debts.

Scunthorpe had just been thrashed 5–0 by rivals Doncaster Rovers and were desperate to get back on the winning trail. Manager Dave Moore in his column called 'Young Moore's Almanack' thought Scunthorpe were the better side for much of the first 45 minutes and that if they'd only lost 3–0 'people would have said we were unlucky and were on the wrong end of some diabolical refereeing decisions'. I wondered how they played for the other 45 minutes! 'Poor,' Moore conceded, acknowledging that they had to 'accept the criticism which came our way'. He added:

> No sooner do we get ourselves into a challenging position for the play-offs than we blow it. And it was particularly galling that we should reserve our worst performance of the season for a vital local derby when everyone was expecting big things of us. Last Saturday's dreadful defeat by Doncaster effectively put paid to our play-off hopes for this season. There can be no excuses, and you can't expect any sympathy after a 5–0 hiding, but I'm sure everyone who was here (all 4,366 of them) would agree that the scoreline did not tell the whole story.

Fortunately, Andy Kiwomya looked dangerous in today's match against Scarborough – the first team to win at Glanford Park back in 1988. He scored the third goal in a 3–1 win, but the home side still lacked ideas. Boro had more possession and were unfortunate to lose by two goals. Not that the home crowd exactly got behind their team. The freezing weather and driving rain didn't help. But it wasn't until the 90th minute, when Kiwomya scored, that they started singing. The travelling fans in the Yorkshire Electricity Stand were more vocal. 'Come on, Boro' was followed by 'Seasiders'.

After the game the receptionist in the club office called a taxi to get me back to the station. Inside the waiting room was a lifelong Scunnies fan in his sixties. He'd braved the rain and made the half-hour walk it takes to get to the station.

'What did you think of Kevin Keegan when he played here?' I asked.

'He was good. But he wasn't the best player we've ever had.'

I was surprised 'Who was, then?' I asked, thinking he might have given Ray Clemence the nod over his Liverpool and England colleague.

'Barrie Thomas. We sold him to Newcastle, but they didn't use him well. He didn't get enough support and didn't fit in. Eventually he came back to Scunthorpe.' I was to come across a picture of Thomas among Newcastle greats like Len Shackleton and Malcolm MacDonald on the wall of the Platinum Club Suite at St James's Park.

Thomas set a new club goalscoring record at Scunthorpe in the 1961–62 season with 31 goals in the Second Division. He was sold to Newcastle for

£40,000 before the end of that season, to the dismay of the Iron's fans. Many were disillusioned and refused to watch Scunthorpe any more, saying the sale of Thomas had cost the club promotion to the First Division. United finished fourth – their best-ever League placing – but not good enough to join the élite. A year later Thomas's replacement John Kaye was also transferred for £40,000, this time to West Brom, after scoring a hat-trick against Chelsea. Clemence was the next bright prospect to leave, followed by Keegan.

Scunthorpe had failed to produce any more world-class players, although Mark Atkins and Neil Cox started out at the Old Showground. The most famous sportsman to wear the Iron's shirt in more recent times was former England cricketer Ian Botham, who made his début away at Bournemouth in April 1980. His all-round ability stretched to the role of centre-forward or defender in the first team or the reserves. I wondered if anyone had seen him play for Scunthorpe?

PLAY-OFF FEVER

Mansfield Town v Torquay United – Field Mill, 29 April 1995

Nine miles. That's how far Mansfield Town's Field Mill ground is from the station. It used to be called Alfreton and Mansfield Parkway Station, but the Mansfield bit was dropped because so many people arrived thinking the town was close by. It's not. There's no public transport either, unless you walk a mile and catch a bus which stops at all the local villages and gets you to the ground an hour and ten minutes later. There's little choice but to go by taxi. The cost: £11.30, though you might get away with a tenner if you're short of change or the driver feels sorry for you.

The fanzine *Follow the Yellow Brick Road* had a section called 'D'ya know what annoys me? Well, I'll tell ya . . .' It included 'people who think Mansfield is in Yorkshire. It's not. It's in Nottinghamshire. Yorkshire is where the Stags take the piss out of teams like Leeds United and Doncaster Rovers (the locals call them Donkey Rovers), and is where those ever so provocative Rotherham policemen behave like savages.'

I didn't think Mansfield was in Yorkshire, but I certainly had no idea how complicated a journey to Field Mill would be when I left Tower Hill tube to catch a train from London's St Pancras Station to Nottingham before changing for Manchester via Alfreton. Tower Hill station, opposite the Tower of London, was full of rugby fans getting an early start on their way to the FA Challenge Cup final between Wigan and Leeds at Wembley Stadium.

Mansfield is described as 'a dull town with hosiery mills and collieries, spanned by a large railway viaduct' in the *Blue Guide to England*. The population of almost 60,000 had therefore looked to their local football team over the years to liven up their lives. Occasionally, to the surprise of many, they had.

Take 1929, for example, when Mansfield were still a non-League club drawn away to Second Division Wolves in the third round of the FA Cup. The Stags won 1–0 and their performance was a factor in their being accepted into the Football

League two years later, when Newport County dropped out of the Third Division (South).

Mansfield's best League placing was 21st in the old Second Division in 1978 – the only season they've spent outside the bottom two divisions. They got there after winning the Fourth Division title in 1975 and the Third Division title in 1977.

Their longest FA Cup run took them to the sixth round in 1969, after beating First Division West Ham, whereas in the League Cup they reached the fifth round in 1976. They won the Freight Rover Trophy in 1987, giving them their only success in a cup competition.

But this year was different. They'd already caused one of the upsets of the season by knocking Leeds out of the Coca-Cola Cup 1–0. Manager Andy King, who took over in 1993, knew his side had character and could battle, but he also thought the gap between the Premier and Third Division had narrowed. King adopted the coaching tactics of the legendary Brian Clough. 'I just go out and play golf and leave the players alone in the afternoons. Cloughie used to play squash so I thought I'd try.'

I walked into reception and asked to see Sandy Whetton, the Mansfield director I'd met on the station platform in Northampton back in October after the last-ever game at the County Ground. Sandy emerged from the boardroom to greet me and the ticket-office manager took me off to get a football signed by the first-team squad. I'd agreed to meet Sandy after the match when he hoped to be celebrating a place in the play-offs.

A quick tour of the ground involved a look at the pitch and a visit to the vice-president's bar to see the club's silverware.

'What's the biggest trophy here?' I asked.

'That one there, the Freight Rover Trophy,' said my guide, referring to the importance of the cup, not its size. There were lots of trophies from Germany too – Mansfield's favourite pre-season destination.

I took up my seat in the steel-framed West Stand, first erected at the Hurst Park racecourse in south London and in 1959 moved to Mansfield where it was reassembled behind the old West Stand. It cost £30,000 but the club spent another £170,000 on new offices, dressing-rooms and a social club in 1961. That £200,000 was four times as much as Sheffield Wednesday had spent on their new cantilevered stand!

The match was always going to be tense. Unfortunately Torquay took the lead after 18 minutes with their first real attack. The home fans were stunned. Silence descended on Field Mill. A crushing blow had just been delivered to their play-off hopes.

But Iffy Onuora eased the home fans' nerves with a diving header after 33 minutes, and then Steve Wilkinson, the club's record £80,000 signing from Leicester, put the Stags in front when he drove the ball home with the outside of his right foot from 20 yards. Wilkinson had earlier been presented with Player of the Year awards from the local newspaper and the supporters club. I could see why.

But the trauma wasn't over for Mansfield. A defensive lapse allowed Torquay's Lee Barrow to equalise when he rose unmarked at the back post after 76 minutes to head home a corner. The last 15 minutes were frantic. Could Mansfield hold out? Would Torquay score again and ruin their play-off dreams? The away side piled on the pressure as the Stags defence struggled to keep them out, kicking the ball as far upfield as they could. Former Preston and Cambridge manager John Beck would have been proud of them. The midfield dropped deeper and the strikers defended.

It was all hands on deck and, as the minutes ticked away, the crowd grew more and more anxious. It was nerve-wracking stuff. Then, after what seemed like hours, the referee blew the final whistle. Mansfield had made it to the play-offs and you could almost feel the relief around the ground. Everyone jumped to their feet to applaud the team. The players embraced each other and clapped the fans. It was time to celebrate.

In the dressing-room the players supped champagne from styrofoam cups or sipped Heineken from the familiar green cans as they celebrated securing the one point needed to guarantee that coveted play-off place. This was the sweet taste of success. The celebrations continued in the players' bar after autographs and photographs for the jubilant supporters outside the main entrance. The players were sharply dressed in black jackets, the MTFC logo picked out in gold on their top pockets. They chatted about the match to the proud gathering of friends and family.

On the way back to Alfreton station the taxi driver said he couldn't understand why supporters travel so far to see their teams, especially in meaningless end-of-season fixtures. 'I picked up a Fulham fan last week. He'd come from Manchester to see them play Mansfield but he didn't get to Alfreton until ten past three. We reached the ground at about 3.30. He must have been mad. And today I took a Torquay fan to the ground. He'd come bloody miles and there's was nothing in it for his team.' He was right, of course. But who said there was anything rational about being a football fan?

SOUL MATE AT CREWE

Crewe Alexandra v Hull City – Gresty Road, 2 May 1995

All trains lead to Crewe. The football club was actually founded by railway workers, who'd previously played cricket and rugby, in 1877. The team is named after the town and either the pub used by locomotive workers or Princess Alexandra. A pub called the Alexandra still stands outside the ground today.

I'd left London's Euston station in the Tuesday-afternoon sunshine looking forward to my visits to Crewe and then Newcastle for the Spurs' game on Wednesday night. Everything went according to plan until the train reached a place called Rugby. We didn't move for ages and the carriage had become stifling hot. There was an announcement that the 'pantograft' had to be checked before the train could leave.

At Crewe I discovered a football fan even more fanatical than me. He may not have covered as much of the country, or seen as many League matches, but he was a true fanatic nonetheless. Crewe fan Terry Harris from Kidsgrove reckoned he'd have watched 220 games at every level since the start of the season by the time I arrived at Gresty Road for a Tuesday-night match against Hull.

The local newspaper, *The Chronicle*, posed the question of how many matches the average football fan watches in a season. Most of my mates see about a dozen. Some loyal home fans get to 15 or 20. Travelling supporters watch 30 to 35. Harris goes to that many games in the pre-season warm-up. I'd reached match number 91 in my record attempt and I thought that was a lot!

If Crewe aren't playing, Harris travels almost anywhere in the country to feed his addiction to the beautiful game. He loves Sundays in the spring when he can watch local-park football in the morning and afternoon before travelling to a local League Cup final in the evening. On the Easter Monday he had seen Crewe win at Chester and then watched Witton Albion against Barrow on the way home for tea.

His own team, Crewe, had already qualified for the play-offs in their first season back in the Second Division following automatic promotion from the Third the previous year when they finished third. The only questions now were who their opponents would be in the play-off semis and whether they could reach Wembley and win promotion. 'Wemberleee, Wemberleee,' sang the joyous home fans in their red and white hats and scarves swaying on the terraces in the Popular Side.

Tonight was their penultimate chance to stand on the 'pop' side. Their last opportunity would come in the final League match at home to Cardiff the following Saturday. After that it would become all-seater. 'What we're doing is upgrading all the terracing; all this is derelict now, it's all coming out and we're going over to seating,' said Cliff Simpson, Crewe's safety officer and stadium manager.

Crewe's previous ground at Nantwich Road once hosted an England–Wales international and the FA Cup semi-final between Aston Villa and Rangers (Glasgow not Queens Park) in 1887 – the last year Scottish teams were allowed to enter the English Cup (Villa won 3–1). Crewe's team of amateurs reached the semi-finals themselves the following year and that remains their most impressive achievement so far, apart from victory in the Welsh Cup in 1936 and 1937.

Once the 'Pop' side was seated the only place fans could stand would be in the Main Stand paddock opposite. The original Main Stand had burned down in the 1930s and was replaced in 1932 when it was opened, ironically, on Bonfire Night. But even those 1,100 standing places wouldn't be preserved for long. Crewe were already negotiating with British Rail to buy the private road behind the Main Stand, which would give them enough room to build a new 6,000 all-seater stand.

So what do the supporters think of the plans for an all-seater stadium? Cliff Simpson replied, 'We've had about 80 complaints, that's all, but they've slowly come round to it. They've had a look at what's going to happen and they're all buying season tickets now.' I wondered whether that had more to do with the prospect of First Division football than with the ground redevelopments. But the club was trying its best to attract supporters. 'We've just put on a cracking deal for season tickets,' Simpson told me. 'For kids it's £45 anywhere in the ground and for adults £130. Pensioners can get in all season for £70.'

The fanzine *Super Dario Land* called the last home match the 'End of an Era'. It was. Dario is the first name of Crewe manager Dario Grady. He was the longest-serving boss in the League after 12 years at Gresty Road and the passage of time hadn't dimmed the supporters' enthusiasm for his brand of attractive, intelligent football. 'He's the Paul Daniels of football, magic,' said Simpson.

The Crewe fans were in full voice as the kick-off approached, particularly on the 'Pop' side where the more vocal fans congregated. 'We're going up, we're going up, you're not, you're not,' they sang in the direction of the hundred or so

Hull fans who'd made the trip down from the North-East. The last time the two sides met, Hull had won 7–1. It wouldn't happen tonight.

Crewe's second goal in a 3–2 come-from-behind win was their 100th League goal of the season and followed the 80 they'd scored in the previous campaign. The defence had leaked goals but the strikers had more than compensated. The Railwaymen were now a force to be reckoned with after years of stagnation in the old Fourth Division.

How the fans would love to get the chance to play arch-rivals Stoke and Port Vale in the First Division. *Super Dario Land* considered the prospect in an editorial: 'Stoke and Vale have now retained their previously precarious status as First Division outfits so, if victorious in the play-off lottery, the Alex have the chance to establish themselves alongside the clayheads "giants". I'm glad they're still there as we'll have the chance to settle a few scores, become the dominant "Potteries" force and enjoy four packed houses as we thrash 'em both at home and away. Who mentioned counting chickens?'

Port Vale are rivals, but Stoke – and Stokies generally – are the Railwaymen's arch-enemy. The fanzine's 'Sexist Joke of the Week' left me in no doubt.

'What do you call a pretty girl in Stoke?'

'A tourist.'

There was also an article called 'Are you a secret Stokie?' It said: 'When you visit a friend's house for tea do you, without thinking, turn over the base of the saucer to see where it was made?' Sad, but true, according to a Stokie I asked. The article went on: 'Is "success" a word you have not used since Saturday 4 March 1972 [when Stoke beat Chelsea 2–1 to win the League Cup]?'

Regional rivalry was something that had fascinated me throughout the season. Many of the main ones I knew well enough. Leeds–Man Utd, Spurs–Arsenal, Liverpool–Everton. But I'd stumbled across others that hadn't occurred to me such as Blackburn–Burnley, Chester–Wrexham and others in areas where any team among many could have been singled out as the enemy. Obviously, the closer the teams are geographically, the stronger the rivalry. It was just that living in London meant I was only aware of what it meant to the bigger clubs.

THRILLER

Newcastle United v Tottenham Hotspur – St James's Park, 3 May 1995

It was my second-last match. Newcastle against Spurs at St James's Park. Should be a great game, I thought, as I caught the train from Crewe. So what sort of game was it between two teams fighting for a UEFA Cup place? A pretty low-key affair, really. Six goals, two sendings-off and a penalty miss by Jürgen Klinsmann. Kevin Keegan described it as 'the greatest advert for football I have seen this season'. It was a true classic, probably one of the best games I've ever been fortunate enough to watch.

The main road outside the ground is called the Gallowgate, but the word originates from the public hangings that once took place from gallows erected where the Gallowgate End now stands. As I sat high up in a smart new executive box looking down at the Gallowgate on a tour of the ground the following morning, I wondered what the atmosphere must have been like at one of the public hangings and whether there was as much noise as there was the night of the Spurs match.

The Gallowgate End was a brand new 11,000-seater stand built in 1994. The two guys sitting next to me at the match had driven for five hours to reach the ground and would head straight back afterwards.

'You won't get home until about 3 o'clock in the morning,' I said, my brain having worked overtime to estimate their time of arrival.

They nodded with a slight grin as if to say, 'Yes, we know we're mad. Great, isn't it?' And it was in a way. One of the fascinating things about football is the lengths people go to so that they can watch their team.

In the past the rivalry between Newcastle and Sunderland has been fierce and as far back as 1901 there was a pitched battle on the St James's Park turf. Things have changed since then, thankfully. 'All the times I've been to Newcastle I've never seen any trouble,' said the Toon Army fan sitting behind me with his son and daughter. That's hardly surprising. The cost of misbehaving inside St James's Park is prohibitively high. Anyone causing trouble has their season ticket taken away. For a Geordie, nothing could be worse. It's probably easier to get inside the Bank of England than to get a ticket for a Newcastle home game.

I walked past the building work that was still going on at the Gallowgate End and made my way along Leazes Terrace in St James's Street past the East Stand. The Georgian terrace must provide the classiest backdrop to any football ground in the country. I turned the corner and passed through the crowds outside the main entrance and into the main foyer of the Milburn Stand, named after the legendary 'Wor Jackie'. Milburn, who came from a famous footballing family, acquired what would now be called cult status. He was a formidable striker with a startling turn of speed but he rarely headed the ball because he suffered with fibrosis. Whenever he used his head the crowd cheered.

Milburn played his first match in 1946 and was the star of the team which won the Cup three times in the 1950s, scoring the fastest-ever FA Cup final goal after 45 seconds in 1955. Milburn scored 10 goals in 13 England appearances, after replacing Tommy Lawton as centre-forward, and 179 goals in 354 League matches. After Wor Jackie died in October 1988, thousands of fans paid their respects at his funeral. Milburn's statue stands outside the main shopping centre in Newcastle, but he would be most proud of the new stand named after him.

Originally expected to cost £4 million, the Milburn, or West, Stand had absorbed £5 million by the time it was finished in 1988. The comparison to the £8,082 14s 11d which the club paid to build the old West Stand in 1906 was striking! The old stand, condemned by the local authority as unsafe, even had a swimming pool for the players, which was later covered over and turned into a reservoir for the sprinkler system used to water the pitch.

Keegan first arrived at St James's Park as a player when he left Southampton for £100,000 in August 1982. He was 31 and Newcastle's first football hero since

Malcolm MacDonald. His best days were probably at Liverpool and Hamburg, but his fading talent flickered brightly for a couple of seasons on Tyneside. The crowds soared and he didn't let them down. He was made captain and scored 21 goals in his first season. Newcastle finished fifth in the Second Division, but Keegan, despite being discarded by England, banged in 27 goals in the 1983–84 season to secure promotion.

He didn't play for the Magpies in the First Division. He'd already announced that he'd retire at the end of the promotion campaign. There was a photograph of the great man, wearing a black and white Newcastle cap and surrounded by hordes of adoring fans, on the wall of the exclusive Platinum Club at St James's Park alongside legends like Hughie Gallagher and Malcolm MacDonald.

The difference between them and Keegan was that he returned to manage the club. 'I have been a manager for not much more than a couple of years and it really seems like ten,' said Keegan. 'So much has happened at St James's Park, which is the only place I wanted to manage anyway. When United asked me to succeed Ossie Ardiles there was no prospect of me turning it down. Having finished my playing career on Tyneside, with promotion to the top flight in 1984, I knew that if I could turn a losing team into a winning one then it would be the most special place in the game to be manager.'

A lot of the credit for the transformation of St James's Park must go to Sir John Hall, whose millions have helped finance the redevelopment of the ground. Surprisingly, he was initially reluctant to get involved. 'I never wanted to become chairman of Newcastle United. They can write that on my gravestone because it's the rock solid truth. I wanted the club to change, of course, because without change and investment it was never going to be the club the most loyal supporters in the game deserved.'

Hall started to get really involved when Newcastle faced relegation to the old Third Division for the first time in their history. 'To have gone down would have been catastrophic.' The rest is history, as they say. Under Hall turnover had soared from £5 million a couple of years ago to three times that amount. Newcastle had spent almost £20 million on ground improvements to comply with the Taylor Report.

The chairman's stand was as packed as the rest of the stadium when the Newcastle and Spurs players came out onto the pitch. An awful song with the refrain 'Howay the Lads' was being played by the club DJ. I'm sure the home fans were as relieved as me when it was time for the game to start – and the song to end! As the teams prepared for the kick-off the noise inside the ground was deafening.

After ten minutes Newcastle were two goals ahead through Gillespie and Peacock, their first for the club, and the atmosphere had risen to new heights. A wall of noise swirled around the stadium as the Toon Army celebrated. Their joy was short-lived. Tottenham hit a purple patch which saw first Barmby, then Klinsmann and, finally, Anderton put Spurs ahead in a six-minute spell midway through the half. Anderton's goal was copybook stuff – a 25-yard curler into the top left-hand corner of Pavel Srnicek's goal. It was unbelievable. The home fans were stunned. It took them a long time to find their voice again but when they did they got behind their team. 'Sing your hearts out for the lads, sing your hearts out for the lads,' sang the faithful.

The second half also began brightly with both sides playing entertaining, attacking football. Then Barmby broke clear, rounded Srnicek and was brought down. Penalty. But worse was to follow for Newcastle. The referee held up the red card and their popular keeper was off. The crowd were in uproar. Boos rang around the ground as the fans reacted angrily to the decision. Former Liverpool keeper Mike Hooper was brought on to replace Ruel Fox (then at Newcastle) and his first job was to face the penalty from Klinsmann. The tall blond German striker ran up and drove the ball towards the centre of the goal. Hooper dived to his left but managed to save the ball with his feet. The home fans went wild, the noisiest they'd been all night. It was the turning-point in a match of turning-points.

In the 65th minute Spurs central defender Colin Calderwood received his second booking for a foul on Malcolm Allen and joined Srnicek in the showers. Hooper then saved brilliantly to keep out another Anderton blockbuster. But the last word was left to the inimitable Peter Beardsley. Spurs defender Sol Campbell failed to cut out a through ball and Beardsley got in behind him like lightening to drive the ball past Ian Walker in the Spurs goal from 15 yards.

Soon afterwards Beardsley collected the ball and walked across to the corner of the Gallowgate and Milburn Stand to take a corner while Keith Gillespie was receiving treatment nearby. The fans applauded and Beardsley clapped them and put up his right thumb. The show of mutual respect and warmth of feeling was genuine. They appreciated his genius, he was grateful for their support. Newcastle pressed for a winner. It was not to be and a draw was probably a fair result.

After the match I stood in the Gallowgate just taking in the feeling of being inside such a magnificent stadium. As I soaked up the last bit of atmosphere, I was starting to get nostalgic. My record attempt nearly over, I realised I'd been living in a fantasy world.

Most people do not watch a League match every two to three days. They don't drive or take trains all over the country to football grounds all week, every week. They live normal lives with jobs and wives and kids. They go down the pub with their mates, or to the cinema or take the missus out for a meal. Me, I'd had little time for anything but football over the past nine months. It would soon be time to return to the real world. As I made my way out into the streets surrounding St James's Park I felt I was leaving behind more than just another football stadium. I was leaving behind a way of life.

After spending the night in South Shields I returned to St James's Park the following morning for a ground tour. The other tourists included a Norwich fan taking a course in Newcastle (the place not the language!). We were taken down some steps towards the tunnel first of all. A black and white sign with the words 'Howay the Lads' stands proudly over the exit like the one at Liverpool which proclaims 'This is Anfield'.

Next it was the dressing-rooms. Each player's number was painted on the wall above his peg with a marker pen. 'We used to have proper numbers, but the kids would peel them off on these tours, so we decided to use a pen. All the first team numbers were there with the exception of number nine. 'When Andy Cole was here the kids rubbed their fingers over his number just to take something of his home with them,' said the guide.

I wasn't sure if I'd ever make it back to St James's Park, but I knew I'd probably never see Klinsmann play there again. When he announced at the end of the season that he would be leaving Spurs for Bayern Munich, I knew I was right. Being there to see the German star score in front of the Gallowgate was worth the journey all on its own. He would be missed.

GLADWYS SINGS THE BLUES

Everton v Southampton – Goodison Park, 6 May 1995

I'd made it at last. Goodison Park was my 93rd football ground. I'd journeyed almost 20,000 thousand miles, seen 372 stands and terraces, more than two thousand players, two broken legs, countless goals, near-misses, ricochets, headers, corners, shots, tackles, penalties, fans and more taxis, buses, planes and trains than some people travel on in a lifetime. And it seemed like a lifetime since I began back in September. But now I'd reached my final game: Everton, about to win the FA Cup, against Premier League survivors Southampton.

Like a relegation-haunted manager I too felt as if I'd only just survived the season. I'd probably seen as many games as the most peripatetic bosses in football. I hadn't taken on the viewing workload of most scouts, but they tend to stick to one area whereas I'd been to every town and city in the country that boasted a League team.

I parked my car in Stanley Park, which separates Goodison from Anfield. I could see Liverpool's ground ahead of me on top of the hill which drops down to Everton's home on the other side of the park. It's ironic that Everton – the name comes from the district to the west of Stanley Park – originally played at Anfield for eight years from 1884 to 1892. They even won their first Championship at the ground in 1891. It was only when Everton left after a dispute with their landlord that Liverpool were formed.

The Toffees, named after a shop called Ye Ancient Toffee House close to the club's Sandon Hotel headquarters, moved to Mere Green, later renamed Goodison Park, on the north side of Stanley Park. They paid just over £8,000 for the new ground – a large sum even in those days. Goodison was to became the country's first major football stadium. In September 1892 Everton beat Bolton 4–2 in the first match played at what was described as 'one of the finest and most complete grounds in the kingdom'.

The main entrance stood opposite a row of terraced houses. Above the various entrances in Goodison Road was a large board with instructions on how to get to each part of the ground – very useful for away fans. I collected my tickets for the Family Area and was taken down the tunnel and out onto the pitch before the match by an official.

The official ran through some of Everton's history, including the fact that they once played at Anfield. Interviews with the players and manager Joe Royle were being played out over the PA along with background on the two teams. 'It can be a nightmare trying to announce the players names,' she told me. 'Our announcer has just been told it's not Amokaachi but Amokatchi, so he's got that wrong all season.' The big Nigerian forward had wandered past us just ahead of David Unsworth as we walked towards the tunnel.

'It's a good job he doesn't have to announce the name of the Portsmouth winger whom everyone calls Precki,' I said.

'Well, he used to play for us, you know, so he's already had practice at getting that one wrong.'

The noise began to pick up as the kick-off approached. Joe Royle was fully aware of the importance of their support. 'Make no mistake, the vocal support, especially at home, has been comparable with anything in the country and it is no coincidence that our home form in particular has been so encouraging with the fans behind us roaring us on,' he said.

I looked across at the Southampton supporters sitting opposite, in the corner of the Bullens Road Stand. They were taunting the Evertonians with chants of 'Down with the Villa. You're going down with the Villa'. The white wooden boards running along the balcony wall which divides the upper and lower tiers of the stand were decorated with a blue criss-cross pattern in steel. It was the hallmark of one of football's unsung heroes, architect Archibald Leitch. He was responsible for the building of many famous grounds including White Hart Lane, Fratton Park, Craven Cottage, Bramall Lane, Villa Park, Roker Park, Old Trafford and others.

The Main Stand contains a portrait of the legendary William Ralph 'Dixie' Dean, Everton's record goalscorer with 349 goals between 1925 and 1937, including the Football League record of 60 in the 1927–28 season, when he was just 21 years old. Next to the picture was a commemorative inscription saying he died in March 1980 after the Merseyside derby, at the age of 73. *The Guardian's* Stephen Bierley quoted a friend's daughter who, on her first visit to Goodison read the plaque and said, 'No wonder. He shouldn't have been playing at that age.' His ashes were scattered at Goodison, scene of his most fruitful years when he was often described as the best centre-forward England has ever produced.

Dean lived in one of the club's terraced houses next to Goodison and was therefore very familiar with the Church of St Luke the Evangelist, which cuts into the ground in the corner between the Main Stand and the Gladwys Street End. The church is only a few feet from the stands and is a well-known landmark in the area. I hadn't noticed it from my seat in the Main Stand, but I had a good look after the match. Everton once tried to have the church removed to acquire extra land, but they failed. It's not always progress to remove long-standing oddities. They're what gives a ground character and distinguishes it from the other 92 League venues around the country.

The Gladwys Street Stand was rebuilt and covered in 1992 to provide the home fans with more modern facilities. The fanzine *Gladwys Sings the Blues* takes its name from the traditional end for home fans, which cost £50,000 when it was built in 1938. George VI and the Queen Mum came to visit the ground to see the stand just after it was completed.

Speaking of royalty, Goodison Park was the first League ground to be visited by royals when George V and Queen Mary came to inspect local schoolchildren in 1913. Goodison was also used by the Territorial Army for drill practice in the First World War and, shortly afterwards, the Chicago White Sox and New York Giants baseball teams played an exhibition match at the ground.

Goodison was the venue for five games in the '66 World Cup including a wonderful quarter-final between Portugal and North Korea, which the Portuguese won 5–3, and the semi-final between West Germany and Russia. Only Wembley was chosen to host more games in the competition than Goodison. Some of the terraced houses originally built by the club for their players were demolished before the World Cup to improve access to the ground from Stanley Park. There would be no such preparations for the 1996 European Championships, however, since Goodison was overlooked in favour of Anfield.

The rivalry with Liverpool is known throughout the football world. It also explains some of the landmarks chalked up over the years involving Everton's arch-rivals. For instance, the record crowd at Goodison was on 18 September 1948 for the First Division match between the two teams. The first floodlights at the ground were used for a friendly against Liverpool on 9 October 1957. And nobody needs reminding of the recent Wembley matches between the two sides starting with the first all-Merseyside final in the Milk (League) Cup of 1984, which Everton lost in a replay at Maine Road, and the two FA Cup finals, in 1986 and 1989, which they also lost. Despite nine Championships, four FA Cups (five including the imminent victory over Manchester United) and a Cup-Winners' Cup, Everton always seem to have been in the shadow of their neighbours across Stanley Park. Those recent Cup final defeats hadn't helped.

Today's game against Southampton was disappointing and didn't hold out much hope that Everton were about to come out of the shadows. Le Tissier was missing from the Saints teamsheet with a sore heel, prompting Derick Allsop in the *Sunday Telegraph* to consider that, 'Southampton without Le Tissier are like the VE celebrations without Vera Lynn.' Well, it's true that he makes the Saints midfield sing! Alan Ball was disappointed that his star player was missing. 'I am sorry because I wanted him to play. I wanted the people here to see him.' Even without the man Ball calls Genius, Southampton still played neat, tidy football and created more than enough chances in the second half to have won. According to Bill Borrows in the *Sunday Times*, 'As Southampton's fluid, hard-working formation went comfortably about its business the Everton midfield, the self-styled Dogs of War, set about imposing themselves on the game and disrupting the rhythm of their opponents.'

From where I was sitting Everton were crap. They struggled to control the ball; couldn't pass it accurately; and generally looked a very poor side. I could see why they were near the bottom of the Premiership and, on this form, they had no chance of overturning the form book against United in the FA Cup final to be played a week on Saturday. The only two Everton players with any flair and skill were on the bench. The biggest cheer of the first half came when one of them, former Spurs star Vinny Samways, out-of-favour since Royle's arrival, was brought on to replace the ineffective John Ebbrell. Anders Limpar, the Swedish international who was to play such an influential role at Wembley, also appeared in the second half to give Everton some width down the right.

Chairman Peter Johnson, writing in the match programme, said Everton were at 'the beginning of a new successful era' and that 'the buzz is positively tangible'. But there was certainly no chance of this Everton side repeating the amazing run of the 1931 team which scored 33 goals in just four games against Sheffield Wednesday, Newcastle, Chelsea and Leicester. Nigerian international

Daniel Amokachi belied his recent good form, which had seen him hit five goals in four games, and was guilty of one particularly glaring miss in which he scooped the ball over the bar from inside the six-yard box. 'Out of Amo' ran the *Sunday Mirror* headline. 'He only scores the difficult ones,' said Royle. Still, a point was better than nothing and, as it turned out, was more than enough to preserve Everton's Premier League status.

After the match I drove to the Dolby Hotel, a new building on the refurbished Albert Dock, scene of my previous visit to see *The Beatles Story* the morning of the Tranmere–Oldham match at Prenton Park back in late January. The weather was considerably warmer now and the water from the Mersey lapped gently against the walls of the dock as I sipped a lager on the hotel terrace. I was feeling quite content now. I had set a new record which would be recorded for posterity in the 1996 *Guinness Book of Records*. Life was sweet.

The next morning I wandered back to the docks and walked along the Mersey. The famous ferries were carrying passengers backwards and forwards and I could hear distant strains of Gerry Marsden's 'Ferry Across the Mersey'. I knew the song, of course, but hadn't realised they actually played it on every ferry crossing. It must drive the captain mad. The docks were also hosting an exhibition on the Liverpool industries of the past, complete with pictures of factories turning out all sorts of useful gadgets. Footballers were still the most prized assets on Merseyside, though.

As I looked out across the Mersey I felt it was fitting that my record attempt should end there. Liverpool Football Club and the Beatles were probably the most famous institutions the city had created. The best players Britain had produced arguably played for Manchester United, but the best team we've ever put together was probably the Liverpool side of the '70s and '80s which conquered Europe so often and collected the games domestic honours almost at will. Merseyside was the heartbeat of football.

The rivalry between the two big Merseyside clubs is thankfully pretty friendly. But victory in those hard-fought derby games means a whole lot to the fans. A few weeks after Everton's Cup success at Wembley I was returning home from work when I heard the faint strains of the song 'Singing the Blues' drifting along a London platform. As I approached the singer his words became clear. 'I never felt more like Singing the Blues when Liverpool win and Everton lose, Oh Everton, You've got me singing the Blues.' The Toffees fan was pretty drunk, but good-natured. He had reason to sing. His team had won the Cup and Europe beckoned. As the venue for my last match Goodison would always have a special place in my heart too. How does it go? 'I never felt more like . . .'

1) Carlisle United v Exeter City – Brunton Park – 10 Sept, 1–0, 6,213
2) Middlesbrough v Sunderland – Ayresome Park – 11 Sept, 2–2, 19,578
3) Wycombe Wanderers v Hull City – Adams Park – 13 Sept, 1–2, 4,626
4) Millwall v Burnley – The New Den – 14 Sept, 2–3, 7,375
5) Doncaster Rovers v Hereford United – Belle Vue – 16 Sept, 3–0, 1,938
6) Leicester City v Tottenham Hotspur – Filbert Street – 17 Sept, 3–1, 21,300
7) Ipswich Town v Norwich City – Portman Road – 19 Sept, 1–2, 17,405
8) Southend United v Bolton Wanderers – Roots Hall – 24 Sept, 2–1, 4,507
9) West Ham United v Arsenal – Upton Park – 25 Sept, 0–2, 18,495
10) West Bromwich Albion v Portsmouth – The Hawthorns – 28 Sept, 0–2, 13,545
11) Colchester United v Bury – Layer Road – 1 Oct, 1–0, 3,286
12) Chelsea v West Ham United – Stamford Bridge – 2 Oct, 2–1, 18,696
13) Southampton v Everton – The Dell – 8 Oct, 2–0, 15,163
14) Coventry City v Ipswich Town – Highfield Road – 10 Oct, 2–0, 9,509
15) Northampton Town v Mansfield Town – The County Ground – 11 Oct, 0–1, 4,993
16) Leeds United v Tottenham Hotspur – Elland Road – 15 Oct, 1–1, 39,362
17) Bolton Wanderers v Oldham Athletic – Burnden Park – 16 Oct, 2–2, 11,106
18) Nottingham Forest v Wimbledon – The City Ground – 17 Oct, 3–1, 20,287
19) Manchester City v Tottenham Hotspur – Maine Road – 22 Oct, 5–2, 25,473
20) Portsmouth v Middlesbrough – Fratton Park – 23 Oct, 0–0, 7,281
21) Fulham v Carlisle United – Craven Cottage – 29 Oct, 1–3, 5,563
22) Wimbledon v Norwich City – Selhurst Park – 30 Oct, 1–0, 8,242
23) Oxford United v Blackpool – The Manor Ground – 1 Nov, 3–2, 5,610
24) Brighton v Bournemouth – The Goldstone Ground – 2 Nov, 0–0, 5,631
25) Blackburn Rovers v Tottenham Hotspur – Ewood Park – 5 Nov, 2–0, 26,933
26) Oldham Athletic v Tranmere Rovers – Boundary Park – 6 Nov, 0–0, 6,475
27) Watford v Southend United – Vicarage Road – 12 Nov, 1–0, 8,551
28) Charlton v West Bromwich Albion – The Valley – 13 Nov, 1–1, 10,876
29) Sheffield United v Southend United – Bramall Lane – 26 Nov, 2–0, 13,405
30) Bristol City v Grimsby Town – Ashton Gate – 3 Dec, 1–2, 6,030
31) Queens Park Rangers v West Ham – Loftus Road – 4 Dec, 2–1, 12,780

32) Reading v Middlesbrough – Elm Park – 6 Dec, 1–1, 10,301

33) Barnsley v Bristol City – Oakwell – 7 Dec, 2–1, 4,305

34) Gillingham v Wigan Athletic – The Priestfield Stadium – 10 Dec, 0–1, 2,257

35) Luton Town v Derby County – Kenilworth Road – 11 Dec, 0–0, 6,400

36) Bournemouth v Wrexham – Dean Court – 16 Dec, 1–3, 2,505

37) Notts County v Portsmouth – Meadow Lane – 17 Dec, 0–1, 6,382

38) Exeter City v Torquay United – St James Park – 26 Dec (11am), 1–2, 5,538

39) Bristol Rovers v Bournemouth – Twerton Park – 26 Dec (3pm), 2–1, 6,913

40) Torquay United v Hartlepool United – Plainmoor – 27 Dec, 2–2, 3,172

41) Cambridge United v York City – The Abbey Stadium – 28 Dec, 1–0, 3,285

42) Peterborough United v Cambridge United – London Road – 31 Dec (12.30pm), 2–2, 7,412

43) Brentford v Oxford United – Griffin Park – 31 Dec (3pm), 2–0 7,125

44) Sheffield Wednesday v Southampton – Hillsborough –2 Jan (3pm), 1–1, 28,424

45) Tottenham Hotspur v Arsenal – White Hart Lane – 2 Jan (8pm), 1–0, 28,747

46) Wrexham v Leyton Orient – The Racecourse Ground – 14 Jan, 4–1, 6,616

47) Port Vale v Tranmere Rovers – Vale Park – 15 Jan, 2–0, 7,944

48) Preston North End v Mansfield Town – Deepdale – 21 Jan, 2–1, 8,448

49) Tranmere Rovers v Oldham Athletic – Prenton Park – 22 Jan, 3–1, 5,581

50) Arsenal v Southampton – Highbury – 24 Jan, 1–1, 27,213

51) Aston Villa v Tottenham Hotspur – Villa Park –25 Jan, 1–0, 40,017

52) Lincoln City v Hereford United – Sincil Bank – 28 Jan, 2–0, 2,545

53) Chester City v Wycombe Wanderers – The Deva Stadium – 31 Jan, 0–2, 1,524

54) Plymouth Argyle v York City – Home Park – 4 Feb, 1–2, 5,572

55) Shrewsbury Town v Plymouth Argyle – Gay Meadow – 7 Feb, 3–1, 3,029

56) Stockport County v Chester City – Edgeley Park – 11 Feb, 2–2, 4,405

57) Chesterfield v Barnet – The Recreation Ground – 14 Feb, 2–0, 2,978

58) Swindon Town v Bristol City – The County Ground – 15 Feb, 0–3, 9,881

59) Hull City v Stockport County – Boothferry Park – 18 Feb, 0–0, 4,576

60) Darlington v Gillingham – Feethams Ground – 21 Feb, 2–0, 1,548

61) Hartlepool United v Exeter City – The Victoria Ground – 25 Feb, 2–2, 1,440

62) Derby County v Bolton Wanderers – The Baseball Ground – 26 Feb, 2–1, 11,003

63) Barnet v Exeter City – Underhill – 28 Feb, 1–1, 1,325

64) Berwick Rangers v Meadowbank – Shielfield Park – 4 Mar, 1–0, 455

65) Sunderland v Tranmere Rovers – Roker Park – 5 Mar, 0–1, 12,043

66) Rotherham United v Cambridge United – The Millmoor Ground – 7 Mar, 1–0, 2,208

67) Wolverhampton Wanderers v Sunderland – Molineux – 8 Mar, 1–0, 25,926

68) Birmingham City v Swansea City – St Andrews – 11 Mar, 0–1, 16,191

69) York City v Wycombe Wanderers – Bootham Crescent – 14 Mar, 0–0, 2,800

70) Manchester United v Tottenham Hotspur – Old Trafford – 15 Mar, 0–0, 43,802

71) Swansea City v Shrewsbury Town – The Vetch Field – 17 Mar, 0–0, 4,130

72) Hereford United v Scarborough – Edgar Street – 18 Mar (12 noon), 2–1, 1,479

73) Stoke City v Reading – The Victoria Ground –18 Mar (3pm), 0–1, 10,006

74) Grimsby Town v Sunderland – Blundell Park – 19 Mar, 3–1, 5,697

75) Norwich City v Ipswich Town – Carrow Road – 20 Mar, 3–0, 17,510

76) Bradford City v Swansea City – Valley Parade – 21 Mar, 1–3, 4,417

77) Bury v Mansfield Town – Gigg Lane – 25 Mar, 2–2, 4,188

78) Burnley v Port Vale – Turf Moor – 28 Mar, 4–3, 10,058

79) Wigan Athletic v Hereford United – Springfield Park – 29 Mar, 1–1, 1,492

80) Rochdale v Barnet – Spotland – 1 Apr, 2–2, 1,834

81) Blackpool v Birmingham City – Bloomfield Road – 4 Apr, 1–1, 4,494

82) Liverpool v Southampton – Anfield – 5 Apr, 3–1, 29,881

83) Cardiff City v Rotherham United – Ninian Park – 8 Apr, 1–1, 6,412

84) Leyton Orient v Bristol Rovers – Brisbane Road – 11 Apr, 1–2, 2,338

85) Crystal Palace v Tottenham Hotspur – Selhurst Park – 14 Apr, 1–1, 18,068

86) Walsall v Rochdale – The Bescot Stadium – 15 Apr, 0–0, 3,766

87) Huddersfield Town v Hull City – The Alfred McAlpine Stadium – 17 Apr, 1–1, 12,402

88) Scarborough v Darlington – The McCain Stadium – 18 Apr, 3–1, 2,182

89) Scunthorpe United v Scarborough – Glanford Park – 22 Apr, 3–1, 2,079

90) Mansfield Town v Torquay United – Field Mill – 29 Apr, 2–2, 3,216

91) Crewe Alexandra v Hull City – Gresty Road – 2 May, 3–2, 3,870

92) Newcastle United v Tottenham Hotspur – St James's Park – 3 May, 3–3, 35,603

93) Everton v Southampton – Goodison Park – 6 May, 0–0, 36,851